THE MIDDLE AGES

VOLUME II

Readings in Medieval History

FOURTH EDITION

BRIAN TIERNEY

Cornell University

McGRAW-HILL, INC.
New York   St. Louis   San Francisco   Auckland   Bogotá
Caracas   Lisbon   London   Madrid   Mexico   Milan   Montreal
New Delhi   Paris   San Juan   Singapore   Sydney   Tokyo   Toronto

THE MIDDLE AGES, Volume II
Readings in Medieval History

1 2 3 4 5 6 7 8 9 0 DOC DOC 9 0 9 8 7 6 5 4 3 2

ISBN 0-07-064612-0

This book was set in ITC New Baskerville
by Waldman Graphics, Inc.
The editors were David Follmer, Niels Aaboe,
and Bernadette Boylan;
the production supervisor was Kathryn Porzio.
The cover was designed by Karen K. Quigley.
R. R. Donnelley & Sons Company was printer and binder.

About the Author

After serving in the Royal Air Force, Brian Tierney received his B.A. and Ph.D. from Cambridge University. He has taught at Catholic University, Washington, D.C., and at Cornell, where he is now Bryce and Edith M. Bowmar Professor in Humanistic Studies. He has been the recipient of Guggenheim Fellowships and of fellowships from the American Council of Learned Societies and the National Endowment for the Humanities. Professor Tierney has been awarded the honorary degrees of Doctor of Theology by Uppsala University, Sweden, and Doctor of Humane Letters by Catholic University. A specialist in medieval church history, he has published many articles and several books, among them *Foundations of the Conciliar Theory; Medieval Poor Law;* and *Origins of Papal Infallibility, 1150–1350.* He is coeditor with Donald Kagan and L. Pearce Williams of *Great Issues in Western Civilization.* His most recent work is *Religion, Law, and the Growth of Constitutional Thought, 1150–1650.*

Contents

N<small>OTE</small> ON THE FOURTH EDITION

A book of *Readings* on medieval history should reflect the current concerns of scholars in the field. The problem for the editor of a new edition is that the range of scholarly interests is always expanding while the book has to stay roughly the same length. Nowadays many students want to know more about family history, women's roles, demographic trends, attitudes about the natural environment. But it remains true that, to understand the Middle Ages at all, we still need to know such things as how feudal institutions worked, what the claims of the medieval papacy were, and how Thomas Aquinas thought he could prove the existence of God. The new interests are a supplement to the old ones, not a substitute for them.

In this new edition I have again tried to maintain a balance between new themes and traditional ones. Some readings have been replaced by alternate ones and some additional readings included. The new readings in this edition are from Harold Berman, Peter Brown, Caroline Bynum, Jeremy Cohen, Norman Cohn, Edith Ennen, Robert Fossier, and Brian Tierney.

PREFACE

This two-volume collection of *Sources of Medieval History* and *Readings in Medieval History* is intended for use in college history courses. The collection was prepared to accompany *Western Europe in the Middle Ages, 300–1475*, by Brian Tierney and Sidney Painter, but it can be used equally well with any of the popular textbooks in the field.

The purpose of the work has helped to determine its form. In particular, the amount of introductory, narrative material has been deliberately kept to a minimum. It seemed more useful to present the widest possible variety of medieval *Sources* and modern *Readings* in these volumes rather than to reproduce routine information that any teacher can supply or that the student can find for himself in any standard textbook. Again, while every anthology must reflect to some degree the taste and judgment of its compiler, I have tried not to emphasize unduly my own idiosyncrasies in making the selections. The *Sources* and *Readings* illustrate topics in the mainstream of medieval history, topics that most instructors will want to discuss with their classes.

The *Sources* are drawn from many different kinds of medieval materials. The *Readings* include essays on social, economic, political, religious, and intellectual history. Some of these modern readings are controversial. In arranging them I have used a "problem-oriented" approach where this seemed appropriate. For example, the section on "The Medieval State" presents sharply conflicting views of modern historians on a central problem of medieval history.

Other sections are intended to illustrate diversity rather than disagreement—to show the various ways in which historians with different backgrounds and different interests will approach the same set of problems. One criterion that I have tried to keep constantly in mind is that of Johann Huizinga—"Unreadable history is no history at all."

Brian Tierney

THE END OF THE ANCIENT WORLD

WHY DID THE Roman empire "fall"? This is the first great problem that a historian of the Middle Ages encounters. The question is one of endless fascination; no simple, satisfactory answer to it has yet been found. We know that the empire was invaded by barbarians and that its people lacked the strength and nerve and will to defend their society effectively. Ever since the Renaissance period (when Machiavelli was much concerned with the problem), historians have tried to explain why this was so. Often the explanations tell us as much about the intellectual prejudices of the historian's own generation as about the affairs of ancient Rome. Each new movement of thought in the modern world gives rise to a new explanation for the decay of classical civilization. Thus, in the writings of the twentieth century, we can find social, economic, religious, racist, demographic, and ecological interpretations of the fall of Rome.

Edward Gibbon, unsurpassed among historians as a literary artist, viewed the late Roman empire from the standpoint of the eighteenth-century Enlightenment. In his day no single power dominated all Europe, and Gibbon was well content with this state of affairs. He attributed the decline of Rome simply to "immoderate greatness." Also he was inclined to think that the rise of Christianity had exercised a debilitating influence on ancient society. Rostovtzeff, a Russian historian, was a professor at the University of St. Petersburg when the communist revolution broke out in 1918. In 1920 he emigrated to America. Rostovtzeff emphasized social conditions, especially class antagonisms, as the underlying cause of Rome's fall. Later historians have suggested that his interpretation, like Gibbon's, was much influenced by the circumstances of his own lifetime.

Some scholars have rejected the description of the fourth and fifth centuries as simply an age of "decline and fall." If there was evident political disintegration, they argue, there was also enormous religious vitality. In the final reading, Peter Brown discusses the interplay of Christian and classical cultures in the late Roman world.

1. General Observations on the Fall of the Roman Empire in the West

EDWARD GIBBON

The rise of a city, which swelled into an empire, may deserve, as a singular prodigy, the reflection of a philosophic mind. But the decline of Rome was the natural and inevitable effect of immoderate greatness. Prosperity ripened the principle of decay; the causes of destruction multiplied with the extent of conquest; and, as soon as time or accident had removed the artificial supports, the stupendous fabric yielded to the pressure of its own weight. The story of its ruin is simple and obvious; and, instead of inquiring why the Roman empire was destroyed, we should rather be surprised that it had subsisted so long. The victorious legions, who, in distant wars, acquired the vices of strangers and mercenaries, first oppressed the freedom of the republic, and afterwards violated the majesty of the purple. The emperors, anxious for their personal safety and the public peace, were reduced to the base expedient of corrupting the discipline which rendered them alike formidable to their sovereign and to the enemy; the vigour of the military government was relaxed, and finally dissolved, by the partial institutions of Constantine; and the Roman world was overwhelmed by a deluge of Barbarians.

The decay of Rome has been frequently ascribed to the translation of the seat of empire; but this history has already shewn that the powers of government were *divided* rather than *removed*. The throne of Constantinople was erected in the East; while the West was still possessed by a series of emperors who held their residence in Italy

From Edward Gibbon, *The Decline and Fall of the Roman Empire,* J. B. Bury, ed., 2d ed. (London: Methuen, 1901), Vol. IV, pp. 161–169.

and claimed their equal inheritance of the legions and provinces. This dangerous novelty impaired the strength, and fomented the vices, of a double reign; the instruments of an oppressive and arbitrary system were multiplied; and a vain emulation of luxury, not of merit, was introduced and supported between the degenerate successors of Theodosius. Extreme distress, which unites the virtue of a free people, embitters the factions of a declining monarchy. The hostile favourites of Arcadius and Honorius betrayed the republic to its common enemies; and the Byzantine court beheld with indifference, perhaps with pleasure, the disgrace of Rome, the misfortunes of Italy, and the loss of the West. Under the succeeding reigns, the alliance of the two empires was restored; but the aid of the Oriental Romans was tardy, doubtful, and ineffectual; and the national schism of the Greeks and Latins was enlarged by the perpetual difference of language and manners, of interest, and even of religion. Yet the salutary event approved in some measure the judgment of Constantine. During a long period of decay, his impregnable city repelled the victorious armies of Barbarians, protected the wealth of Asia, and commanded, both in peace and war, the important straits which connect the Euxine and Mediterranean seas. The foundation of Constantinople more essentially contributed to the preservation of the East than to the ruin of the West.

As the happiness of a *future* life is the great object of religion, we may hear, without surprise or scandal, that the introduction, or at least the abuse, of Christianity had some influence on the deline and fall of the Roman empire. The clergy successfully preached the doctrines of patience and pusillanimity; the active virtues of society were discouraged; and the last remains of the military spirit were buried in the cloister; a large portion of public and private wealth was consecrated to the specious demands of charity and devotion; and the soldiers' pay was lavished on the useless multitudes of both sexes, who could only plead the merits of abstinence and chastity. Faith, zeal, curiosity, and the more earthly passions of malice and ambition kindled the flame of theological discord; the church, and even the state, were distracted by religious factions, whose conflicts were sometimes bloody, and always implacable; the attention of the emperors was diverted from camps to synods; the Roman world was oppressed by a new species of tyranny; and the persecuted sects became the secret enemies of their country. Yet party-spirit, however pernicious or absurd, is a principle of union as well as of dissension. The bishops, from eighteen hundred pulpits, inculcated the duty of passive obedience to a lawful and orthodox sovereign; their frequent assemblies, and perpetual correspondence, maintained the communion of distant churches: and the benevolent temper of the gospel was strengthened, though confined, by the spiritual alliance of the Catholics. The sacred indolence of the monks was devoutly embraced by a servile and effeminate age; but, if superstition had not afforded a decent retreat, the same vices would have tempted the unworthy Romans to desert, from baser motives, the standard of the republic. Religious precepts are easily obeyed, which indulge and sanctify the natural inclinations of their votaries; but the pure and genuine influence of Christianity may be traced in its beneficial, though imperfect, effects on the Barbarian proselytes of the North. If the decline of the Roman empire was hastened by the conversion of Constantine, his victorious religion broke the violence of the fall, and mollified the ferocious temper of the conquerors.

This awful revolution may be usefully applied to the instruction of the present age. It is the duty of a patriot to prefer and promote the exclusive interest and glory of his native country; but a philosopher may be permitted to enlarge his views, and to consider Europe as one great republic, whose various inhabitants have attained almost the same level of politeness and cultivation. The balance of power will continue to fluctuate, and the prosperity of our own or the neighbouring kingdoms may be alternately exalted or depressed; but these partial events cannot essentially injure our general state of happiness, the system of arts, and laws, and manners, which so advantageously distinguish, above the rest of mankind, the Europeans and their colonies. The savage nations of the globe are the common enemies of civilized society; and we may inquire with anxious curiosity, whether Europe is still threatened with the repetition of those calamities which formerly oppressed the arms and institutions of Rome. Perhaps the same reflections will illustrate the fall of that mighty empire, and explain the probable causes of our actual security.

I.   The Romans were ignorant of the extent of their danger, and the number of their enemies. Beyond the Rhine and Danube, the northern countries of Europe and Asia were filled with innumerable tribes of hunters and shepherds, poor, voracious, and turbulent; bold in arms, and impatient to ravish the fruits of industry. The Barbarian world was agitated by the rapid impulse of war; and the peace of Gaul or Italy was shaken by the distant revolution of China. The Huns, who fled before a victorious enemy, directed their march towards the West; and the torrent was swelled by the gradual accession of captives and allies. The flying tribes who yielded to the Huns assumed in *their* turn the spirit of conquest; the endless column of Barbarians pressed on the Roman empire with accumulated weight; and, if the foremost were destroyed, the vacant space was instantly replenished by new assailants. Such formidable emigrations can no longer issue from the North; and the long repose, which has been imputed to the decrease of population, is the happy consequence of the progress of arts and agriculture. Instead of some rude villages, thinly scattered among its woods and morasses, Germany now produces a list of two thousand three hundred walled towns; the Christian kingdoms of Denmark, Sweden, and Poland, have been successively established; and the Hanse merchants, with the Teutonic knights, have extended their colonies along the coast of the Baltic, as far as the Gulf of Finland. From the Gulf of Finland to the Eastern Ocean, Russia now assumes the form of a powerful and civilized empire. The plough, the loom, and the forge, are introduced on the banks of the Volga, the Oby, and the Lena; and the fiercest of the Tartar hordes have been taught to tremble and obey. The reign of independent Barbarism is now contracted to a narrow span; and the remnant of Calmucks or Uzbecks, whose forces may be almost numbered, cannot seriously excite the apprehensions of the great republic of Europe. Yet this apparent security should not tempt us to forget that new enemies, and unknown dangers, may *possibly* arise from some obscure people, scarcely visible in the map of the world. The Arabs or Saracens, who spread their conquests from India to Spain, had languished in poverty and contempt, till Mahomet breathed into those savage bodies the soul of enthusiasm.

II.   The empire of Rome was firmly established by the singular and perfect coalition of its members. The subject nations, resigning the hope, and even the wish, of independence, embraced the character of Roman citizens; and the provinces of the West were reluctantly torn by the Barbarians from the bosom of their mother-country. But this union was purchased by the loss of national freedom and military spirit; and the servile provinces, destitute of life and motion, expected their safety from the mercenary troops and governors, who were directed by the orders of a distant court. The happiness of an hundred millions depended on the personal merit of one or two men, perhaps children, whose minds were corrupted by education, luxury, and despotic power. The deepest wounds were inflicted on the empire during the minorities of the sons and grandsons of Theodosius; and, after those incapable princes seemed to attain the age of manhood, they abandoned the church to the bishops, the state to the eunuchs, and the provinces to the Barbarians. Europe is now divided into twelve powerful, though unequal, kingdoms, three respectable commonwealths, and a variety of smaller, though independent, states; the chances of royal and ministerial talents are multiplied, at least with the number of its rulers; and a Julian, or Semiramis, may reign in the North, while Arcadius and Honorius again slumber on the thrones of the South. The abuses of tyranny are restrained by the mutual influence of fear and shame; republics have acquired order and stability; monarchies have imbibed the principles of freedom, or, at least, of moderation; and some sense of honour and justice is introduced into the most defective constitutions by the general manners of the times. In peace, the progress of knowledge and industry is accelerated by the emulation of so many active rivals: in war, the European forces are exercised by temperate and undecisive contests. If a savage conqueror should issue from the deserts to Tartary, he must repeatedly vanquish the robust peasants of Russia, the numerous armies of Germany, the gallant nobles of France, and the intrepid freemen of Britain; who, perhaps, might confederate for their common defence. Should the victorious Barbarians carry slavery and desolation as far as the Atlantic Ocean, ten thousand vessels would transport beyond their pursuit the remains of civilized society; and Europe would revive and flourish in the American world, which is already filled with her colonies and institutions.

III.   Cold, poverty, and a life of danger and fatigue, fortify the strength and courage of Barbarians. In every age they have oppressed the polite and peaceful nations of China, India, and Persia, who neglected, and still neglect, to counterbalance these natural powers by the resources of military art. The warlike states of antiquity, Greece, Macedonia, and Rome, educated a race of soldiers; exercised their bodies, disciplined their courage, multiplied their forces by regular evolutions, and converted the iron which they possessed, into strong and serviceable weapons. But this superiority insensibly declined with their laws and manners; and the feeble policy of Constantine and his successors armed and instructed, for the ruin of the empire, the rude valour of the Barbarian mercenaries. The military art has been changed by the invention of gunpowder; which enables man to command the two most powerful agents of nature, air, and fire. Mathematics, chymistry, mechanics, architecture, have been applied to the service of war; and the adverse parties oppose to each other the most elaborate modes of attack and of defence. Historians may indignantly observe that the preparations of a siege would found and maintain a flourishing colony; yet we cannot be displeased that the subversion of a city should be a work of cost and difficulty, or that an industrious people should be protected by those arts, which survive and supply the decay of military virtue. Cannon and fortifications now form an impregnable barrier against the Tartar horse; and Europe is secure from any future irruption of Barbarians; since, before they can conquer, they must cease to be barbarous. Their gradual advances in the science of war would always be accompanied, as we may learn from the example of Russia, with a proportionable improvement in the arts of peace and civil policy; and they themselves must deserve a place among the polished nations whom they subdue.

Should these speculations be found doubtful or fallacious, there still remains a more humble source of comfort and hope. The discoveries of ancient and modern navigators, and the domestic history, or tradition, of the most enlightened nations, represent the *human savage*, naked both in mind and body, and destitute of laws, of arts, of ideas, and almost of language. From this abject condition, perhaps the primitive and universal state of man, he has gradually arisen to command the animals, to fertilise the earth, to traverse the ocean, and to measure the heavens. His progress in the improvement and exercise of his mental and corporeal faculties has been irregular and various, infinitely slow in the beginning, and increasing by degrees with redoubled velocity; ages of laborious ascent have been followed by a moment of rapid downfall; and the several climates of the globe have felt the vicissitudes of light and darkness. Yet the experience of four thousand years should enlarge our hopes, and diminish our apprehensions; we cannot determine to what height the human species may aspire in their advances towards perfection; but it may safely be presumed that no people, unless the face of nature is changed, will relapse into their original barbarism. The improvements of society may be viewed under a threefold aspect. 1. The poet or philosopher illustrates his age and country by the efforts of a *single* mind; but these superior powers of reason or fancy are rare and spontaneous productions, and the genius of Homer, or Cicero, or Newton, would excite less admiration, if they could be created by the will of a prince or the lessons of a preceptor. 2. The benefits of law and policy, of trade and manufactures, of arts and sciences, are more solid and permanent; and *many* individuals may be qualified, by education and discipline, to promote, in their respective stations, the interest of the community. But this general order is the effect of skill and labour; and the complex machinery may be decayed by time or injured by violence. 3. Fortunately for mankind, the more useful, or, at least, more necessary arts can be performed without superior talents or national subordination; without the powers of *one* or the union of *many*. Each village, each family, each individual, must always possess both ability and inclination to perpetuate the use of fire and of metals; the propagation and service of domestic animals; the methods of hunting and fishing; the rudiments of navigation; the imperfect cultivation of corn or other nutritive grain; and the simple practice of the mechanic trades. Private genius and public industry may be extirpated; but these hardy plants survive the tempest, and strike an everlasting root into the most unfavourable soil. The splen-

did days of Augustus and Trajan were eclipsed by a cloud of ignorance; and the Barbarians subverted the laws and palaces of Rome.
But the scythe, the invention or emblem of Saturn, still continued
annually to mow the harvests of Italy: and the human feasts of the
Laestrygons have never been renewed on the coast of Campania.

Since the first discovery of the arts, war, commerce, and religious
zeal have diffused, among the savages of the Old and New World,
those inestimable gifts: they have been successively propagated; they
can never be lost. We may therefore acquiesce in the pleasing conclusion that every age of the world has increased, and still increases,
the real wealth, the happiness, the knowledge, and perhaps the virtue, of the human race.

2. The Decay of Ancient Civilization

MICHAEL ROSTOVTZEFF

Every reader of a volume devoted to the Roman Empire will expect the author to express his opinion on what is generally, since Gibbon, called the decline and fall of the Roman Empire, or rather of ancient civilization in general. I shall therefore briefly state my own view on this problem, after defining what I take the problem to be. The decline and fall of the Roman Empire, that is to say, of ancient civilization as a whole, has two aspects: the political, social, and economic on the one hand, and the intellectual and spiritual on the other. In the sphere of politics we witness a gradual barbarization of the Empire from within, especially in the West. The foreign, German, elements play the leading part both in the government and in the army, and settling in masses displace the Roman population, which disappears from the fields. A related phenomenon, which indeed was a necessary consequence of this barbarization from within, was the gradual disintegration of the Western Roman Empire; the ruling classes in the former Roman provinces were replaced first by Germans and Sarmatians, and later by Germans alone, either through peaceful penetration or by conquest. In the East we observe a gradual Orientalization of the Byzantine Empire, which leads ultimately to the establishment, on the ruins of the Roman Empire, of strong half-Oriental and purely Oriental states, the Caliphate of Arabia, and the Persian and Turkish empires. From the social and economic point of view, we mean by decline the gradual relapse of the

From Michael Rostovtzeff, *The Social and Economic History of the Roman Empire*, 2d ed. (Oxford: Clarendon Press, 1957), Vol. I, pp. 532–541. Reprinted by permission of the Clarendon Press, Oxford.

ancient world to very primitive forms of economic life, into an almost pure "house-economy." The cities, which had created and sustained the higher forms of economic life, gradually decayed, and the majority of them practically disappeared from the face of the earth. A few, especially those that had been great centres of commerce and industry, still lingered on. The complicated and refined social system of the ancient Empire follows the same downward path and becomes reduced to its primitive elements: the king, his court and retinue, the big feudal landowners, the clergy, the mass of rural serfs, and small groups of artisans and merchants. Such is the political, social, and economic aspect of the problem. However, we must not generalize too much. The Byzantine Empire cannot be put on a level with the states of Western Europe or with the new Slavonic formations. But one thing is certain: on the ruins of the uniform economic life of the cities there began everywhere a special, locally differentiated, evolution.

From the intellectual and spiritual point of view the main phenomenon is the decline of ancient civilization, of the city civilization of the Greco-Roman world. The Oriental civilizations were more stable: blended with some elements of the Greek city civilization, they persisted and even witnessed a brilliant revival in the Caliphate of Arabia and in Persia, not to speak of India and China. Here again there are two aspects of the evolution. The first is the exhaustion of the creative forces of Greek civilization in the domains where its great triumphs had been achieved, in the exact sciences, in technique, in literature and art. The decline began as early as the second century B.C. There followed a temporary revival of creative forces in the cities of Italy, and later in those of the Eastern and Western provinces of the Empire. The progressive movement stopped almost completely in the second century A.D. and, after a period of stagnation, a steady and rapid decline set in again. Parallel to it, we notice a progressive weakening of the assimilative forces of Greco-Roman civilization. The cities no longer absorb—that is to say, no longer hellenize or romanize—the masses of the country population. The reverse is the case. The barbarism of the country begins to engulf the city population. Only small islands of civilized life are left, the senatorial aristocracy of the late Empire and the clergy; but both, save for a section of the clergy, are gradually swallowed up by the advancing tide of barbarism.

Another aspect of the same phenomenon is the development of a new mentality among the masses of the population. It was the mentality of the lower classes, based exclusively on religion and not only indifferent but hostile to the intellectual achievements of the higher classes. This new attitude of mind gradually dominated the upper classes, or at least the larger part of them. It is revealed by the spread among them of the various mystic religions, partly Oriental, partly Greek. The climax was reached in the triumph of Christianity. In this field the creative power of the ancient world was still alive, as is shown by such momentous achievements as the creation of the Christian church, the adaptation of Christian theology to the mental level of the higher classes, the creation of a powerful Christian literature and of a new Christian art. The new intellectual efforts aimed chiefly at influencing the mass of the population and therefore represented a lowering of the high standards of city-civilization, at least from the point of view of literary forms.

We may say, then, that there is one prominent feature in the development of the ancient world during the imperial age, alike in the political, social, and economic and in the intellectual field. It is a gradual absorption of the higher classes by the lower, accompanied by a gradual levelling down of standards. This levelling was accomplished in many ways. There was a slow penetration of the lower classes into the higher, which were unable to assimilate the new elements. There were violent outbreaks of civil strife: the lead was taken by the Greek cities, and there followed the civil war of the first century B.C. which involved the whole civilized world. In these struggles the upper classes and the city-civilization remained victorious on the whole. Two centuries later, a new outbreak of civil war ended in the victory of the lower classes and dealt a mortal blow to the Greco-Roman civilization of the cities. Finally, that civilization was completely engulfed by the inflow of barbarous elements from outside, partly by penetration, partly by conquest, and in its dying condition it was unable to assimilate even a small part of them.

The main problem, therefore, which we have to solve is this. Why was the city civilization of Greece and Italy unable to assimilate the masses, why did it remain a civilization of the *élite*, why was it incapable of creating conditions which should secure for the ancient world a continuous, uninterrupted movement along the same path of urban civilization? In other words: why had modern civilization to be built up laboriously as something new on the ruins of the old, instead of being a direct continuation of it? Various explanations have been suggested, and each of them claims to have finally solved the problem. Let us then review the most important of them. They may be divided into four classes.

(1) The political solution is advocated by many distinguished scholars. For Beloch the decay of ancient civilization was caused by the absorption of the Greek city-states by the Roman Empire, by the formation of a world-state which prevented the creative forces of Greece from developing and consolidating the great achievements

of civilized life. There is some truth in this view. It is evident that the creation of the Roman Empire was a step forward in the process of levelling, and that it facilitated the final absorption of the higher classes. We must, however, take into consideration that class war was a common feature of Greek life, and that we have not the least justification for supposing that the Greek city-community would have found a solution of the social and economic problems which produced civil war in the various communities. Further, this view suggests that there was only one creative race in the ancient world, which is notoriously false. Another explanation, tending in the same direction, has been put forward by Kornemann. He regards as the main cause of the decay of the Roman Empire the fact that Augustus reduced the armed forces of the Empire, and that this reduction was maintained by his successors. The suggestion lays the whole emphasis on the military side of the problem, and is therefore a return to the antiquated idea that ancient civilization was destroyed by the barbarian invasions, an idea which should not be resuscitated. Besides, the maintenance of a comparatively small army was imperatively imposed by the economic weakness of the Empire, a fact which was understood by all the emperors. Still less convincing is the idea of Ferrero, that the collapse of the Empire was due to a disastrous event, to an accident which had the gravest consequences. He holds that by transmitting his power to his son Commodus instead of to a man chosen by the senate, M. Aurelius undermined the senate's authority on which the whole fabric of the Roman state rested; that the murder of Commodus led to the usurpation of Septimius and to the civil war of the third century; and that the usurpation and the war destroyed the authority of the senate and deprived the imperial power of its only legitimacy in the eyes of the population which was its main support. Ferrero forgets that legally the power of the emperors in the third century was still derived from the senate and people of Rome, that it was so even in the time of Diocletian, and that the same idea still survived under Constantine and his successors. He also forgets that the subtle formula of Augustus, Vespasian, and the Antonines was incomprehensible to the mass of the people of the Empire, and was a creation of the upper classes, completely outside the range of popular conceptions. Finally, he fails to understand the true character of the crisis of the third century. The struggle was not between the senate and the emperor, but between the cities and the army—that is to say, the masses of peasants—as is shown by the fact that the lead in the fight was taken not by Rome but by the cities of the province of Africa. A deeper explanation is offered by Heitland. He suggests that the ancient world decayed because it was unable to give the masses a share in the government, and even gradually restricted the numbers of those who participated in the life of the state, ultimately reducing them to the emperor himself, his court, and the imperial bureaucracy. I regard this point as only one aspect of the great phenomenon which I have described above. Have we the right to suppose that the emperors would not have tried the plan of representative government if they had known of it and believed in it? They tried many other plans and failed. If the idea of representative government was foreign to the ancient world (and as a matter of fact it was not), why did the ancient world not evolve the idea, which is not a very difficult one? Moreover, the question arises, Can we be sure that representative government is the cause of the brilliant development of our civilization and not one of its aspects, just as was the Greek city-state? Have we the slightest reason to believe that modern democracy is a guarantee of continuous and uninterrupted progress, and is capable of preventing civil war from breaking out under the fostering influence of hatred and envy? Let us not forget that the most modern political and social theories suggest that democracy is an antiquated institution, that it is rotten and corrupt, being the offspring of capitalism, and that the only just form of government is the dictatorship of the proletariat, which means a complete destruction of civil liberty and imposes on one and all the single ideal of material welfare, and of equalitarianism founded on material welfare.

(2) The economic explanation of the decay of the ancient world must be rejected completely. In speaking of the development of industry in the ancient world, I have dealt with the theory of K. Bücher, accepted with modifications by M. Weber and G. Salvioli. If the theory fails to explain even this minor point, much less will it serve to explain the general phenomenon. Those who defend this theory forget that the ancient world went through many cycles of evolution, and that in these cycles there occur long periods of progress and other long periods of return to more primitive conditions, to the phase of economic life which is generally described as "house-economy." It is true that the ancient world never reached the economic stage in which we live. But in the history of the ancient world we have many epochs of high economic development: certain periods in the history of many Oriental monarchies, particularly Egypt, Babylonia, and Persia; the age of the highest development of the city-states, especially the fourth century B.C.; the period of the Hellenistic monarchies, where the climax was reached in the third century B.C.; the period of the late Roman Republic and of the early Roman Empire. All these periods show different aspects of economic life and different aspects of capitalism. In none of them did the forms of house-economy prevail. We may compare the economic

aspect of life during these periods to that of many European countries in the time of the Renaissance and later, although in no case would the comparison be perfect, as there is no identity between the economic development of the modern and that of the ancient world. According to the different economic conditions of these several periods in the history of the ancient world, the relations between house-economy and capitalistic economy varied, and they frequently varied not only in the different periods but also in different parts of the ancient world during the same period. The ancient world was in this respect not unlike the modern world. In the industrial countries of Europe, such as England and some parts of Germany and France, economic life nowadays is by no means the same as it is in the agricultural countries, like Russia and the Balkan peninsula and large parts of the Near East. The economic life of the United States of America is not in the least identical with the economic life of Europe or of the various parts of South America, not to speak of China, Japan, and India. So it was in the ancient world. While Egypt and Babylonia had a complex economic life, with a highly developed industry and wide commercial relations, other parts of the Near East lived a quite different and much more primitive life. While Athens, Corinth, Rhodes, Syracuse, Tyre, and Sidon in the fourth century B.C. were centres of a developed commercial capitalism, other Greek cities lived an almost purely agricultural life. In the Hellenistic and Roman periods it was just the same. The main fact which has to be explained is why capitalistic development, which started at many times and in many places, and prevailed in large portions of the ancient world for comparatively long periods, yielded ultimately to more primitive forms of economic life. Even in our own times it has not completely ousted those forms. It is evident that the problem cannot be solved by affirming that the ancient world lived throughout under the forms of primitive house-economy. The statement is manifestly wrong. We might say exactly the same of large areas of the modern world, and we are not at all sure that a violent catastrophe might not bring the modern capitalistic world back to the primitive phase of house-economy.

To sum up what I have said, the economic simplification of ancient life was not the cause of what we call the decline of the ancient world, but one of the aspects of the more general phenomenon which the theories mentioned above try to explain. Here, just as in the other spheres of human life, the political, social, intellectual, and religious, the more primitive forms of life among the masses were not absorbed by the higher forms but triumphed over them in the end. We may select one of these phenomena and declare it to be the ultimate cause; but it would be an arbitrary assumption which would not convince any one. The problem remains. Why was the victorious advance of capitalism stopped? Why was machinery not invented? Why were the business systems not perfected? Why were the primal forces of primitive economy not overcome? They were gradually disappearing; why did they not disappear completely? To say that they were quantitatively stronger than in our own times does not help us to explain the main phenomenon. That is why many economists, who are aware that the usual explanation only touches the surface and does not probe the problem to the bottom, endeavour to save the economic explanation, and the materialistic conception of historical evolution in general, by producing some potent physical factor as the cause of the weakness of the higher forms of economic life in the ancient world. Such a factor has been found by some scholars in the general exhaustion of the soil all over the ancient world, which reached its climax in the late Roman Empire and ruined the ancient world. I have dealt with this theory above. There are no facts to support it. All the facts about the economic development of the ancient world speak against it. Agriculture decayed in the ancient world just in the same way and from the same causes as the other branches of economic life. As soon as the political and social conditions improved in the various parts of the Empire, the fields and gardens began to yield the same harvests as before. Witness the flourishing state of Gaul in the time of Ausonius and of Sidonius Apollinaris; witness the fact that in Egypt, where the soil is inexhaustible and those parts of it which are not flooded are very easily improved by the most primitive methods, agriculture decayed in the third and fourth centuries, just as in the other provinces. It is plain that the economic explanation does not help us, and that the investigations of the economists reveal, not the cause of the decline of the ancient world, but merely one of its aspects.

(3) The rapid progress of medicine and of biological science has had its influence on the problem of the decay of ancient civilization. A biological solution has been often suggested, and the theories of degeneration and race-suicide have been applied to the ancient world. The biological theory supplies us with an apparently exhaustive explanation of the decline of the assimilative forces of the civilized upper classes. They gradually degenerated and had not the power to assimilate the lower classes but were absorbed by them. According to Seeck, the cause of their degeneration and of their numerical decline was the "extermination of the best" by foreign and civil wars. Others, like Tenney Frank, think of the contamination of higher races by an admixture of the blood of inferior races. Others, again, regard degeneration as a natural process common to all civilized communities: the best are neither exterminated nor con-

taminated, but they commit systematic suicide by not reproducing and by letting the inferior type of mankind breed freely. I am not competent to sit in judgment on the problem of degeneration from the biological and physiological point of view. From the historical point of view, I venture to remark against Seeck that in wars and revolutions it is not only the best that are exterminated. On the other hand, revolutions do not always prevent the succeeding period from being a period of great bloom. Against Frank I may suggest that I see no criterion for distinguishing between inferior and superior races. Why are the Greek and Latin races considered the only superior races in the Roman Empire? Some of the races which "contaminated" the ruling races, for instance, the pre-Indo-European and pre-Semitic race or races of the Mediterranean, had created great civilizations in the past (the Egyptian, the Minoan, the Iberian, the Etruscan, the civilizations of Asia Minor), and the same is true of the Semitic and of the Iranian civilizations. Why did the admixture of the blood of these races contaminate and deteriorate the blood of the Greeks and the Romans? On the other hand, the Celts and the Germans belonged to the same stock as the Greeks and the Romans. The Celts had a high material civilization of their own. The Germans were destined to develop a high civilized life in the future. Why did the admixture of their blood corrupt and not regenerate their fellow Aryans, the Greeks and the Romans? The theory of a natural decay of civilization by race-suicide states the same general phenomenon of which we have been speaking, and gradual absorption of the upper classes by the lower and the lack of assimilative power shown by the upper. It states the fact, but gives no explanation. The problem this theory has to solve is, Why do the best not reproduce their kind? It may be solved in different ways: we may suggest an economic, or a physiological, or a psychological explanation. But none of these explanations is convincing.

(4) Christianity is very often made responsible for the decay of ancient civilization. This is, of course, a very narrow point of view. Christianity is but one side of the general change in the mentality of the ancient world. Can we say that this change is the ultimate cause of the decay of ancient civilization? It is not easy to discriminate between causes and symptoms, and one of the urgent tasks in the field of ancient history is a further investigation of this change of mentality. The change, no doubt, was one of the most potent factors in the gradual decay of the civilization of the city-state and in the rise of a new conception of the world and of a new civilization. But how are we to explain the change? Is it a problem of individual and mass psychology?

None of the existing theories fully explains the problem of the decay of ancient civilization, if we can apply the word "decay" to the complex phenomenon which I have endeavoured to describe. Each of them, however, has contributed much to the clearing of the ground, and has helped us to perceive that the main phenomenon which underlies the process of decline is the gradual absorption of the educated classes by the masses and the consequent simplification of all the functions of political, social, economic, and intellectual life, which we call the barbarization of the ancient world.

The evolution of the ancient world has a lesson and a warning for us. Our civilization will not last unless it be a civilization not of one class, but of the masses. The Oriental civilizations were more stable and lasting than the Greco-Roman, because, being chiefly based on religion, they were nearer to the masses. Another lesson is that violent attempts at levelling have never helped to uplift the masses. They have destroyed the upper classes, and resulted in accelerating the process of barbarization. But the ultimate problem remains like a ghost, ever present and unlaid: Is it possible to extend a higher civilization to the lower classes without debasing its standard and diluting its quality to the vanishing point? Is not every civilization bound to decay as soon as it begins to penetrate the masses?

3. The Impact of Christianity

PETER BROWN

The expansion of Christianity was not a gradual, ineluctable process beginning with St Paul and ending with the conversion of Constantine in 312. Its expansion in the third century was impressive, because it had been totally unexpected. Very suddenly, the Christian Church became a force to be reckoned with in the Mediterranean towns. The very seriousness of the measures taken against the Church as a body, and not merely against individual Christians, in the persecutions of 257 and after 303, shows that something was lacking in the life of a Roman town, which Christianity was threatening to fulfil.

The Christian Church differed from the other oriental cults, which it resembled in so many other ways, through its intolerance of the outside world. The cults were exclusive and, often, the jealously guarded preserve of foreigners; but they never set themselves up against the traditional religious observances of the society round them. They never enjoyed the publicity of intermittent persecution. While the oriental cults provided special means to salvation in the next world, they took the position of their devotees in this world for granted. The Christian Church offered a way of living in this world. The skillful elaboration of the ecclesiastical hierarchy, the sense of belonging to a distinctive group with carefully prescribed habits and increasing resources heightened the impression that the Christian Church made on the uncertain generations of the third century.

From Peter Brown, *The World of Late Antiquity* (London: Thames and Hudson, 1971), pp. 65–68, 82–89. Reprinted by permission of Thames and Hudson Ltd.

Seldom has a small minority played so successfully on the anxieties of society as did the Christians. They remained a small group: but they succeeded in becoming a big problem.

Christian missionaries made most headway in just those areas where Roman society was most fluid. The seedbeds of the Church were the raw new provinces of the hinterland of Asia Minor. In a province such as Lycaonia, the arrival of Greek civilization had virtually coincided with the arrival of St Paul. The religious leader Marcion, who brought the Christian community in Rome some 200,000 sesterces, was a contemporary from the same region as the Phrygian merchant who had made this journey seventy-two times.

It is part of the appeal of a religious group that it can be a little ahead of social developments. It was possible to achieve in a small group, "among the brethren," relationships that were being achieved in society at large at a heavy cost of conflict and uncertainty. As a member of a church, the Christian could cut some of the more painful Gordian knots of social living. He could, for instance, become a radical cosmopolitan. His literature, his beliefs, his art and his jargon were extraordinarily uniform, whether he lived in Rome, Lyons, Carthage or Smyrna. The Christians were immigrants at heart—ideological *déracinés*, separated from their environment by a belief which they knew they shared with little groups all over the empire. At a time when so many local barriers were being painfully and obscurely eroded, the Christians had already taken the step of calling themselves a "non-nation."

The Church was also professedly egalitarian. A group in which there was "neither slave nor free" might strike an aristocrat as utopian, or subversive. Yet in an age when the barriers separating the successful freedman from the *déclassé* senator were increasingly unreal, a religious group could take the final step of ignoring them. In Rome the Christian community of the early third century was a place where just such anomalies were gathered and tolerated: the Church included a powerful freedman chamberlain of the emperor; its bishop was the former slave of that freedman; it was protected by the emperor's mistress, and patronized by noble ladies.

For men whose confusions came partly from no longer feeling embedded in their home environment, the Christian Church offered a drastic experiment in social living, reinforced by the excitements and occasional perils of a break with one's past and one's neighbours.

This intense sense of the religious community was the legacy of Judaism. It saved the Christian Church. Because it thought of itself as "the true Israel," the Christian community was able to remain rooted in every town in which it was established, like a limpet on a rock when the tide recedes. In the late third century, the public religious ceremonies of the towns diminished; the dislocation of trade starved the oriental cults of immigrant devotees; but the Christian bishop remained, with a stable community and a long past behind him, to reap his harvest in the towns.

The wealth of the local notables was not so much impaired by the crisis of the late third century, as redirected: sums of money that had been spent on the townsfolk in the previous century were invested in more private living and on more frankly egotistical forms of competition for status. Naturally, the gods were affected by this change in the tempo of social life. Public competition in the second century had involved a large amount of religious activity—rites, processions, dedications of statues and temples. The Late Antique style of life, by contrast, was more blatantly personal, and so more secular: a magnate spent lavishly, but he gave shows and processions in order to emphasize his personal standing, his *potentia*; he did not care for reinforcing communal activities, such as religious festivals. Not surprisingly, therefore, the lavish inscriptions in honour of the traditional gods come to a halt after 250.

The Christian community suddenly came to appeal to men who felt deserted. At a time of inflation, the Christians invested large sums of liquid capital in people; at a time of increased brutality, the courage of Christian martyrs was impressive; during public emergencies, such as plague or rioting, the Christian clergy were shown to be the only united group in the town, able to look after the burial of the dead and to organize food-supplies. In Rome, the Church was supporting fifteen hundred poor and widows by 250. The churches of Rome and Carthage were able to send large sums of money to Africa and Cappadocia, to ransom Christian captives after barbarian raids in 254 and 256. Two generations previously, the Roman state, faced by similar problems after an invasion, had washed its hands of the poorer provincials: the lawyers declared that even Roman citizens would have to remain the slaves of the private individuals who bought them back from the barbarians. Plainly, to be a Christian in 250 brought more protection from one's fellows than to be a *civis romanus*.

But the true measure of the crisis of the towns is not to be found in the appeal of a few spectacular public gestures by the Christian Church. What marked the Christian Church off, and added to its appeal, was the ferociously inward-looking quality of its life. The Church did not scatter its alms indiscriminately: collected from the Christian community, they were presented by the bishop to God as the special "sacrifice" of the group. (The "sacrifice" of alms was quite as much part of the sacrificial offering of the Christians as was the Eucharist; this, in itself, was a most significant departure from pagan practice.) Thus blessed, the wealth of the community returned to the members of the community alone, as part of the "loving-kindness" of God to His special people.

Nor was Christian propaganda indiscriminate. The Christians did not adopt the market-place preaching of the Cynic philosophers. Instead, applicants for membership were supposed to be carefully scrutinized; they were slowly prepared for initiation; and, once initiated, a formidable penitential system made them constantly aware of the awesome chasm between belonging and not belonging to the religious group.

In the mid-third century, an educated Roman, Cyprian of Carthage, could simply disappear into this exotic and self-contained world. From 248 to 258 he spent the last part of his life performing feats of organization and diplomacy in order to maintain the Christian "faction" in Carthage. The appeal of Christianity still lay in its radical sense of community: it absorbed people because the individual could drop from a wide impersonal world into a miniature community, whose demands and relations were explicit.

The Christian Church enjoyed complete tolerance between 260 and 302. This, the "Little Peace of the Church," was of crucial importance, as we shall see . . . for the future development of Christianity in the Roman empire. As for the emperors, they were too preoccupied with the frontiers to care about the Christians. This is a sign of how far away the Rhine and the Danube were from the heart of the classical world; for a generation, the emperors and their advisers turned their backs on what was happening in the Mediterranean cities. When Diocletian finally established his palace in Nicomedia in 287, he was able to look out at a basilica of the Christians standing on the opposite hill. The Roman empire had survived; but in this Roman empire, Christianity had come to stay.

• • •

"If all men wanted to be Christians," the pagan Celsus wrote in 168, "the Christians would no longer want them." By 300 this situation had changed entirely. Christianity had put down firm roots in all the great cities of the Mediterranean: in Antioch and Alexandria the Church had become probably the biggest, certainly the best-organized single religious group in the town. The Christian gains had been made in just that part of the Roman world that had emerged comparatively unscathed from the troubles of the late third century. Silence descended on the stoutly pagan provinces of the West. By contrast, Syria and Asia Minor, with their vocal Christian elements, stood out more sharply than ever before as provinces of undimmed prosperity and intellectual ferment.

The most decisive change of that time, however, cannot be reduced to a matter of the size of the Christian communities. It was more significant for the immediate future of Christianity that the leaders of the Christian Church, especially in the Greek world, found that they could identify themselves with the culture, outlook and needs of the average well-to-do civilian. From being a sect ranged against or to one side of Roman civilization, Christianity had become a church prepared to absorb a whole society. This is probably the most important *aggiornamento* in the history of the Church: it was certainly the most decisive single event in the culture of the third century. For the conversion of a Roman emperor to Christianity, of Constantine in 312, might not have happened—or, if it had, it would have taken on a totally different meaning—if it had not been preceded, for two generations, by the conversion of Christianity to the culture and ideals of the Roman world.

Origen of Alexandria (*c.* 185–*c.* 254) was the towering genius whose works summed up the possibility of such a venture in assimilation. His work, continued by a succession of Greek bishops, culminated in the writings of a contemporary and adviser of the emperor Constantine, Eusebius, bishop of Caesarea, from about 315 to about 340. For Origen and his disciples, Christianity was the "natural," the "original" religion. The "seeds" of Christian doctrine had been sown by Christ in every man. Ever since the Creation they had been variously tended by Him. Christ, therefore, had "tended" the best in Greek culture—especially Greek philosophy and ethics—as deliberately as He had revealed the Law to the Jews; the foundation of the universal Christian Church by Christ had been expressly synchronized with the foundation of a universal Roman peace by Augustus. A Christian, therefore, could reject neither Greek culture nor the Roman empire without seeming to turn his back on part of the divinely ordained progress of the human race. Christ was the "schoolmaster" of the human race, and Christianity was the peak of His education, the "true" *paideia*, the "true" culture. Origen and his successors taught the pagan that to become a Christian was to step, at last, from a confused and undeveloped stage of moral and intellectual growth into the heart of civilization. On the sarcophagi and frescoes of the late third century, Christ appears as the Divine Schoolmaster, dressed in the simple robes of a professor of literature, lecturing—as Origen must have done—to a quiet circle of well-groomed disciples. The Christian bishop had become part of the intelligentsia of many a great Greek town: he, also, sat on a professor's "chair"—his *cathedra;* and he was thought of as "lecturing" his *didaskaleion,* his study-group, on simple and elevating ethical themes.

The early fourth century was the great age of the Christian Apologists—Lactantius (*c.* 240–*c.* 320), writing in Latin, and Eusebius of Caesarea, in Greek. Their appeals to the educated public coincided with the last, the "Great Persecution of the Church," from 302 to 310, and with the conversion and reign of Constantine as a Christian emperor from 312 to 337. The Christianity of the Apologists was not merely a religion that had found a *modus vivendi* with the civilization that surrounded it. They presented it as something far more than that. They claimed that Christianity was the sole guarantee of that civilization—that the best traditions of classical philosophy and the high standards of classical ethics could be steeled against barbarism only through being confirmed by the Christian revelation; and that the beleaguered Roman empire was saved from destruction only by the protection of the Christian God.

Such a message played on the "Great Fear" of the townsmen of the Mediterranean world of the late third century. One should always remember that classical civilization was the civilization of a fragile veneer: only one man in ten lived in the civilized towns. At no time did this urban crust feel its hold over a wide world to be more precarious than at the end of the third century. The townsmen had maintained their privileges. But they were dwarfed by a countryside whose face had become less recognizable to classical men. In many rural areas, from Britain to Syria, archaic cults, far removed from the classical Olympians, reared their heads more insistently than ever before. The primitive tribes from beyond the frontiers had made their presence felt in terrifying *razzias.* Furthermore, the traditional protectors of the towns, the emperors and their army, had never seemed so alien. The Roman army was stationed among, and recruited from, the populations of the frontiers. It had always been an outsider in the Mediterranean world: in the generation before the accession of Diocletian, in 284, it was in danger of becoming a foreign body. The Danubian provincials who saved the empire needed to be told by their commanders that they did so to preserve, not to terrorize, the civilians. When we compare the rough, uniformed figures of Diocletian and his colleagues with the exquisitely classical sarcophagi of contemporary upper-class Christians, we realize that, against the gulf which threatened to open between the new masters of the empire and the traditions of the ancient cities, the old division between pagan and Christian civilian might seem insignificant. By 300, the Christian bishop had at least become part of the landscape of most towns: in the civilized Greek world it was the Latin-speaking soldier who was the outsider.

With the return of peace after the accession of Diocletian, the wound began to close between the new, military governing class and the urban civilization of the Mediterranean. But there were now two groups who claimed to represent this civilization: the traditional pagan governing class, whose resilience and high standards had been shown in the revival and spread of Platonic philosophy in the late third century, were in danger of being outbid by the new, "middlebrow" culture of the Christian bishops, whose organizing power and adaptability had been proved conclusively in the previous generation.

At first, organization for survival was more important to the emperors than culture. Diocletian was a sincere, *borné* Roman traditionalist; yet he ruled for nineteen years without giving a thought to the Christians. The "Great Persecution," which began in 302 and continued spasmodically for a decade, came as a brutal shock to respectable Christians. They found themselves officially outcastes in the society with which they had so strenuously identified themselves. It was a terrifying and, on the whole, a deeply demoralizing experience. They were saved by an obscure event. In 312, a usurping emperor, Constantine, won a battle over his rival at the Milvian Bridge, outside Rome. He ascribed this victory to the protection of the Christian God, vouchsafed in a vision.

If God helps those who help themselves, then no group better deserved the miracle of the "conversion" of Constantine in 312 than did the Christians. For the Christian leaders seized their opportunity with astonishing pertinacity and intelligence. They besieged Constantine in his new mood: provincial bishops, notably Hosius of Cordova (*c.* 257–357), attached themselves to his court; other bishops, from Africa, swept him into their local affairs as a judge; Lactantius emerged as tutor to his son; and, when Constantine finally conquered the eastern provinces in 324, he was greeted by Eusebius of Caesarea, who placed his pen at the emperor's disposal with a skill and enthusiasm such as no traditional Greek rhetor had seemed able to summon up for Constantine's grim and old-fashioned predecessors—Diocletian and Galerius.

This prolonged exposure to Christian propaganda was the true "conversion" of Constantine. It began on a modest scale when he controlled only the under-Christianized western provinces; but it reached its peak after 324, when the densely Christianized territories of Asia Minor were united to his empire. Its results were decisive. Constantine could easily have been merely a "god-fearing" emperor, who, for reasons of his own, was prepared to tolerate the Christians: there had been many such in the third century (one of whom, Philip (244–249), was even regarded as a crypto-Christian).

Given the religious climate of the age, there was no reason, either, why this decision to tolerate the Church might have been ascribed to intimations from the Christian God. Constantine rejected this easy and obvious solution. He came to be the emperor we know from his speeches and edicts: a crowned Christian Apologist. He viewed himself and his mission as a Christian emperor in the light of the interpretation of Christianity that had been presented to the average educated layman by the Christian Apologists of his age. In becoming a Christian, Constantine publicly claimed to be saving the Roman empire; even more—in mixing with bishops, this middle-aged Latin soldier sincerely believed that he had entered the charmed circle of "true" civilization, and had turned his back on the Philistinism of the raw men who had recently attacked the Church.

One suspects that Constantine was converted to many more aspects of Mediterranean life than to Christianity alone. The son of a soldier, he threw in his lot with a civilian way of life that had been largely ignored by the grey administrators of the age of Diocletian. From 311 onwards, Constantine put the landed aristocracy on its feet again: he is the "restorer of the Senate," to whom the aristocracy of the West owed so much. In 332, he gave these landowners extensive powers over their tenants. After 324, he grouped a new civilian governing class round himself in the Greek East. . . . He gave the provincial gentry of Asia Minor what they had long wanted: Constantinople, a "new" Rome, placed within convenient range of the imperial court as it moved along the routes connecting the Danube to Asia Minor. For the Greek senator and bureaucrat, roads that had long ceased to lead to Rome converged quite naturally at this new capital.

Constantine, very wisely, seldom said "no." The first Christian emperor accepted pagan honours from the citizens of Athens. He ransacked the Aegean for pagan classical statuary to adorn Constantinople. He treated a pagan philosopher as a colleague. He paid the travelling expenses of a pagan priest who visited the pagan monuments of Egypt. After a generation of "austerity" for everyone, and of "terror" for the Christians, Constantine, with calculated flamboyance, instituted the "Great Thaw" of the early fourth century: it was a whole restored civilian world, pagan as well as Christian, that was pressing in round the emperor.

In this restored world, the Christians had the advantage of being the most flexible and open group. The bishops could accept an uncultivated emperor. They were used to autodidacts, to men of genuine eccentric talent who—so they claimed—were taught by God alone. Constantine, one should remember, was the younger contemporary of the first Christian hermit, St Anthony. . . . Neither the

Latin-speaking soldier nor the Coptic-speaking farmer's son would have been regarded as acceptable human material for a classical schoolmaster: yet Eusebius of Caesarea wrote the life of Constantine the soldier, and Athanasius of Alexandria—an equally sophisticated Greek—the life of Anthony the Egyptian. It was over the wide bridge of a "middlebrow" identification of Christianity with a lowest common denominator of classical culture, and not through the narrow gate of a pagan aristocracy of letters, that Constantine and his successors entered the civilian civilization of the Mediterranean.

THE MAKING OF EUROPE

IN THE FOURTH century "Western Europe" did not exist as a political or cultural entity. Most of modern Germany lay outside the borders of the Roman state. Northern Gaul and Britain were mere outlying provinces of a Mediterranean empire which found its greatest centers of wealth and population in the East. By the time of Charlemagne's coronation (A.D. 800) a new, distinctively European society had emerged. It included numerous Germanic peoples; its main centers of power were in the north; it formed a political-religious unit clearly distinguished from the Byzantine civilization to the east and the Islamic civilization to the south.

Between A.D. 400 and A.D. 800 two basic processes of change—one religious, one economic—contributed to this outcome of events. Virtually all the people of Western Europe came to accept a common religion, Roman Christianity. And the trading activity which had linked the western provinces of the Roman empire to a Mediterranean system of commerce dwindled almost to nothing. Traditionally these changes have been seen as the slow working out of the consequences of the Germanic invasions. In 1925 the great economic historian Henri Pirenne proposed a radically different interpretation upon which he elaborated in several subsequent works. The unity of the Mediterranean world survived the Germanic invasions, he maintained. The decisive changes which led to the emergence of Charlemagne's Europe were initiated by the Islamic conquests of the seventh and eighth centuries. Pirenne's thesis was argued mainly in terms of economic history, and it stimulated a great body of new work by other historians on the economic life of the early Middle Ages. In the following readings D. C. Dennett criticizes Pirenne's arguments; Christopher Dawson reminds us of the religious foundations of the new European civilization; and Bryce Lyon presents a contemporary summing-up of the whole controversy.

4. Mohammed and Charlemagne

HENRI PIRENNE

The Mediterranean

The Roman Empire, at the end of the third century, had one out-standing general characteristic: it was an essentially Mediterranean commonwealth. Virtually all of its territory lay within the watershed of that great landlocked sea; the distant frontiers of the Rhine, the Danube, the Euphrates, and the Sahara, may be regarded merely as an advanced circle of outer defenses protecting the approaches.

The Mediterranean was, without question, the bulwark of both its political and economic unity. Its very existence depended on mastery of the sea. Without that great trade route, neither the government, nor the defense, nor the administration of the *orbis romanus* would have been possible.

As the Empire grew old this fundamentally maritime character was, interestingly enough, not only preserved but was still more sharply defined. When the former inland capital, Rome, was abandoned, its place was taken by a city which not only served as a capital but which was at the same time an admirable seaport—Constantinople.

The Empire's cultural development, to be sure, had clearly passed its peak. Population decreased, the spirit of enterprise waned, bar-barian hordes commenced to threaten the frontiers, and the increasing expenses of the government, fighting for its very life, brought in their train a fiscal system which more and more enslaved men to the State. Nevertheless this general deterioration does not seem to have appreciably affected the maritime commerce of the Mediterranean. It continued to be active and well sustained, in marked contrast with the growing apathy that characterized the inland provinces. Trade continued to keep the East and West in close contact with each other. There was no interruption to the intimate commercial relations between those diverse climes bathed by one and the same sea. Both manufactured and natural products were still extensively dealt in: textiles from Constantinople, Edessa, Antioch, and Alexandria; wines, oils, and spices from Syria; papyrus from Egypt; wheat from Egypt, Africa, and Spain; and wines from Gaul and Italy. There was even a reform of the monetary system based on the gold *solidus,* which served materially to encourge commercial operations by giving them the benefit of an excellent currency, universally adopted as an instrument of exchange and as a means of quoting prices.

• • •

The appearance of the Germanic tribes on the shore of the Mediterranean was by no means a critical point marking the advent of a new era in the history of Europe. Great as were the consequences which it entailed, it did not sweep the boards clean nor even break the tradition. The aim of the invaders was not to destroy the Roman Empire but to occupy and enjoy it. By and large, what they preserved far exceeded what they destroyed or what they brought that was new. It is true that the kingdoms they established on the soil of the Empire made an end of the latter in so far as being a *State* in Western Europe. From a political point of view the *orbis romanus,* now strictly localized in the East, lost that ecumenical character which had made its frontiers coincide with the frontiers of Christianity. The Empire, however, was far from becoming a stranger to the lost provinces. Its civilization there outlived its authority. By the Church, by language, by the superiority of its institutions and law, it prevailed over the conquerors. In the midst of the troubles, the insecurity, the misery, and the anarchy which accompanied the invasions there was naturally a certain decline, but even in that decline there was preserved a physiognomy still distinctly Roman. The Germanic tribes were unable, and in fact did not want, to do without it. They barbarized it, but they did not consciously germanize it.

Nothing is better proof of this assertion than the persistence in the last days of the Empire—from the fifth to the eighth century— of that maritime character pointed out above . . . the economic organization of the world lived on after the political transformation.

In lack of other proofs, the monetary system of the Frankish kings would alone establish this truth convincingly. This system, as is too well known to make necessary any lengthy consideration here, was purely Roman or, strictly speaking, Romano-Byzantine. This is shown by the coins that were minted: the *solidus*, the *triens*, and the *denarius*—that is to say, the *sou*, the *third-sou*, and the *denier*. It is shown further by the metal which was employed: gold, used for the coinage of the *solidus* and the *triens*. It is also shown by the weight which was given to specie. It is shown, finally, by the effigies which were minted on the coins. In this connection it is worth noting that the mints continued for a long time, under the Merovingian kings, the custom of representing the bust of the Emperor on the coins and of showing on the reverse of the pieces the *Victoria Augusti* and that, carrying this imitation to the extreme, when the Byzantines substituted the cross for the symbol of that victory they did the same. Such extreme servility can be explained only by the continuing influence of the Empire. The obvious reason was the necessity of preserving, between the local currency and the imperial currency, a conformity which would be purposeless if the most intimate relations had not existed between Merovingian commerce and the general commerce of the Mediterranean. In other words, this commerce continued to be closely bound up with the commerce of the Byzantine Empire.

• • •

Merovingian times knew, thanks to the continuance of Mediterranean shipping and the intermediary of Marseilles, what we may safely call a great commerce. It would certainly be an error to assume that the dealings of the Oriental merchants of Gaul were restricted solely to articles of luxury. Probably the sale of jewelry, enamels, and silk stuffs resulted in handsome profits, but this would not be enough to explain their number and their extraordinary diffusion throughout all the country. The traffic of Marseilles was, above all else, supported by goods for general consumption such as wine and oil, spices, and papyrus. These commodities, as has already been pointed out, were regularly exported to the north.

The Oriental merchants of the Frankish Empire were virtually engaged in wholesale trade. Their boats, after being discharged on the quays of Marseilles, certainly carried back, on leaving the shores of Provence, not only passengers but return freight. Our sources of information, to be sure, do not tell much about the nature of this freight. Among the possible conjectures, one of the most likely is that it probably consisted, at least in good part, in human chattels—that is to say, in slaves. Traffic in slaves did not cease to be carried on in the Frankish Empire until the end of the ninth century. The wars waged against the barbarians of Saxony, Thuringia, and the Slavic regions provided a source of supply which seems to have been abundant enough. Gregory of Tours speaks of Saxon slaves belonging to a merchant of Orleans, and it is a good guess that this Samo, who departed in the first half of the seventh century with a band of companions for the country of Wends, whose king he eventually became, was very probably nothing more than an adventurer trafficking in slaves. And it is of course obvious that the slave trade, to which the Jews still assiduously applied themselves in the ninth century, must have had its origin in an earlier era.

If the bulk of the commerce in Merovingian Gaul was to be found in the hands of Oriental merchants, their influence, however, should not be exaggerated. Side by side with them, and according to all indications in constant relations with them, are mentioned indigenous merchants. Gregory of Tours does not fail to supply information concerning them, which would undoubtedly have been more voluminous if his narrative had had more than a merely incidental interest in them. He shows the king consenting to a loan to the merchants of Verdun, whose business prospers so well that they soon find themselves in a position to reimburse him. He mentions the existence in Paris of a *domus negociantum*—that is to say, apparently, of a sort of market or bazaar. He speaks of a merchant profiteering during the great famine of 585 and getting rich. And in all those anecdotes he is dealing, without the least doubt, with professionals and not with merely casual buyers or sellers.

The picture which the commerce of Merovingian Gaul presents is repeated, naturally, in the other maritime Germanic kingdoms of the Mediterranean—among the Ostrogoths of Italy, among the Vandals of Africa, among the Visigoths of Spain. The Edict of Theodoric contained a quantity of stipulations relative to merchants. Carthage continued to be an important port in close relations with Spain, and her ships, apparently, went up the coast as far as Bordeaux. The laws of the Visigoths mentioned merchants from overseas.

In all of this is clearly manifest the vigorous continuity of the commercial development of the Roman Empire after the Germanic invasions. They did not put an end to the economic unity of antiquity. By means of the Mediterranean and the relations kept up thereby between the West and East, this unity, on the contrary, was preserved with a remarkable distinctiveness. The great inland sea of Europe no longer belonged, as before, to a single State. But nothing yet gave reason to predict that it would soon cease to have its time-honored importance. Despite the transformations which it had undergone, the new world had not lost the Mediterranean character of the old. On the shores of the sea was still concentrated the better part of its activities. No indication yet gave warning of the end of the common-wealth of civilization, created by the Roman Empire from the Pillars of Hercules to the Aegean Sea. At the beginning of the seventh century, anyone who sought to look into the future would have been unable to discern any reason for not believing in the continuance of the old tradition.

Yet what was then natural and reasonable to predict was not to be realized. The world-order which had survived the Germanic inva-sions was not able to survive the invasion of Islam.

It is thrown across the path of history with the elemental force of a cosmic cataclysm. Even in the lifetime of Mahomet (571–632) no one could have imagined the consequences or have prepared for them. Yet the movement took no more than fifty years to spread from the China Sea to the Atlantic Ocean. Nothing was able to with-stand it. At the first blow, it overthrew the Persian Empire (637–644). It took from the Byzantine Empire, in quick succession, Syria (634–636), Egypt (640–642), Africa (698). It reached into Spain (711). The resistless advance was not to slow down until the start of the eighth century, when the walls of Constantinople on the one side (713) and the soldiers of Charles Martel on the other (732) broke that great enveloping offensive against the two flanks of Christianity.

But if its force of expansion was exhausted, it had none the less changed the face of the world. Its sudden thrust had destroyed an-cient Europe. It had put an end to the Mediterranean common-wealth in which it had gathered its strength.

The familiar and almost "family" sea which once united all the parts of this commonwealth was to become a barrier between them. On all its shores, for centuries, social life, in its fundamental char-acteristics, had been the same; religion, the same; customs and ideas, the same or very nearly so. The invasion of the barbarians from the North had modified nothing essential in that situation.

But now, all of a sudden, the very lands where civilization had been born were torn away; the cult of the Prophet was substituted for the Christian Faith, Moslem law for Roman law, the Arab tongue for the Greek and the Latin tongue.

The Mediterranean had been a Roman lake; it now became, for the most part, a Moslem lake. From this time on it separated, instead of uniting, the East and the West of Europe. The tie which was still binding the Byzantine Empire to the Germanic kingdoms of the West was broken.

The Ninth Century

The tremendous effect the invasion of Islam had upon Western Europe has not, perhaps, been fully appreciated.

Out of it arose a new and unparalleled situation, unlike anything that had gone before. Through the Phoenicians, the Greeks, and finally the Romans, Western Europe had always received the cultural stamp of the East. It had lived, as it were, by virtue of the Mediterranean; now for the first time it was forced to live by its own resources. The center of gravity, heretofore on the shore of the Mediterranean, was shifted to the north. As a result the Frankish Empire, which had so far been playing only a minor role in the history of Europe, was to become the arbiter of Europe's destinies.

There is obviously more than mere coincidence in the simultaneity of the closing of the Mediterranean by Islam and the entry of the Carolingians on the scene. There is the distinct relation of cause and effect between the two. The Frankish Empire was fated to lay the foundations of the Europe of the Middle Ages. But the mission which it fulfilled had as an essential prior condition the overthrow of the traditional world-order. The Carolingians would never have been called upon to play the part they did if historical evolution had not been turned aside from its course and, so to speak, "de-Saxoned" by the Moslem invasion. Without Islam, the Frankish Empire would probably never have existed and Charlemagne, without Mahomet, would be inconceivable.

This is made plain enough by the many contrasts between the Merovingian era, during which the Mediterranean retained its time-honored historical importance, and the Carolingian era, when that influence ceased to make itself felt. These contrasts were in evidence everywhere: in religious sentiment, in political and social institutions, in literature, in language, and even in handwriting. From whatever standpoint it is studied, the civilization of the ninth century shows a distinct break with the civilization of antiquity. Nothing would be more fallacious than to see therein a simple continuation of the preceding centuries. The *coup d'etat* of Pepin the Short was considerably more than the substitution of one dynasty for another. It marked a new orientation of the course hitherto followed by history. At first glance there seems reason to believe that Charlemagne, in assuming the title of Roman Emperor and of Augustus, wished to restore the ancient tradition. In reality, in setting himself up against the Emperor of Constantinople, he broke that tradition. His Empire was Roman only in so far as the Catholic Church was Roman. For it was from the Church, and the Church alone, that came its inspiration. The forces which he placed at her service were, moreover, forces of the north. His principal collaborators, in religious and cultural matters, were no longer, as they had previously been, Italians, Aquitanians, or Spaniards; they were Anglo-Saxons—a St. Boniface or an Alcuin—or they were Swabians, like Einhard. In the affairs of the State, which was now cut off from the Mediterranean, southerners played scarcely any rôle. The Germanic influence commenced to dominate at the very moment when the Frankish Empire, forced to turn away from the Mediterranean, spread over Northern Europe and pushed its frontiers as far as the Elbe and the mountains of Bohemia.[1]

In the field of economics the contrast, which the Carolingian period shows to Merovingian times, is especially striking. In the days of the Merovingians, Gaul was still a maritime country and trade and traffic flourished because of that fact. The Empire of Charlemagne, on the contrary, was essentially an inland one. No longer was there any communication with the exterior; it was a closed State, a State without foreign markets, living in a condition of almost complete isolation.

To be sure, the transition from one era to the other was not clear-cut. The trade of Marseilles did not suddenly cease but, from the middle of the seventh century, waned gradually as the Moslems advanced in the Mediterranean. Syria, conquered by them in 633–638, no longer kept it thriving with her ships and her merchandise. Shortly afterwards, Egypt passed in her turn under the yoke of Islam (638–640), and papyrus no longer came to Gaul. A characteristic consequence is that, after 677, the royal chancellery stopped using papyrus.[2] The importation of spices kept up for a while, for the monks of Corbie, in 716, believed it useful to have ratified for the last time their privileges of the *tonlieu of Fos.* A half century later, solitude reigned in the port of Marseilles. Her foster-mother, the sea, was shut off from her and the economic life of the inland regions which had been nourished through her intermediary was definitely extinguished. By the ninth century Provence, once the richest country of Gaul, had become the poorest.

More and more, the Moslems consolidated their domination over the sea. In the course of the ninth century they seized the Balearic Isles, Corsica, Sardinia, Sicily. On the coasts of Africa they founded new ports: Tunis (698–703); later on, Mehdia to the south of this city; then Cairo, in 973. Palermo, where stood a great arsenal, became their principal base in the Tyrrhenian Sea. Their fleets sailed it in complete mastery; commercial flotillas transported the products of the West to Cairo, whence they were redispatched to Bagdad, or pirate fleets devastated the coasts of Provence and Italy and put towns to the torch after they had been pillaged and their inhabitants captured to be sold as slaves. In 889 a band of these plunderers even laid hold of Fraxinetum (the present Garde-Frainet, in the Department of the Var) not far from Nice, the garrison of which, for nearly a century thereafter, subjected the neighboring populace to continual raids and menaced the roads which led across the Alps from France to Italy.

The efforts of Charlemagne and his successors to protect the coasts from Saracen raiders were as impotent as their attempts to oppose the invasions of the Norsemen in the north and west. The hardihood and seamanship of the Danes and Norwegians made it easy for them to plunder the coasts of the Carolingian Empire during the whole of the eleventh century. They conducted their raids not only from the North Sea, the Channel, and the Gulf of Gascony, but at times even from the Mediterranean. Every river which emptied into these seas was, at one time or another, ascended by their skilfully constructed barks, splendid specimens whereof, brought to light by recent excavations, are now preserved at Oslo. Periodically the valleys of the Rhine, the Meuse, the Scheldt, the Seine, the Loire, the Garonne, and the Rhône were the scene of systematic and persistent pillaging. The devastation was so complete that, in many cases indeed, the population itself disappeared. And nothing is a better illustration of the essentially inland character of the Frankish Empire than its inability to organize the defense of its coasts, against either Saracens or Norsemen. For that defense, to be effective, should have been a naval defense, and the Empire had no fleets, or hastily improvised ones at best.

Such conditions were incompatible with the existence of a commerce of first-rate importance. The historical literature of the ninth century contains, it is true, certain references to merchants (*mercatores, negociatores*), but no illusions should be cherished as to their importance. Compared to the number of texts which have been preserved from that era, these references are extremely rare. The capitularies, those regulations touching upon every phase of social life, are remarkably meagre in so far as applies to commerce. From this it may be assumed that the latter played a rôle of only secondary, negligible importance. It was only in the north of Gaul, that, during the first half of the ninth century, trade showed any signs of activity.

Of a regular and normal commercial activity, of steady trading carried on by a class of professional merchants, in short, of all that constitutes the very essence of an economy of exchange worthy of the name, no traces are to be found after the closing off of the Mediterranean by the Islamic invasion. The great number of markets (*mercatus*), which were to be found in the ninth century, in no way contradicts this assertion. They were, as a matter of fact, only small local marketplaces, instituted for the weekly provisioning of the populace by means of the retail sale of foodstuffs from the country. As a proof of the commercial activity of the Carolingian era, it would be equally beside the point to speak of the existence of the street occupied by merchants (*vicus mercatorum*) at Aix-la-Chapelle near the palace of Charlemagne, or of similar streets near certain great abbeys such as, for example, that of St. Riquier. The merchants with whom we have to do here were not, in fact, professional merchants but servitors charged with the duty of supplying the Court or the monks. They were, so to speak, employees of the seignorial household staff and were in no respect merchants.

There is, moreover, material proof of the economic decline which affected Western Europe from the day when she ceased to belong to the Mediterranean commonwealth. It is furnished by the reform of the monetary system, initiated by Pepin the Short and completed by Charlemagne. That reform abandoned gold coinage and substituted silver in its place. The *solidus* which had heretofore, conforming to the Roman tradition, constituted the basic monetary unit, was now only nominal money. The only real coins from this time on were the silver *deniers*, weighing about two grams, the metallic value of which, compared to that of the dollar, was approximately eight and one-half cents. The metallic value of the Merovingian gold *solidus* being nearly three dollars, the importance of the reform can be readily appreciated. Undoubtedly it is to be explained only by a prodigious falling off of both trading and wealth.

If it is admitted, and it must be admitted, that the reappearance of gold coinage, with the florins of Florence and the ducats of Venice in the thirteenth century, characterized the economic renaissance of Europe, the inverse is also true: the abandoning of gold coinage in the eighth century was the manifestation of a profound decline. It is not enough to say that Pepin and Charlemagne wished to remedy the monetary disorder of the last days of the Merovingian era. It would have been quite possible for them to find a remedy without giving up the gold standard. They gave up the standard, obviously, from necessity—that is to say, as a result of the disappearance of the yellow metal in Gaul. And this disappearance had no other cause than the interruption of the commerce of the Mediterranean. The proof of this is given by the fact that Southern Italy, remaining in contact with Constantinople, retained like the latter a gold standard, for which the Carolingian sovereigns were forced to substitute a silver standard. The very light weight of their *deniers*, moreover, testifies to the economic isolation of their Empire. It is inconceivable that they would have reduced the monetary unit to a thirtieth of its former value if there had been preserved the slightest bond between their States and the Mediterranean regions where the gold *solidus* continued to circulate.

But this is not all. The monetary reform of the ninth century not only was in keeping with the general impoverishment of the era in which it took place, but with the circulation of money which was noteworthy for both lightness and inadequacy. In the absence of centers of attraction sufficiently powerful to draw money from afar, it remained, so to speak, stagnant. Charlemagne and his successors in vain ordered that *deniers* should be coined only in the royal mints. Under the reign of Louis the Pious, it was necessary to give to certain churches authorization to coin money, in view of the difficulties, under which they labored, of obtaining cash. From the second half of the ninth century on, the authorization to establish a market was almost always accompanied by the authorization to establish a mint in the same place. The State could not retain the monopoly of mint-ing coins. It was consistently frittered away. And that is again a man-ifestation, by no means equivocal, of the economic decline. History shows that the better commerce is sustained, the more the monetary system is centralized and simplified. The dispersion, the variety, and in fact the anarchy which it manifests as we follow the course of the ninth century, ends by giving striking confirmation to the general theory here put forward.

There have been some attempts to attribute to Charlemagne a farseeing political economy. This is to lend him ideas which, however great we suppose his genius to have been, it is impossible for him to have had. No one can submit with any likelihood of truth that the projects which he commenced in 793, to join the Rednitz to the Altmuhl and so establish communication between the Rhine and the Danube, could have had any other purpose than the transport of troops, or that the wars against the Avars were provoked by the desire to open up a commercial route to Constantinople. The stipulations, in other respects inoperative, of the capitularies regarding coinages, weights and measures, the market-tolls and the markets, were inti-mately bound up with the general system of regulation and control which was typical of Carolingian legislation. The same is true re-garding the measures taken against usury and the prohibition en-joining members of the clergy from engaging in business. Their pur-pose was to combat fraud, disorder, and indiscipline and to impose a Christian morality on the people. Only a prejudiced point of view can see in them an attempt to stimulate the economic development of the Empire.

We are so accustomed to consider the reign of Charlemagne as an era of revival that we are unconsciously led to imagine an identical progress in all fields. Unfortunately, what is true of literary culture, of the religious State, of customs, institutions, and statecraft is not true of communications and commerce. Every great thing that Charlemagne accomplished was accomplished either by his military strength or by his alliance with the Church. For that matter, neither the Church nor arms could overcome the circumstances in virtue of which the Frankish Empire found itself deprived of foreign markets. It was forced, in fact, to accommodate itself to a situation which was inevitably prescribed. History is obliged to recognize that, however brilliant it seems in other respects, the cycle of Charlemagne, considered from an economic viewpoint, is a cycle of regression.

The financial organization of the Frankish Empire makes this plain. It was, indeed, as rudimentary as could be. The poll tax, which the Merovingians had preserved in imitation of Rome, no longer existed. The resources of the sovereign consisted only in the revenue from his demesnes, in the tributes levied on conquered tribes, and in the booty got by war. The market-tolls no longer contributed to the replenishment of the treasury, thus attesting to the commercial decline of the period. They were nothing more than a simple extortion brutally levied in kind on the infrequent merchandise transported by the rivers or along the roads. The sorry proceeds, which should have served to keep up the bridges, the docks, and the highways, were swallowed up by the functionaries who collected them, the *missi dominici*, created to supervise their administration, were impotent in abolishing the abuses which they proved to exist because the State, unable to pay its agents, was likewise unable to impose its authority on them. It was obliged to call on the aristocracy which, thanks to their social status, alone could give free services. But in so doing it was constrained, for lack of money, to choose the instruments of power from among the midst of a group of men whose most evident interest was to diminish that power. The recruiting of the functionaries from among the aristocracy was the fundamental vice of the Frankish Empire and the essential cause of its dissolution, which became so rapid after the death of Charlemagne. Surely, nothing is more fragile than that State the sovereign of which, all-powerful in theory, is dependent in fact upon the fidelity of his independent agents.

The feudal system was in embryo in this contradictory situation. The Carolingian Empire would have been able to keep going only if it had possessed, like the Byzantine Empire or the Empire of the Caliphs, a tax system, a financial control, a fiscal centralization, and a treasury providing for the salary of functionaries, for public works, and for the maintenance of the army and the navy. The financial impotence which caused its downfall was a clear demonstration of the impossibility it encountered of maintaining a political structure on an economic base which was no longer able to support the load.

NOTES

1. The objection may be raised that Charlemagne conquered in Italy the kingdom of the Lombards and in Spain the region included between the Pyrenees and the Ebro. But these thrusts towards the south are by no means to be explained by a desire to dominate the shores of the Mediterranean. The expeditions against the Lombards were provoked by political causes and especially by the alliance with the Papacy. The expedition in Spain had no other aim than the establishing of a solid frontier against the Moslems.

2. Imports, however, had not completely ceased at that date. The last reference we know to the use of papyrus in Gaul is in 737; see M. Prou, *Manuel de paléographie*, 3rd edit., p. 17. In Italy, it was continued to be used up to the eleventh century; see A. Giry, *Manual de diplomatique*, p. 494. It was imported there either from Egypt or, more probably, from Sicily (where the Arabs had introduced its manufacture) by the shipping of the Byzantine cities of the South of the Peninsula, or by that of Venice.

5.   *Pirenne and Muhammad*

DANIEL C. DENNETT

A critic of Pirenne's theses must begin by asking the following six questions:

1. Was it the policy and the practice of the Arabs to prohibit commerce either at its source or on the normal trade routes of the Mediterranean? Can we indicate an approximate date, accurate within twenty-five years, for the ending of commerce between the Christian Occident and the Orient?
2. Is is possible to find another explanation for the disappearance of the wines of Gaza, the papyrus of Egypt, and the spices of the Orient?
3. Is is true that Gaul had no appreciable foreign commerce after the beginning of the Carolingian period?
4. Is it true that the civilization of Merovingian Gaul, considered in its broadest social and political aspects, was determined by trade? Is it possible that internal factors conversely may have been of importance in determining the prosperity of industry and trade? How extensive was Mediterranean commerce before 650?
5. Was "Romania" in fact a true cultural unity of ideas, law, language, foreign policy, common interest?
6. What is the real significance and true cause of the transition from a gold to a silver coinage?

From Daniel C. Dennett, "Pirenne and Muhammad," *Speculum*, Vol. 23 (1948), pp. 167–181, 185–190. Reprinted by permission of the Medieval Academy of America.

43

I

We must affirm that neither in the Koran, nor in the sayings of the Prophet, nor in the acts of the first caliphs, nor in the opinions of Muslim jurists is there any prohibition against trading with the Christians or unbelievers. Before Muhammad, the Arabs of the desert lived by their flocks and those of the town by their commerce. To these two sources of livelihood the conquest added the income of empire and the yield of agriculture, but the mercantile career remained the goal of many, as the caravan still crossed the desert and the trading vessel skirted the coast line of the Red Sea, the Persian Gulf, and the Indian Ocean. Pirenne has asserted that "it is a proven fact that the Musulman traders did not install themselves beyond the frontiers of Islam. If they did trade, they did so among themselves." This statement is a serious misrepresentation of fact. Arab merchants had established trading colonies which were centers not only for the exchange of goods but the propagation of the faith in India, Ceylon, the East Indies, and even China, by the close of the eighth century, and if one wishes to know why they did not establish similar centers in Gaul, let him ask the question—would Charlemagne have permitted a mosque in Marseilles?

In this respect the Muslims themselves were more tolerant and placed few obstacles in the path of Christian traders who came to their territory. Within the lands that had formerly submitted to the Emperor, the Christians were now subjects of the Muslim state, yet they were protected by law, and in return for the payment of their taxes and the discharge of obligations stipulated in the original terms of capitulation, they were specifically and formally guaranteed the freedom of Christian worship, the jurisdiction of Christian bishops in cases not involving Muslims, and the pursuit of trades and professions. The civil service and the language of administration remained Greek, and Arabic did not universally displace Greek in the government bureaus until the end of the first century following the conquest. In Egypt, at least, the change of rule brought an improvement in the social and economic life of the population, and the church of Alexandria enjoyed a liberty of faith which it had hitherto not experienced.

In consideration of the fact that it has formerly been believed that internal causes produced a decline of industry and trade in Gaul, the burden of proof in Pirenne's thesis must show that the Arab raids were of a frequency and intensity *in themselves* to destroy the commerce of the western Mediterranean. It is not a just argument merely to assert that these raids were disastrous because commerce in Gaul declined. We have already noticed that in order to connect the decline of the Merovingian monarchy with the activity of the Arabs, Pirenne has been obliged to assign the date 650 as that point when Arab naval activity became formidable. What are the facts?

There may have been a raid on Sicily in 652. We are told that it was led by Muawia ibn Hudajj and resulted in taking much booty from unfortified places, but was called off when plague threatened the invaders. As Amari shows, there is a great deal of confusion among the Muslim authorities both as to the date (for an alternative, 664 A.D. is given), as to the leader (since it is highly probable that not Muawia but his lieutenant Abdallah ibn Quis commanded the actual expedition), and as to the port of embarkation (either Tripoli in Syria or Barka in North Africa). Becker does not accept the date 652 and argues that the first raid took place only in 664, but it is possible that there were two different expeditions, one in 652, the second in 664.

Three years after the presumed earliest assault on Sicily, the Emperor Constans II, in 655, received a serious blow to his prestige when the Byzantine fleet was beaten in the Aegean by the new Muslim navy in the first real test of sea power. The Arabs did not follow up their victory, but its consequence demonstrated to the Emperor the need for a vigorous naval policy, for, although Constantinople and the straits might be held against siege, the strategically vulnerable point of the Empire was not in the Aegean, but in the West, since (as events were to show two centuries later) once the enemy had a base in Sicily, South Italy would then be within easy grasp, and if South Italy were securely held, only immense navel exertions could protect Greece proper, and if Greece fell under Muslim control, a combined blockade by land and sea of the imperial city would be possible. Bury holds that this consideration, the guarding of the rear against attack from the West, was a strong motive in inducing Constans to concentrate naval power in the West and to go himself to Sicily in 662, where he reigned for six years until his assassination in 668.

The Arabs took advantage of the chaos following the assassination to raid the coasts of Sicily the next year, but when order was reestablished Sicily remained at peace again for thirty-five years.

Meanwhile the Greek fleet itself was far from inactive, raiding Egypt in 673 and, in a successful attack on Barka in 689, putting the Arabs to a rout in which the governor of North Africa, Zuheir ibn Qais, perished. Early attempts to take Carthage were frustrated because the Greeks had control of the seas, and the city fell in 698 only because the Arabs had constructed a fleet for the purpose and the

Greek naval force was in the Aegean. Following Bury's argument, if the Emperor had established a permanent naval base at Carthage, the city would never have been taken.

Therefore, in view of the facts that the Arabs made only two (possibly three) raids on Sicily before 700, that these raids resulted in a vigorous naval policy of the Greeks in the West, that it was not until 698 that the Arabs had a fleet strong enough to operate at Carthage, and that they had not yet seized the straits of Gibraltar or occupied Spain, we are bound to acknowledge the absence of any evidence to indicate the closing of the Mediterranean thereby weakening the basis of royal power in Gaul before 700. Pirenne himself acknowledges this fact by admitting that spices and papyrus could be procured by the monks of Corbie in 716. Indeed, anyone who reads Pirenne closely will notice that he is careless with chronology and mentions results which were produced by the Arab conquest as beginning at various points within a period of 150 years.

• • •

Finally, let us consider the possibility that Gaul was cut off from the East by military occupation.

The Arabs crossed the Pyrenees in 720, occupied Narbonne, and controlled the extreme southern part of the country bordering on the Mediterranean—Septimania. In 726 they occupied Carcassonne. The next great advance, coming in 732, was turned back by Charles Martel in the celebrated battle of Tours. In 736 they reached the Rhone for the *first* time at Arles and Avignon but were hurled back the next year by Charles. We have already mentioned the period of chaos after 740 which shelved all plans of aggression; when domestic order was restored, a new power existed in Gaul; Pippin recaptured Narbonne in 759. Pirenne himself says, "This victory marks, if not the end of the expeditions against Provence, at least the end of the Musulman expansion in the West of Europe." Charlemagne, as is well known, carried the war with indifferent success across the Pyrenees, but the Arabs did not again renew their assaults until after his death. In 848 they raided Marseilles for the first time, and later, spreading out from the base at Fraxinetum, pushed into Switzerland, where in 950 they held Grenoble and the St. Bernard Pass. The consequences of this activity, however, fall long after the period under discussion and need not be considered here.

To summarize: It is not correct to assume, as Pirenne does, that a policy of economic blockade played as principal a role in the warfare of antiquity and the Middle Ages as it does today, unless there is a positive testimony to that effect, as for example, the instance when the Persians cut the Greeks off from the supply of Eastern silk. With the exception of two brief intervals, the Byzantine fleet was master of the Aegean and the eastern Mediterranean not only in the seventh century but in the following centuries. This same fleet defended the West so well that only two raids are known to have been attempted against Sicily before 700. After the conquest of Spain had been accomplished, the Arabs embarked in 720 on an ambitious policy which took them for one brief year to the Rhone, and exactly coinciding in time with these military attacks came a series of raids on Sicily; but by 740 dismal failure was the reward everywhere, and throughout the last fifty years of the century the Arabs were either at peace or on the defensive.

II

Did the Arab conquest of Egypt in 640–642 end the exportation of papyrus? The evidence is to the contrary. It was not until 677 that the royal chancery of Gaul adopted parchment and it would be difficult to imagine that the Frankish government had a supply on hand to last for thirty-seven years. Actually, papyrus was employed in Gaul until a much later epoch, since the monks of Corbie obtained fifty rolls in 716, but the last specimen, dated 787, discovered in the country, had been written in Italy. Papyrus was traditionally employed by the Papacy. Still preserved on papyrus are numerous papal documents, together with a letter of Constantin V to Pippin and a breviary of Archbishop Peter VI (927–971) describing the possessions of the Church of Ravenna. That papyrus was the customary material used by the popes seems to be indicated by numerous references, e.g., the glossator of the panegyrist of Berengar comments on the word papyrus "secundum Romanum morem dicit, qui in papiro scribere solent."

In light of the evidence, there can be no other conclusion than that "the conquest of Egypt by the Arabs brought no immediate change. The manufacturing of papyrus continued." Relying on a statement of Ibn Haukal who referred to the cultivation of papyrus in Sicily in 977, some have held that in the tenth and eleventh centuries, the papal chancery obtained its supplies in Sicily and not in Egypt. In this connection it is worth noting that the process of making rag paper was introduced from China into the Eastern Caliphate shortly after 750, and we hear of a paper factory in Bagdad in 794. About this time there was a decline in Egyptian production of papyrus, and political disturbances in the country so interfered with a supply which paper had not yet made dispensable, that the caliph was forced to establish his own papyrus factory at Samarra in 836. T. W. Allen suggests that inasmuch as the earliest known Greek minuscule occurs in the Uspensky Gospels of 835, one may accept as a hypothesis that a known temporary shortage of papyrus may have induced the world of the Isaurian monarchy to give up the use of papyrus, to write on vellum only, in book form, on both sides, in a small hand permitting the most to be made of the space. Papyrus continued to be produced until the competition of paper finally destroyed the industry in the middle of the eleventh century, and the fact that the last Western document to employ it, a bull of Victor II, is dated 1057 and coincides with the end of production in Egypt, leads us to believe that it was on Egypt, and not on Sicily, that the Papacy depended.

Parchment, of course, was not unknown in Merovingian Gaul, Gregory of Tours mentions it, as Pirenne points out. It was regularly employed in preference to papyrus in Germany from the earliest times.

Since the Arab conquest of Egypt did not cut off the supply of papyrus at its source, because this material was still found in Gaul a century later and was regularly employed by the Papacy until the eleventh century, it is difficult to say that its disappearance in Gaul is a conclusive proof that the Arabs had cut the trade routes. In the absence of all direct evidence one way or another, it would appear that as a possible hypothesis one might conclude that because parchment could be locally produced, because it was preferable as a writing material, and because, owing to a depreciated coinage, it *may* not have been more expensive than papyrus, the people of Gaul preferred to employ it.

The wines of Gaza undoubtedly were no longer exported, or even produced on a large scale, since it is not an unreasonable assumption that the Arabs, following the well known Koranic injunction against wine, discouraged its manufacture. Some vineyards certainly remained, for the Christian churches of Palestine and Syria still used wine in celebrating the mass, and certain of the later Umayyad Caliphs were notorious drunkards. But inasmuch as papyrus and (as we shall presently show) spices were still exported, the *argumentum ad vinum* cannot be seriously advanced.

III

Is it true that with the Carolingians the former commerce of Gaul came to an end and the importation of Eastern luxuries ceased?

Everyone agrees—even Pirenne—that Gaul was surrounded by countries actively engaged in commerce. In Italy, for example, Venetian traders were selling velvet, silk, and Tyrian purple in Pavia by 780. Early in the ninth century they had trading connections with

Alexandria, since the Doge issued an edict in conjuction with Leo V (813–820) forbidding this trade—an edict which had little effect in view of the fact that Venetian merchants translated the body of St. Mark in 827. Venice exported armor, timber for shipbuilding, and slaves—the latter despite the interdicts of Charlemagne and Popes Zacharias and Adrian I and imported all the usual Eastern products: spices, papyrus, and silks, large quantities of which were purchased by the Papacy.

Confronted with the alternative of defending Christendom or co-operating with the Saracens in return for trading rights, Naples, Amalfi, Salerno, and Gaeta chose the latter course.

North of Gaul, the Scandinavian countries and the region about the Baltic maintained an active intercourse with Persia via the water routes of Russia. The Arabs purchased furs (sable, ermine, marten, fox, and beaver), honey, wax, birch bark (for medicinal purposes), hazel nuts, fish glue, leather, amber, slaves, cattle, Norwegian falcons, and isinglas (made from sturgeons' bladders), and they sold jewelry, felt, metal mirrors, luxury goods, and even harpoons for the whale fisheries, besides exporting large quantities of silver coin to balance an unfavorable trade. The evidence for the really great prosperity of this commerce is to be found in the enormous coin hoards, the contents of tombs excavated in Scandinavia, the accounts of Arab geographers, and the incidental references in the writings and lives of men like Adam of Bremen and St. Ansgar. Pirenne testifies to the importance of commerce in this period for the Netherlands.

We now come to the crucial point. If Gaul was surrounded by neighbors actively engaged in commerce, did not some of their activity embrace Gaul as well? Pirenne denies this and asserts that no mention of spices is to be found after 716 in Gaul and that no *negotiator* of the Merovingian type—a man who lent money at interest, was buried in a sarcophagus, and bequeathed property to the poor and the church—existed.

Now spices could be obtained at the time of Charlemagne, but at a high price, according to a statement of Alcuin. . . . Augsburg, from the beginning of the tenth century, imported Oriental products via Venice. In 908 we read of a gift of Tyrian purple by the bishop of Augsburg to the monastery of St. Gall. . . .

Einhard, in his account of the translation of the blessed martyrs, Marcellinus and Peter, mentions that the holy relics on arrival were placed on *new* cushions of silk and that the shrine was draped with fine linen and silk. Abbo, in his epic of the siege of Paris by the Northmen in 885–886, scorned those whose manners were softened by Eastern luxuries, rich attire, Tyrian purple, gems, and Antioch leather. Similar references are to be found in the work of the cele-

brated monk of St. Gall. Are we certain that this credulous retailer
of myth completely falsified the local color as well? A far more interesting example is a long list of spices to be found appended to a
manuscript of the statutes of Abbot Adalhard. These statutes are
certainly dated in 822, but the manuscript is a copy of 986, so scholars have assumed the possibility that the list of spices may have been
inserted at any period between 822 and 986. If this were true, Pirenne's case would certainly be shaken and he has not hesitated to
deny the authenticity of the document, which he places in the Merovingian period. But he can produce not a single argument to support his view—except the usual one—the document could not date
from 822 or after because the Arabs had cut the trade routes of the
Mediterranean. Such a reason is inadmissible.

That Carolingian Gaul traded with her neighbors we may gather
from a capitulation issued by Charlemagne in 805 regulating commerce with the East in which specific towns were named where merchants might go. Louis the Pious confirmed the bishop of Marseilles
as collector of tariff at the port. An edict of Charles III in 887 mentions merchants at Passau on the Danube who were exempt from
customs duties. A pact of Lothar in 840 regulated trade with Venice.

Charles the Bald in a charter of immunity given to St. Denis in
884 exempted from all exactions boats belonging to the monks engaged in trade or to their commercial agents, "qui pro orum utilitate
ad Massiliam . . . seu per diversos portus. . . . mercatus negotiandi
gratia advenissent" [i.e., agents traveling to Marseilles or other
ports].

Sabbe has discovered an example of at least one *negotiator* who
died in Bonn in 845 and disposed of a large estate—a man who
certainly would seem to be included in Pirenne's definition of a
Merovingian merchant. We have a continuous record of Mainz as a
trading center from the ninth to the eleventh century: Einhard mentions grain merchants who were accustomed (*solebant*) to make purchases in Germany. The *Annales Fuldenses,* for the famine year of 850,
mention the price of grain there; Frisian merchants founded a
colony in the city in 866. Otto I sent a wealthy merchant of Mainz—
iustitor ditissimus—as ambassador to Constantinople in 979. An Arab
geographer of the next century describing the city says, "It is strange,
too, that one finds there herbs which are produced only in the far-
thest Orient: pepper, ginger, cloves, etc." Sabbe has collected much
evidence, from which he concludes that in the ninth and tenth centuries there were merchants, men of fortune, making long voyages,
transporting cargoes in ships they owned personally and speculating
on the rise of prices.

It should be unnecessary to repeat further evidence collected by

Dopsch, by Erna Patzelt and by Thompson. Any notion that Gaul was separated from commercial contacts with the East in the ninth and tenth centuries can be contradicted by irrefutable evidence.

IV

Is it true that the culture and stability of Merovingian Gaul was largely determined by its commerce? The answer to this question is to be found in a brief survey of the economic history of the country. From the Roman conquest until the end of the second century of our era, Gaul enjoyed an immense prosperity based on natural products. Wheat and barley were produced in exportable quantities. Flax and wool were woven into textiles famous throughout the Mediterranean world. Cicero tells us (*De Republica*, III, 9, 16) that Rome, to safeguard Italian interests from competition, forbade the production of wine and olives, but the prohibition was ineffective as vineyards and olive orchards multiplied. The wine of Vienne was especially prized in Rome and in the middle of the second century Gaul exported both oil and olives. Forests yielded timber which was sawed into planking or exported to feed the fires of the baths of the imperial city. In Belgium horses were bred for the Roman cavalry. Ham, game birds, and the oysters of Medoc were prized by Roman gourmets.

Mines yielded copper, lead, and iron, and quarries in the Pyrenees, marble. Especially famous was Gallic pottery and glass, large quantities of which have been found at Pompeii and Naples and Rome. The names of hundreds of free workers are known from autographs on sherds. The principal industries were textiles and ironware, for Gallic swords, armor, and metal utensils were highly valued. Leather and skin containers for oil were widely manufactured. One fact is of the *utmost* importance: the merchants and shipowners who carried this commerce were of Gallo-Roman birth. The merchants of Narbonne had a *schola* at Ostia as did those of Arles. An inscription in Narbonne tells us that a native merchant of that city who traded in Sicily was an honorary magistrate of all the important Sicilian ports. Another inscription found in Beirut, dated 201, contains a letter of the prefect to representatives of the five corporations of *navicularii* of Arles. It should be especially noted that all the commodities mentioned above have one characteristic in common: they are either bulky or heavy objects of low intrinsic value which depend of necessity for profitable export on cheap transportation and relative freedom from onerous tariffs.

The accession of Commodus in 180 marks the beginning of serious civil disturbances in Gaul. Robber bands pillaged the country.

After his assassination in 192, the struggle between Clodius and Septimus Severus was settled in the battle of Lyon, in the course of which the city was sacked and burned. Political disorder in this and ensuing periods was always an invitation for the barbarians to cross the frontier. They now came in bands, inflicting damage everywhere. Alexander Severus restored some semblance of order and initiated a policy of settling the new arrivals in military colonies on the frontier, but assassination stayed his hand and the infamous Maximin, who dominated the scene after 235, systematically confiscated all property within his grasp. He reduced the most illustrious families to poverty, seized the property of the different societies and charitable foundations, and stripped the temples of their valuables. A treasure hoard uncovered in 1909 in Cologne, of 100 gold aurei and 20,000 silver pieces, dating from Nero to 236, testifies to the unhappy fate of the owner, who preserved his goods but doubtless lost his life. Maximin shortly was slain, but civil war continued from 238 to 261, with new invasions of Franks and Alemans in 253–257. In 267 the German soldiery murdered the emperor, who had forbidden them the sacking of Mainz. When Aurelian died in 275 more barbarians entered Gaul, to be checked until Probus died in 282, when Alemans and Burgundians ravaged the country and pirates harried the coasts. At the same time the terrible Bagaudes, robber bands of peasants, wreaked havoc wherever they went. It is highly significant that in the debris scattered about Roman ruins in France today are to be found coins and scattered inscriptions dating about, but rarely after, the second half of the third century, thus fixing the date of the greatest damage. Adrian Blanchet, in a study of 871 coin hoards uncovered in Gaul and northern Italy, by tabulating the results in chronological and geographical form has concluded that there is a remarkable correspondence between the places and periods of disorder and invasion, and the location, numbers, and size of the hoards.

When order was restored in the fourth century, the cities had been reduced to a size which could be easily fortified and defended, and they became important rather as military centers with a population of officials, soldiers, clerics, and a few merchants, than as the once thriving, proud, free cities of happier eras. An attempt was made at reconstruction, as in the case of Autun, ravaged in 269 and restored in the years after 296. Testifying to the lack of skilled labor was the importation of masons from Britain to assist in the rebuilding. Yet when Constantine visited Autun in 311 it was still poor and sparsely settled, while the citizens who survived complained of the crushing taxation.

Renewed civil war followed the death of Constantine in 337, culminating in the Frankish invasion of 355. Julian's campaigns brought peace and a revitalized life, but the year following his death, 363, the Alemans again invaded the country and in 368 sacked Mainz. After 395 Gaul was virtually abandoned by the Empire.

In addition to these civil disturbances, the depreciation of the Roman coinage in the third century was a powerful factor in leading to the institution of the colonnate and compulsory services of the fourth century with attendant hardships on the poor and middle classes. The severity of their circumstances urged them to seek relief through the relationship of the *precarium* and *patrocinium*, producing as the result the dominating class of the great landholders of the senatorial aristocracy and a general weakening of all imperial authority.

One would imagine that the final product of these disturbances and regulations would be the serious, if not catastrophic deterioration of the once flourishing economic activity of the country, and our information leads us to believe that such was the case. Some cloth was still made at Treves, Metz, and Reims; but, if we except the beautiful jewelry of the Merovingian age, the glass industry alone may be said to have flourished, although the pieces that have survived are poor in quality and design and characterized by imperfect purification of the glass. Technical skill in masonry was limited, and the crudity of lettering on inscriptions bears witness to a decline of craftsmanship. During the earlier period of the empire, there were frequent references to Gallic sailors, as we have shown, but in the fourth century we hear only of African, Spanish, Syrian, and Egyptian sailors, and it is, of course, well known that Syrians and Orientals henceforth play an increasingly dominant role in trade and commerce. It would be a serious mistake to exaggerate this decline. Arles was still a busy port for the entrance of Eastern commodities, as an edict of Honorius of 418 testifies, and some possessors of large estates were extremely wealthy not only in land, but in large sums of gold; however, the accumulative testimony of writers, archaeology, and legislation indicates a far smaller scale of activity in industry and commerce than two centuries earlier.

Consequently, if after the Gothic invasions of North Italy, Southern Gaul, and Spain, and the Vandal conquest of North Africa and pirate raids in the western Mediterranean in the fifth century, we wish to speak of commerce as a determining factor in Merovingian Gaul, we would have to show that the reigns of Clovis and his successors produced a considerable economic revival, rather than that they maintained purely the status quo. This is, of course, one of the major parts of Pirenne's thesis: that there was an important identity in all the significant aspects of life, government, and culture between East and West, a true unity which effected a real survival—indeed revival—of prosperity until the Muslim conquest. Consequently, a comparison of West and East is necessary, and if possible an attempt should be made to show whether Merovingian government acted to encourage or discourage commerce.

V

The government of Merovingian Gaul was a monarchy, absolute in all respects, and if one may judge from the conduct of its rulers as revealed in the history of Gregory of Tours, the monarch had a very imperfect grasp of the "antique" notion of the state as an instrument designed to promote the common welfare. True, Clovis and his successors preserved many of the features of the Roman administrative system—particularly the method of deriving revenue, but there was certainly not the slightest reason for altering the machinery of an institution designed to raise the maximum of taxes when the principal aim of the ruler was to acquire as much wealth as possible. But even the operation of this part of the government became increasingly inefficient, particularly in the collection of the taxes on land, for the registers were in the greatest disorder and rarely revised, and the powerful did not pay at all. Thus, it came about that the easiest imposts to collect were the indirect tolls on commerce, for officers could be stationed on bridges, at cross roads, in the ports, and along the principal waterways to waylay all who passed. All the old levies of the later empire remained or were multiplied, and we read of the *foratica, laudatica, salutatica, pulveratica, rotatica, timonatica, ripatica, portatica,* and *pontatica* among others. The internal free trade of a bygone era was a thing of the past, and it should be obvious that while such tariffs could be borne by goods of high intrinsic value and small bulk, or by goods going short distances, they would certainly put an intolerable burden on those products which once constituted the basis of Gaul's prosperity.

True, Latin was still the language of administration, but after the death of Justinian, Greek replaced Latin in the East.

• • •

In a wild and bloody period where one Merovingian fought another, the reckless expenditure of money, the destruction of property, the escape of the nobility from taxation, the conciliation of partisans by lavish gifts,—these, and similar factors weakened the royal authority.

Pirenne asserts that "the foreign policy of the Empire embraced all peoples of Europe, and completely dominated the policy of the Germanic State." The fact that on certain occasions embassies were sent to Constantinople or that the Emperor at one time hired the Franks to attack the Lombards is the chief basis of this assertion. Clovis may have been honored by the title of "consul," but would anyone maintain that he considered himself answerable to the will of the Emperor? Insofar as for much of the time the conduct of the kings either in their domestic or foreign affairs can hardly be honored by the term "policy," it would be probably true to say that the Emperor was the *only* one to have a foreign policy.

Again, Pirenne makes a great point of the fact that the Merovingians for a long time employed the image of the Emperor on their coins. So did the Arabs, until Abdul Malik's reform, and for the same reason.

In fact, in matters of law, of policy domestic and foreign, of language, of culture, of statecraft and political vision, the kingdom of the Franks and the empire of the Greeks were as independent of one another as two different sovereign states can be, and if one is reduced to speaking of the mystical "unity of Romania" as a dominant historical fact, one has reduced history itself to mysticism.

VI

... Pirenne turns to the problem of money and says, "In any case, the abundant circulation of gold compels us to conclude that there was a very considerable export trade." Now, in the absence of any banking system for settling by the shipment of bullion an accumulated disparity between exports and imports, one would certainly be prepared to believe it quite possible that the export of some products would bring foreign gold into the country, although the total supply might be diminishing due to larger imports, and this was undoubtedly the case, but Pirenne goes much farther and makes it very plain that he believes the exports from Gaul in early Merovingian days exceeded in value, or at least equalled, the imports of eastern products, since "if it [gold] had been gradually drained away by foreign trade we should find that it diminished as time went on. But we do not find anything of the sort." He argues that when the Muslim conquest closed the trade routes, gold became a rarity and was abandoned for silver as a medium of exchange. The employment of silver was the real beginning of the Middle Ages and is a witness of a reversion to natural economy. When gold reappeared, the Middle Ages were over, and "Gold resumed its place in the monetary system only when spices resumed theirs in the normal diet."

A natural question arises. If gold remained the medium of currency, unimpaired in quantity due to a favorable export balance until the Arabs cut the trade routes, what happened to it then? It could not have flowed East after the catastrophe on the assumption that exports suffered before imports, because Pirenne is insistent, and all the evidence he has collected is designed to show that it was the import of Eastern products which first disappeared. If gold *could not* flow East, why did it not remain in Gaul as a medium of local exchange?

There are at least three factors in the problem.

1. From the earliest times small quantities of gold were found in the beds of certain streams flowing from the Pyrenees, and even in the sands of the Rhine, but the supply was so negligible that one may assert that the West produced no gold. On the other hand, there were substantial deposits of silver, and there were silver mines at Melle in Poitou and in the Harz mountains.

2. It should be unnecessary to point out that we have not the slightest idea of the total amount of gold in Gaul at any period. We occasionally hear of an amount confiscated by a king, of a loan given by a bishop, of a sum bequeathed the church by a landholder or merchant, of the size of booty or tribute, of a subsidy of 50,000 *solidi* sent by the Emperor, but that is all. In many cases, without doubt, a figure or instance is mentioned, not because it was usual, but because it was extraordinary. The number and importance of coin finds are not in any proportion to the probable facts and may not be relied on. Therefore when Pirenne speaks of "large" amounts of gold, he is merely guessing. Furthermore, as is well known, there was in general circulation a bronze and silver currency for use in smaller transactions.

3. Gregory the Great (590–604) testifies that Gallic gold coins were so bad that they did not circulate in Italy, and an examination of coins shows a progressive debasement before the Arab conquest. Since these coins did not come from the royal mint, but were struck by roving minters for people in more than a hundred known localities, one has evidence of the chaotic decentralization of the government and lack of interest in orderly financial administration, together with a possible indication of a growing scarcity of gold.

If gold disappeared in Gaul, this disappearance could be due to the following causes:

a. It might have been hoarded, buried, and lost.

b. It might have been exchanged or used for the purchase of silver.

c. It might have been drained off in purchase of commodities in a one sided trade, or paid in tribute.

d. Through the operation of Gresham's law, foreign merchants might have hoarded and removed the good gold coinage, leaving a debased coinage in local circulation.

There is no evidence to support the first two hypotheses, and considerable evidence for the last two—both of which amount to this same fact: gold *was* drained out of the country. This hypothesis is strongly supported by the best known authority and Bloch gives good reasons for accepting it. Gold, of course, did not completely disappear in the West, as the manufacture of jewelry and occasional references show, and it would be interesting to possess the full facts about the gold coin counterfeiting the Arab dinar—the *mancus*. However, it is difficult to accept the thesis advanced by Dopsch that there was enough gold to constitute with silver a truly bimetallic currency. But it is even more difficult to accept the proposition of Pirenne that the change from gold to silver meant a change from money to natural economy. The numerous instances which prove conclusively that money continued as a medium of exchange have been diligently collected by Dopsch (*Naturalwirtschaft und Geldwirtschaft*, pp. 110–145) and need not be repeated. It is not clear why silver coinage should equal natural economy. China and Mexico use silver today, and the coins of Arab mintage found in the Baltic regions are also silver, yet no one would pretend that in these instances we are dealing with a system of natural economy. Had a system of natural economy prevailed we might have expected an absence of all kinds of money, and the fact that the Carolingians introduced a pure, standard, centrally minted silver coinage would seem logically to prove just the contrary of Pirenne's thesis. . . .

To conclude: There is no evidence to prove that the Arabs either desired to close, or actually did close the Mediterranean to the commerce of the West either in the seventh or eighth centuries. Islam was hostile to Christianity as a rival, not as a completely alien faith, and the Muslims were invariably more tolerant than the Christians, but Islam as a culture, as the common faith of those who submitted and spoke Arabic, though not necessarily by any means of Arab blood, had far more in common with the Hellenized East and with Byzantium than did the Gaul of Pirenne's Romania. Much of what he says of Gaul was true of Islam. The Merovingians took over the administrative and particularly the taxation system of Rome intact. So did the Arabs. The Merovingians preserved Latin as the language of administration. The Arabs used Greek. Western art was influenced by Byzantine forms. So was Arab. But these are smaller matters. The crude Western barbarians were not able to develop—indeed, they were too ignorant to preserve the state and the culture they took by conquest, while the Arabs on the contrary not only preserved what they took but created from it a culture which the world had not known for centuries, and which was not to be equalled for centuries more. This culture was based on that of the Hellenized Eastern Mediterranean in one part and on that of Persia strongly permeated with both Hellenic and Indian elements, on the other. Arab theology, Arab philosophy, Arab science, Arab art—none was in opposition to late antique culture, as Pirenne seems to imagine, but was a new, fertile, virile, and logical development of long established forms. The decadence of the West—the so-called Middle Ages—was due to a complexity of causes, mostly internal, and largely connected with social and political institutions. Rostovtzeff, writing of economic conditions of the later Roman Empire, frequently warns against mistaking an aspect for a cause, and most of the economic factors of the Middle Ages are aspects and not causes. Thus, the man—whether he be a Pirenne or a Dopsch—who attempts to understand and to interpret either the Merovingian or Carolingian period in terms *purely* of an economic interpretation of history will be certain to fail, for the simple reason that economic factors play a subsidiary role and present merely aspects in the great causative process.

6.   *Charlemagne and the Roman Church*

CHRISTOPHER DAWSON

. . . There has never been an age in which England had a greater influence on continental culture. In art and religion, in scholarship and literature, the Anglo-Saxons of the eighth century were the leaders of their age. At the time when continental civilisation was at its lowest ebb, the conversion of the Anglo-Saxons marked the turn of the tide. The Saxon pilgrims flocked to Rome as the centre of the Christian world and the Papacy found its most devoted allies and servants in the Anglo-Saxon monks and missionaries. The foundations of the new age were laid by the greatest of them all, St. Boniface of Crediton, "the Apostle of Germany," a man who had a deeper influence on the history of Europe than any Englishman who has ever lived. Unlike his Celtic predecessors, he was not an individual missionary, but a statesman and organiser, who was, above all, a servant of the Roman order. To him is due the foundation of the mediaeval German Church and the final conversion of Hesse and Thuringia, the heart of the German land. With the help of his Anglo-Saxon monks and nuns he destroyed the last strongholds of Germanic heathenism and planted abbeys and bishoprics on the site of the old Folkburgs and heathen sanctuaries, such as Buraburg, Amoneburg and Fulda. On his return from Rome in 739 he used his authority as Papal Vicar in Germany to reorganise the Bavarian Church and to establish the new dioceses which had so great an importance in German history. For Germany beyond the Rhine was

From Christopher Dawson, *The Making of Europe* (London: Sheed and Ward, 1946), pp. 166–171. Reprinted by permission of Christina Scott as the literary representative of the Estate of Christopher Dawson.

still a land without cities, and the foundation of the new bishoprics meant the creation of new centres of cultural life. It was through the work of St. Boniface that Germany first became a living member of the European society.

This Anglo-Saxon influence is responsible for the first beginnings of vernacular culture in Germany. It is not merely that the Anglo-Saxon missionaries brought with them their custom of providing Latin texts with vernacular glosses, nor even that the earliest monuments of German literature—the old Saxon *Genesis* and the religious epic *Heliand*—seem to derive from the Anglo-Saxon literary tradition. It is that the very idea of a vernacular culture was alien to the traditions of the continental Church and was the characteristic product of the new Christian cultures of Ireland and England, whence it was transmitted to the continent by the missionary movement of the eighth century.

But in addition to this, Boniface was the reformer of the whole Frankish Church. The decadent Merovingian dynasty had already given up the substance of its power to the mayors of the palace, but in spite of their military prowess, which saved France from conquest by the Arabs in 735, they had done nothing for culture and had only furthered the degradation of the Frankish Church. Charles Martel had used the abbeys and bishoprics to reward his lay partisans, and had carried out a wholesale secularisation of Church property. As Boniface wrote to the Pope, "Religion is trodden under foot. Benefices are given to greedy laymen or unchaste and publican clerics. All their crimes do not prevent their attaining the priesthood; at last rising in rank as they increase in sin they become bishops, and those of them who can boast that they are not adulterers or fornicators, are drunkards, given up to the chase, and soldiers, who do not shrink from shedding Christian blood," Nevertheless, the successors of Charles Martel, Pepin and Carloman, were favourable to Boniface's reforms. Armed with his special powers as Legate of the Holy See and personal representative of the Pope, he undertook the desecularisation of the Frankish Church.

In a series of great councils held between 742 and 747, he restored the discipline of the Frankish Church and brought it into close relations with the Roman see. It is true that Boniface failed to realise his full programme for the establishment of a regular system of appeals from the local authorities to Rome and for the recognition of the rights of the Papacy in the investiture of the bishops. But, though Pepin was unwilling to surrender his control over the Frankish Church, he assisted St. Boniface in the reform of the Church and accepted his ideal of co-operation and harmony between the Frankish state and the Papacy. Henceforward the Carolingian dynasty was to be the patron of the movement of ecclesiastical reform, and found in the Church and the monastic culture the force that it needed for its work of political reorganisation. For it was the Anglo-Saxon monks and, above all, St. Boniface who first realised that union of Teutonic initiative and Latin order which is the source of the whole mediaeval development of culture.

• • •

The historical importance of the Carolingian age far transcends its material achievement. The unwieldy Empire of Charles the Great did not long survive the death of its founder, and it never really attained the economic and social organisation of a civilised state. But, for all that, it marks the first emergence of the European culture from the twilight of pre-natal existence into the consciousness of active life. Hitherto the barbarians had lived passively on the capital which they had inherited from the civilisation which they had plundered; now they began to co-operate with it in a creative social activity. The centre of mediaeval civilisation was not to be on the shores of the Mediterranean, but in the northern lands between the Loire and the Weser which were the heart of the Frankish dominions. This was the formative center of the new culture, and it was there that the new conditions which were to govern the history of mediaeval culture find their origin. The ideal of the mediaeval Empire, the political position of the Papacy, the German hegemony in Italy and the expansion of Germany towards the East, the fundamental institutions of mediaeval society both in Church and State, and the incorporation of the classical tradition in mediaeval culture—all have their basis in the history of the Carolingian period.

The essential feature of the new culture was its religious character. While the Merovingian state had been predominantly secular, the Carolingian Empire was a theocratic power—the political expression of a religious unity. This change in the character of the monarchy is shown by the actual circumstances of the installation of the new dynasty; for Pepin obtained Papal authority for the setting aside of the old royal house and was anointed king in the year 752 by St. Boniface according to the religious coronation rite which had grown up under ecclesiastical influence in Anglo-Saxon England and Visigothic Spain, but which had hitherto been unknown among the Franks. Thus the legitimation of the rule of the Carolingian house sealed the alliance between the Frankish monarchy and the Papacy which St. Boniface had done so much to bring about, and henceforward the Frankish monarchy was the recognised champion and protector of the Holy See. The Papacy had already been alienated from the Byzantine Empire by the Iconoclastic policy of the Isaurian emperors, and the extinction of the last survival of the Byzantine power at Ravenna by the Lombards in 751 forced the Pope to look for support elsewhere. In 754 Stephen II visited Pepin in his own dominions, and obtained from him a treaty which secured to the Papacy the Exarchate of Ravenna and the former Byzantine possessions in Italy, together with the duchies of Spoleto and Benevento. In return the Pope reconsecrated Pepin as King of the Franks, and also conferred on him the dignity of Patrician of the Romans. This was an epoch-making event, for it marked not only the foundation of the Papal State which was to endure until 1870, but also the protectorate of the Carolingians in Italy, and the beginning of their imperial mission as the leaders and organisers of Western Christendom.

The Carolingians were naturally fitted to undertake this mission since they were themselves the representatives of both sides of the European tradition. They traced their descent from Gallo-Roman bishops and saints as well as from Frankish warriors, and they combined the warlike prowess of a Charles Martel with a vein of religious idealism, which shows itself in Carloman's renunciation of his kingdom in order to enter the cloister, and Pepin's sincere devotion to the cause of the Church. But it is in Pepin's successor, Charles the Great, that both these elements find simultaneous expression. He was above all a soldier with a talent for war and military enterprise which made him the greatest conqueror of his time. But in spite of his ruthlessness and unscrupulous ambition he was no mere barbaric warrior; his policy was inspired by ideals and universal aims. His conquests were not only the fulfillment of the traditional Frankish policy of military expansion; they were also crusades for the protection and unity of Christendom. By his destruction of the Lombard Kingdom he freed the Papacy from the menace which had threatened its independence for two hundred years and brought Italy into the Frankish Empire. The long drawn out struggle with the Saxons was due to his determination to put an end to the last remains of Germanic heathenism as well as of Saxon independence. His conquest of the Avars in 793–794 destroyed the Asiatic robber state which had terrorised the whole of Eastern Europe, and at the same time restored Christianity in the Danube provinces, while his war with the Saracens and his establishment of the Spanish March were the beginning of the Christian reaction to the victorious expansion of Islam. In the course of thirty years of incessant warfare he had extended the frontiers of the Frankish monarchy as far as the Elbe, the Mediterranean and the Lower Danube, and had united Western Christendom in a great imperial state.

The coronation of Charles as Roman Emperor and the restoration of the Western Empire in the year 800 marked the final stage in the reorganisation of Western Christendom and completed the union between the Frankish monarchy and the Roman Church which had been begun by the work of Boniface and Pepin.

7. *Pirenne's Thesis Today*

BRYCE LYON

What, then, can be said for the Pirenne theory? Much of the sub-sequent research has weakened his thesis. He obviously overempha-sized Merovingian economic activity and its continuity with the Ro-man, and may have underemphasized Carolingian economic activity. He seems also to have assigned to the Arabs too decisive a role in the destruction of Mediterranean economic unity and, conse-quently, in the emergence of the Middle Ages. His treatment of pol-itics and institutions is victim to the same weaknesses as his interpre-tation of economic and social history—overemphasis regarding the continuity of Roman institutions in the German kingdoms and some delusion in believing that the German chiefs took the Roman em-perors as models. Although correct in stressing the exclusively secu-lar bases of German political authority prior to Charlemagne and his father Pepin, Pirenne perhaps attributed too much to the spir-itual sanction of secular authority given by the church. It is true that his bent toward social and economic causation caused him to slight the cultural and religious differences separating the ancient from the medieval world or to place such differences out of focus as in distorting Theodoric's love of classical culture and his patronage of such as Boethius and Cassiodorus. Undoubtedly there was more re-ligious and educational reform and more cultural achievement in the so-called Carolingian renaissance than Pirenne admits, but not in the inflated proportion that many historians would have it. Like

Reprinted from *The Origins of the Middle Ages, Pirenne's Challenge to Gibbon,* by Bruce Lyon, by permission of W. W. Norton & Company, Inc.

most theories concerned with the explanation of vast historical transformations, Pirenne's suffers from over and understatement, generalizes at times upon evidence too scant and cryptic, and explicates too much from certain types of evidence. Later research suggests that the Carolingian and post-Carolingian periods were not as dark socially and economically as Pirenne portrayed, that in the ninth and tenth centuries there were important economic and technological developments from which emerged in the eleventh century such economic phenomena as the town, international trade, and the middle class of merchants and artisans, all of which Pirenne allegedly regarded as springing up rapidly without antecedents.

But Pirenne's theory has by no means been completely discredited. His grand tableau of the early Middle Ages has actually been little changed. It is not wholly accurate to say that he had western Europe leaping into economic revival in the eleventh century without any period of preparation. He traces the momentum for the revival back to the late ninth and tenth centuries which he clearly identified as a preparatory period. From the middle of the tenth century he discerned a rise in population; increased cultivation resulting from the clearance of forests and the reclamation of land from swamps, moors, and coastal waters; a growing political stability essential for economic activity; and a surge in trade along the waterways and overland routes converging on such points as Venice and Flanders. For Pirenne these were the roots of the economic flowering in the eleventh century.

Scholars continue to under and overemphasize the cultural vigor of the Merovingian and Carolingian periods and to distort Christian influence on pagan thought. Some see St. Augustine imbibing in classical thought. Others see him at its fringes, sabotaging it and preparing the way for a completely new view of man and his use of knowledge. Some see Pope Gregory the Great as a competent continuator of good Latin and an admirer of the classical tradition. Others point to his simple Latin compositions, seeing him as epitomizing the difference between sophisticated, rational, classical thought and simple, mystical, Christian thought. These scholars in cultural and religious history with their subjective evaluations will continue to agree or disagree with Pirenne.

Dawson's conclusions, however, parallel those of Pirenne. Like Pirenne, he interpreted Charlemagne's coronation as symbolizing the beginning of the Middle Ages. Pierre Riché's recent study of education and culture in the barbarian West has confirmed the main lines of Pirenne's interpretation of the cultural and religious transition from the ancient to the medieval world. Like Pirenne, Riché sees a transformation in education and thought during the late imperial period that was even given impetus with the advent of the Germans. In spite of the decline of classical culture and its conversion to serve Christian truth, Riché believes that the aristocratic contemporaries of the Merovingians Chilperic and Dagobert still lived in an antique atmosphere, that Merovingian Gaul remained a part of the Mediterranean cultural community into the first half of the seventh century, and that not until the second half of that century did cultured men become scarce and barbarism sweep over the West. By Charlemagne's time Roman education and thought were dead in western Europe.

Some historians have found Pirenne deficient in his analysis of the evidence but most, except perhaps classical historians, admit that his large picture or synthesis has credibility. He was, after all, not the first historian to perceive that after the empire in the West no longer existed politically some features of its civilization continued. He did not deny that during the third and fourth centuries political disintegration, social and economic misfortunes, cultural malaise, and a profound shift in religious values occurred, but he did not believe that they alone ended Graeco-Roman civilization. Despite the German conquests with their turmoil and new political arrangements, no new civilization arose because the Germans were generally willing to partake of the Mediterranean civilization and the unity upon which it depended. What impressed Pirenne was how much all this had changed in the West by the time of the Carolingians. He noticed that after 600 Italy lay prostrate with the Ostrogothic kingdom destroyed by Justinian's unfortunate attempt to reconquer the West; that all the lands ringing the Mediterranean, except for some in southern Europe, were under Arab dominion; and that the Carolingian state was oriented northward rather than southward to the Mediterranean, its center lying between the Loire and the Rhine. He sensed also that there was much less trade, especially on the Mediterranean between the West and the East, that few real towns still existed, that the economy was much more agrarian, and that culturally, Europe was relatively barren. But why had such change come after 600? For Pirenne the logical reason was the Arab conquest of the Mediterranean, which made it a barrier rather than a boulevard for East-West exchanges, causing the orbit of power in the East to shift to Baghdad and in the West, to the north. This transformation isolated western Europe and presaged seignorialism, feudalism, and the domination of the church, all of which were consecrated by the coronation of Charlemagne in 800.

Although giving the Arabs too decisive a part in this change, Pirenne was the first to understand that they had exercised a profound influence upon the Mediterranean and the West. In comparing the culture of the Arab lands with that of the West, he saw an improverished and underdeveloped West facing in the East a thriving, creative culture rooted in a money economy. This picture was little changed until the West revived and pushed its way back into the Mediterranean during the eleventh century, a push climaxed by the First Crusade. For the first time in centuries the West again traded on the Mediterranean and established regular contacts with the East. Without this development the extraordinary achievements of the twelfth and thirteenth centuries would have been inconceivable. One may fault Pirenne for his details, but in terms of western history his synthesis is both credible and imaginative. Its hypotheses account for the relative darkness of the early Middle Ages and for the recovery and vigorous achievements of western Europe in the High Middle Ages. By placing in proper perspective those centuries between 400 and 1000 that had been ignored by classical historians and slighted by medievalists, Pirenne dramatically reminded historians that in this period lie the answers to the uniqueness of western history. Historiographically he did even more. He delivered medievalists from Gibbon's spell by forcing them to acknowledge that they must repudiate much of what Gibbon had argued, and that this meant reexamination of a historiographical tradition dating back to the Renaissance. For this reason alone Pirenne's *Mahoment et Charlemagne* ranks among the historical classics. It compels every student of the Middle Ages to wrestle with its concepts because within their framework rests a truer understanding and appreciation of the Middle Ages.

It may well be that what Gibbon referred to as the world's great debate will never end because we lack the evidence for a real solution. For the whole period from the third to the ninth century there are gaps and uncertainties. To lessen these gaps and to remove some uncertainties further research by Arabists and Byzantinists is definitely needed. Too much of the research so far has been done by specialists in western history using the evidence of western Europe and viewing the problem through western eyes. For a truer perspective there must be greater focus on Arab and Byzantine evidence. But even with further research by Byzantinists and Arabists and assistance from the classical and medieval archaeologist, the numismatist, and the art historian, some of the fundamental questions will never be resolved. What new evidence and insights emerge will little alter our present understanding. The large gaps in our knowledge can never be appreciably narrowed. Each historian working on this problem will need to use his historical imagination to recreate what happened, to suggest the known for the unknown, and to assemble the meager facts in proper perspective.

Did Pirenne, knowing what he did about the evidence, think that he had resolved the great debate? He himself has answered this question. Although he had no philosophy of history and rarely wrote about method, he clearly expressed his view of the historian's task. The historian must grasp all that he can of the concrete with the realization that he can never directly observe past events. He must then relate these concrete facts to collective phenomena if he would attain his highest objective—the study of the development of human societies in space and time. For each historian, criticism and proper appreciation of evidence is an essential first step that must lead always to asking whether the conclusions drawn from the evidence meet the standards of credibility. If he is satisfied that his analysis of the sources is credible, he should then advance to historical narrative which must combine synthesis and hypothesis. The proper end of all research is historical synthesis, but it cannot stand alone; it must be animated and given its *raison d'etre* by hypothesis. History, therefore, is a conjectural or a subjective discipline. It has to be, not only because of what each historian brings to it, but because it contains the element of chance. Finally, the historian must realize that a synthesis incorporating these qualities and allowing for human deficiencies will ever be unfulfilled unless it is comparative. Only by comparison of events, institutions, societies, and civilizations can the historian achieve a balanced perspective.

Elaborating upon this view of the historian's task, Pirenne stated on one occasion: "All those engaged in searching for the truth understand that the glimpses they have of it are necessarily fleeting. They glow for an instant and then make way for new and always more dazzling brightness. Quite different from that of the artist, the work of the scholar is inevitably provisional. He knews this and rejoices in it because the rapid obsoleteness of his books is the very proof of the progress of his field of knowledge." And, again, upon completion of the final volume of his *Histoire de Belgique,* he wrote: "If it is true that every attempt at a synthesis is necessarily provisional, it is also true that by the hypotheses it proposes, the connections it establishes, and the problems it poses, it is able to assist in scientific progress. There is only a science of the general and this is true of history as for the other fields of knowledge. To call upon a historian to delay his construction until all the material of his subject has been assembled and all the questions involved elucidated, is to condemn him to a perpetual waiting, because the materials will never be completely known, nor the questions definitively resolved, because as a field of knowledge develops it is always uncovering new problems. What should be demanded of an author is that he utilize all the resources at his disposal at the moment he writes."

When he wrote *Mahomet et Charlemagne,* Pirenne met these de-mands. He was under no illusion that he was in command of all the evidence or that what he wrote would completely resolve the cen-turies-old debate, but he knew that he brought to the problem a different perspective which he hoped would bring new understand-ing and inspire historians to reexamine it. He would probably be disappointed in learning that his theory has generally been ignored by classical historians who continue blithely along, serene in their faith that most of what Gibbon told them is the truth, that they need have no concern for what happened after 330, 395, 410, 455, or 476 because this was when the ancient world ended, but that he failed to convince all his peers, that his facts have been corrected, or that his theory has been revised, would not distress but delight him be-cause it would be a measure of how much his work had advanced our knowledge of western civilization. And yet Pirenne's theory, though revised, has not yet been replaced by any other more credi-ble or convincing on the enigma of the end of the ancient world and the beginning of the Middle Ages.

APPROACHES TO FEUDALISM

CHARLEMAGNE'S EMPIRE DISINTEGRATED in the ninth century. Out of the near-anarchy that ensued there emerged a new ordering of society that modern historians describe by the word "feudal." David Herlihy discusses below the problems inherent in the use of this vague term. Some historians, notably Karl Marx, have seen feudalism as a necessary stage in the evolution of all civilizations. Others have regarded it as a specifically European phenomenon. This is largely a question of definition. If, like Marx, we mean by the term "feudal society" essentially a society that is based on the exploitation of a subject peasantry, then evidently many feudal regimes have existed in many different times and places. But modern Western historians more commonly use the word "feudal" to describe the relationships existing among the medieval nobility, among the knights and greater lords. Here we find an aristocracy of mounted warriors, holding fiefs from overlords to whom they are bound by oaths of personal loyalty, and exercising substantial rights of government over the lands they control. This is a much more rare—perhaps unique—form of social structure.

The readings that follow illustrate the basic characteristics of Western feudalism. Whatever its universal significance, feudalism certainly represents an important, formative stage in the growth of Western institutions. Primitive Teutonic societies were organized primarily by kinship groupings; modern societies depend on the loyalty of citizens to the state. In feudal society we can find an intermediate form of organization. This approach to feudalism is explored in the reading from Marc Bloch. He describes the persistence of kinship ties and the growth of new forms of personal allegiance in the early feudal age. Joseph Strayer's discussion is concerned with the political aspects of feudalism. He argues that the "informal and flexible" arrangements of feudal society made possible the emergence of new kinds of governmental institutions in the Western world.

8. Feudalism: Meanings and Methodologies

DAVID HERLIHY

Meanings

... With the Enlightenment and the French Revolution, a certain bifurcation becomes evident in the meaning and uses of the word "feudal," and this variance has persisted to the present, to the frequent confusion of students and the annoyance of scholars. To some historians, then and now, feudalism retains its late-medieval, early-modern, essentially juridic sense as the aggregate of those institutions connected with the support and service of knights. To investigate feudalism therefore requires a consideration of the relationships, personal and proprietary, between the ruler or the chief and the warriors who attended and served him. Feudalism in this reconstruction is a system of law, of government, and of military organization, but not of economic production. "Manorialism" is the term usually used to connote the system of large estates which frequently, although not always, accompanied the "feudalism" of the aristocracy. This concept of feudalism thus exclusively describes the political and social relations within the free, ruling, and preeminently fighting classes. Serfs, who were not free and thus could not enter into the feudal contract, should therefore be excluded from consideration under the feudal rubric. To write "feudal" is necessarily to think of an aristocracy.

But there remains a second, quite different use of the word; it was

From David Herlihy, ed., *The History of Feudalism* (New York: Harper & Row, 1970), pp. xvii–xxvii. From *The History of Feudalism* edited by David Herlihy. Copyright © 1970 by David Herlihy. Reprinted by permission of HarperCollins Publishers.

later in emerging but was already established in the writings of Adam Smith and the reformers of the eighteenth century. Tautologically defined, feudalism is a system of economic production founded upon "feudal rent," which means in turn reliance on force and not on incentives to secure labor and support from the workers. It is not exactly slavery, as the peasant was not chattel and could not be moved about at the lord's will; there were, moreover, traditional limits set upon the services and payments the lord could demand. But it was a survival of bondage, and of course it contrasted greatly with the wage system and the "cash nexus" of the capitalistic economy, which stimulated and disciplined the worker not by direct power but by the incentive of monetary payments.

In the nineteenth century, the socialists borrowed this conception of feudalism (as they did much else) from the liberal economists. Marx and Engels in particular made it a part of their sweeping characterization of the stages of human development. In the beginning there was primitive communism, poor and unproductive; there followed slavery, which allowed greater wealth at the cost of human degradation; feudalism came next, and then capitalism; finally, communism returned, now wealthy and triumphant. The word "feudal" is scattered through the Communist Manifesto of 1848 ("feudal society," "feudal property," "feudal system of industry," and the like). It is viewed of course with opprobrium, but often favorably compared with the subsequent, still crueler exploitations of the bourgeois state.

This understanding of feudalism has remained canonical for Marxists and has retained considerable appeal to some other, especially economic historians, who find the concept of feudal rent a valid one and a cornerstone in the social and economic structure of medieval society. Disagreement over the meaning of this basic term has produced a major anomaly in the historical literature concerning feudalism. Marxist scholars have professed that they were investigating feudalism and have written extensively on tenures, rents, and the methods by which the peasants were allegedly exploited. Many non-Marxists have professed the same intent and have not gone beyond a consideration of the services owed by knights and the means used to support them.

Today, many historians, anxious to avoid battles over terminology which soon become idle, prefer not to offer rigorous definitions of feudalism, but rather to describe feudal society, in the sense of listing those characteristics which seem central to it. This descriptive approach avoids the implication that one factor—whether the practices of the aristocracy or the organization of production—necessarily determined all others.

As summarized by Marc Bloch, one of the great historians of the medieval world, whose work we shall subsequently consider, the following characteristics may justifiably earn for a society the name "feudal":

A subject peasantry; widespread use of the service tenement (i.e. the fief) instead of salary; supremacy of a class of specialized warriors; ties of obedience and protection which bind man to man; fragmentation of authority; and, in the midst of all this, survival of other forms of association, family and State.

Bloch's large and loose definition of the essential characteristics of feudal society effectively combines much of what both Marxists and non-Marxists alike have said about it or have written concerning it. Although his words may be criticized as lacking both conceptual and methodological rigor, they offer a good working description, to which most scholars would readily give assent. In stressing the importance of investigating not feudalism alone, or feudal institutions, but feudal society, Bloch also laid great stress on the importance of comparative history. It was his hope and expectation that a careful comparison of western Europe in the Middle Ages with, for example, the lands of east Asia, Japan especially, would deepen our understanding of feudal institutions and our appreciation of the place a "feudal stage" might hold in human development. Although the results of a comparative history of feudal societies have not so far been spectacular, it remains fair to say that the quest is only now beginning and that with time Marc Bloch's great faith in its potential may prove justified.

Historians, over the centuries, have differed not only in their interpretations of the word "feudalism," but also in the methods they have used to investigate the feudal centuries. An appreciation of those methods is similarly needed to understand the nature of feudal society, or at least what historians have discovered concerning it.

Methodologies

The lawyers who made the earliest efforts to find dimension and order in the array of feudal customs were not primarily concerned with the historic origins of the practices they studied. Much in contrast, the social commentators and reformers who continued the effort were vitally concerned, as they wished to know when and why their society had adopted the institutions which most of them regarded as deplorable. We have already mentioned that the writers in the age of the Enlightenment concluded variously that feudalism was the product either of Roman decadence, German arrogance, or medieval brutality. In the course of the nineteenth century, the methods of historical research changed drastically, but the interest remained. This age marked the birth and development of scientific history, in the sense of a discipline which was rigorously exact, ingeniously critical, and powerful enough to uncover knowledge about the past which even contemporaries had not realized or recognized. This development of historical science has continued to the present, and in the course of its growth historians have made use of various approaches to their documents and to the realities behind them. Specifically in regard to feudal society, it is possible to discern in modern analysis three distinct methods, each with its own purposes and advantages.

THE GENEALOGY OF TRADITIONS

One of the oldest and still today one of the most cultivated of the scholarly approaches to feudalism is to establish the line along which the basic institutions, customs, and traditions associated with it grew and changed. Historians, for example, have for long carefully investigated the changes in military institutions between the ancient and medieval worlds, and especially the replacement of the foot soldier of antiquity by the mounted warrior or knight as the main support of armies. They have studied with equal care the character and the history of the personal tie between warriors and their chiefs known as vassalage, and of the distinctive sort of land grant known as the fief. For both institutions, they have succeeded in finding antecedents in the Roman and barbarian worlds. So also, for a later period, scholars have investigated, and still investigate, the influences upon the legal systems and governments of Europe which the revived knowledge of Roman law or new philosophical ideas concerning nature or society may have exerted. On a more restricted scale, the question of origins has long posed one of the great problems of medieval English history: what impact did the Norman conquest and Norman policies have upon the growth of English government?

History conceived and pursued as a genealogy of institutions or of traditions offers several advantages to the scholar. The problems are usually well defined, and the method—chiefly the careful collation of documents—is proven and reliable. Moreover, the principal institutions of society are usually well illuminated, even in medieval sources. A strong documentary record, clearly delineated problems, and precise methods thus enable the historian of institutions to proceed with a rigor that is often the envy of scholars working in other areas of human culture. As a result of generations of research, we today possess a rather good idea concerning the development of the chief institutions of feudalism; we can date with some accuracy the major changes in them and observe with some detail how these institutions functioned.

But institutional history also possesses some limitations, as even its most accomplished practitioners have recognized. Institutions rarely explain themselves. Often the very sources which illuminate them appear only after the institutions have acquired a certain stability and maturity; law, someone has remarked, is born late. To investigate their formation, the historian must also consider why these institutions acquired certain characteristics rather than others, or developed in one direction rather than in another. At this point, the kind of history he is pursuing becomes less a consideration of the lines of institutional development and more an analysis of the causes and factors which explain social change.

THE SKEIN OF CAUSES

A second, major interest of historians concerned with feudalism has therefore been this: Why, at a certain point in time, did there occur changes in the social and political institutions of western Europe? If feudalism by definition consisted of those institutions concerned with the service and support of knights, to know its origin was primarily to determine when and why knights came to play so decisive a role in Western warfare, and hence in Western society and government. The armies of the ancient world—the Macedonian phalanxes or the Roman legions—had relied primarily upon foot soldiers to wage and win the wars. Medieval armies relied on the heavily armed, mounted warrior. When and why did the change occur?

In 1887, a German historian of law, Heinrich Brunner, advanced one of the most ingenious and still one of the most influential explanations for this shift in military tactics. Brunner argued that this fundamental change to cavalry occurred in the eighth century. In 755, King Pepin the Short ordered that the Frankish army be mustered in May instead of March. May offered more fodder, and this must have meant that more Frankish soldiers were coming on horseback. Shortly afterward, in 758, he changed the tribute imposed on the subject Saxons from cattle to horses, for which the Frankish army had an apparently greater need. Why was this happening? Brunner himself pointed to the penetration of the horse-riding Arabs through Spain and across the Pyrenees in the early eighth century; the Carolingian mayor of the palace, Charles Martel, repulsed them at the battle of Poitiers (732), but even afterward their menace continued. To resist the invaders required that the Franks adopt their tactics, and particularly enlarge and strengthen their cavalry. This military reform necessarily brought about a number of profound political, social, and economic changes. Horses were expensive engines of war, and the Carolingians had to find economic support for them and for the men who rode them. Charles Martel seized part of the possessions of the churches, or ordered ecclesiastical institutions to provide his soldiers with land, by grants known as *precaria* or *beneficia.* This was the origin of the fief, and the Carolingians further insisted that the mounted fighters assume toward their superiors and toward themselves the obligations of vassals.

The military change further made fighting an enterprise of the aristocracy, even its monopoly. The few freemen who had the means to afford the expensive horses and armor, or were favored with grants of land by the rulers, became the new feudal nobility. To fight was the great mark of freedom in early medieval society, and the poor who could no longer afford to fight sank into the ranks of full-time peasants and serfs. As the direct result of these ninth-century military reforms, medieval society thus acquired the basic feudal traits: a dependent peasantry and a warrior aristocracy tied to its chief or king, and he to them, by bonds created by the fief and by vassalage.

Scholars have since mounted a barrage of objections against Brunner's theory of the origins of the military fief, and hence of feudalism, in the West. It now appears that the Muslim cavalry was not nearly so important as Brunner maintained, and probably could not have served as so powerful an incentive for Frankish military reform. Rather, mounted horsemen seem to have been growing in numbers on both sides of the religious frontier in the eighth century at an almost equal pace.

But if this interpretation would tend to excise the prime mover from Brunner's link of causes, his views are by no means dead, and have recently been given a new breath of life by the researches of a historian of technology, Lynn White, Jr. In his *Medieval Technology and Social Change,* White has replaced the Saracen challenge with the introduction of a new tool, the stirrup, but he has otherwise left largely intact the sequence of causes leading to the formation of the feudal system. This stirrup, White maintains, was adopted for the Frankish army by Charles Martel, who learned of it from the East. For the first time, this deceptively simple device permitted a man on horseback to deliver a powerful blow without the danger of unseating himself. Feudalism was thus created by the Franks, "presumably led by the genius of Charles Martel," who recognized the military potential of the new tool and reorganized the Frankish army, and indirectly government and society, to take advantage of it.

Both Brunner and White thus offer an interpretation of feudalism which attributes its fundamental institutions to specific causes and links them together in a rational pattern. Martel (in White's reconstruction) adopted the stirrup, revolutionized warfare, and gave su-premacy to the mounted horseman or knight. To support the new warrior class, fiefs were introduced and personal obligations im-posed upon the persons who held them. The nobility had to train its sons from an early age in the difficult skills of mounted shock combat, and this educational and professional experience produced among the warrior class a kind of subculture, chivalry, a name ap-propriately deriving from the late Latin word for horse (*caballus*). Western society was thus transformed militarily, socially, and cultur-ally, all because of the introduction of a small iron implement sup-porting the feet of horsemen.

There are other, comparable attempts to explain feudalism in the West through a reputed sequence of causes. One of the most famous was that advanced between the two world wars by a Belgian historian, Henri Pirenne. Pirenne's contention was that the classical world had been founded on the unity of the Mediterranean Sea and the vig-orous trade which this unity made possible. Commerce provided the Roman state with an abundance of money, with which it supported the two chief pillars of the empire, a paid bureaucracy and a profes-sional army. That unity and that trade survived the barbarian inva-sions of the fourth and fifth centuries. But in the seventh century, the Arab followers of Muhammad broke into the Mediterranean, built a fleet, and turned an avenue of peaceful trade into a battle-field. The West was cut off from the East and from its life-giving trade. It was therefore thrown back upon its own, exclusively agrarian resources. Charlemagne (king of the Franks, 768–814) recognized the realities of the new situation and reorganized the army and his state in conformity with them. Without money revenues, he took to supporting his soldiers through granting them pieces of land in fief. Thus he created the new feudal state and society, and with these changes the Middle Ages was born. In a famous phrase, Pirenne affirmed that without Muhammad, Charlemagne would have been inconceivable. He meant that the economic and social order of the Middle Ages—the feudal order, in sum—was unthinkable without the intervention of the Saracen expansion and the destruction of the Mediterranean unity. By a series of brilliantly linked arguments, the dazzled reader is led from cause to cause, until he finds himself confronting the unlikely, nearly incredible conclusion that the prime cause of feudalism in the West was the Koran.

These reconstructions offer the student numerous insights into the origins of feudalism. Their validity has been endlessly but fruit-fully discussed, and we shall content ourselves here with some com-ment on their methodological implications and some of the diffi-culties implicit in them. In locating the causes of feudalism in the

Saracen horse, or the Asian stirrup, or the Arabian prophet, these arguments assume an answer to the most fundamental question of all the social sciences: What really causes or explains human behavior? For example, even if the recognized value of the stirrup prompted Charles Martel to reorganize the Frankish army and distribute land among his soldiers, the explanation remains evidently incomplete. Why did he place so much importance on a military decision? Was he influenced by a present and pressing military need or a traditional cultural value? Why could he not have supported the army by other means? His response to the problems which confronted him was clearly conditioned by many factors, by the economic, administrative, and cultural resources at his disposal, and further by the fundamental character of his own society. To understand human decisions and human behavior requires something more than an appreciation of immediate stimuli. It requires, too, a consideration of the totality of forces, material and spiritual, which condition, influence, or direct human responses. And because we are dealing with human beings, the forces which helped shape their actions must be recognized as multiple, subtle, and infinitely complex.

Thus, efforts to explain feudalism through single and simple causes, whether through horses or tools or prophets, are open to the criticism that they are founded on too simple a conception of human behavior. To explain what happened (at least according to some critics), the historian should function as does the social scientist. He should not try to isolate apparent causes, as these will often prove specious. Rather, he should seek to combine them, thus reconstructing the total social milieu, the total life situation, in which the events occurred. Only then will the actions of past generations become not explained but understandable.

In France, between the two world wars, a group of historians associated with a journal which today bears the name *Annales-Economies-Sociétés-Civilisations* took issue with the traditional methods of history which then dominated the schools. They called for a new historical method which would make use of the other social sciences and the insights they offer. They argued that the academic historians, for all their admitted power in establishing what happened in the past, were still guilty of self-deception. They pretended to write "definitive" works, in the sense of exploring, once and for all, given historical topics; they claimed that they could explain not only what happened but the causal relations among events. Definitive history, for these critics, was dehumanized history, as it pretended to a knowledge of the past and a mastery of human behavior which not even the most advanced social sciences possessed.

THE ANALYSIS OF A SITUATION

One of the prominent figures among these critics was also one of the great historians of feudalism. This was Marc Bloch, who died a hero's death in 1944 as a member of the French resistance in World War II. His great work, *Feudal Society*, characteristically begins with an extended treatment of the feudal environment. To understand how men act, one must know how they live, not only economically or politically, but culturally, intellectually, and religiously. Every human action is a product of many causes and many influences, and it would be naïve for a historian to rank them by supposed importance. Rather, he should seek to reconstruct the entire social milieu, the total life situation of the period he is studying.

Bloch's book on feudal society is one of the most influential historical works to have been written in this century, and its influence is by no means confined to medieval history. Many historians of many periods have sought to follow Bloch's advice, to reconstruct the "total social environment" of a past society. To be sure, this approach is itself not without some weaknesses. To reconstruct the total life situation, the tone and style of a past epoch, the historian must frequently propose conclusions beyond the power of traditional historical methods to prove or disprove; he must, in other words, resort to impressions. Bloch himself, in describing characteristics of the feudal period, frequently cited examples or evidence well beyond the chronological limits of the age he was examining. Because specific causes are all but lost in the total milieu, so specific events and specific personalities lose their importance. A kind of chronological vagueness hovers over the analysis. Bloch, as we shall see, distinguishes two fundamentally different feudal ages, but he shifts the division between them, according to his context, backwards and forwards, over a century or more. Finally, Bloch's approach has also developed a rhetoric of its own. The rhetorical question, suggesting a conclusion, frequently replaces the confident affirmation of the older academic historian. Historians inspired by the spirit of the *Annales*, anxious to avoid the pretense of writing definitive studies, now often parade an exaggerated modesty. Like the medieval authors who announce in excellent Latin their inability to write excellent Latin, they often claim that their chief purpose in writing is only to pose questions and to inspire others to carry the work a little further.

But in spite of some weaknesses, it is probably fair to say that this effort to reconstruct and to understand a total human situation has proved its merit in the past generation, and scholars are far from exhausting its potential. More rigorous use of the sources and a better exploitation of the other social sciences promise abundant harvests in the future.

The history of feudal society, illuminated by this and other methods, should attract not only those interested in the Western past but all who are concerned with the dynamics of human change. If the feudal society of the Middle Ages has left us comparatively few sources, its history has one advantage which the history of the modern age cannot duplicate. It has time; it permits the study of human change over centuries, amounting to a millennium. The legal issues involving the fief, the moral and social need for reform, which first brought men to the study of feudal society, have all but faded in our modern world. But the fascination of this lengthy chapter in Western history, and in human history, remains.

9. Kinship and Lordship

MARC BLOCH

The Structure of the Family

Vast *gentes* or clans, firmly defined and held together by a belief—
whether true or false—in a common ancestry, were unknown to western Europe in the feudal period, save on its outer fringes, beyond
the genuinely feudalized regions. On the shores of the North Sea
there were the *Geschlechter* of Frisia or of Dithmarschen; in the west,
Celtic tribes or clans. It seems certain that groups of this nature had
still existed among the Germans in the period of the invasions. There
were, for example, the Lombard and Frankish *farae* of which more
than one Italian or French village continues today to bear the name;
and there were also the *genealogiae* of the Alemans and Bavarians
which certain texts show in possession of the soil. But these excessively large units gradually disintegrated.

The Roman *gens* had owed the exceptional firmness of its pattern
to the absolute primacy of descent in the male line. Nothing like
this was known in the feudal epoch. Already in ancient Germany
each individual had two kinds of relative, those "of the spear side,"
and those "of the distaff side," and he was bound, though in different degrees, to the second as well as to the first. It was as though
among the Germans the victory of the agnatic principle had never
been sufficiently complete to extinguish all trace of a more ancient

From Marc Bloch, *Feudal Society*, L. A. Manyon, trans. (Chicago: University of Chicago Press, 1961), pp. 137–141, 145–147, 157–162. English translation copyright
1961 by Routledge & Kegan Paul Ltd. Reprinted by permission of The University
of Chicago Press and Routledge & Kegan Paul Ltd.

system of uterine filiation. Unfortunately we know almost nothing of the native family traditions of the countries conquered by Rome. But, whatever one is to think of these problems of origins, it is at all events certain that in the medieval West kinship had acquired or retained a distinctly dual character. The sentimental importance with which the epic invested the relations of the maternal uncle and his nephew is but one of the expressions of a system in which the ties of relationship through women were nearly as important as those of paternal consanguinity. One proof of this is the clear evidence from the practices of name-giving.

The majority of Germanic personal names were formed by linking two elements, each of which had a meaning of its own. So long as people continued to be aware of the distinction between the two stems, it was the common custom, if not the rule, to mark the filiation by borrowing one of the components. This was true even in Romance-speaking regions where the prestige of the conquerors had led to the widespread imitation of their name system by the native peoples. Children took their names either from the father or the mother; there seems to have been no fixed rule. In the village of Palaiseau, for example, at the beginning of the ninth century, the peasant *Teud-ricus* and his wife *Ermen-berta* baptized one of their sons *Teut-hardus,* another *Erment-arius,* and the third, by way of a double memorial, *Teut-bertus.* Then the practice developed of handing down the whole name from generation to generation. This was done again by taking the name from each side alternately. Thus of the two sons of Lisois, lord of Amboise, who died in 1065, one was named after his father but the other, who was the elder, was named Sulpice like his maternal grandfather and uncle. Still later, when people began to add patronymics to Christian names, they vacillated for a long time between the two modes of transmission. "I am called sometimes Jeanne d'Arc and sometimes Jeanne Romée," said the daughter of Jacques d'Arc and Isabelle Romée to her judges. History knows her only by the first of these names; but she pointed out that in her part of the country it was customary to give daughters the surname of their mother.

This double link had important consequences. Since each generation thus had its circle of relatives which was not the same as that of the previous generation, the area of the kindred's responsibilities continually changed its contours. The duties were rigorous; but the group was too unstable to serve as the basis of the whole social structure. Worse still, when two families clashed it might very well be that the same individual belonged to both—to one of them through his father and to the other through his mother. How was he to choose between them? Wisely, Beaumanoir's choice is to side with the nearest relative, and if the degrees are equal, to stand aloof. Doubtless in practice the decision was often dictated by personal preference. When we come to deal with feudal relations in the strict sense, we shall encounter aspects of this legal dilemma in the case of the vassal of two lords. The dilemma arose from a particular attitude of mind and in the long run it had the effect of loosening the tie. There was great internal weakness in a family system which compelled people to recognize, as they did in Beauvaisis in the thirteenth century, the legitimacy of a war between two brothers, sons of the same father (though by different marriages), who found themselves caught up in a vendetta between their maternal relatives.

How far along the lines of descent did the obligations towards "friends by blood" extend? We do not find their limits defined with any precision save in the groups that maintained the regular scale of compensation, and even here the customs were set down in writing only at a relatively late date. All the more significant is the fact that the zones of active and passive solidarity which they fixed were surprisingly large, and that they were, moreover, graduated zones, in which the amount of the indemnity varied according to the closeness of the relationship. At Sepulveda in Castile in the thirteenth century it was sufficient, in order that the vengeance wreaked on the murderer of a relative should not be treated as a crime, for the avenger to have the same great-great-grandfather as the original victim. The same degree of relationship entitled one to receive a part of the blood money according to the law of Oudenarde and, at Lille, made it obligatory to contribute to its payment. At Saint-Omer they went so far as to derive the obligation to contribute from a common founder of the line as remote as a grandfather of a great-grandfather. Elsewhere, the outline was vaguer. But, as has already been pointed out, it was considered only prudent in the case of alienations to ask the consent of as many collaterals as possible. As for the "silent" communities of the country districts, they long continued to gather together many individuals under one roof—we hear of as many as fifty in eleventh-century Bavaria and sixty-six in fifteenth-century Normandy.

On close examination, however, it looks as if from the thirteenth century onwards a sort of contraction was in process. The vast kindreds of not so long before were slowly being replaced by groups much more like our small families of today. Towards the end of the century, Beaumanoir felt that the circle of people bound by the obligation of vengeance had been constantly dwindling—to the point where, in his day, in contrast with the previous age, only second cousins, or perhaps only first cousins (among whom the obligation continued to be very strongly felt), were included. From the latter years of the twelfth century we note in the French charters a tendency to restrict to the next of kin the request for family approval. Then came the system under which the relatives enjoyed the right of redemption. With the distinction which it established between acquired possessions and family possessions and, among the latter, between possessions subject, according to their origin, to the claims of either the paternal or the maternal line, it conformed much less than the earlier practice to the conception of an almost unlimited kinship. The rhythms of this evolution naturally varied greatly from place to place. It will suffice here to indicate very briefly the most general and most likely causes of a change which was pregnant with important consequences.

Undoubtedly the governmental authorities, through their activities as guardians of the peace, contributed to the weakening of the kinship bond. This they did in many ways and notably, like William the Conqueror, by limiting the sphere of lawful blood-feud; above all, perhaps, by encouraging refusal to take any part in the vendetta. Voluntary withdrawal from the kindred group was an ancient and general right; but whilst it enabled the individual to avoid many risks, it deprived him for the future of a form of protection long regarded as indispensable. Once the protection of the State had become more effective, these "forswearings" became less dangerous. The government sometimes did not hesitate to impose them. Thus, in 1181, the count of Hainault, after a murder had been perpetrated, forestalled the blood-feud by burning down the houses of all the relatives of the guilty man and extorting from them a promise not to give him succour. Nevertheless the disintegration and attenuation of the kindred group, both as an economic unit and as an instrument of the feud, seems to have been in the main the result of deeper social changes. The development of trade conduced to the limitation of family impediments to the sale of property; the progress of inter-communication led to the break-up of excessively large groups which, in the absence of any legal status, could scarcely preserve their sense of unity except by staying together in one place. The invasions had already dealt an almost mortal blow at the much more solidly constituted *Geschlechter* of ancient Germany. The rude shocks to which England was subjected—Scandinavian inroads and settlement, Norman conquest—were doubtless an important factor in the premature decay in that country of the old framework of the kindred. In practically the whole of Europe, at the time of the great movement of land reclamation, the attraction of the new urban centres and of the villages founded on the newly cleared lands undoubtedly broke up many peasant communities. It was no accident if, in France at least, these brotherhoods held together much longer in the poorest provinces.

• • •

The Man of Another Man

To be the "man" of another man: in the vocabulary of feudalism, no combination of words was more widely used or more comprehensive in meaning. In both the Romance and the Germanic tongues it was used to express personal dependence *per se* and applied to persons of all social classes regardless of the precise legal nature of the bond. The count was the "man" of the king, as the serf was the "man" of his manorial lord. Sometimes even in the same text, within the space of a few lines, radically different social stations were thus evoked. An instance of this, dating from the end of the eleventh century, is a petition of Norman nuns, complaining that their "men"—that is to say their peasants—were forced by a great baron to work at the castles of his "men," meaning the knights who were his vassals. The ambiguity disturbed no one, because, in spite of the gulf between the orders of society, the emphasis was on the fundamental element in common: the subordination of one individual to another.

If, however, the principle of this human nexus permeated the whole life of society, the forms which it assumed were none the less very diverse—with sometimes almost imperceptible transitions, from the highest to the humblest. Moreover there were many variations from country to country. It will be useful if we take as a guiding thread one of the most significant of these relationships of dependence, the tie of vassalage; studying it first in the most highly "feudalized" zone of Europe, namely, the heart of the former Carolingian Empire, northern France, the German Rhineland and Swabia; and endeavoring, before we embark on any inquiries into its origins, to describe the most striking features of the institution at the period of its greatest expansion, that is to say, from the tenth to the twelfth century.

Homage in the Feudal Era

Imagine two men face to face; one wishing to serve, the other willing or anxious to be served. The former puts his hands together and places them, thus joined, between the hands of the other man—a plain symbol of submission, the significance of which was sometimes further emphasized by a kneeling posture. At the same time, the person proffering his hands utters a few words—a very short declaration—by which he acknowledges himself to be the "man" of the person facing him. Then chief and subordinate kiss each other on the mouth, symbolizing accord and friendship. Such were the gestures—very simple ones, eminently fitted to make an impression on minds so sensitive to visible things—which served to cement one of the strongest social bonds known in the feudal era. Described or mentioned in the texts a hundred times, reproduced on seals, miniatures, bas-reliefs, the ceremony was called "homage" (in German, *Mannschaft*). The superior party, whose position was created by this act, was described by no other term than the very general one of "lord." Similarly, the subordinate was often simply called the "man" of his lord; or sometimes, more precisely, his "man of mouth and hands" (*homme de bouche et de mains*). But more specialized words were also employed, such as "vassal" or, till the beginning of the twelfth century at least, "commended man" (*commendé*).

In this form the rite bore no Christian imprint. Such an omission, probably explained by the remote Germanic origins of the symbolism, in due course ceased to be acceptable to a society which had come to regard a promise as scarcely valid unless God were guarantor. Homage itself, so far as its form was concerned, was never modified. But, apparently from the Carolingian period, a second rite—an essentially religious one—was superimposed on it; laying his hand on the Gospels or on relics, the new vassal swore to be faithful to his master. This was called fealty, *foi* in French (in German *Treue*, and, formerly, *Hulde*).

The ceremony therefore had two stages, but they were by no means of equal importance. For in the act of fealty there was nothing specific. In a disturbed society, where mistrust was the rule and the appeal to divine sanctions appeared to be one of the few restraints with any efficacy at all, there were a great many reasons why the oath of fealty should be exacted frequently. Royal or seignorial officials of every rank took it on assuming their duties; prelates often demanded it from their clergy; and manorial lords, occasionally, from their peasants. Unlike homage, which bound the whole man at a single stroke and was generally held to be incapable of renewal, this promise—almost a commonplace affair—could be repeated several times to the same person. There were therefore many acts of fealty without homage: we do not know of any acts of homage without fealty—at least in the feudal period. Furthermore, when the two rites were combined, the pre-eminence of homage was shown by the fact that it was always given first place in the ceremony. It was this alone that brought the two men together in a close union; the fealty of the vassal was a unilateral undertaking to which there was seldom a corresponding oath on the part of the lord. In a word, it was the act of homage that really established the relation of vassalage under its dual aspect of dependence and protection.

The tie thus formed lasted, in theory, as long as the two lives which it bound together, but as soon as one or other of these was terminated by death it was automatically dissolved. We shall see that in practice vassalage very soon became, in most cases, hereditary; but this *de facto* situation allowed the legal rule to remain intact to the end. It mattered little that the son of the deceased vassal usually performed this homage to the lord who had accepted his father's or that the heir of the previous lord almost invariably received the homage of his father's vassals: the ceremony had none the less to be repeated with every change of the individual persons concerned. Similarly, homage could not be offered or accepted by proxy; the examples to the contrary all date from a very late period, when the significance of the old forms was already almost lost. In France, so far as it applied to the king, this privilege was legalized only under Charles VII and even then not without many misgivings. The social bond seemed to be truly inseparable from the almost physical contact which the formal act created between the two men.

The general duty of aid and obedience incumbent on the vassal was an obligation that was undertaken by anyone who became the "man" of another man. But it shaded off at this point into special obligations, which we shall discuss in detail later on. The nature of these corresponded to conditions of rank and manner of life that were rather narrowly defined, for despite great differences of wealth and prestige, vassals were not recruited indiscriminately from all levels of society. Vassalage was the form of dependence peculiar to the upper classes who were characterized above all by the profession of arms and the exercise of command. At least, that is what it had become. In order to obtain a clear idea of the nature of vassalage, it will be well at this point to inquire how it had progressively disentangled itself from the whole complex of personal relationships.

• • •

Carolingian Vassalage

The policy of the Carolingians—by which of course is meant not only the personal plans of the monarchs, some of whom were remarkable men, but also the views of their leading counsellors—may be said to have been dominated both by acquired habits and by principles. Members of the aristocracy who had attained power after a long struggle against the traditional royal house, they had gradually made themselves masters of the Frankish people by surrounding themselves with bands of armed dependants and by imposing their *maimbour* on other chiefs. Is it surprising that once they had reached the pinnacle of power they should continue to regard such ties as normal? On the other hand their ambition, from the time of Charles Martel, was to reconstitute the power of the central government which at the outset they, along with the rest of the aristocracy, had helped to destroy. They wanted to establish order and Christian peace throughout their realms. They wanted soldiers to spread their dominion far and wide and to carry on the holy war against the infidel, an enterprise both conducive to the growth of their own power and beneficial for souls.

The older institutions appeared inadequate for this task. The monarchy had at its disposal only a small number of officials: but these were in any case not very reliable men and—apart from a few churchmen—they lacked professional tradition and culture. Moreover, economic conditions precluded the institution of a vast system of salaried officials. Communications were slow, inconvenient and uncertain. The principal difficulty, therefore, which faced the central government was to reach individual subjects, in order to exact services and impose the necessary sanctions. Thus there arose the idea of utilizing for the purposes of government the firmly established network of protective relationships. The lord, at every level of the hierarchy, would be answerable for his "man" and would be responsible for holding him to his duty. This idea was not peculiar to the Carolingians. It had already been the subject of legislation in Visigothic Spain; after the Arab invasion the many Spanish refugees at the Frankish court may have helped to make the principle known and appreciated there, and the very lively mistrust of the "lordless man" which is reflected later in the Anglo-Saxon laws reflects a similar attitude. But hardly anywhere was the policy more consciously pursued and—one is tempted to add—the illusion more consistently maintained than in the Frankish kingdom about the year 800. "Each chief must constrain his subordinates in order that the latter may with increasing willingness obey the Emperor's commands and instructions"—these words from a capitulary of 810 sum up with expressive brevity one of the fundamental principles of the edifice constructed by Pepin and Charlemagne. In the same way, it is said that in Russia in the days of serfdom the Tsar Nicholas I boasted that in his *pomeshchiks* (lords of villages) he had "a hundred thousand police superintendents."

In the execution of this policy, the most urgent step was clearly to fit vassalage into the legal system and at the same time to give it the stability that alone could make it a firm bulwark of the royal power. At an early date, persons of humble status had commended themselves for life—like the starveling of the Tours formula. But though in practice (and this had no doubt long been the case) many war-companions had also continued to serve their masters to the end of their lives—whether as the result of an express undertaking or in obedience to the dictates of social convention or self-interest—nothing proves that under the Merovingians this had been the general rule. In Spain, Visigothic law had never ceased to recognize the right of private fighting-men to change their masters: for, as the law said, "the free man always retains control of his person." Under the Carolingians, on the other hand, various royal or imperial edicts were concerned with defining precisely the offences which, if committed by the lord, would justify the vassal in breaking the contract. This meant that, with the exception of such cases and apart from separations by mutual agreement, the tie lasted for life.

The lord, moreover, was made officially responsible for the appearance of the vassal in court and when required for his military service. If he himself took part in a campaign, his vassals fought under his orders. It was only in his absence that they came under the direct command of the king's representative, the count.

Yet what was the use of this scheme whereby the lords exacted loyalty from the vassals if these lords, in their turn, were not solidly attached to the sovereign? It was in trying to realize this indispensable condition of their great design that the Carolingians helped to push to the extreme limit the penetration of all social relations by the principle of vassalage.

Once in power, they had had to reward their "men." They distributed lands to them. Furthermore, as mayors of the palace and then as kings they had to get supporters and above all create an army. So they attracted into their service—frequently in return for gifts of land—many men who were already of high rank. Former members of the military following, established on property granted by the ruler, did not cease to be regarded as his vassals; and his new followers were considered to be bound to him by the same tie, even if they had never been his companions-in-arms. Both groups served in his army, followed by their own vassals, if they had any. But, since most of their time was spent away from their master, the conditions under which they lived were very different from those of the household warriors of but a short time before. Each one of them was the centre of a more or less widely scattered group of dependants whom he was expected to keep in order; if necessary, he might even be required to exercise a similar supervision over his neighbours. Thus, among the populations of the vast empire, there became distinguishable a relatively very numerous class of "vassals of the Lord"—that is, "of the Lord King" (*vassi dominici*). Enjoying the special protection of the sovereign and being responsible for furnishing a large part of his troops, they also formed, through the provinces, the links of a great chain of loyalty. When in 871 Charles the Bald, having triumphed over his son Carloman, wished to re-establish the allegiance of the young rebel's accomplices, he could conceive of no better way of doing it than by compelling each of them to select from among the royal vassals a lord of his own choosing.

There was another consideration. Experience had seemed to prove the strength of the tie of vassalage, and the Carolingians planned to extend its use to their officials, for the purpose of stabilizing their constantly wavering loyalty. The latter had always been regarded as being in the special *maimbour* of the sovereign; they had always taken an oath to him; and they were more and more frequently recruited from men who, before their appointment, had already served him as vassals. The practice gradually became more general. From the reign of Louis the Pious, at the latest, there was no office at court, no great command, no countship especially, whose holder had not been obliged, on assuming office, if not earlier, to bind himself in the most solemn fashion as vassal of the monarch. Even foreign rulers, if they recognized the Frankish protectorate, were required from the middle of the eighth century to submit to this ceremony and they also were called vassals of the king or emperor. Of course no one expected these distinguished personages to mount guard in the house of their master, like the followers of former days. In a manner, nevertheless, they belonged to the military household since they owed him first and foremost—along with their fealty—aid in war.

Now the magnates, for their part, had long been accustomed to see in the good companions of their household following men whom they could rely on, ready to carry out the most varied missions. What happened if a distant appointment, the gift of an estate or a heritage led one of these loyal fellows to withdraw from personal service? The chief none the less continued to regard him as his sworn follower. Here again, in short, vassalage by a spontaneous development tended to break out from the narrow circle of the lord's household. The example of the kings and the influence of the legal enactments they had promulgated gave stability to these changing customs. Lords as well as dependants could not fail to favour a form of contract which henceforth would be provided with legal sanctions. The counts bound to themselves by the ties of vassalage the officials of lower rank; the bishop or abbot similarly bound the laymen on whom they relied to assist them in administering justice or to lead their subjects when the latter were called up for service in the army. Powerful individuals, whoever they were, thus strove to draw into their orbit increasing numbers of petty lords and these in their turn acted in the same way towards those weaker than themselves. These private vassals formed a mixed society which still comprised elements of fairly humble status. Among those whom the counts, bishops, abbots and abbesses were authorized to leave in the district when the host was summoned, there were some to whom—like *vassi dominici* on a small scale—the noble task of maintaining the peace was entrusted. Others, again, had the more modest duty of guarding the house of the master, watching over the harvest and supervising the lord's domestic arrangements. These were positions of authority and consequently positions worthy of respect. Around the chiefs of every rank, as around the kings, the purely household service of earlier times had provided the mould in which thenceforward every form of honourable dependence would be cast.

The Formation of the Classical Type of Vassalage

The collapse of the Carolingian state represented the swift and tragic defeat of a little group of men who, despite many archaisms and miscalculations but with the best of intentions, had tried to preserve some of the values of an ordered and civilized life. After them came a long and troubled period which was at the same time a period of gestation, in which the characteristics of vassalage were to take definitive shape.

In the state of perpetual war—invasions as well as internal strife—in which Europe henceforth lived, men more than ever looked for chiefs, and chiefs for vassals. But the extension of these protective relationships no longer redounded to the benefit of the kings. Private ties now increased in number, especially in the neighbourhood of the castles. With the beginning of the Scandinavian and Hungarian invasions, more and more of these fortresses sprang up in the country districts, and the lords who commanded them—either in their own name or in that of some more powerful personage—endeavored to assemble bodies of vassals for their defence. "The king has now nothing save his title and his crown . . . he is not capable of defending either his bishops or the rest of his subjects against the dangers that threaten them. Therefore we see them all betaking themselves with joined hands to serve the great. In this way they secure peace." Such is the picture which, about 1016, a German prelate drew of the anarchy in the kingdom of Burgundy. In Artois, in the following century, a monk pertinently explains how among the "nobility" only very few have been able to avoid the ties of seignorial domination and "remain subject to the public authority alone." Even here it is obviously necessary to understand by this term not so much the authority of the crown, which was much too remote, as that of the count, the repository, in place of the sovereign, of all that remained of a power by its very nature superior to personal ties.

It goes without saying that these ties of dependence spread through all ranks of society and not only among those "nobles" to whom our monk refers. But the lines of demarcation which the Carolingian age had begun to trace between the different kinds of relationships, characterized by different social atmospheres, were now more firmly drawn.

Certainly language and even manners for a long time preserved vestiges of the old confusion. Some groups of very modest manorial subjects, dedicated to the despised labours of the soil and tied to responsibilities which from now on were considered servile, continued till the twelfth century to bear that name of "commended men" which the author of the *Chanson de Roland* applied to the greatest vassals. Because the serfs were the "men" of their lord, it was often said of them that they lived in his "homage." Even the formal act by which an individual acknowledged himself the serf of another was sometimes described by this name and indeed at times, in its ritual, recalled the characteristic gestures of the homage "of hands."

This servile homage, however, where it was practised, was in sharp contrast with vassal homage; it did not have to be renewed from generation to generation. Two forms of attachment now began to be distinguished more and more clearly. One was hereditary. It was marked by all manner of obligations considered to be of a rather low order. Above all, it allowed of no choice on the part of the dependant, and so was regarded as the opposite of what was then called "freedom." It was in fact serfdom, into which most of those of inferior status who commended themselves descended imperceptibly, in spite of the "free" character which had marked their original submission in a period when social classifications were based on different principles. The other relationship, which was called vassalage, terminated in law, if not in fact, on the day when one or other of the two lives thus bound together came to an end. By this very characteristic, which relieved it from the stigma of an hereditary restriction on the individual's liberty of action, it was well suited to the honourable service of the sword. And the form of aid which it involved was essentially warlike. By a characteristic synonymity the Latin charters from the end of the eleventh century speak almost indifferently of a man as being the vassal, or the *miles*, of his lord. Literally, the second term should be translated by "soldier." But the French texts, from the moment of their appearance, rendered it by "knight" and it was certainly this vernacular expression which the notaries of an earlier day had had in mind. The soldier was typically a man who served on horseback in heavy armour, and the function of the vassal consisted above all in fighting in this manner for his lord. So that, by another avatar of the old word which not long before had been so humble, "vassalage" in popular speech came into common use as a name for the finest of the virtues known to a society perpetually at war—to wit, bravery. The relation of dependence thus defined was formally sealed by homage with joined hands, which was henceforth almost entirely restricted to this use. But, from the tenth century, this rite of profound dedication seems generally to have been completed by the addition of the kiss which, by placing the two individuals on the same plane of friendship, lent dignity to the type of subordination known as vassalage. In fact, this relationship was now confined to persons of high—sometimes even of very high— social status. Military vassalage had emerged by a slow process of differentiation from the ancient and disparate practice of commendation, and had come in the end to represent its highest form.

10. Feudalism in Western Europe

JOSEPH R. STRAYER

Feudalism, in Western European history, is a word which has been given many meanings,[1] but most of them can be brought into two general categories. One group of scholars uses the word to describe the technical arrangement by which vassals became dependents of lords, and landed property (with attached economic benefits) became organized as dependent tenures or fiefs. The other group of scholars uses feudalism as a general word which sums up the dominant forms of political and social organization during certain centuries of the Middle Ages.

There are difficulties with both usages. In the first category there is no agreement on the relationships which are to be considered typically feudal. Is it the act of becoming a vassal, or the act of granting a fief, or a combination of the two which makes feudalism? Retainers, clients, armed dependents of a great man—all these we have in both Germanic and Roman society from the fourth century on, but does that entitle us to speak of the late Roman or primitive German feudalism? Under Charlemagne there are vassals, and these vassals receive dependent tenures. Yet the king still keeps close control over all men and all lands, and the relationships of dependency are not necessarily hereditary. If this is feudalism, then we need another word to describe conditions in the eleventh century. In the seventeenth century, in both France and England all the technical forms of feudalism survive—most nobles are vassals and much of their land is held as fiefs. Yet it is only the form which has survived; the ideas which control the relationship of king and noble no longer conform to the feudal pattern. In short, the difficulty in concentrating on the technical aspects of feudalism is that it sets no chronological limits and provides no standards by which feudalism can be clearly distinguished from preceding and succeeding types of organization.

In the second category this difficulty is overcome by assuming at the onset that there is a "feudal age," a "feudal period" with definite chronological limits. The limits may vary, but there is general agreement on the core of the period—all authorities would admit that feudalism reached its height in the eleventh and twelfth centuries. But while this approach clears up the chronological confusion, it introduces a functional confusion by applying the feudal label to all social phenomena between the tenth and the thirteenth centuries. For example, the class structure of the late Middle Ages was very different from that of the early Middle Ages—are they both feudal? Lords used a different technique in exploiting their lands in 1200 from that in vogue in 1000—which technique should be accepted as typical of feudalism? We meet the sort of difficulties here that a modern historian would find if he assumed that the factory system were an integral part of democracy.

To obtain a usable concept of feudalism we must eliminate extraneous factors and aspects which are common to many types of society. Feudalism is not synonymous with aristocracy—there have been many aristocracies which were not feudal and there was no very clear concept of aristocracy in the early days of feudalism. Feudalism is not a necessary concomitant of the great estate worked by dependent or servile labor—such estates have existed in many other societies. Feudalism is not merely the relationship between lord and man, nor the system of dependent land tenures, for either can exist in a non-feudal society. The combination of personal and tenurial dependence brings us close to feudalism, but something is still lacking. It is only when rights of government (not mere political influence) are attached to lordship and fiefs that we can speak of fully developed feudalism in Western Europe. It is the possession of rights of government by feudal lords and the performance of most functions of government through feudal lords which clearly distinguishes feudalism from other types of organization.

This means that Western European feudalism is essentially political—it is a form of government. It is a form of government in which political authority is monopolized by a small group of military leaders, but is rather evenly distributed among members of the group.

As a result, no leader rules a very wide territory, nor does he have complete authority even within a limited territory—he must share power with his equals and grant power to his subordinates. A fiction of unity—a theory of subordination or cooperation among feudal lords—exists, but government is actually effective only at the local level of the country or the lordship. It is the lords who maintain order, if they can, who hold courts and determine what is the law. The king, at best, can merely keep peace among the lords and usually is unable even to do this.

The men who possess political power also possess important sources of wealth—land and buildings, markets and mills, forests and rivers—and this wealth is naturally useful in maintaining or increasing their political authority. Yet wealth alone does not give political power—loyal vassals and courageous retainers are more important. Any sensible feudal lord will surrender much of his land in order to increase the number of his vassals, and the most powerful lords, such as the Duke of Normandy, actually possess relatively few estates. It is also true that political and economic rights do not always correspond. A lord may have rights of government where he has no land and may hold land where some other lord has superior political authority. No one finds this inconsistent, because the distinction which we have been making between political and economic rights has almost no meaning for the early Middle Ages. Public authority has become a private possession. Everyone expects the possessor of a court to make a profit out of it, and everyone knows that the eldest son of the court-holder will inherit this profitable right, whatever his qualifications for the work. On the other hand, any important accumulation of private property almost inevitably becomes burdened with public duties. The possessor of a great estate must defend it, police it, maintain roads and bridges and hold a court for his tenants. Thus lordship has both economic and political aspects; it is less than sovereignty, but more than private property.

Effective feudal government is local, and at the local level public authority has become a private possession. Yet in feudalism the concepts of central government and of public authority are never entirely lost. Kingship survives, with real prestige though attenuated power, and the Church never forgets the Roman traditions of strong monarchy and public law. The revival of Roman law in the twelfth century strengthens these traditions and by the thirteenth century most lawyers insist that all governmental authority is delegated by the king and that the king has a right to review all acts of feudal lords.

Feudal lordship occupies an intermediate place between tribal leadership and aristocratic government. It differs from tribal leadership in being more formalized and less spontaneous. The feudal lord is not necessarily one of the group whom he rules; he may be a complete stranger who has acquired the lordship by inheritance or grant. It differs from aristocracy in being more individualistic and less centralized. The feudal lord is not merely one of a group of men who influence the government; he *is* the government in his own area. When feudalism is at its height, the barons never combine to rule jointly a wide territory but instead seek a maximum degree of independence from each other. One of the signs of the decay of feudalism in the West is the emergence of the idea of government by a *group* of aristocrats.

As the last paragraphs suggest, we must distinguish between an earlier and a later stage of Western feudalism. In the early stage feudalism was the dominant fact in politics, but there was almost no theoretical explanation or justification of the fact. In the later stage feudalism was competing with and slowly losing ground to other types of political organization, and many able writers tried to explain how and why it functioned. The great law-books of the thirteenth century—the Norman *Summa de Legibus,* Bracton, Beaumanoir—fit the facts of feudalism into a logical and well-organized system of law and government. Naturally most writers of secondary works have relied on these treatises and as a result the modern concept of feudalism is largely that of feudalism in the late twelfth and thirteenth centuries—a feudalism which was much better organized, much more precise, and much less important than that of the earlier period.

The first period of feudalism is best exemplified by the institutions of northern France about 1100. In northern France the one basic institution was the small feudal state dominated by the local lord. He might bear any title (the ruler of Normandy was called at various times duke, count, or marquis) and he was usually, though not always, the vassal of a king. But whatever his title, whatever his nominal dependence on a superior, he was in fact the final authority in his region. No one could appeal from his decisions to a higher authority; no one could remain completely indifferent to his commands. His position was based on his military strength. He had a group of trained fighting men in his service; he held fortified strategic positions throughout his lands; he possessed sufficient economic resources to pay for both the army and the fortifications. There might be lesser lords within his sphere of influence who had accepted his leadership in order to gain protection or because his military power left them no choice but submission. Some of his retainers—not necessarily all—would have fiefs for which they rendered service, in which they had limited rights of government. Relations between the lord and these subordinates were still undefined. The exact amount of service to be rendered by the vassal, the rights of government which he could exercise, the degree to which these rights could be inherited by his descendants depended far more on the power and prestige of the lord than on any theory of law. It was up to the lord to defend his territory and his rights; if he failed he would either lose his lands to a stronger neighboring lord or to his more powerful subordinates. There could be great fluctuations in power and in amount of territory controlled, not merely from one generation to another, but even from one decade to another. The only thing which was relatively stable was the method of government. The customs of a region remained the same, even if the lordship changed hands, and every lord had to govern through and with his vassals. They formed his army; they made up the court in which all important acts of government were performed; they performed most of the functions of local government in their fiefs.

The second stage of feudalism—the stage described by the great lawyers of the thirteenth century—bears a closer resemblance to the neat, pyramidal structure of the textbooks. The bonds of vassalage have been tightened at the upper and relaxed at the lower level; the ruler of a province now owes more obedience to his superior and receives less service from his inferiors. Early feudalism might be described as a series of overlapping spheres of influence, each centered around the castles of some strong local lord. Later feudalism is more like a series of holding corporations; the local lord still performs important functions but he can be directed and controlled by high authority. Appeals from the local lord to his superior are encouraged; petty vassals are protected against excessive demands for service or attempts to seize their fiefs; the central government in some cases deals directly with rear-vassals instead of passing orders down a long chain of command. Royal law-courts play a great role in this reorganization. The institution of the assizes at the end of the twelfth century in England protected the rear-vassal and brought him into direct contact with the king. The development of appeals to the king's court at Paris gave the same results in thirteenth-century France. In this much more highly organized feudalism rights and duties are spelled out in great detail. The amount of service owed is carefully stated, rules of inheritance are determined, the rights of government which can be exercised by each lord are defined and regulated. Force is still important, but only the king and the greatest lords possess sufficient force to gain by its use; the ordinary lord has to accept judicial solutions to his controversies.

There is obviously a great difference between these two stages of feudalism, and yet the transition from one to the other was made so smoothly, in many places, that it was almost imperceptible. It is true that in the later stage rulers were aided by concepts which were not derived from early feudalism, such as the revived Roman law and the Church's ideas of Christian monarchy. Yet, giving due weight to these outside influences, there must still have been some principle of order and growth in early feudalism which made possible the rapid development of relatively advanced systems of political organization in the twelfth and thirteenth centuries. Early feudal society, turbulent as it was, was never pure anarchy. There was always some government, even if rudimentary and local; there were always some centers of refuge and defense. Early feudal government, primitive as it was, was still more sophisticated and complicated than tribal government. There was a higher degree of specialization—the fighting men and the men with rights of government were clearly marked off from the rest of the group. There was a little more artificiality in political organization. Feudal government was not (necessarily) part of the immemorial structure of the community; it could be imposed from the outside; it could be consciously altered by the lord and his vassals. Early feudalism was rough and crude, but it was neither stagnant nor sterile. Flexible and adaptable, it produced new institutions rapidly, perhaps more rapidly than more sophisticated systems of government.

To understand the real vitality of feudalism we shall have to consider briefly the circumstances in which it first appeared in Europe. The Roman Empire had collapsed in the West, largely because none of its subjects cared enough for it to make any great effort to defend it. The Germanic rulers who succeeded the Emperors were not hostile to Roman civilization. They preserved as much of it as they were able; they kept together as large political units as they could. They were not entirely successful in these efforts, but they did preserve real power for the central government and they did thwart the growth of independent local lordship. The greatest of the Germanic rulers, Charlemagne, even united a large part of Western Europe in a new Empire. This was a *tour de force* which has impressed men for over a thousand years; he made his bricks not only without straw but very nearly without clay. The Latin and Germanic peoples he united had no common political tradition, no common cultural tradition and very few economic ties. Their interests were predominantly local, as they had been for centuries; only the clergy remembered with longing the peace and good order of Rome. With the moral support of the Church and the physical support of the army of his own people, the Franks, Charlemagne held his Empire together, but it was always a shaky structure. The Church profited by its existence to extend the parish system and to improve the education of the higher clergy. These developments helped to soften some of the cultural differences among Western European peoples, and to lay the foundations for a common European civilization, but the forces of localism were still stronger than those which worked for unity. Local government was in the hands of counts, men of wealth and high social position who held their authority from the king but who were not always fully obedient to him. The counts, in turn, were not always able to dominate the great landowners of their districts. Vassalage was becoming common and something very like fiefs held of the king or of lords appeared about the middle of the eighth century. Charlemagne tried to reinforce the doubtful loyalty of his subjects by making the great men his vassals, but this expedient had only temporary success. The ties between the magnates and their retainers were far closer than those between Charlemagne and the magnates, for the retainers lived with their lords while the lords visited the imperial court only occasionally. As a result the magnates had great power in their own provinces, subject only to the intermittent intervention of the king. This was not yet feudalism: there was still public authority, and the great men held political power by delegation from the king and not in their own right. But it was very close to feudalism; a strong push was all that was needed to cross the line.

The push came in the fifty years which followed Charlemagne's death. His heirs were less competent than he and quarreled among themselves. The magnates took advantage of these quarrels to gain independence; they began to consider their offices private possessions, to be inherited by their sons. Meanwhile invasions from outside threatened the security of all inhabitants of the Empire. The Saracens raided the south coast of France, the west coast of Italy, and even established a permanent fort at Garde-Frainet which interfered seriously with overland travel between France and Italy. The Magyars occupied Hungary, and from this base sent great cavalry expeditions through southern Germany, eastern France and northern Italy. Worst of all were the Northmen. For over a century their shallow-draft ships pushed up all the rivers of northern Europe and sent out raiding parties which plundered the countryside. The central government was almost helpless; it could not station troops everywhere on the vast periphery of the Empire and it could seldom assemble and move an army quickly enough to catch the fast-moving raiders. Defense had to become a local responsibility; only the local lord and his castle could provide any security for most subjects of the Empire.

It was in these conditions that feudal governments began to appear in northern France—a region which had suffered heavily from both civil war and Viking raids. We could hardly expect these early feudal governments to be well organized and efficient—they were improvised to meet a desperate situation and they bore all the signs of hasty construction. But they did have two great advantages which made them capable of further development. In the first place, feudalism forced men who had privileges to assume responsibility. In the late Roman Empire, the Frankish kingdom, and the Carolingian monarchy wealthy landlords had assisted the central government as little as possible while using their position and influence to gain special advantages for themselves. Now they had to carry the whole load; if they shirked they lost everything. In the second place, feudalism simplified the structure of government to a point where it corresponded to existing social and economic conditions. For centuries rulers had been striving to preserve something of the Roman political system, at the very least to maintain their authority over relatively large areas through a hierarchy of appointed officials. These efforts had met little response from the great majority of people; large-scale government had given them few benefits and had forced them to carry heavy burdens. Always there had been a dangerous discrepancy between the wide interests of the rulers and the narrow, local interests of the ruled. Feudalism relieved this strain; it worked at a level which was comprehensible to the ordinary man and it made only minimum demands on him. It is probably true that early feudal governments did less than they should, but this was better than doing more than was wanted. When the abler feudal lords began to improve their governments they had the support of their people who realized that new institutions were needed. The active demand for more and better government in the twelfth century offers a sharp contrast to the apathy with which the people of Western Europe watched the disintegration of the Roman and Carolingian Empires.

Feudalism, in short, made a fairly clean sweep of obsolete institutions and replaced them with a rudimentary government which could be used as a basis for a fresh start. Early feudal government was informal and flexible. Contrary to common opinion, it was at first little bound by tradition. It is true that it followed local custom, but there were few written records, and oral tradition was neither very accurate nor very stable. Custom changed rapidly when circumstances changed; innovations were quickly accepted if they seemed to promise greater security. Important decisions were made by the lord and his vassals, meeting in informal councils which followed no strict rules of procedure. It was easy for an energetic lord to make experiments in government; for example, there was constant tinkering with the procedure of feudal courts in the eleventh and twelfth centuries in order to find better methods of proof. Temporary committees could be set up to do specific jobs; if they did their work well they might become permanent and form the nucleus of a department of government. It is true that many useful ideas came from the clergy, rather than from lay vassals, but if feudal governments had not been adaptable they could not have profited from the learning and skill of the clergy.

Feudalism produced its best results only in regions where it became the dominant form of government. France, for example, developed her first adequate governments in the feudal principalities of the north, Flanders, Normandy, Anjou and the king's own lordship of the Ile de France. The first great increase in the power of the French king came from enforcing his rights as feudal superior against his vassals. Many institutions of the French monarchy of the thirteenth century had already been tested in the feudal states of the late twelfth century; others grew out of the king's feudal court. By allowing newly annexed provinces to keep the laws and institutions developed in the feudal period, the king of France was able to unite the country with a minimum of ill-will. France later paid a high price for this provincial particularism, but the existence of local governments which could operate with little supervision immensely simplified the first stages of unification.

England in many ways was more like a single French province than the congeries of provinces which made up the kingdom of France. In fact, the first kings after the Conquest sometimes spoke of the kingdom as their "honor" or fief, just as a feudal lord might speak of his holding. As this example shows, England was thoroughly feudalized after the Conquest. While Anglo-Saxon law remained officially in force it became archaic and inapplicable; the law which grew into the common law of England was the law applied in the king's feudal court. The chief departments of the English government likewise grew out of this court. And when the combination of able kings and efficient institutions made the monarchy too strong, it was checked by the barons in the name of the feudal principles expressed in Magna Carta. Thus feudalism helped England to strike a happy balance between government which was too weak and government which was too strong.

The story was quite different in countries in which older political institutions prevented feudalism from reaching full development. Feudalism grew only slowly in Germany; it never included all fighting men or all lands. The German kings did not use feudalism as the chief support of their government; instead they relied on institutions inherited from the Carolingian period. This meant that the ruler acted as if local lords were still his officials and as if local courts were still under his control. In case of opposition, he turned to bishops and abbots for financial and military aid, instead of calling on his vassals. There was just enough vitality in this system to enable the king to interfere sporadically in political decisions all over Germany, and to prevent the growth of strong, feudal principalities. But while the German kings of the eleventh and twelfth centuries showed remarkable skill in using the old precedents, they failed to develop new institutions and ideas. Royal government became weaker, and Germany more disunited in every succeeding century. The most important provincial rulers, the dukes, were also unable to create effective governments. The kings were jealous of their power, and succeeded in destroying or weakening all the great duchies. The kings, however, were unable to profit from their success, because of their own lack of adequate institutions. Power eventually passed to rulers of the smaller principalities, not always by feudal arrangements, and only after the monarchy had been further weakened by a long conflict with the papacy. Thus the German kings of the later Middle Ages were unable to imitate the king of France, who had united his country through the use of his position as feudal superior. Germany remained disunited, and, on the whole, badly governed, throughout the rest of the Middle Ages and the early modern period.

Italy also suffered from competition among different types of government. The German emperor was traditionally king of (north) Italy. He could not govern this region effectively but he did intervene often enough to prevent the growth of large, native principalities. The Italian towns had never become depopulated, like those of the North, and the great economic revival of the late eleventh century made them wealthy and powerful. They were too strong to be fully controlled by any outside ruler, whether king or feudal lord, and too weak (at least in the early Middle Ages) to annex the rural districts outside their walls. The situation was further complicated by the existence of the papacy at Rome. The popes were usually on bad terms with the German emperors and wanted to rule directly a large part of central Italy. In defending themselves and their policies they encouraged the towns' claims to independence and opposed all efforts to unite the peninsula. Thus, while there was feudalism in Italy, it never had a clear field and was unable to develop as it did in France or England. Italy became more and more disunited; by the end of the Middle Ages the city-state, ruled by a "tyrant," was the dominant form of government in the peninsula. There was no justification for this type of government in medieval political theory, and this may be one reason why the Italians turned with such eagerness to the writings of the classical period. In any case, the Italian political system was a failure, and Italy was controlled by foreign states from the middle of the sixteenth to the middle of the nineteenth century.

There are certainly other factors, besides feudalism, which enabled France and England to set the pattern for political organization in Europe, and other weaknesses, besides the absence of fully developed feudalism, which condemned Germany and Italy to political sterility. At the same time, the basic institutions of France and England in the thirteenth century, which grew out of feudal customs, proved adaptable to changed conditions, while the basic institutions of Italy and Germany, which were largely non-feudal, had less vitality. Western feudalism was far from being an efficient form of government, but its very imperfections encouraged the experiments which kept it from being a stagnant form of government. It was far from being a just form of government, but the emphasis on personal relationships made it a source of persistent loyalties. And it was the flexibility of their institutions and the loyalty of their subjects which enabled the kings of the West to create the first modern states.

NOTE

1. Pollock and Maitland, *History of English Law*, 2nd ed. (Cambridge, 1923), I, 66–67: "... *feudalism* is an unfortunate word. In the first place it draws our attention to but one element in a complex state of society and that element is not the most distinctive: it draws our attention only to the prevalence of dependent and derivative land tenure. This however may well exist in an age which can not be called feudal in any tolerable sense. What is characteristic of 'the feudal period' is not the relationship between letter and hirer, or lender and borrower of land, but the relationship between lord and vassal, or rather it is the union of these two relationships. Were we free to invent new terms, we might find *feudo-vassalism* more serviceable than *feudalism*. But the difficulty is not one which could be solved by any merely verbal devices. The impossible task that has been set before the word *feudalism* is that of making a single idea represent a very large piece of the world's history, represent the France, Italy, Germany, England, of every century from the eighth or ninth to the fourteenth or fifteenth. Shall we say that French feudalism reached its zenith under Louis d'Outre-Mer or under Saint Louis, that William of Normandy introduced feudalism into England or saved England from feudalism, that Bracton is the greatest of English feudists or that he never misses an opportunity of showing a strong antifeudal bias? It would be possible to maintain all or any of these opinions, so vague is our use of the term in question."

ECONOMIC LIFE AND SOCIAL CHANGE

IN THE TENTH and eleventh centuries a great economic recovery took place in Western Europe; eventually it provided the material foundations for a new civilization.

Population increased. New patterns of trade became established. Once a profitable market for surplus agricultural products existed, lords and peasants found a new incentive to expand agricultural production, and great tracts of wasteland were brought under cultivation for the first time. Total output rose very substantially, mainly because of this extension of arable land but also because of the use of improved farming methods. The readings in this section illustrate different aspects of these widespread changes.

The excerpt from Georges Duby describes the social and economic structure of an early medieval manor. Léopold Génicot discusses the demographic expansion that made possible all the other achievements of the age. A. B. Hibbert considers the emergence of the new merchant class. Finally, H. S. Bennett's essay provides a vivid recreation of day-to-day life in a medieval English village.

11. Manorial Economies

GEORGES DUBY

The Great Landed Estates

Some tenants of the manor were rich and some were poor, but all tilled the land of a master who was far wealthier than they. It was for the benefit of this landed aristocracy that the documents which illuminate the rural scene for us were put together; and they are solely concerned with their possessions.

The picture they reflect is that of a highly stratified society, in which power was vested in a small group of people who controlled from above the activities of the vast mass of country folk. It is true that there existed between tenants and lords a class of modest farmers who succeeded in preserving at least some of their economic independence. [There was] a peasant family numbering twenty souls whose existence is known to us by accident because their forebear had recently presented his land to a great monastery. Before this act of charity the family's possessions had been free from any overlordship. From other sources, and particularly from those which recorded service in the royal army, we catch glimpses of the existence and vitality of this class of peasants who farmed their own *manses.**

---

*The term *villa* refers to a great landed estate. The *manse* was a peasant's small-holding on the estate, i.e., his dwelling and a surrounding plot of land. The more well-to-do peasants also held strips of land in the open fields. These are referred to as *appendicia.*—Ed.

From Georges Duby, *Rural Economy and Country Life in the Medieval West,* Cynthia Postan, trans. (Columbia, S.C.: University of South Carolina Press, 1968), pp. 33–42, 48–52. Reprinted by permission of the University of South Carolina Press and Edward Arnold (Publisher) Limited.

It was more than likely that what enriched the great abbeys of south Germania in the ninth century were donations from such small farmers, each gift a modest one but commensurate with the donor's means. But however they were assembled it cannot be denied that very large accretions of *manses* and waste were concentrated in the hands of the ruling princes, the great ecclesiastical establishments and a few wealthy families. Enormous landed estates thus came into existence. The part of the temporal property of St. Bertin which was devoted to the support of the monks in the ninth century consisted of 25,000 acres, and the area of the lay estate of Leeuw St. Pierre in Brabant was reckoned to be more than 45,000 acres in extent.

Of all the forms which rural activity took at that time, these great estates were the first—and indeed very nearly the only—ones to be clearly revealed by written evidence. These carefully ordered institutions, run for the profit of their owners, were called in the scholarly parlance of the time *villae,* the same word which had been used in classical Latin texts. Those situated in the region of Carolingian civilization between Loire and Rhine, or in Lombardy, which can be more satisfactorily observed, belonged to the great monasteries. Inventories and descriptions have enabled historians to trace the characteristics of this economic organization which it is convenient to call "the manorial system." As it has been the subject of many studies, often very detailed, we shall not need to linger long over it.

The aspects of the system revealed by the most famous of the documents, the first to be described by scholars and represented by them as the "classical" type, are the two, complementary, halves of the *villa.* One of these was farmed by direct management. French historians have been accustomed to call this part *la réserve,* but when medieval lords and peasants spoke of it, they used the word *le domaine*—the demesne—and I, too, shall use the same word. The second half of the *villa* was composed of tenancies; small holdings let out on lease.

A demesne bore the same appearance as a *manse,* for it was after all the *manse* of the master, *manse indominicatus.* But it was an outsize *manse,* because it corresponded to a specially numerous, productive and demanding "household" or *familia.* Even so, its structure was no different from that of other *manses.* At the centre was an enclosure, the courtyard, the space surrounded by a solid palisade, enclosing as well as the orchard and kitchen garden a collection of buildings which amounted to a hamlet. Here is a description of Annapes, which belonged to the king. Around a well-built stone palace containing three halls on the ground floor and eleven rooms upstairs stood a cluster of wooden buildings, a cowhouse, three stables, kitchen, bakehouse and 17 huts to shelter the servants and store the food. As for the *appendicia,* attached to the central plot, there were extensive stretches of arable and meadow, as many vineyards as possible, and finally huge tracts of waste. The farm of Somain, near Annapes, had attached to it fields measuring 625 acres, meadow measuring 110 acres and 1,970 acres of woods and pasture. Other "farms" were not always so well provided for; the one belonging to the abbey of St. Pierre-du-Mont-Blandin at Ghent possessed less than 250 acres.

However, generally speaking, the *mansus indominicatus* was equal in size to several dozen peasant *manses* held as tenancies. And the picture most frequently given by the evidence is of a number of tenanted *manses* supporting the one farmed by the master. The area of arable possessed by the tenanted *manses* varied very greatly in size, as we have seen, but was always less than the quantity of land which theoretically corresponded to the physical capacity of a peasant family. Those holdings called "free" were on the average endowed with attached fields larger in extent than the "servile" holdings—but the status of the *manse* was not always the same as the personal status of its tenant.

The primary function of the great demesnes was to allow a few men to live in idleness, abundance and the exercise of power. They maintained a narrow circle of the magnates in a magnificent way of life. In a society still primitive, and at a time when food supplies were limited, the "man of power" showed himself first of all as the man who could always eat as much as he wished. He was also open handed, the man who provided others with food, and the yardstick of his prestige was the number of men whom he fed, and the size of his "household." Around the great lay and religious leaders congregated vast retinues of relatives, friends, people receiving patronage (the latter were known officially at the court of Charlemagne as *les nourris*), guests welcomed with liberality who would spread tales of the greatness of a house, and a host of servants, amongst whom would be found those artists in metal, woodcarving and weaving who could fashion weapons, jewellery and ornaments, and thereby enhance the luxurious setting appropriate to the exalted rank of the ruler. This way of life assumed housekeeping on a gigantic scale; barns and cellars filled to overflowing; well tended and fruitful gardens, trellises and vineyards; the cultivation of fields of almost limitless extent to provide sufficient grain in spite of low yields; and lastly the existence of enormous forests and wastes to harbour game and give pasture to the riding and warhorses which were the mark of the aristocrat. The springs of wealth had to be inexhaustible. It was the privilege of the noble at all times to avoid any appearance of shortage. He had to be prodigal in the midst of famine, but, as harvests fluctuated from year to year, his steward, anxious never to find himself in short supply, naturally tried to increase output, especially of corn.

• • •

Farming the Demesne

Scholars have in recent years constructed economic "models" of what they choose to call the classic demesne system (*le régime domanial classique*), based on the evidence of the few authoritative documents, and in this ideal system the *villa* is shown as a centre for the direct exploitation of the land: a widely spread centre, it is true, because agricultural yields were so low. At the beginning of the tenth century the monastery of San Giulia of Brescia consumed 6,600 *muids* of grain per annum. To assure themselves of this quantity the monks had to sow 9,000 *muids*. So rudimentary was agricultural technique that a single aristocratic family needed for its support a vast arable area, usually the extensive *appendicia* of several *villae*. Consequently the chief problem which faced estate managers was that of manpower.

The solution of this problem was much simplified by the existence of slavery. At that period the whole of western Europe practised slavery, and probably nowhere more actively than on the less advanced fringes closer to pagan lands, such as England and Germania. In any case there were very large numbers of men and women described in Latin texts by the classical names of *servus, ancilla*, or the collective noun of neuter gender, *mancipium*. Their legal condition, only slightly ameliorated by a Christian environment, was the same as that of Roman or heathen slaves. Their marriages were recognized, they could save small sums of money and acquire land. But their bodies were entirely at the lord's disposal and could be bought and sold: they, together with their offspring and their possessions, formed part of the equipment of the household. Their duty to obey was unlimited and their labour was without reward. Many were set up by their masters on *manses* where they could raise families and make a living, and these enjoyed a degree of freedom. But many more lived and worked in the lord's house where their position was the same as that of the farm animals. They were fed and looked after and became objects of capital value, and they worked at the lord's will. It may be that household slaves were more numerous than other slaves, and there is some evidence to show that some peasants employed them in their homes. The man of modest means who managed the demesne of the monks of St. Bertin at Poperinghe had four slaves in his service; his neighbour who managed a *manse* of 62 acres of arable at Moringhem kept a dozen slaves for his own personal use. In the houses of the nobles and the headquarters of the *villae,* there were of course hordes of them.

Our documents seldom mention the farm personnel as such. Slaves working with their hands (*servi manuales*), from whom these workers were drawn, and the *mancipia non casata*—the slaves who had no habitation in which to lead a separate family life but who were lodged in outhouses in the courtyard, and were also known as "prebendaries," since their master gave them food—all these were lumped together in a capitulary of 806 with household movables which were not always listed in inventories. Personnel of this character existed everywhere and agricultural production everywhere depended primarily on them. On a demesne *manse* of about 60 acres which had just been presented to St. Germain-des-Pres when the *polyptyque* of Irminon was drawn up the work was done by three *mancipia.* And 22 household slaves worked on the 200 acres of demesne arable on the *villa* of Ingolstadt presented by Louis the Pious to the abbey of Niederalteich. On the Lombardy possessions of the abbey of San Giulia of Brescia there were in the years 905–906 between eight and forty-nine slaves in each household.

The support of these servants was not an insurmountable problem. On estates where there were mills, the profits of multure were often sufficient to maintain the servile *familia.* Nor must it be thought that recruitment of domestics was difficult. It is true that the spread of Christianity somewhat hindered the slave traffic, but the market remained well supplied. Furthermore, some of the servants were married (as was the case with two of the *homines manuales* who worked in the household of one of the abbey of Farfa's *villae*) and many had legitimate or illegitimate children. It was probably not thought profitable to bring these children up in the master's household, since it would have meant feeding them until they were old enough to work. On the other hand it is more than likely that the lord's personal servants, both male and female, were the offspring of the slaves who had been settled on the servile *manses.* The latter could have been nurseries for rearing young domestic servants, and perhaps this was one of their chief economic functions.

There was one overwhelming reason, nevertheless, why masters did not leave all the fieldwork in the hands of their household staff. This was because the work itself was unequally spread over the agricultural calendar. Unlike animal husbandry or viticulture, cereal-growing alternates long seasons of inactivity with feverish periods when fieldworkers are needed in extraordinary numbers. Ploughing, harvesting and making hay to feed the draught animals in winter had to be accomplished with great speed in uncertain weather, and were times of frantic activity. To have enough personal servants to fulfill all the needs of the moment would have meant maintaining them in virtual idleness throughout the rest of the year. The food they ate would have been wasted and would have reduced the already restricted yield of agriculture. As a consequence the delicately poised economy of the demesne would have been disturbed. A far better solution was to supplement the small domestic labour force required to perform the daily tasks with the seasonal appointment of some hired labourers.

Economic conditions of the time did not absolutely preclude the possibility of wage labour. At Corbie the official in charge of cultivating the garden employed helpers for digging the borders, for planting and for weeding. Every year he was given towards the upkeep of these dayworkers 100 loaves, one *muid* of peas and beans and one of barley beer (which proves that these workers by the day were paid with meals), but 60 *deniers* were set aside as well "to take on men." But even so the monetary medium lacked flexibility, and money wages remained exceptional. It was much more convenient to reward the temporary farmworkers of the demesne with a plot of land, and to settle them upon a *manse*. The productive effort of these men and their families was thus divided. One part was left to provide themselves and their families with a living from their own plot of land. But the other had to remain at the disposal of the landlord. Here then was another economic function of the satellite holdings of the demesne.

In return for their endowment the peasant "households" owed to the "household" of their master various dues the nature of which was usually the same for each category of *manses* on the *villa* and also on other *villae* belonging to the same landowner. There were to begin with the various dues which had to be taken to the lord's hall on certain days of the year. The amounts were fixed, a few pieces of money, some chickens, eggs, one or two small animals such as sheep or pigs. These payments can be taken either as payments for the use of the woods and wastes of the lord, or as taxes of public origin. Some of them were the relics of the charges formerly imposed on peasants for supplies to the royal armies. It was the duty of the landlord to collect these, and in time he appropriated them for himself. These different dues were never heavy and the profit of the recipient was minimal. Their impact on the economy of the *villa* cannot have affected the real struggle for existence, the toil connected with garnering the main food supply, but was more a marginal matter of backyard poultry and small surplus items of diet. They formed only a superficial charge on the tenants' own farm production; and to the lord, as well, these odd amounts of food and small sums of money were trifling matters which contributed little if anything to his standard of living.

On the other hand the labour services imposed on the holdings were the essential economic link between them and the demesne and formed the very nexus of the demesne system. The manpower available on each satellite farm unit was, as we have seen, greater than that required to cultivate its fields. And this surplus manpower had to go to the demesne. It might take the form of periodic deliveries of objects upon which labour had been expended: thus, each *manse* might have to prepare a load of firewood, or a certain number of stakes, beams or planks, or perhaps some of those simple tools which could be constructed by any unskilled person. On servile holdings the women would weave cloth for the demesne. But the main tasks were agricultural, and they took three distinct but often interconnected forms.

1. The *manse* could in the first place be charged with a definite task. It could be responsible, for instance, for erecting in springtime a certain length of temporary fencing to protect the crops and the hay. More usually it was given the responsibility for an entire season's cultivation of a given plot of land, the *ansange*, taken from the demesne arable; activities which began with preliminary ploughing and continued right until storing of the grain in the lord's barn. In this way, every year some parcels of the demesne arable which needed cultivating were temporarily detached from the rest and were joined to the *appendicia* of the peasant *manses*. They rounded off the latter and absorbed the underemployed productive effort of the tenant population.

2. Other obligations were more exacting, since they left the workers less freedom. To perform them they were periodically taken away from the family group and put to join a team of workers on the lands attached to the demesne. The demands—the *corvées* in the real sense of the term, since the word means "demand" or "requisition"— only affected one labour unit in each *manse*, a worker either by hand or with a draught animal, i.e. a man or a plough team. If a *manse* was occupied by several families, or if the tenants themselves owned servants, as was fairly frequent, the service would be much lightened. Sometimes the *manse* owed a fixed number of days either at certain seasons, or else each week, and sometimes the man subject to the *corvée* assisted in a definite task until it was completed. In certain cases it was really manual labour (*manoperae*), for the man in question would come in the morning to the lord's hall to join the farm servants and await his orders whilst his implements and plough team were left behind at the *manse*. Another kind of forced labour was

specially assigned to certain tasks. The work of the women from the servile *manses* in the demesne workshops was of such a kind, and so were the errands and cartage requiring the use of cart and draught animals, which were usually the responsibility of the better-equipped, so-called "free" *manses.*

3. Tasks referred to in the inventories as "nights" were the third kind of work which might be required. These placed the tenant at the service of the lord for several days at a stretch without the certainty of returning home each evening. This enabled him to be employed at a distance or to be sent away on a mission, and it is clear that these obligations of an indeterminate nature provided the demesne with a reserve of immediately available and reliable labour in cases of unforeseen need.

These different tasks were often combined. But for the free *manse* they were usually lighter, more limited, and of less degrading nature. The free *manses* were generally occupied by peasants of free status, whose ancestors had often been independent, but who, because they were poor or weak, had allowed their lands to become part of the economic system of the *villa* in exchange for help and protection. But even where rural migration, mixed marriages and the alienation of land had obliterated the connection between the "freedom" of the tenancy and the free status of the tenants, the holdings were of sufficient size to support the larger domestic animals. To be able to provide oxen or a horse, and thus to take part in ploughing, cartage and contacts with the outside world, was probably their most valuable contribution to the demesne activities; they could supply ploughmen, drivers and horsemen, rather than unskilled labourers. On the other hand, it is easy to believe that when landlords created servile *manses* to house some of their domestic serfs in order to be rid of responsibility for their maintenance and to let them bring up their own children, they did not for one moment relax their right to command obedience or to use them at their will. They had to do manual labour because they did not usually possess draught animals. It was they who guarded the headquarters of the demesne at night, did the laundry, dipped and sheared sheep, while their wives and daughters worked in the demesne workshops. Servile manses were also burdened with the weekly labour services of undefined nature. In Germania they had usually to put a man at the disposal of the lord for three days a week; or in other words each *manse* had to provide one half-time servant throughout the year. This explains their smaller allocation of arable land than that of the free *manses.* Their holders were forced to work away from home for longer and could thus devote less time to their own farms, but on the other hand, when performing forced labour in the demesne they ate in the refectory, and their consumption of food at home was accordingly reduced.

Since the profit to be derived from a tenancy did not correspond to the services which it owned, the tenancy was not exactly a wage. The letting out of the *manses* ought primarily to be thought of as a way of relieving the demesne management of the necessity to provide the servants with board and lodging. The demesne could in this way have an abundant source of labour at its disposal. It has been calculated that the 800 dependent families of the abbey of San Giulia of Brescia at the beginning of the tenth century owed service to their masters amounting to 60,000 working days. The lord, here as elsewhere, wanted to dip into a bottomless well, to be permanently able to command instant service in the event of unforeseen need. But in normal times it is unlikely that all the labour services owing were actually called upon.

This then was the manorial system. The surplus productive effort of the peasant families was appropriated by the lord, to whose rule they were subject, for the purpose of farming his lands. But since human labour could by itself produce so little, this surplus was also limited. And because of this, the demesne needed a large number of satellite *manses*.

12. On the Evidence of Growth of Population in the West

LÉOPOLD GÉNICOT

Economic expansion, religious ferment, renaissance of letters and development of science, creation of an original art, territorial gains at the expense of the infidel world, all these phenomena of which the life of Christian Europe was woven between the 11th century and the 13th are in some way related to a net growth of the population. Consequently, almost all historians hold that, during what Marc Bloch called the second feudal age, the West went through a strong demographic surge.

This virtual unanimity is, however, a little deceptive: no one ordinarily doubts the fact or its importance yet we really know little about it. Actually, no one has had the courage to study it very closely. The documentation is so poor as at first sight to seem unable to sustain more than vague general conclusions. It has not been interrogated methodically, for fear that the effort would be futile. Perhaps this pessimism is justified, but how can we tell? We cannot be certain until at least one scholar has carried out systematic and exhaustive research in some definite region, and has then tried to draw together all the forms of evidence that reveal the shape of demographic trends from the post-Carolingian period up to the end of the Middle Ages.

This article tries to show what types of research would be feasible.

From Léopold Génicot, "On the Evidence of Growth of Population in the West from the Eleventh to the Thirteenth Century," Sylvia L. Thrupp, trans., in *Change in Medieval Society* (New York: Appleton-Century-Crofts, 1964), pp. 14–23. Article from the *Journal of World History*, Vol. 1:2. Copyright 1953 by Unesco. Reproduced by permission of Unesco.

It offers, not a finished history of the population of the different regions of the West between the years 1000 and 1300—indeed, the present state of knowledge would barely permit of an outline—but a list of the various indices of population growth that the monographs we need ought to collect and analyze. We shall illustrate the uses and the significance of each of these indices. Perhaps this will stimulate more careful research into "demographic prehistory." In any case I hope it will show that, although some historians may have exaggerated in speaking of the "demographic revolution of the 11th, 12th, and 13th centuries" and although our knowledge is still far from precise, the impression that population was growing is well founded.

To speak of demography means that we must seek quantitative measures, even though the figures may only partially reflect the reality and be no more than a basis for interpretation. Accordingly, we shall classify the numerous and varied indices of population growth in order of decreasing precision, that is to say, according as they may be expressed in more or less rigorous mathematical form, or better still—for history is concerned with evolution—in statistical series. They might be ranged as follows: the evidence given in military or fiscal documents; information gained from inventories of seigneurial property and rights; birth rates to be deduced from genealogical study and from the descriptions of families to be found in many charters; long-term price trends, in particular of agricultural prices; the multiplication and expansion of towns; land clearance, technological advances, and the fragmentation of traditional land holdings; changes in ecclesiastical geography and construction or alteration of public buildings, especially of churches and chapels; and colonization of the vast regions seized from the Infidel.

Medievalists do not hope to find a complete census of any population. They are happy enough to find incomplete or indirect data, such as lists of men liable to military service, or accounts of hearth taxes or poll taxes. The former are rather rare and late; only in Italy do we have any that antedate the 14th century. Again, they concern only the towns and we cannot be certain that urban population fluctuated in the same way as rural population. And their use depends on the calculation of a multiplier, usually on uncertain grounds, that will represent the ratio between the number of men capable of bearing arms and the total population. The second type of data, as presented by the celebrated "Etat des paroisses et des feux" of 1328 and the poll tax returns of 1377, is more valuable because it ordinarily covers a wide region, not just a single town. But it raises even more difficult problems. What was a hearth and what is the average number of individuals it indicates? Or what was the ratio between the number of adults who paid a poll tax and the number of children? What percentage of the population did exempt groups form— clergy, often nobles and their households, and vagrants? Were the enumerators and collectors conscientious? Was it hard to evade payment? How are we to fill the frequent gaps in the records? To what extent and under what conditions is it legitimate to argue from the part to the whole? All these questions are extremely delicate. On the other hand, again with exceptions in Italy (the *generales subventiones* of Frederick II and Charles of Anjou), the fiscal records, like the military lists, are all later than 1300. Yet for our purpose they are still relevant and useful, even for the earlier period. They furnish figures which, when compared with earlier data from other sources, show very convincingly that the population of the West had grown before the 14th century, and they help us to form a rough idea of the amplitude and the rhythm of this growth. Without the poll tax referred to above, J. C. Russell would not have been able to establish so firmly the fact that the population of England more than tripled in some 250 years, between 1086 and 1346.

Among the oldest of the other auxiliary sources are the surveys known as the polyptyques. Sometimes these give a fully detailed inventory of all the lands and dues belonging to a lay or ecclesiastical lord. In the 13th century many great and middling lords whose classical manorial regime had weathered a crisis drew up surveys of this kind in order, so to speak, to take their bearings. Sometimes the survey is merely a concise description of a single manor, compiled on the occasion of a pious donation or of a dispute or of what was later called a *dénombrement* of a fief. But whatever their form or scope, the polyptyques all contain similar statistical data: the number of settlements on the estate, for at least from the 11th century this often comprised more than one; the number of holdings of each type; the total area, in the ancient and the current measures, of fields and meadows; the number of tenants and the average extent of their holdings; and finally, in so far as one can tell from figures based on dues levied on individuals or on hearths, the total population and its density. If one has, then, for all or part of an estate, several polyptyques or related documents, such as accounts, it is possible to establish these facts at a series of dates and hence to deduce, more or less exactly, the demographic trend of the period and region in question. New settlements may appear, or the older ones may come to be more densely populated. For example, the 81 people living on the lands of Weedon Beck in 1248 had by 1300 grown to 110. Such a record is a valid measure of population growth if all other things remain equal at the two dates, namely, the area of land in question and the hearth or household unit. We must also be certain that an increase in one item is not offset by a decrease in another, for example, that an increase in the number of tenants does not simply reflect a decrease in the number of subtenants or of landless people.

Another way of measuring population change is through calculations of the average number of children per household. With luck, if our documentation is good enough, there will be two ways of doing this. One is through compiling genealogies. If genealogies compiled in the Middle Ages are used they of course have to be checked, and may sometimes be amplified, by new research. In this way it was discovered that the eldest branches of two of the greatest families of the region of Namur in each generation between the dates 1000 and 1250 had respectively a minimum of 5.75 and 4.30 children who came of age. The method is however applicable only in the case of great families. And the average number of children surving may have varied considerably between one social level and another. There is however another procedure, one that to my knowledge has never been tried, namely, the gathering of the descriptions of complete families to be found in charters. These quite often, when referring to pious donations of land, or in the case of *liberi* who donated themselves or of serfs who were donated to a religious foundation, name parents and their children. This information should be classified by date, by social class, by regions, etc. It would then show how the average number of children altered between one period and another. It might also resolve other problems, especially the question whether, as many historians have maintained, the serfs died out through having a particularly low birth rate. Having obtained the average by one or the other of these methods, one then has to estimate the number of children per couple, in the period and region in question, that would have been requisite simply to maintain the population level. Ideally one would deduce this from local documents of the period. In practice the best plan is to take a coefficient calculated by modern specialists, say 2.7, modifying it in the light of differences in the relevant variables. We are unable to take account of infant mortality, because the documents mention only children who have lived for some years, indeed usually only those who have grown up. But we have to take account of the nuptuality rate. This was undoubtedly lower in the Middle Ages than today because of a more pronounced disequilibrium between the sexes and because of more frequent entry into religious orders. Again, we have to bear in mind that the average duration of life was also lower in that age of all too frequent famine and epidemic.

Price trends, especially in agricultural prices, also demand attention. They are or may be, to an extent which has to be determined for every case, a function of demographic change. A fall in the rent of fields and meadows, accompanied by a rise in wages, especially of farm hands, such as we see in 14th-century England, is an unequivocal sign of a fall in population. Inversely, a rise in the value of arable land, above all if it is accompanied by a fall in wages, is a clue to population increase. Although we may never be able to trace the course of wages with any exactness before 1300, it is possible to form a general idea of their movement in the regions that are better documented. As to land values, at least in the 13th century, it is quite easy to show that they were rising: one may do so either by comparing average figures in successive years or, more surely, by charting the course of the rents on specific pieces of land.

Other indices lend themselves less easily to measurement, chief among these being the growth of towns. In some regions, such as the Low Countries, these probably originated in the 9th century; in others, such as Lombardy, they were revivified in the 10th century; everywhere they were in full expansion between the 11th century and the 13th. Proof of this lies in the continual enlargement of their bounds that is revealed by the successive construction of new outworks and by the reordering of their ancient parish divisions. The extension of their areas was not, however, exactly proportionate to increase in the number of inhabitants, for the density of urban population was not a constant. It varied from one town to another and within the same town, not only from one period to another but from one quarter to another, as, for example, between the market quarter and what modern architects would call the residential quarters, or from the ancient *civitas* to newly built suburbs. Besides, the walled area was seldom if ever completely built up; especially towards the close of the Middle Ages, it might include fields and meadows and other vacant sites. Yet in default of any more exact measure, the extension of the area enclosed is of some significance. To cite only two instances, the area enclosed by the fortifications of Ghent, one of the greatest towns of the age, had by the 14th century grown from 80 hectares to 644; the fortified area of Aix, a lesser town, grew from 50 hectares to 175.

Parallel with this urban movement ran another which some historians overlook: the transformation of villages into little towns. Places that had hitherto been simply agricultural acquire market rights and a market place, and sometimes a fair. They become petty commercial centers.

One should beware of exaggerating the demographic significance of these urban phenomena. Urban growth is not a precise index of total population growth. Even if the area of Ghent grew almost tenfold in 250 years or the population of some town in central Italy grew in the same period from 5,000 to 30,000, it does not follow that the population of Flanders or of Tuscany or of Umbria had grown tenfold or sixfold. Towns have always tended to absorb the people of their immediate environs; in some regions, as in Italy, they have attracted the artisans of whole regions, and even the peasants. They have continually drained the open country. All the same, and this is the point to be emphasized here, they did not empty the countryside. They drained off only its surplus human output.

They did not even take the whole of that surplus. Between the 11th and the 13th century, the rural population grew appreciably. The considerable extension of arable land during this period is sufficient evidence of this. For this was the age of the great work of dyking and drainage in fenlands. In Flanders, nature and man combined in the 11th century to push back the sea. In Lombardy, bishops, monasteries, and finally communes, endeavoured to tame the Po and make its valley fertile. By 1250 the work was finished: Milan by then, for instance, had its great irrigation canal, the Muzza, while downstream, between the tributaries of the Oglio and the Molinella, the river was well under control.

This is also, notably in such regions of France as the Parisian basin, the great age of the "villes neuves." The "villes neuves" were new settlements founded on open waste and in forest clearings by enlightened lords and their colonists (*hôtes*). We have the foundation charters of some of these places. For others the place name attests their origin by referring to new foundation (the French *Villeneuve*) or to the proprietor (Créon, Libourne), or by indicating their privileged status (the Italian *Villafranca*), or by copying the name of some great city far off (Bruges or Ghent in Béarn), or above all, by preserving the memory of the ancient forests and of the clearing process which eroded it, as in the German place names ending in *rade, raut, rode, roth, reut, riet, holz, wald, forst, hausen, hain, hagen, bruch, brand, scheid, schlag*, etc. Often the ground plan is our evidence, a grid pattern or the angling of intersections proving that the whole place was laid out in one operation.

Even where there was no dyking, no drainage, and no planting of new settlements, there was still new activity, although it may be more difficult for us to trace it. Yet careful examination of the old landscapes and attentive reading of the documents relating to them will often reveal that arable and pasture areas were being enlarged. Sometimes the structure of villages is significant, as in the intercalary type of settlement. Here there is a nucleus around which lie hamlets, scattered houses, or, less frequently, isolated manors. Records and source data prove these to be relatively new. They may, for example, be mentioned as inhabited places only rather late; they may be served by a little chapel dependent on the church in the central settlement, or they may be located in the middle of a huge tract of land owned by a single tenant, while the surrounding lands lie in open fields cultivated in strips, etc. Sometimes holdings are classified in such a way as to indicate that new clearing has taken place. A 13th century polyptyque, for instance, distinguishes the older tenements—manses, *més*, quarters, and *masale* land—from the assarts (newly broken land). Or study of the names of fields and holdings reveals the presence of *courts*, *vents*, *artigues*, *arsis*, and *mesnils*, dating from Roman or early Frankish times. Again, the documents may speak of the tithes known as *novales*, those levied on newly cultivated land, which may go back to a 9th century origin but more often only to the 11th century. Finally, a charter or a saint's life may mention the new development of forest or wasteland: for example, a property may be deeded to an individual or to a religious foundation to be cleared (*ad extirpandum*), or someone struck by paralysis has to lease out land that he had brought under cultivation.

All of these indices of the advance of cultivation have been known to us for a long time. The need now is to examine them in a more methodical and rigorous way. Research should focus on clearly defined areas and should exploit every existing source of information. Local study should deal simultaneously with water problems, with the appearance, the number and the importance of *villes neuves*, and with clearing operations within older lands in order to identify and date each assart. By doing so, it would be possible to measure the advance of cultivation in the region in question as accurately as possible.

The increase of the cultivated area would be a main clue to the degree of population growth. Yet although the two phenomena certainly move together, there is nothing to show that they must vary equally. Conceivably the breaking in of more land might be due less to an increase in population than to a fall in the number of the landless, or to a general rise in standards of living. The problem in each case would be to decide how far the movement was the result of population pressure. To know the motivation of the people or the communities concerned would be helpful. The founding of a *ville neuve* by a king or a territorial prince whose aims were political, strategic, or fiscal rather than truly economic and whose call for immigrants drew a response mainly from more or less remote countries, or the creation of a grange (outlying farm) by some Cistercian abbey would be less significant for the region we were studying than clearing planned by the cadets of seigneurial families or by peasants. Work of this kind was often more important than has been generally recognized.

To attack forest and wasteland is one means of dealing with population pressure. Another way is to improve technique. Agricultural methods progressed through fallowing every third year instead of every second and, on some plots, by sowing legumes in the fallow, through plowing more frequently and more deeply and fertilizing the soil more, and by specialization, for example, in vine culture or market gardening. All this was going on in the valley of the Rhine in the 12th and 13th centuries. What was achieved there may have been achieved elsewhere. In studying the demographic history of a region, it is important to look into all this.

But not everyone with too many children made an effort to get more land or to farm better. When population began to grow families at first continued to live on their patrimony. After a time, if juridical and other customs permitted, they would simply divide it. Fragmentation of manorial units, both of a whole vill and of the peasant *mansus,* was thus to some extent a consequence of population growth. It is one of our indices. It is true that the movement began well before 1100; in some places, for example in Lorraine, it was by then general. Of greater interest for us is the further fragmentation of the units, especially the quarter, into which the ancient manse had been split, but its occurrence is not easy to date.

Population growth bore not only on the secular "cell" of the social organism, the vill, but also on its religious "cell", the parish. Sometimes the parish disintegrated, though less often than has been supposed. The proprietors and the incumbents of the old churches, both rural and urban, defended their privileges fiercely and often victoriously. Thus the spiritual problems consequent on the growth of the flock had to be met by other means than subdivision of parishes. The old churches, and the bodies of clergy serving them, had to be enlarged or else new *loci religiosi* had to be set up, that is, chapels served more or less regularly by a priest, so that the faithful could at least hear Sunday Mass. Construction or alteration of churches and chapels is thus evidence of population growth; here the historian should consult the archeologist.

Finally, along with chance references to the development of this or that rural industry, we have clear proof of a rise in the population curve—in the expansion of the West. *Reconquista,* the feudal operations of the Hautevilles and their rivals in Southern Italy and Sicily, Crusades, and the *Drang nach Osten*—these movements are too familiar and too far-reaching to be discussed here. Between the 11th century and the 13th, and even into the 14th century, they were drawing colonists from all parts of the Christian West. In research in the population history of a region one must never forget to find out whether any of its people emigrated—either in large groups, like the Flemish peasants who went off to the Baltic fenlands, or singly, like the barons of Perche or of Béarn who straggled off to Spain. One should also try to find out why they went. Land hunger need not have been the only motive.

These then are the kinds of evidence which tend to show that from 1000 or 1050 to 1300 or 1350 the Christian West was becoming more thickly settled. Taken by itself, each piece of evidence is debatable. For example, the clearing of new land is not in itself "decisive evidence of an unusual growth of population, of a demographic revolution." It is the consistency of the evidence that brings conviction. Increase in the number of households or of individuals within a given area, birth rates higher than would have been necessary to mere maintenance of the population, a rise in land values coinciding with a probable fall in wages, growth in the size and number of towns, the promotion of more and more villages to the status of a little town and the rise of God knows how many new villages and hamlets, the pushing back of seas, marshes, wasteland, and forest by the advance of fields and pastures, improvements in the yield of land, fragmentation of old manorial units, subdivision of parishes or enlargement of churches and building of chapels, the expansion of the West to the South and to the East—how are we to explain all this going on at the same time, except by a net increase of population?

But though the nature of the process is clear enough, its working is in many respects still hazy. The evidence has not been systematically interrogated. We are still much in the dark about the starting points, the duration, the intensity and the phasing of the movement. When did it begin? We say, in the mid-11th century. But is this true of Italy? Or of Germany? Or of the Low Countries, Flanders or Normandy? When did it die down? Most historians would say, in the 14th century; many towns were then stagnating or declining, while marginal lands and even whole villages were being deserted. But there is still controversy as to whether these developments came in the early or middle years of the century. Those who believe that they came around 1300 point to the impossibility of bringing any more land under wheat, and to evidence of soil exhaustion on many of the assarts. They argue that in these circumstances population must already have ceased to grow and may already have begun to fall. But the majority still holds to the contrary thesis that the Black Death was responsible for reversing the trend. Again, some researchers take an entirely different view of the phasing of the movement. One writer claims that the Bavarian plain was already fully exploited by the end of the 13th. Another claims, after comparing two fiscal records, that between 1312 and 1427 the population of the Tirol grew by 50%.

The extent to which population grew is also a matter of debate. To speak of a revolution is perhaps to exaggerate. Even by the rather generous estimates of Levasseur or of Lamprecht, the average annual increase comes out far below that of England or Germany between 1800 and 1850—a percentage of 3.8 or 4.8 instead of 14 or 11. As to the possible phases of the movement, we are still unable to distinguish and describe them.

Almost everything that we know or postulate on this subject therefore requires to be verified and restated in quantitative terms. This can be done only through meticulously careful regional study. We cannot even be certain of reaching precise quantative results. But the attempt has to be made, for although it has been long neglected, the problem is nonetheless important. Indeed, in all medieval history there are few questions so fundamental as this one.

P.S. On reading the manuscript of this article my esteemed colleague and friend Professor Philippe Wolff of the University of Toulouse suggested to me that the improvement in the status of peasants, especially the relaxation of the bonds attaching them to the soil, may equally be a consequence of population growth. This is certainly true, yet the interpretation of this index is a particularly delicate matter, one that does not lend itself well to statistical study.

·13. The Origins of the Medieval Town Patriciate

A. B. HIBBERT

This article is concerned with the theory advanced by Henri Pirenne to explain the origins and early history of medieval towns. This theory may be summarized as follows.[1] During the 9th and much of the 10th centuries long-distance trade in Europe was at its lowest ebb, and during this period the only settlements which were not purely agricultural were the ecclesiastical, military and administrative centres which served the major needs of the feudal ruling classes: fortresses, monasteries, episcopal seats, royal residences and the like.[2] These had none of the characteristics of true towns and knew neither commercial nor industrial activity, but when long-distance trade revived in the 10th and 11th centuries the merchants and artisans produced by changing economic conditions settled round them. The influx of such people made it possible for true town life to develop.

From the very beginning the incoming traders differed from the older inhabitants. They were set apart by their origins, for they were "new men" and indeed outsiders to the feudal order itself, living on the margins of that society; they were set apart in a purely physical sense, for they lived outside the walls of the old feudal settlement or "pre-urban nucleus" in a separate trading and manufacturing colony, the suburb.

The feudal "core" of such double settlements remained static,

From A. B. Hibbert, "The Origins of the Medieval Town Patriciate," *Past and Present,* No. 3 (February 1953), pp. 15–27. World copyright The Past and Present Society, 175 Bauxbury Road, Oxford England. This article is reprinted with the permission of the Society and the author from *Past and Present, A Journal of Historical Studies.*

inert, but the colony formed by the newcomers grew in numbers and in strength. Finally a time came when the traders and craftsmen felt themselves strong enough to challenge the control which the feudal element had hitherto exercised over them. They or their leaders struggled for independence, and by money or force of arms established a new regime which contrasted in all essentials with the old order. A distinctive social, economic and legal unit was brought into being, the medieval town, and this was the work of the merchants and artisans alone.

A group of the more important merchants commonly took the lead in the struggle to achieve these various changes, and after the town had thrown off or modified feudal control, this group developed into the characteristic medieval "patriciate." This patriciate was an increasingly narrow class which enjoyed social, political and economic control in the town and whose power and influence rested on the control of the wholesale and long-distance trades of the town. The changing relations between this dominant element and the rest of the townsmen were to determine a great deal of later town history.

This theory is certainly both powerful and fertile, and yet it may be questioned at many points. What follows is not an original or exhaustive examination of the hypothesis. I intend merely to probe some of its weak points in a preliminary way. I shall only deal with one theme in detail, that of the origin of the patriciate, and shall choose my facts and arguments from among those likely to be familiar to students of the subject.

We can most profitably criticise Pirenne's views in two ways: on theoretical grounds and by reference to fact. In the first instance we may ask whether he was right in his view of the role of the revival of long-distance trade in the 10th and 11th centuries, and in his views on the relationship between trade and feudal society in general. In the second, we may ask whether a sharply contrasted feudal "nucleus" and a trading suburb really occurred in the early stages of all towns and whether the patriciate really developed along the lines he suggested.

I shall make the only the briefest reference to the effects and nature of the expansion of long-distance trade from the late 10th century onwards. Has long-distance trade as opposed to local trade any special virtue as a stimulant of town growth? Was long-distance trade before 1000 A.D. as unimportant as Pirenne's theory assumes? We may leave these questions aside, though Pirenne's answers to them may be, and have been challenged. There are other grounds for disquiet. Pirenne treats a trade revival as though it were something which happens of itself, independent of surrounding circumstance.[3] Such treatment of historical fact is often justifiable, it is a useful piece of shorthand to prevent an infinite regress from cause to cause but it loses its justification if instead of condensing argument to a convenient size, it involves the elimination of arguments vital to the discussion.

Just such a difficulty arises here. Pirenne's theory leans heavily on the idea that there is a natural incompatibility between arrangements of society suited to feudal lords and those suited to merchants and artisans, or between a "feudal" settlement and one allowing the development of trade and industry. One cannot deny that such an antagonism between "feudal" and "burgess" interests did develop later in the Middle Ages. It may even be granted that it was potential or latent from the beginning. If, however, we consider how trade *must* originally have developed in the context of a feudal society, and how the earlier concentrations of merchants and artisans must equally have been the outcome of feudal circumstance, we may properly question any theory which assumes that the two were originally and inherently incompatible.

Both fact and theory suggest that in earlier medieval times trade was by no means a solvent of feudal society, but that it was a natural product of that society and that feudal rulers up to a point favoured its growth. There is the simple fact that whatever area and whatever century we may choose to take as being most typically "feudal" there is still trade and there are still merchants. Feudalism could never dispense with merchants. The very structure, technical level and economic habits of society always made some local and long-distance trade necessary. It is possible to press this point further. It can be argued that the development of feudal lordships and of related changes in agricultural organization both increased total productivity and concentrated the wealth so produced. Ever greater and wealthier feudal establishments appeared and these acted as ever greater and more demanding consumers—thus directly stimulating trade and concentrating those who supplied the goods for them. Again, a substantial class of merchants and craftsmen had to be fed by the agricultural labours of the other groups; these therefore had to provide extra food. It may thus be suggested that growth of such a class depended essentially on changes in rural society which made either for increased productivity or lower consumption per head among the tillers, thus providing more food. Such changes must have been wrought *within* the "feudal" structure and were a basic prerequisite of any town development.

The mass of evidence about what attitude feudal lords took in practice towards towns and trade adds weight to these arguments. They founded towns, encouraged merchant and artisan settlement, sketched out a staple policy in their attempts to direct trade through centres under their own control and, especially in Southern Europe, took an active and direct part in town life. There were two obvious reasons why they should do this. They had to provision large private and public establishments, and they wished to gain profit from trade and industry, either by becoming traders themselves or by tapping the wealth produced by trade and industry through levies and charges upon goods or upon those who produced and distributed them.

Portions of Pirenne's theory can be tested by a more direct appeal to facts. Two questions seem particularly prominent: the nature and role of the "pre-urban" or "feudal" nucleus and the origins of the patriciate. For the sake of brevity I shall discuss only the second of these here. Pirenne's description of the social history of the burgess class and the rise among them of an urban patriciate is of prime importance in his theory. For him the patricians were the main creators and moulders of urban life and institutions; they were the mainspring of town development. It is therefore of some consequence to establish who and what they were.

Pirenne answers this question in a fairly simple way. The more prosperous burgesses were the descendants of those newcomers who in the 11th century and onwards had settled round fortresses, monasteries and similar centres for the sake of security. Each had originally been "a little pedlar, a sailor, a boatman, a docker" or something of the sort.[4] Those who had prospered had become great merchants and from among the most notable of these was recruited, during the 12th and 13th centuries, the ruling clique of the towns, a patriciate whose class dominance was based on their position as great wholesale traders.[5]

Any attempt to find out whether the patriciate really did originate among merchants and "new men" encounters very great difficulties, above all the sheer lack of documentary material. The obvious way to answer the question would be to sample the family histories of members of the early patriciate, but in practice this is almost impossible. Of course this difficulty cuts both ways and Pirenne himself has to rely more on inference than on direct evidence for his own theory. The career of St. Godric of Finchale, which he uses as a picturesque illustration, is a rather shaky foundation on which to build a great theoretical edifice.[6]

The basic facts about many Italian towns are perhaps too well known to need much comment. There the petty nobility and the greater among the free landowners played a part which Pirenne himself admits to be different from that generally allotted to them in this theory.[7] They were favourably disposed towards the development of trade, they took a direct part in commercial activities and they were sometimes the most prominent subscribers of capital and the final controllers of commercial life.

At *Genoa* for example where the first trading partnerships are found in the documents of the early 11th century, the typical sleeping partner is a landowner who has some surplus capital to invest, presumably derived from land rents, loot from expeditions against the Moslems, or from feudal office. Later, during the course of the 11th and 12th centuries, it becomes even clearer that the greatest leaders of trade expansion were the men who already possessed influence and money because of their high position in a feudal society, men who received larger revenues from rents or customs or market dues. In the very front rank, commercially as well as socially and politically, were great 12th century vice-comital families like the Burone, della Volta, Mallone and di Castro. They and people of the same general standing, such as the Embriaco family, dominated all aspects of Genoese life during this period. Then, in the later 12th and 13th centuries, their position was challenged by new men who had risen from the lower ranks of society by the ladder of successful trade. Such newcomers were the Doria, Cigala and Lercari families who were to be so important in the period of Genoese maturity.[8]

This class of lesser nobles and landowners were equally important in the constitutional development of Italian towns. They took a prominent part, and characteristically the lead, in the struggle against episcopal control. We find them to be the essential element of many of the earliest urban ruling groups; they provided the membership of the earliest Italian patriciates. From the earliest date *Milan* chose its consuls from the "capitanei," "valvassores" and "cives."[9] Elsewhere the "grandi" were typically recruited from the lesser nobility and great landlords, from the group which had usurped seignorial control. This group was so little composed of great merchants alone that these latter had subsequently to lead revolutions to secure a share of control with the earlier patriciate. Long after the towns had achieved a marked degree of independence, in the 13th century, great merchants combined against the old patriciate of semi-feudal nature in revolutionary movements at *Florence* and elsewhere. Few things could be more significant, for if the patriciate had already been simply composed of great merchants such struggles would have been superfluous. Hence A. Sapori, summing up the present state of investigations into Italian town history, sees town development as due to the formation of a group stronger and richer than the rest, which usurped the public and financial functions of the overlord and gave its personal and class unity a territorial basis. It was essentially formed, he holds, of petty vassals, great emphyteutic tenants and large-scale "farmers," all of whom had developed a direct interest in trading matters.[10]

It therefore seems no exaggeration to say that in Italy the first stages of urban history in the Middle Ages were associated with the formation of a ruling group of largely aristocratic and feudal origin, which controlled town life and trading conditions. The later history of this patriciate would vary. Sometimes the original patriciate adapted itself to the changing volume and nature of trade by taking an interest in its development or by recruiting members from among the merchants themselves. In such cases an upper group, part feudal-aristocratic, part mercantile would arise, a group of mixed nature like the "magnates" of *Bologna* formed of nobles made *bourgeois* by business and *bourgeois* ennobled by city decree, both fused together in law.[11] In other towns the old patriciate would prove too unadaptable and powerful new groups would build up outside its ranks. Then the day would come when the controllers of the great trades either overthrew the rule of the "grandi" or else forced them to share their powers. In the first case the history of the patriciate clearly consists, in various proportions, of the transformation of the old ruling group of feudal origin and the recruitment of new men into it. Even when events had the most revolutionary appearance, however, we have still to face two facts. An aristocratic patriciate held sway in the earlier and most formative period, and the supplanting group usually made little change in town organization and quickly formed itself into a body barely distinguishable from that which it had replaced.

Leaving aside the evidence of other southern regions, which is often so similar to the Italian, let us turn to northern Europe, for Pirenne in fact based his theory on the evidence of northern towns.

J. W. F. Hill has collected the information available about the families which dominated *Lincoln* immediately after it achieved some degree of self-government.[12] Take the three most prominent families of all, those which provided the first three mayors to be known by name. Adam, mayor between 1210 and 1216, had as grandfather a landowner and church benefactor, as uncles the holder of a fee and a bailiff of the lord; his father was a property owner, a man who leased houses to tradesmen, and supervisor of repairs of the castle gaol. His brothers-in-law were lords' bailiffs and considerable landowners within the city and in surrounding villages, his cousin another landowner. He himself possessed numerous lands, houses and rents, including land in the Bail, the area which remained under the feudal jurisdiction of the constable of the castle. His nephew, John Fleming de Holm, held a lordship at Langton as well as being an alderman of Lincoln, and John's son and grandson followed in his footsteps. The latter, Peter de Holm, held property within the Bail by homage and fealty to the Bishop of Durham, and his case is the first in which we *may* have evidence that the family engaged in trade: in 1268 he was granted life exemption from all tallages assessed in the city provided that he did not trade in town. This seems very dubious and negative evidence on which to base a claim that the family was one of merchants. We must not make too much of an argument from silence, but it remains true that between 1150 and 1250 the family was one of important landowners, rentiers and feudal officials, on the fringe of the nobility.

The second known mayor, William "nephew of Warner," had relatives of the same generation who held the rectory of St. Paul in the Bail, held half a Knight's fee from the bishop, were owners of houses and market stalls, bailiffs and great landowners. William himself was bailiff to the lord on several occasions and a rich rentier into the bargain. There were trading interests in the family however; a certain Osbert, probably William's uncle, and owner of considerable landed property, was once fined for selling wine contrary to the assize. Even so it is very arguable whether trade or land and office-holding ranked as the original and basic activity, and Osbert's sons and grandsons figured as prominently as bailiffs, landed proprietors and rent holders as they did as men with commercial interests. The third family, that of the mayor Peter de Ponte, conformed more closely to the pattern of the first. This family "had its roots in the Bail," contained two bailiffs in Peter's father's generation, and was characteristically made up of large landowners and rentiers in the 12th and early 13th centuries.

Naturally such evidence is not conclusive as to the origins of the 13th century patriciate of Lincoln. Somewhere in an unrecorded past these men *may* have first climbed to fortune by the profits of the Scandinavian trade. What the facts do tell us is that at its very first documented appearance the patriciate has the character of a land-owning and rentier group, holding feudal office and then town office without a break, merging with the smaller kind of feudal noble and landlord. If we can discriminate at all on such slender evidence we are shown that trading was at least as likely to be something taken up as time went on, as something to be dropped as part of a shameful family past.

Evidence of varied nature comes from other places. In *Poland* Rutkowski derives the trading patriciate of those towns whose population remained on the whole Polish, from the feudal nobles who settled in the towns while retaining their interests as great landholders.[13] In *Norway* the chief merchants in the 12th and 13th centuries were great ecclesiastics and great landowners, while the ruling class of *Bergen* and its dominant trading clique before the days of Hanseatic hegemony, was made up of important officials and the principal owners of "gaards" (curtes) within the town, to whom were joined as more recent and less substantial elements, some professional merchants and shipowners.[14] Pirenne himself goes so far as to agree that in the 11th century there was at least some fusion between the knightly class and the upper rank of traders to form the patriciate in the northern towns, and he has also to admit that in some towns of his area, and especially in the episcopal cities of the *Rhineland* and the *Liége* region, the "ministeriales" of the lord entered into the patriciate.[15]

It is interesting that the evidence for his own theory is so very dubious in the one town on which Pirenne has published a detailed study—*Dinant*.[16] Here, under the presidency of the "villicus" of the bishop of Liége, the chief officials were the "monetarii" who acted as judges in the town court and were the instruments of episcopal control. Pirenne describes this feudal group as "gradually giving way before the slow but irresistible invasion of the bourgeoisie,"[17] the echevinage replacing the "monetarii" in the 12th and 13th centuries. Pirenne's case would be firmer if the "monetarii-judices" survived by the side of the "échevins" as a contrasted group. As it is, their disappearance allows us to guess that both groups might in fact have been recruited from the same class of men and that one was transformed into the other. In fact, the evidence suggests just this. In 1227 when the four "monetarii" are mentioned for the last time, two of them *were* "échevins," and another almost certainly belonged to a family which provided more than one "échevin" later in the century. In other words, three out of the four episcopal officials furnished direct proof of continuity and fusion with the echevinage. It should be noted that "échevins" were probably still elected by the bishop, that the law they administered was seigneurial, that they clung above all other things to competence in cases involving real estate. If the echevinage was the original form of the *bourgeois* patriciate as Pirenne says, then it must be conceded that it derived in great part, if not entirely from the same class as the original feudal officials. "Their possession in the city and its surrounds of vineyards, curtileges, houses and land rents" was a primary basis of their economic power and their large-scale trading interests were probably derivative.

J. Lestocquoy's researches into the great patrician families of *Arras*[18] provide most important direct evidence. He examines in detail five of the families who were in the top rank from the 12th century onwards and in no case does he find their origins among landless newcomers or among a population of professional merchants some of whom gradually improved their position. Instead they seem to spring from a group who were feudal officials and moderately important landowners in the 11th century. The Crespin family, which produced some of the greatest financiers of the Middle Ages and lent several times their annual income to most of the cities of Flanders, first appeared as modest landed proprietors and possessors of a mill in the mid-12th century. They took up money-lending on a moderate scale about the 1220s. The Huquedieu family started in the service of St. Vaast monastery, as officials of the Count of Flanders and as cathedral canons about the same time. They may have had a military origin, and seem to have been high feudal officials; one of them was an échevin in 1111 when these officers receive their first mention.

Similar cases can be multiplied. At *Cambridge* we find that the alderman of the Gild Merchant and perhaps the first mayor of the town, Hervey Dunning, held land in half-a-dozen villages, claimed the rank of knight and twice demanded wagers of battle in suits concerning landed property. His father, uncle and grandfather were all land owners.[19] At *Brussels* the patriciate dominated the Gild Merchant at the beginning of the 14th century and contained the most prominent merchant-employers in the drapery industry; yet no 13th century document shows the patrician "lignages" engaged in trade. Of course this is in part due to the chances of documentary survival, yet the further back patrician family histories are pushed, the more clearly the patricians appear as landholders and lesser feudatories. Families like the Clutines and Eggluys were farmers of tithes, tenants of castellanies, holders of ducal fiefs—they owed their wealth to lands, rents and the farming of feudal revenues.[20]

Perhaps there is much more similar evidence to be found. Who were the 11th and early 12th century aldermen of *London?* Who were the "possessores" who lived near *Ghent* in the 11th century and took their wool to the town to be woven? Who were the leading citizens of early *Douai,* two of whom can be found in the 12th century selling their share in the town tolls to the Abbey of Andin?[21] The whole problem of patrician origins requires much more detailed investigation, but the evidence does seem to call for an interim revision of Pirenne's theory.

This revision must take account of two main facts: the evidence which shows that old-established families could adapt themselves to new economic conditions, and use their old power to achieve power in a new context; and the truth in Pirenne's contention that the more successful merchants among the newcomers to a town could make their way into the ruling class. Two processes are involved in the formation of the patriciate, the internal transformation of an old dominant class and the recruitment of new families from the more successful merchants and artisans, who were often immigrants or the descendants of immigrants. Let us take each process in turn.

In the earlier stages of town development there was often a class between the actual lords on the one hand, and agricultural workers, craftsmen, petty traders, porters, innkeepers and the like, on the other. This group comprised large freeholders and emphyteutic tenants, sometimes the lower grades of the nobility (especially in Italy), prominent officials in the service of a lay or ecclesiastical lord, like the more important among the "ministeriales" in Germany, and, possibly, such elements as burhthegns, cnihts, lawmen, or members of a witan, dimly discernible in early English towns. The economic position of the group was intimately associated with the possession of land and feudal office. At the same time its members were willing to take advantage of any opportunity to improve their position—by leasing their land or renting the buildings they had constructed on it, by letting out stalls in the market place, by farming mints, tolls or mills from the lord, by raising loans wherever required, and by engaging their capital in commercial and industrial enterprises beyond the scope of lesser men.

Two things would happen to such a group, made up of quite wealthy men, used to freedom and possessing initiative, men accustomed also to running the affairs of the town on the lord's behalf, or at least to being consulted by him. What more natural than that they should be in the lead of movements for freedom from seigneurial control? The new municipal powers created economic and political opportunities of which they were in the best position to take advantage. Psychologically, socially and politically they were in the most suitable position to conduct a successful attack.

Secondly, these men would probably have had an interest in trade from the earliest times. As seigneurial officials many of them were well placed for controlling supplies to one of the best of the early markets, the feudal households, and the group as a whole possessed land and land rents, one of the greatest potential sources of liquid capital during the Middle Ages. They would therefore include the capitalization of trade among their varied activities, and where trade developed quickly they might be merchant capitalists among other things at a very early date. As M. Postan comments: "It can well be doubted whether the conventional picture of a vagrant trader, travelling with his goods . . . ever represented the upper strata of the medieval merchant class."[22] At first, however, trading, if present at all, would not normally be the greatest or most typical of their economic activities; but as economic change proceeded in Europe, trade and finance would come to rival, perhaps to overshadow, other means of gaining wealth. The leading families, or the more adaptable among them, invested proportionately more in the new activities, because men of their group characteristically seized all opportunities of advancement of any kind. They would retain, and even intensify their old land-owning and office-holding interests by means of the new wealth, as methods of social and financial investment. By and large, however, the influence and power of the class increasingly depended on commerce and finance.

Thus the formation of the 12th and 13th century patriciate involved *internal transformation* of a dominant class which already existed, and which was opportunist enough to shift the emphasis of its activities as conditions changed. Some of the leading townsfolk were, however, too conservative and rigid in outlook to adapt themselves. They were left as survivals of an older stage, like the "grandi" in Italy, opposing the great trades rather than merging with them; or like the échevins in some towns of the *Liége* group who refused to join their more progressive fellows in leadership of the new council of jurés; or like the Avvocato and Gavi families of 12th century *Genoa* who failed to join the rush of many of their social equals into trade. Sometimes the class as a whole failed in adaptability, especially when it was faced with fundamental economic changes like those of the late 13th and 14th centuries. Then there were challenges of varying seriousness, and the ensuing battles filled much of town history in the later Middle Ages.

These problems cannot be treated here. Instead we must complete the explanation of patrician origins by looking at the recruitment of new men. Outsiders, and especially those merchants and artisans who had made more than a modest competence through their ability and good fortune, could and did enter the patriciate. Such recruitment could take two principal forms. There was the normal continuous inflow of rich parvenus into the ruling group, which was all the more easily assimilated when the patriciate itself had developed large trading interests. The rate of recruitment however would vary greatly and depended particularly on the attitude of the patricians themselves. This suggests the second form. If the ruling group proved unadaptable and exclusive, a class of nouveaux riches was likely to build up in opposition to them, particularly when economic conditions had opened up new ways of obtaining wealth. Recruitment was, so to speak, dammed back, and would therefore produce tensions and greater or lesser crises in which the new men would try to seize power or at least to share it with the old.

A satisfactory explanation of the origin of the medieval patriciate seems possible along these lines. Moreover, the explanation can be adjusted to suit the divergent circumstances of different towns and regions by allowing for variations in the relative importance of the two main processes, the internal transformation of a "feudal" upper class and the recruitment of the new man.

Sometimes for instance the social constitution of an early town did not favour any large number of men of the "feudal" type. This type seems to have been especially common in Southern Europe, and particularly where there was substantial continuity of town life from late Roman times. It was fairly common in most of the episcopal centres and other large and old-established settlements in the North. But the old "feudal" group might be weaker, and the association of the "new" merchants coming up from below the stronger, for many social reasons. Then "recruitment" would be a major factor and merchants rising from among the commons more important than an element of officials and landowners who had taken to trade. In the South such conditions may have obtained exceptionally, as in *Venice*, but in the non-episcopal towns of the North they were much more common, especially in England and "new" Germany, where they were often associated with the peculiar importance of the merchant gild. It is on such evidence that Pirenne founds his theory, on part of the evidence for part of Europe. We may freely admit that in certain cases his explanation seems close to the truth, but what matters is that the explanation, appropriate to cases at one end of the spectrum, is applied to the whole range. In fact even those examples best suited to Pirenne's theory usually show some small effects due to another type of development. Even in the North of Europe there are many important towns in which "transformation" was at least as important as "recruitment," and most towns in the South require a different approach altogether. Further, if there is a Pirennian extreme at one end of the scale, there seems to be an equally "feudal" extreme at the other. This is constituted by such towns as those in northern Italy and especially in *Piedmont* where communes sprang from seigneurial families whose multiplying offspring formed themselves into an association, each the nucleus of a town commune.

We may in conclusion note a few auxiliary advantages of the foregoing explanation. Trade revival and economic change generally are retained as integral parts of the scheme of development, and merchant capitalists keep an important role though a different one from that postulated by Pirenne. The explanation tallies well with what we know of the forms of economic and political power actually exercised by established patriciates. It allows for a source of mercantile capital additional to or alternative to the windfalls of petty pedlars and porters. Finally it will allow for the idea that novel techniques or fresh markets might first be exploited by new men who in order to expand relied on association with wealthy men of older standing so that capital was gradually shifted from an older to a new use.

NOTES

1. H. Pirenne's theory was first advanced in articles on "L'Origine des Constitutions Urbaines au Moyen Age" in the *Revue Historique* 1895, and expanded in various later works. All these can be most conveniently consulted in the collection of his writings on urban history published as *"Les Villes et les Institutions Urbaines"* (2 vols.), henceforward quoted as V.I.U.

2. The word "feudal" will be used in this article to refer to a kind of society in which economic and political power derive from large-scale land-holding, and where there is direct and indirect exploitation of this land by means of dependent cultivators.

3. "Que l'origine des villes du Moyen Age se rattache directement, comme un effet à la cause, à la renaissance commerciale . . . c'est ce dont il est impossible de douter," V.I.U., I, p. 376. "L'idée fondamentale . . . qui voit dans le commerce la cause essentielle de la formation des villes, est incontestablement vraie," *Ibid.*, II, p. 259.

4. H. Pirenne, *Economic and Social History of Medieval Europe,* p. 48.

5. *Ibid.,* p. 201.

6. *Ibid.,* p. 47.

7. *Ibid.,* p. 48.

8. Y. Renouard, *Les Hommes d'Affaires Italiens,* pp. 24, 47–54.

9. V.I.U., p. 400.

10. A. Sapori, article in *International Historical Congress* 1950, Vol. I, Rapports.

11. *Ibid.*

12. J. W. F. Hill, *Medieval Lincoln,* Appendix V.

13. J. Rutkowski, *Histoire Economique de la Pologne avant les Partages,* p. 39.

14. J. A. Gade, *The Hanseatic Control of Norwegian Commerce,* pp. 27–8.

15. V.I.U., I, pp. 54, 103–4, 216.

16. *Histoire de la Constitution de la Ville de Dinant au Moyen Age;* V.I.U., II, pp. 1–94.

17. J. Lestocquoy, *Les Dynasties Bourgeoises d'Arras du XIe au XVe Siècle.* Since writing this article, I have been able to see Lestocquoy's *Les Villes de Flandre et d'Italie sous le gouvernement des patriciens XIe–XVe siècles,* which attacks the Pirenne thesis in greater detail along lines similar to those here indicated.

18. H. Cam, *Liberties and Communities of Medieval England*, pp. 23–4.

19. Favresse, *Le Régime Démocratique à Bruxelles*, pp. 32–3.

20. V.I.U., I, p. 137 n. 1.

21. G. Espinas, *Douai*, I, p. 306.

22. Power and Postan, *English Trade in the Fifteenth Century*, p. 146.

14. Life on the English Manor

H. S. BENNETT

The writing of a book on medieval life necessitates the scrutiny, assembly, and arrangement of innumerable documents and pieces of evidence, from which, by slow degrees, some coherent pictures emerge. In this way a writer is enabled to build up a series of studies, each revealing some facet of his subject. But, while this enables him to put these various aspects into focus the more clearly, it is apt to divert him from what many will hold to be his chief duty—to see life steadily and see it whole, and to present this vision to his readers. Such a vision, however, is even more difficult to communicate than it is to receive. It is comparatively easy to assemble detailed accounts of various sides of the peasant's life, but each of these accounts must deal with the mass, so that the individual tends to recede into the background. Yet it is as an individual human being, living his normal life, that he is of interest.

Thomas Hardy's poem, *In Time of "The Breaking of Nations,"* tells us of his fundamental place in the scheme of things:

> Only a man harrowing clods
> In a slow silent walk
> With an old horse that stumbles and nods
> Half asleep as they stalk.
> Only thin smoke without flame
> From the heaps of couch-grass;
> Yet this will go onward the same
> Though Dynasties pass.

From H. S. Bennett, *Life on the English Manor* (London: Cambridge University Press, 1937), pp. 3–25. Reprinted by permission of the author and publisher.

This is the man our ideal picture would show us. Short of this, in an attempt to show what I believe to have been his normal life, I make bold at the outset to draw an imaginary picture of one such man during a few days of the year. In doing so, I have not chosen one of the most well-to-do of the manorial peasants, nor do I forget that many lacked even the rudimentary comforts and the limited possessions which this man had. And although my picture is frankly imaginary, it is based on a wealth of definite evidence and backed up by an almost equal wealth of suggestions and hints, none of them in themselves clear or weighty enough, perhaps, to be vouched as evidence, but, nevertheless, possessed of a cumulative power which could not be denied.

The sun rose early, for it was late June, but not much earlier than the peasants of the little village of Belcombe, in the year 1320. As the light strengthened, bit by bit the village became visible, and the confused medley, in which here a roof and there a bit of wall stood out, began to arrange itself as a narrow street with flimsy houses dotted about in little groups. In the centre of it all the stone-built church loomed up high and very new looking above everything about it, and made the peasants' houses appear small and insignificant. On closer view, the village was seen to radiate from the church and down each of the winding ways that led up to it the peasants had built their homes. There they stood, some neat and trim, with their thatched roofs and roughly finished walls in good repair, while others were dilapidated and showed evident signs of neglect and decay. The larger houses stood a little back from the lane, so that the ground in front of each of them was roughly enclosed and set with young cabbage, onions and parsley, and here and there a few herbs were growing along the sides of the pathway to the house. Most of them had a rudely constructed shed or lean-to at the back of the house, and running away from this stretched another enclosed piece of ground. This was mainly broken up and planted with vegetables, and both here and in the rough grass beyond there were a few apple and cherry trees. At the bottom of the garden where it ran down to the stream the pigs had their styes, and any villager fortunate enough to own a cow tethered it there in among the rankly growing grass. Smaller houses had meagre plots about them, with sparse room for cabbage or onion, and only rarely a pig or a few fowls.

Within most of these houses men were stirring, and before long began to appear at their cottage doors, taking a look at the sky before they ate a brief meal (if such it might be called) of a lump of bread and a draught of ale. Then they came out again, fetched their scythes and rakes from the sheds, and started off down the street, so that for a few minutes the noisy chatter and greetings of neighbours broke the silence. They soon passed by the church and came out into open country, for no hedges or fences were to be seen. One large tract, however, had clearly been cultivated recently, for as they passed they saw how it was divided into narrow plots, each with grassy raised strips dividing it from its neighbours. Now, however, this field was fallow, and, early as it was, one of their fellows was there before them, and was guarding the sheep which were quietly feeding on such sparse vegetation as was to be found, for the first ploughing had already taken place, and next month any weeds the sheep might leave would all be ploughed in.

A little farther on they passed a stone cross. Almost unconsciously (some even in perfunctory fashion) they crossed themselves, and a moment later turned from the main path to follow a track which led to a piece of meadow land. This, unlike the fallow, was enclosed on three sides with a hedge, whilst a little stream formed its other boundary. On entering the field the peasants broke up in little groups, some going to one and some to another part of the meadow, for amongst the long grass there were little pegs and twigs marking off one portion of the field from another. By this time the sun was well up and the dew was drying rapidly as they prepared for work. The wide blade of the scythe was sharpened with the whetstone, and then they turned, and with rhythmic movement began to mow the grass in wide sweeping swathes.

In one corner of the field John Wilde and his two sons, Richard and Roger, kept to their task for some time without pause. The younger son moved steadily across the strip, turning the hay which had been cut on the previous morning, while his brother Richard worked on side by side with his father at the mowing. Save for a pause when the scythes were re-sharpened they worked without resting and with but little to say, for there was much to do and time was short, since this was Sunday, and ere long they would have to leave their work for Mass. Indeed, they were fortunate to be on the field at all on such a day, but Sr. William, their vicar, had always been lenient in times of harvest; and, although he looked with concern at such work, he did not absolutely forbid it, so long as the Mass itself were not neglected. So all three continued until the sun was getting well up in the heavens, when they stopped their work and left the field together with many others. As they passed the church John glanced at the Mass clock on its wall near the door, and saw by the shadow of its style that they had good time before the service, as it was not yet eight.

During their absence the house had not been untended, and after a while the good wife Agnes and her daughter Alice appeared from a room which led out of the main living room. Alice ran out in the garden close, and soon the clucking of the hens was heard, and a little later she returned and set down on the wooden bench inside the door a rough earthenware jar of milk which she had just taken from the cow. Meanwhile, her mother had brushed up the embers and had piled together the kindling and few logs, and already a fire was burning cleanly, and over it hung a large metal pot of water. Then she and her daughter went into the small inner room, which was cleaner and less sooty than its neighbour, and pulled back the thick coverlets and remade the only two beds that stood there. Once this was done, the rough earthen floors of both rooms were swept out with a brush of large twigs, and then the trestle-table was put in its place near the side of the room. Some bread and a little ale satisfied Agnes' hunger, while Alice took a drink of the milk she had just brought in. All being done, they turned to prepare for Mass. A large wooden tub on the trestle-table served for a wash-bowl, and after a little washing they occupied themselves for some time in plaiting and arranging their hair, before they drew out of a wooden chest, that stood at the foot of the bed, the bright coloured dresses which they wore only on Sundays and festivals. There were other childish garments in the chest, but they had not been worn these many days, for they were those of the two little girls, both dead now for ten years and more, one of the plague, and one lost by what the coroner called "misadventure." What this was exactly her mother never knew; for, while she was at play, she had fallen from the bridge over the big river, but no one could be found to say what had taken her so far from home, or how the end had come. Other children there had been, like so many others they had died at birth or very soon after, and were no more than distant memories.

The return of the men-folk threw the cottage into confusion, for there was little room, and they all tried to wash and dress themselves for Mass at the same time. It did not take them long, however—the old "tabard" or sleeveless smock with all its traces of weekday work ("baudy tabard" Chaucer called it) was discarded for that kept for Sundays and special occasions, and they were ready. The bell was already ringing, and they moved off and were soon joined by friends and neighbours as they made their short journey to the church. John noticed that the low wall which enclosed the church and the graveyard was rapidly breaking down in several places: for many months now it had been cracking and stones falling away from it here and there, but nothing had been done to repair it, in spite of the archdeacon's periodical warnings. On two or three occasions John had noticed that pigs and sheep had wandered into the graveyard itself and had started to graze among the tombs. But he had little time to reflect on this, for his neighbours were pressing into the church since the time for service had come, and even the men-folk, who habitually lingered outside in little groups till the last moment, had turned to go in.

So he entered with his wife through that selfsame door at which they had stood when the priest had married them over twenty-five years ago. They touched the holy water, and crossed themselves as they moved into the nave, and there they parted to take up their places on either side of the aisle. They remained standing, as there were not yet even rudimentary seats or pews for them, for this was not one of the richest village churches. Only behind the chancel-screen were there any seats, but these were reserved for the clergy, although the lord of Hemings Manor and his family, when they were at the manor house, were also privileged to seat themselves there. Hubert Longfellow, the parish clerk, was the only other parishioner who had his seat within the chancel, and that because he was a bachelor. His predecessor had been a married man, and therefore, although he was in Minor Orders, he was kept out and had to stand with the ordinary congregation in the nave.

While they were waiting an animated conversation was going on, but at last Sir William, the vicar, entered followed by the parish clerk, and for a moment the congregation was still. As the service began, however, many resumed their whispering and mutterings, while some lounged by pillars and seemed to be taking but small notice of the service. The priest's voice droned on: here and there it was raised for a moment while he intoned a prayer, or while he and the clerk sang their versicles and brief responses. But, for the most part, even the keenest ear could catch little more than an unintelligible murmur, interspersed with a *Dominus vobiscum,* or *Oremus,* or *Amen,* which, by countless repetitions, had familiarised itself to the ear. Even in those churches where traditionally the priest read the service aloud, it was not audible even to a Latinist, and the village congregation rarely had any such lettered person among its number. So the service went on its way, and John meditated awhile. It was all very familiar to him, for ever since he was a child he had faithfully attended the Sunday Mass—now these fifty years and more—and, when his lord's service did not forbid it, he frequently came on holy-days as well. He understood little, but yet there was something about it all that was dear to him. He knew that in some mysterious way Christ's body was made anew at this service: the bell would ring while the priest prayed, and then, after a pause, Sir William would then hold up before them all the blessed bread and wine now made God. But that great moment had not yet come, and his thoughts wandered as he looked about him in the high-roofed church. For a moment his eyes fell on the painting of the Last Judgment which had recently been renewed on the wall over the chancel arch. It fascinated him to contemplate the calm and severe majesty of Christ, as He sat enthroned in glory and meting out doom. The ecstasy of the saved as they were caught up in the arms of the angels, or the three naked souls cosily nestling in Abraham's bosom, were so vividly portrayed that his eyes lingered on them, and only with reluctance turned to gaze on those damned souls, who stood on the left hand of the throne of grace, and in varying attitudes of pleading, fear and bewilderment expressed their horrible condition. Others, even more fearful to behold, were already enduring the tortures destined for them, as the devils savagely seized them with flesh-hooks and pitched them into the cauldron and the everlasting fire.

Other pictures painted on the walls also told their story, and recalled to him fragments of sermons and tales, especially some of those told in the vivid and understandable language of a passing friar. Their own priest had no such gift. Indeed, how should he have such powers? The marvel was that now, at this very minute, the Latin phrases were flowing from his lips and he was God's minister to them all. Yet he had been born in this selfsame village, and was the youngest brother of John's own wife Agnes. He had always been about the church as a boy, and was taught how to read and to sing the service by their old priest Sir John Walters. Then, he had become the holy-water carrier, and, little by little, had learnt all Sir John could teach him, and had been sent away to school. And now, here he was, back in the parish, and living in the vicar's house with its garden and stone wall round it, hard by the church, and standing at the head of them all. As John looked at him he recalled some of his kindly actions: no parishioner was too distant for him to visit if need arose, and no one led a more model life than he. "If gold rust, what shall iron do?," was his watchword, and he taught his flock more by what he was than by anything he was able to say. All men knew him to be their friend, and yet there was something about him which forbade men to be too familiar. Even his sister regarded him with the awe born of more than one snibbing he had administered to her, and which her conscience admitted to be just.

By this time, however, the Creed had been said, and Sir William had come from the altar steps to the door of the rood-screen. He looked grave, for it was but seldom that he attempted to teach his flock in a set discourse, rather than by short explanation of the main points of the Faith. But the bishop was constantly urging upon the clergy the need for more sermons, and he must obey. As he waited, his people settled themselves down, most of them squatting in the rushes which covered the floor, while a few lounged against the pillars and seemed to care little for what was to come. When all were settled, he reminded them of earlier sermons he had preached at intervals on the seven deadly sins, and then turned to speak of the fourth of these, namely sloth. Slothfulness kept men from church, and encouraged them to be inattentive at Mass, and to put off the day of repentance till it was too late. All this, as he said, would inevitably have to paid for in purgatory, unless they were truly penitent and shriven. Not only in church, but in ordinary worldly affairs, idleness was to be shunned, and young men and women should be made to work and serve their masters with love and cheerfulness. Therefore, parents must chastise naughty children, or they would grow up idle and disobedient as were the sons of Eli. The tale of the death of the prophet and his two sons followed, and Sir William concluded his short sermon by bidding his hearers to think on Eli and his sons, and to chastise their children, and to see they learnt to labour well and truly while there was yet time, and further to think how best to labour for their souls as well as their bodies.

All this was listened to in comparative quiet, although a few took but little notice of the discourse, and kept up a desultory conversation among themselves; and throughout the nave there was more whispering and occasional chatter than Sir William liked to hear, but he was powerless to stop it, for no one could remember when a little talking or even joking in church had been forbidden. When the sermon was ended he went back to the altar, and the service continued. Ere long the ringing of the bell called even the most inattentive to their devotions, since the great moment of the Mass had now come. *Paternoster, Ave* and Creed were all that John could say, but these he repeated again and again; and later, when he heard the priest intoning the *Paternoster,* he joined in heartily. Then, while Sir William was rinsing his holy vessels, he prayed silently again until the service came to an end with its *Ite, missa est,* and after the priest had retired, he too rose to leave. Many "sons of Belial" had not waited so long, and had hurried off, as soon as the communion had been finished, as if they had seen not God but the Devil, for some wanted to get to their work again, while others were only concerned to cross the green to the ale-house where they might refresh themselves and gossip at their ease.

Once out in the churchyard again John stopped to talk with his neighbours. One group was looking with interest at the platform, which was as yet but half-erected, at the one end of the churchyard. Here, in a week's time, they would see the actors from the neighbouring town, as well as some of their own fold performing in the Miracle Plays. Hubert, the parish clerk, was particularly skilful, and all remembered his performance as Herod, "that moody King," two years before, and also how masterful it had been. Besides this, however, there had been much to amuse them in the rough boisterous performances of many of the actors. They hoped to see Cain bullying his boy at the plough and ranting at his brother Abel, or Pilate shouting and raging as he had done the last time the plays had come. On the other hand, John recalled the affecting scenes in which the players had presented to them many of the poignant moments of the Gospel story, and he and his mates discussed with zest the scenes they would like to see again.

When he left this group he was stopped by two neighbours who wanted him to join with them in some work waiting to be done on their strips which lay side by side in the great east field. This he promised to do towards the end of the week when he had carried his hay; and, with a parting look at the sundial, he moved from the churchyard, and caught up his wife and daughter near their home. Agnes was full of news she had gleaned from her gossips: Cicely Wode was to marry John Freman of the neighbouring town, and she and her old mother were to leave the manor as soon as the marriage could take place. Matilda, the reeve's daughter, was in trouble, and would be accused at the next Manor Court of incontinency. Agnes Atwater had scalded her legs badly by overturning a vat of boiling water in her brewhouse—and so on.

They soon reached their cottage; and, while the women-folk went indoors to prepare the midday meal John went behind the house and down to the bottom of the close where the pig was kept. He emptied into the trough the remainder of a bucket containing some sour milk and scraps of household waste, and pulled up a few rank-growing weeds and threw them into the trough. Then he turned to his garden and worked at this and that, for he had a good conscience, and his brother-in-law, Sir William, took a reasonable view of the Fourth Commandment. At last Roger came to call him in to dinner. Meanwhile, Agnes and her daughter had been busy in the house. The fire had been made up, and the large pot, in which the soup of peas and beans had been prepared on the previous day, was hung over it and heated. The trestle-table was now standing in the middle of the room, and the beechen bowls and spoons arranged on it. A few mugs and an earthen jug filled with good ale stood ready, for John was not one of those landless labourers in whom it was presumptuous to drink anything more than penny ale. They all sat down, and soon were supping noisily the thick pottage and eating with it large hunks of a dark coloured bread. A good lump of home-made green cheese followed, and with this and mugs of the good ale they made their simple meal.

There was much to be done in the garden at this time of year, and John and his sons spent part of the afternoon in weeding and thinning out their cabbages. Some of their neighbours returned to the meadows and continued their haymaking, but John knew how much Sir William disliked this, and how often he had spoken against Sunday work, unless it were absolutely necessary to avoid spoiling the crop. Hence he stayed at home, and did a little here and there to clear things up in his garden. In this way the afternoon wore on, and when John went into the house he found that his wife and daughter had gone off to Vespers at the church. Sir William liked to see a good congregation at this service, especially on Sundays, and most of the women, and a considerable number of men, attended this short simple service as the day began to close. John's sons, however, had but little thought for this, for they were more interested in the pleasure they hoped for a little later in the evening, and after a while both left the house to forgather with their companions. When Agnes returned, the evening meal was soon on the table, for as it was Sunday they had already eaten the most substantial meal of the day. Now they fared on a few eggs, a bit of oatcake and some cheese. Both the women drank milk, but John refused this, and said he preferred a mug of ale since some still remained of his wife's last brewing.

As the shadows lengthened they left the house, and a short walk brought them on to the green, which looked at its best in the evening light, and already many of the villagers were there. Soon, to the sound of a rebeck and pipe the dancing began, for here again Sir William's moderate and friendly rule did not prohibit the dance, although he had a sharp word for any whose behaviour on these occasions seemed to call for correction. The measures were simple, and were trodden with an unaffected grace which seemed to recall a happier and more innocent age—far removed from the toil and difficulties of everyday life. Young men and maidens with linked hands went through the evolutions of the dance and smiled one at the other, and "dallied with the innocence of love." Yet, even so, there were some matrons who looked on with but half-approving eye, as if underneath the seeming innocence there lurked who knew what dangers? Agnes, partly from native prudery and partly as Sir William's sister, would not let Alice join in the dances, although her friends called to her from time to time, and she darted envious eyes on Joan and Cicely as they moved in concert to the music. Even while they stood there the airs seemed to grow a little less restrained, and very soon Alice and her mother moved away towards home. The dances, however, went on, and as dusk fell and journeys to the alehouse on the edge of the green became more common, the shrill cries of the rebeck were answered by the shrill cries and laughter of

the girls, and by the lower laughter and snatches of song of some of
the men. John watched all this with an indulgent eye, and sat for a
while with some of his cronies on the ale-house bench, and listened
to the shouts and sounds of revelry coming from within the devil's
chapel, as a friar had once called it, in a sermon which told of how
three men, after drinking and dicing there, had set off to find Death
so that they might slay him, and of what had befallen them. The
noise within grew louder: "there was laughing and lowering, and 'let
the cup go,' " and at last Clement Cooke, notorious in the village
for his inability to carry his liquor, got up to go

> . . . like a gleeman's bitch,
> Sometimes aside and sometimes backwards,
> Like one who lays lures to lime wild-fowl.
> As he drew to the door all dimmed before him,
> He stumbled on the threshold and was thrown forwards.

John thought it was time for him also to get home, for there was
a good day's work to do with the hay on the morrow, and with a
"Goodnight" to his friends set off quickly. He soon came to the
church, which seemed very tall and new in the fast fading light, and
then, in a few minutes, he was once again at his door. The house
was dark, since for some time now their scanty stock of rush-lights
had been spent, though this was of small moment for they were
seldom to be found out of bed long after dusk. He turned to go in,
when a glance down the street showed him Walter, the beadle, going
from door to door. He knew well what that meant, and had half
feared his coming, so that he waited only for a moment while Walter
called out to him that the lord had asked for a "love-boon" on the
morrow. His own hay, he reflected, would have to wait, and with a
last look at the sky and a hope for a few fine days, he went in and
closed the door.

The next morning saw another early start, for John knew well the
Lord Prior's officers would be on the look-out for late-comers; and
indeed, it was only a few years since they had tried to insist on every
one appearing at dawn. Though that had been declared contrary to
the custom of the manor when it had been discussed at the Manor
Court, and therefore had been quietly dropped, nevertheless, it was
still unwise to appear much later than the neighbours. So John
roused up the two boys, and Alice as well, for on these days every
one, save the housewife, had to appear, and help with the lord's hay.
As they started they soon met many neighbours; it was a far larger
party than that of yesterday, all making their way to the lord's great
meadow (for on this manor all the Prior's pasture was in one im-

mense field) which lay in the little valley to the west of the village, and through the midst of which the streamlet flowed so sweetly. Soon after they arrived they had been divided up into groups, and placed in different parts of the field by the reeve and the hayward, who bustled about from place to place to see that all was well and that work was beginning in good earnest.

So to the music of whetstone striking on scythe the work began, and the mowers bent to their task, sweeping down the grass in wide swathes, as they slowly moved from side to side of the piece allotted to them. John was glad to see old William Honiset already in the field. He could no longer use a scythe, but he was very crafty in the straightening and sharpening of obstinate blades, and the whole day long sat under a great beech tree in one corner of the field with hammer and stone and put a new edge on many a scythe before nightfall. As the sun rose higher and higher the blades swung to and fro, while up and down the field moved a man, with a stave in his hand, whose duty it was to oversee the workers. John looked at him as he passed, recalling his own early days, and how often he and the father of this man who now stood over him had worked together in this very meadow, for they had been partners, or "marrows," as the country people termed it, and so did whatever was possible to help one another. But, in his old age, his friend had bought his freedom at a great price, for he had paid to the Lord Prior six marks of silver, the savings of a lifetime, and as much as the yearly income of Sir William, the vicar, himself. Now, therefore, his son was free of everything except a few small services from time to time, of which this was one.

The workers paused to sharpen their scythes, or for a momentary rest, or better still to listen while some belated arrival poured his tale into the ear of an incredulous reeve, or while some careless fellow, who was working in lazy or incompetent fashion, was soundly berated by the hayward. At other moments, again, there was most welcome respite, for this was fortunately a "wet boon," and old Alice atte Mere, who had only a tiny cot on the edge of the village, held it on the homely tenure of carrying ale to the workers at these boons. Hence, she was continuously going to and fro from the manor house for reinforcements of ale which the thirsty labourers seemed to consume almost as soon as it was doled out to them. Although this was only the drink rationed out to the manorial servants, and was not exactly the corny ale—the *melior cervisia*—brewed for the brethren of the priory, yet, perhaps this *secunda cerevisia* was a more prudent drink for the labourers, and certainly it seemed doubly delicious in the heat of the day. Steadily the work went on till wellnigh noon, when at last the hayward's horn was heard. John straightened himself, and made for the shade with his companions. There they threw themselves down, and soon the manor servants appeared, some carrying great loaves and cheeses, while others brought the ever-welcome barrels of ale. John and his family were given four of the loaves for themselves, and as they cut them open they saw that these were the good wheaten loaves, which so seldom came their way. They ate ravenously of these and of the cheese after their six hours in the open air, and called again and again for ale, of which there was no stint, for this was one of the few days of the year on which the customal specified that they were to "drink at discretion."

After this meal there was a short welcome rest, and then they went back to the field once more. Steadily the work went on, and from time to time the now tiring mowers looked at the sky, and watched the slow course of the sun over the big trees which bordered the field. The girls and women busied themselves in raking and turning the first cut hay, while the officials were moving busily from place to place trying to keep the workers at their tasks. At last the long-awaited sound of the hayward's horn was heard, and in a few minutes the field was deserted, and old and young were making their way and chattering together as they went toward the manor house. The toil of the day was over, and all that remained was the good evening meal that the Lord Prior always gave them as a reward for their labours. As they reached the manor house they saw that one of the large outhouses had been made ready with trestle-tables down the centre and at the sides of the building, and platters and mugs were soon laid out ready for the repast. In the courtyard the great cauldrons were steaming, and the hungry people were busy carving into hunks the remainder of their midday loaves. Soon the manorial servants brought in the cauldrons, and a mess of thick pease pottage was served out, to which had been added a little meat for flavouring. This, and a draught of ale, took the sharp edge off their hunger, and they awaited with pleasurable anticipation the next course. The winter had been a hard one, and few of them had been able to buy flesh, or to expect more than a bit of boiled bacon from time to time. Some could afford to keep but few chickens or geese, and had to exist as best they might on their scanty produce, and on cheese and curds, with oatmeal cake or thick oatmeal pottage to satisfy their ever-hungry children. This and a sour bread of peas and beans had been the lot of many for several months, so that the entry of the servants with great dishes of roast meat caused a hum of satisfaction to go up around the room. Each group tackled the portion set down before them with eagerness, and with many a call to a friend here and joke with a neighbour at another table, the meal wore on. Ale flowed liberally, and there was "cheese at call" for those who were still hungry. When some of the women showed signs of wishing to leave, the hayward blew his horn for silence, and the reeve announced that if the weather remained fine there would be two more boons on the Wednesday and the following Monday, and by then he hoped all the hay would be cut and carried into the great manor courtyard. Little by little the company dispersed, most of them ready enough to get home and do whatever was necessary about the house before they went to bed. John and his family walked back together, and saw as they passed their own meadow that Agnes had been at work during the day. The hay that was dry had been raked up into small cocks, and she had turned most of that which had only been cut the previous morning.

Much of their time in the next few days was spent by the peasants either on the lord's hayfield or on their own. John had but little more to cut on his alloted portion, and all was done by the Wednesday evening. The following Friday he and his boys spent the afternoon in loading it onto a wagon they borrowed from a friend, Roget the ox pulled it home, and they stored it away in the little shed behind the house.

What little time John and his sons had from the haymaking seemed to go all too rapidly in a variety of tasks. The work which he had promised to do in the east field with his neighbours took up the Thursday afternoon, and besides this they were hard at work on an "assart" or clearing they were making near the edge of the great wood. The prior had granted this to John only the previous autumn; and, although it was but three acres in extent, the work of grubbing up the furze and briars and cleaning the land so that they could sow it this coming autumn seemed endless. Richard spent all the time he could at this, for he hoped one day to make this plot the site of a home for himself, since he was now fully grown and eager to marry Johanna, the daughter of William Sutton, an old friend of his father.

The other two days of work on the lord's meadow passed much like the first, except that there was no ale provided at the second boon, for it was a "dry reap," but they had to work only till midday. The last boon, however, surpassed all the rest, for not only was there ale again, but other pleasures as well. As the last load was carried from the field the hayward loosed a sheep in their midst. All watched this poor frightened beast with interest, for if it remained quietly grazing they could claim it for a feast of their own, but if it wandered out of the field they lost it, and it remained the lord's property. As they looked on, restraining the children from noise or sudden movement, the sheep gazed around and then began to eat what it could find. Little did it think how in lingering over this Esau's mess it had sealed its fate.

All was not yet over, however. Indeed, many thought the best was yet to come, and John and the other householders next moved off to a part of the field where the reeve stood by a very large cock of hay. Everyone knew what was to be done, and no one wished to be the first to start. At last the reeve called on Robert Day to begin, and with a sly look at some of his neighbours he gathered together a great mass of hay, and rapidly bound it into a bundle. Then, carefully placing his scythe-head under the bundle, he slowly raised it from the ground amidst the encouraging cries of the onlookers. Others were not so fortunate, and some through greed or lack of skill were unable to raise the load without letting the scythe-handle touch the ground, or still more unfortunate, without breaking the handle altogether. Accompanied by the laughter and rude criticisms of their fellows, they retired in confusion. So the ceremony went on till all had had a sporting chance. Once this was over the farm servants rapidly forked the remainder into a small cart, and accompanied by the reeve and hayward left the field. John and his friends, bearing their trophies aloft in victory, started happily for home. For them it was a moment for rejoicing: the three "boons" were over, and they knew that there were no further calls to be made on them beyond the weekly service that went on from year end till year end. Not before the Gules of August would any extra works be again demanded of them.

Their happiness, however, was a little dashed within a few minutes, for as they rounded a corner a small cavalcade rapidly drew towards them. As the riders came nearer, John and his friends recognized them, and when the party reached them all the peasants doffed their hats and louted low, for the imperious looking man who rode at their head, clothed in flowing garments of fine black cloth, was none other than the cellarer himself. Two others of the brethren rode just behind him, followed by two servants. A few moments later John overtook old Margery who had been at work at the Manor Court all day strewing the rooms with rushes, and making the beds with sheets and counterpanes—for these great ones demanded every comfort. On the morrow the Manor Court would be held, and much time would be lost, so John and his friends hurried on to do what they could overnight.

On the next morning John was up and about his close from an early hour, and this kept him busy until it was time to go to the Manor Court. He called his two sons, for it was no ordinary court, but a Leet Court, at which all over twelve years of age were bound to attend. Thus they started out, and reached the manor house a little before eight, and waited about outside chatting aimlessly with their friends. At last the beadle came out, and summoned them all into the court room. They entered, and found themselves in a long panelled room with a fine timber roof which showed up well from the light that streamed in from the large east window, as well as from the smaller mullioned windows on either side. They took up their places on the rush-strewn floor, and chattered away until the reeve and hayward entered, followed by the beadle, whose command for silence was still echoing in the hall when the cellarer entered from a side door at the west end of the room. He took his seat on a raised dais with his clerk by his side, and after the clerk had unfolded the great parchment Court Roll, and had begun to write with his quill the day and year of the Court, the cellarer nodded, and the beadle cried out an "Oyez" thrice repeated, and ordered all who had business and owed service to the Lord Prior of Honiwell to draw near.

At once several men stepped forward: one asked for a neighbour to be excused attendance since he was sick in bed; another pleaded that his friend was absent in the King's wars, while others told the cellarer that their man was unable to attend for various reasons, and pledged themselves to produce him at the next Court. All these facts were noted by the clerk on his roll, and then the reeve was told to put forward his pleas. First, he presented Roger le Bacheler to the cellarer, and said that he asked permission to take over the land of Alice Tunstall since she was a widow with no children, and could not work the twenty acres which were her holding. The cellarer allowed this, and told Roger that he might hold the land at the same rent and services as had Alice's husband, and that he would have to pay 6s. 8d. as a fine for entry. Since he willingly agreed to this, he was called forward, and the cellarer formally admitted him to the holding, handing him, in token of the exchange, a white wand. This done, Roger fell on his knees, and placing his hands between those of the cellarer, swore "so help me God and all His Saints" that from this day forth he would be true and faithful to the Lord Prior, and should owe fealty for the land which he held of him in villeinage, and that he would be justified by him in body and goods, and would not take himself off the lord's manor.

Next, the reeve told a long tale of many dilapidations that had accrued since the last Court: some houses were falling into serious disrepair; the path outside certain cottages was continuously foul; many men had taken timber from the Lord Prior's wood without leave; three men. . . . So he droned on, and John paid but slight attention, for he was not conscious of having broken any of the manorial laws, and only noticed with dismay that the name of his brother Henry was constantly mentioned. All these matters took but a short time, for no one denied his guilt, and a fine of twopence or threepence was generally imposed by the cellarer. The reeve then told the cellarer of the misdemeanours of several men at the recent hay-making—of their late-coming, their laziness or their impudence. These received short shrift, and were fined twopence each, all except Richard Cook, who spoke opprobrious words to the cellarer, for which he was sternly rebuked and fined sixpence. Lastly, the reeve brought forward Thomas Attegate, who told the cellarer how his son was eager for book-learning, and how Sir William thought so well of him that he wanted to send him to the grammar school in the near-by town if this were allowed. After some questions the cellarer gave his consent, on the assurance that the boy wished to devote himself to learning in the hope of rising to the dignity of the priesthood in due course. His father thanked the cellarer in halting words, and paid the sixpence demanded of him for the permission, and then fell back among his fellows once more.

After this the beadle called for the tithing men to come forward and make their reports. Each in turn told the steward of how matters stood in so far as he was responsible. William Sleford presented that Richard Tubbing and Johanna atte Grene were common brewers and had broken the prior's orders about the sale of ale, and they were each fined twelvepence. John Morgan presented that a stray horse had been found by one of his tithing and surrendered to the beadle and was now in the village pound. He also asked that William Bonesay might be enrolled in his tithing as he was now twelve years of age. William Cook complained that Richard Jamys had received one John Freeman into his house, and that John was not in any tithing and was suspected of being a night-walker and eavesdropper. Richard was ordered to produce John at the next Court and to be ready to answer for him. Lastly, John atte Hethe was removed from his office of tithing man, and in his place William Craft was elected and sworn.

So the proceedings came to an end; and, after the cellarer had reminded them that the next Court would be held on that day six weeks, he withdrew to his private chamber, and amid a general chattering the peasants began to disperse. John left the Court with his sons who soon joined their own friends and set off homewards. He, however, made a roundabout circuit so as to pass by the great west field, for he was anxious to see how things were coming on, for the whole week past had been so taken up with haymaking and work elsewhere that he had no time even to do an hour's work there. As he came round by the field his eye rapidly moved from strip to strip and he saw there was much to be done. St. John's Day was already past, so they must set to work at once at the weeding, he thought, and he determined to spend the rest of the day at this. For a few minutes before turning homeward to his midday meal he sat down and looked across the great field at the village as it straggled over the neighbouring slope—a familiar sight, but dearer to him than any other place on earth. There stood the church, clean and white in the midday sun, and there a few hundred yards to the right his own little house and its narrow close which, with his land in the common fields, represented all he had in the world.

It seemed little enough, yet, he reflected, things might be worse. The last winter had been hard, and the death of his only cow had made life even harder. Now, however, his twenty-four half-acre pieces were all ploughed and planted with crops which promised well, but everyone knew that twelve acres was none too much, if more than the barest existence was hoped for. Last year the crops had been poor, and for several months food had been scarce, so that many of his neighbours had been half starved, and nearly everyone in the village was forced to live on victuals lacking in flavour or variety. The oats had been their salvation: with oatcake and porridge, and with the bread they had made from a mixed corn of barley and rye they had been able to hold off the worst pangs of hunger; but for weeks on end no meat or flesh, except an occasional chicken or something snared by night in the prior's woods, had come their way. Since then, however, the summer had come, and the hay crop had been a good one, and hope sprang up once again. At the next Court, he thought he would ask for leave to build a little cot on the piece of new land they had been clearing near by the great wood. Then Richard and Johanna could be married and live there, and could grow something on the three acres to help them all to live. His wife would know how to make the best of everything that came into the house: no one could make a bushel of corn go farther than she. That was the root of his brother Harry's trouble. His wife had been careless and slatternly, and their home was always uncared for and the meals ill-prepared. And yet, despite it all, Harry had been heartbroken when she went off with Thomas Oxenden, a rising burgess of Thorpston near by. Since then, Harry had gone down hill fast: his holding was badly kept, his house a disgrace, while his time was mainly spent with bad friends snaring in the prior's woods, or in drinking and "Hi tooral hay" at the ale-house. John reflected sadly as to the end of all this, but what was to be done to stay it he could not tell. Life was strange and in his fifty odd years he had seen ups and downs in the village. Some he had played with as a boy had stolen away by night, and had been heard of no more; some, like his wife's brother, had become priests, and were now important people; some, like his own brother, had lost their grip on life, and had become a byword in the village. But there it was, and each must abide his fate. As Sir William had often told them, they were in the hand of God, and He and His holy angels would protect them all their days. Then, as he rose to go, the sound of the midday bell rang out clear over the fields. He crossed himself, and after repeating an *Ave,* went quickly to his own home.

HUMANISM AND "RENAISSANCE" IN THE TWELFTH CENTURY

THE IDEA OF a medieval "Renaissance" was popularized by Charles Homer Haskins in a book called *The Renaissance of the Twelfth Century*. Haskins presented his thesis thus: "There was an Italian Renaissance, whatever we choose to call it. . . . But—this much we must grant—the great Renaissance was not so unique or decisive as has been supposed. The contrast of culture was not nearly so sharp as it seemed to the humanists and their modern followers, while within the Middle Ages there were intellectual revivals whose influence was not lost to succeeding times, and which partook of the same character as the better known movement of the fifteenth century."

This argument attracted a good deal of comment and criticism. Erwin Panofsky dissented from it in a study titled *Renaissance and Renascenses in Western Art*. Panofsky preferred to use words such as "renascence" or "proto-Renaissance" for the medieval revivals of culture in Carolingian times and in the twelfth century in order to distinguish them from the Italian Renaissance—which he regarded as the only real Renaissance—that came later. He maintained that "the two medieval Renascences were limited and transitory; the Renaissance was total and permanent." Panofsky added, "Since the Renaissance the Antique has been constantly with us whether we like it or not. It lives in our mathematics and natural sciences. It has built our theatres and cinemas as opposed to the mediaeval mystery stage. It haunts the speech of our cab driver—not to mention the motor mechanic or radio expert—as opposed to that of the medieval peasant."

At first this dispute seems to be a rather sterile squabble, mere quibbling about how historians ought to use the word "Renaissance." But it really involves the whole problem of how we look at the course of Western history. Is the emergence of modern civilization really due to the revival of classical culture in the Italian Renaissance? Did the Middle Ages produce any distinctive ideas or institutions that have survived to help shape the modern world? The role of humanism in present-day culture (usually in the guise of "secular humanism") is often debated nowadays. What types of humanism existed in earlier periods, and how are we to evaluate them? These are some of the serious questions raised by the initial dispute about a "twelfth-century Renaissance."

In the following readings, David Knowles finds evidence of a real humanism in the twelfth century, but holds that this humanism was short-lived. It was soon overwhelmed by the rise of scholasticism. Richard Southern argues that the scholastic culture of the thirteenth century was itself humanistic. Eva M. Sanford discusses the views of Haskins and Panofsky and other contributors to the debate.

15. The Humanism of the Twelfth Century

DAVID KNOWLES

The two centuries that follow the millennium, which have been so closely studied by the historians of politics, economics and art, have perhaps not yet yielded up all their secrets in the realm of cultural life. It is only too easy to regard the medieval period as a prelude and preparation for the modern world, and to consider the history of Western civilization as that of an ordered progress towards the material and intellectual perfection of man; within the medieval centuries themselves it is equally inviting to discover a steady and straightforward evolution from barbarism to enlightenment. Yet even in constitutional, legal and economic history where such a view is least misleading, the conception of an ordered and unhalting progress, familiar to Victorian writers, must receive modification in more than one respect; in the history of intellectual development and the changes of religious sentiment any idea of an unfaltering advance is wholly false.

This, perhaps, is particularly true in respect of the first great flowering of culture in Western Europe which began shortly after the year 1000. This age, save for its artistic life, had until recently been unduly neglected by historians of thought. The great moral and intellectual leaders—Anselm, Abelard and Bernard, and their lesser contemporaries such as Peter the Venerable or John of Salisbury—were indeed familiar figures, but they had been treated only in isolation; and even during the last twenty years, when the various

From David Knowles, "The Humanism of the Twelfth Century," *Studies*, Vol. 30 (1941), pp. 43–58; reprinted in Knowles, *The Historian and Character and Other Essays* (Cambridge, 1963), pp. 16–30. Reprinted by permission of Professor C. N. L. Brooke, the author's literary executor, and the publisher.

schools of medieval philosophy and theology have at last attracted
something of the attention they deserve, there has been a tendency
to regard the eleventh and twelfth centuries as but a dawning, a
prelude, to the thirteenth, the "greatest of centuries," which
opened with Innocent III and St. Francis, which saw the earliest and
purest masterpieces of Gothic architecture spring into being at
Chartres, at Paris, at Salisbury and at Westminster, which embraced
all the glories of scholastic theology, and which closed upon the year
in which Dante, waking in the hillside forest, passed in imagination
through the realms beyond the grave. In consequence, even those
who, like the late Professor Haskins, have done most to extend our
knowledge of the twelfth century or who, like Denifle and Ehrle and
Mandonnet and Grabmann, have studied the growth of the universities, the origins of scholasticism and the pre-history of the friars—
even these, when treating of earlier years, have given their attention
to the seeds that were still to bear fruit rather than to the ripe ears
of the summer's harvest. Yet to a careful observer the latter half of
the twelfth century appears as a decline as well as a dawn, and as he
looks back over the brilliant creative achievement of the hundred
years between 1050 and 1150 and notes its deep and sympathetic
humanism, which anticipated to an extraordinary degree much that
is considered typical of the age of the Medici and of Erasmus, he
becomes sensible of a very real change and declension between 1150
and 1200 which helped to make the culture of the thirteenth century, for all its intense speculative force and abiding power, less universal, less appealing and, in a word, less humane than what had
gone before.

It is the purpose of these pages to direct attention to the earlier
years, to the brilliant and original creative energies of the late eleventh century, and to the wide and sympathetic humanism which
between 1050 and 1150 made its appearance for the first time in
Western Europe. This first great re-birth—the proto-Renaissance as
it has sometimes been called by historians of art and architecture—
took place earlier than is generally supposed; the movement reached
maturity between 1070 and 1130; it changed and declined in the fifty
years between the death of St. Bernard and the pontificate of Innocent III, and the intellectual atmosphere of the thirteenth century
which followed, though it was in some ways more rare, more bracing
and more subtle, lacked much of the kindly warmth and fragrant
geniality of the past. The culture of the schools was, in fact—to drop
the language of metaphor—without many of the elements that make
a society fully humane, and that the preceding age had possessed
for a time and subsequently lost.

The first stages of all great creative movements are hard to trace.

The pre-Socratic philosophy, the sculpture which preceded the age of Ictinus and Pheidias, the constitutional legislation of Solon and Cleisthenes, though in many ways more original and admirable than the later developments in the golden age of Pericles, have but partially and recently been rescued from oblivion and reconstructed from the fragmentary monuments that survive. Similarly, few decades in European history are darker than those between 970 and 1030 in which the first generations of the new age were growing to maturity, and only those familiar with the writings and artistic achievements of the previous centuries can appreciate the change that then began. Consequently, there has been a general tendency to set the dawn too late—when, in fact, it is no longer dawn but a sunlight visible to all, at the end of the century, and in northern France. Yet it is clear that the real moving of the waters was in the decades immediately before the millennium, and in northern Italy.

That the schools of Italy, and in particular those of Lombardy, were the first by some thirty or forty years to develop new life, is clear not only from the calibre of their alumni but from the express testimony of contemporaries. How solid the literary training was may be seen from Peter Damian, who had himself been a master in the schools during early manhood. Damian after his conversion inveighed ceaselessly against secular learning and the poets, but in doing so he used, even in spite of himself, the very instruments against which his attack was turned; for all his writings are those of one who has not only been well trained in all the arts of expression and persuasion, but who is, besides, gifted with a real sense of the beauty of language in both prose and verse, and who is possessed of oratorical and poetic powers of a high order.

While the revival of intellectual life was a reality in Italy already between 1000 and 1020, the tide did not reach Touraine, Maine and the Ile de France till about the middle of the century; but, when it came, the spring there was even more brilliant than in Italy. Historians have often noted that while the Italian revival speedily developed into an intensive cultivation of civil and canon law, the French schools turned almost at once to dialectic. Neither of these developments was, properly speaking, humanistic in character; but whereas in Italy the purely literary education was soon abbreviated into a preparation for the study of law, in France, for almost a century, some of the monasteries and a group of schools, of which Chartres is the most important, kept to a purely literary culture, looking to philosophy, such as they knew it, for a general illumination of life and conduct rather than for a lifelong intellectual pursuit and the key to the understanding of the deepest mysteries of the faith.

The three notes of the new humanism, which set the great men of the eleventh and twelfth centuries apart from those who had gone before and those who came after, may be put out as: first, a wide literary culture; next, a great and what in the realm of religious sentiment would be called a personal devotion to certain figures of the ancient world; and, finally, a high value set upon the individual, personal emotions, and upon the sharing of experiences and opinions within a small circle of friends.

Since the ideas and emotions thus shared were often of a religious or, at least, of a philosophical character, and since the writers were in every case men who wrote little or nothing that could be called pure poetry or secular literature, the fundamental humanism of their outlook has been overlooked or, at best, has been recognized only in those who, like John of Salisbury or Hildebert of Lavardin, were classical scholars of an eminence that would attract notice in any age. In one celebrated case, indeed, it has been obscured by the persistent attempts that have been made to romanticize the past in a totally unhistorical fashion. Nevertheless, the men of the early twelfth century, if they are regarded with attention and sympathy, show themselves as possessed of a rare delicacy of perception and warmth of feeling. It is to the sixteenth century, not to the thirteenth, that one looks for the spiritual kin of Anselm, of John of Salisbury, and of Héloïse.

The hall-mark of the revival, and the accomplishment that was most widely possessed by all whom it affected, was a capability of self-expression based on a sound training in grammar and a long and often loving study of the foremost Latin writers. The great ecclesiastics, one and all, who flourished between 1030 and 1180, could express themselves not only in fluent, correct and often elaborate language, but also in phrases and sentences of true dignity and eloquence. Peter Damian, John of Fécamp, Anselm, Abelard, Bernard, William of Malmesbury, Peter the Venerable, John of Salisbury—all these, and a hundred others, were masters of a flexible style and a wide vocabulary; they can be read with ease and pleasure; they are capable of giving adequate expression to their ideas and emotions, and do not fail to do so. Indeed, a student of the period comes to take this for granted—just as, in the use of contemporary manuscripts, he takes for granted the uniform, clear and beautiful script. Yet all this is in contrast alike to the age which had gone and to that which was to follow. Even the most learned men of the previous century, such as Abbo of Fleury, are narrow in the range of their ideas and awkward in their utterance; in England, among those who write Latin, the ideas are still less mature and the expression often laboured to the point of incomprehensibility. As for the century that came after, it may seem paradoxical to suggest that the great churchmen and thinkers of the age were inarticulate; yet those who have read in their entirety the correspondence of Adam Marsh, Robert Grosseteste and John Pecham, or who have endeavored to pierce through to the personal experience and intimate characteristics of Albert the Great, Thomas Aquinas or Robert Kilwardby—to say nothing of the enigmatic Roger Bacon or Duns Scotus—will readily admit that in all the arts of language, in all manifestations of aesthetic feelings or personal emotions, in fine, in all the qualities of self-revealing intimacy, the great men of the thirteenth century are immeasurably poorer than their predecessors a hundred years before. And though the luminous and adequate expression of ideas and emotions does not of itself alone constitute a character which we call humanist—for neither Anselm nor Bernard, past masters of the craft of letters, are precisely humanists—yet the power of self-expression grounded upon, or at least reinforced by, a wide literary culture is a condition *sine qua non* of a humanist's growth.

The second trait of the humanism of the twelfth century was, it is suggested, a personal devotion to one or more of the great figures of the distant past. To look to the past as to an age wider and more accomplished than the present, to imitate its masterpieces and hand on its doctrine, had been a common tendency in every country since the end of the Empire wherever any sort of enlightenment found scope. To rediscover and repeat the past had been the watchword of Charlemagne, as it was to be the watchword, differently understood, of Hildebrand, of the early fathers of Cîteaux and of the early promulgators of the newly revived civil and canon law. What was peculiar to many of the humanists, and at the same time a striking anticipation of the sentiment of leading circles in the later Italian Renaissance, was a reverence for the precepts and a conscious endeavour to imitate the lives of celebrated writers or characters of antiquity considered as human beings or sages, rather than precisely as saints or legislators. If we wish to see the more intimate aspects of this trait, we cannot perhaps do better than consider the ways of thinking and acting of three individuals, all endowed with eminent intellectual gifts and exquisite emotional sensibilities and all eager to give expression to a part, at least, of their experience.

Abelard, Héloïse and Ailred of Rievaulx are among the comparatively few personalities of the early twelfth century whose lives and words will continue to attract and move the minds of men throughout the ages. All three are, though in very different ways, essentially of their own period and remote from ours in the circumstances of their lives and in the cast of their thought. The problems, the catastrophe and the fate of Abelard and Héloïse are, quite as much as the austere monastic life of Ailred, typical of the twelfth century and remote from the experience of the twentieth. All three, on the other hand, by reason of their intense sensibility to emotions shared in some degree by all civilized mankind, and by reason also of a vivid power of self-expression, are not only of an age but for all time. With neither of the characteristics just mentioned are we concerned here, however, but with a third: the peculiar cast, that is, given to their thoughts and emotions by the humanistic training which they had undergone.

This appears, as has been said, most clearly in the reverence and devotion with which they regarded certain great figures of antiquity. With Abelard and Héloïse it is Cicero, Seneca, Lucan and St. Jerome who are principally revered; with Ailred it is Cicero (at least in youth) and St. Augustine. That in the case of all three the influence has a strong religious colour and that its primary object is a saint (for St. Jerome is the exemplar to whom both Abelard and Héloïse turn most readily) does not affect its peculiar character. There is a world of difference between Abelard's attitude to Jerome or Ailred's to Augustine and the liturgical, quasi-feudal devotion of so many of their contemporaries to an apostle or an eponymous saint; equally, the reverence paid to the word of Seneca or Cicero is something personal, something coloured by emotion, and quite distinct from the immense but purely scientific authority given to Aristotle by St. Thomas or to Cicero by the grammarians. It is Jerome the man, inveighing against marriage or counselling Paula and Eustochium; it is Cicero the friend and the philosopher as pictured (however unhistorically) by the imagination of the twelfth century; it is "my own Augustine" of Ailred, the Augustine who loved and was loved by others, the Augustine of the *Confessions,* not the Doctor of Grace. Yet we may see a difference between Ailred and the other two. He is a humanist to the extent that he chooses out and turns for counsel to those minds of the past who had felt and suffered and striven as he had. Abelard and Héloïse "date" more clearly than Ailred because they, like their scholar-successors of the later Renaissance, take for masters and guides and models a few great men of the past chosen with a scholar's rather than with a Christian's mind, and set them on a pedestal, not indeed opposed to that on which Christ and His saints stand, but without direct reference to revealed, supernatural religion. Both, when coming to closest grips with their own tragic and most real and keenly felt problems, find their securest counsel and stay in the Stoics of the Empire—Seneca, Persius and Lucan— and in the letters of Jerome. Héloïse, indeed, who was at once the more absolute and final in her self-surrender and the one less susceptible of any spiritual influence, frankly turned for a model to

Lucan and his Cornelia at the moment when she devoted herself irrevocably to the life for which she had no spiritual vocation. The passage in which Abelard described this crisis is so vivid as to deserve quotation in full:

And she, as I remember well, when many full of sympathy for her youth were vainly endeavoring to deter her from submission to the monastic Rule as though it were an unbearable punishment—she, I say, breaking out as best she could amid her tears into Cornelia's famous lament, cried aloud: "O most renowned of husbands! O thou deemed unworthy of my bed! Had fortune, then, power thus far over such a one as thee? Why did I marry so rashly above my star, only to make him unhappy? Accept from me the penalty which I pay of my free choice." And with these words she hastened to the altar, and took from it the veil blessed by the bishop, and before all bound herself with the monastic vows.

It is hard to conceive a scene less characteristic than this of the monastic life of the twelfth century as commonly pictured: the despairing self-immolation of Héloïse, with the Stoic's cold phrases ringing in her ears, would be more in character in a heroine of Corneille or in some tragic story of a noble Roman house of the fifteenth century.

The third trait common to Abelard, Héloïse and Ailred, though again issuing in very different courses of action, is the importance which all attached to their personal emotions. With Abelard the crisis came comparatively late in life, when he was near his fortieth year. Previously, we may suppose, the vivid interests and brilliant successes of his intellectual life had kept all else suppressed; for the deterioration of character, due to wealth and fame, to which he attributed his fall, may supply a moral explanation, but does not of itself reveal the psychological background of the drama. In any case, his passion ran a not unusual course, though the genius of the man and the tragical *dénouement* of the affair have to some extent sublimated it in the eyes of posterity. From frank sensuality he rose to a deeper, if still wholly selfish, emotion; self-centered as he was, he must give his every mood expression (for in this, as in much else, he resembled a Newman or a Cicero), and the most acute dialectician of the schools, the successful rival of William of Champeaux and Anselm of Laon, became a singer of love lyrics which by their words and melody carried the name of Héloïse beyond the barriers of land and sea. All have perished, but when we read the hymns which Abelard wrote in a still later phase, we are not disposed to accuse of partiality the judgement passed upon his earlier verses by the one who was the theme of their praise.

Abelard's love for Héloïse long remained selfish; the sacrifices which it entailed were, as he himself pointed out somewhat coldly, the unwilled consequences and punishments of his fault, not a willing gift of self-surrender. Only when he had become a monk and a priest and was, partially at least, "converted" to the religious life, did his affection for Héloïse show itself in actions inspired by a genuine and selfless devotion. Indeed, it is by reason of the care shown by this strange ex-abbot for his wife who still more strangely found herself abbess, rather than by the earlier phases of his emotional drama, that Abelard stands among the humanists, in contrast to the more conventional religious sentiments of his day.

Héloïse, on the other hand, at once greater and not so great as her lover, gave all in a very real sense from the beginning. With her, motives of the intellectual order meant nothing, and those of the spiritual order little more. Héloïse in truth, so far as her own deepest utterances go, has nothing of the Christian in her. What renders her unique and gives her nobility and even sublimity is the combination of exceptional mental power and unshakable resolve with the most complete and voluntary self-sacrifice—not, indeed, the surrender of her own will and life to God or to any ethical demand, but the surrender of herself in totality to another. Clinging to this sacrifice with an intensity worthy of a heroine of Scandinavian legend—and indeed the blood of the pagan North may well have flowed in her veins—she found her model not in any saint of the Christian or even of the Hebrew centuries, but in the haughty and despairing women of ancient Rome, as they were depicted by the Stoic poet.

The life story of St. Ailred, when compared with those of Abelard and Héloïse, may have appeared tranquil enough to those who saw the distinguished abbot of the Yorkshire Rievaulx only on his travels up and down England or at his appearances at court. Yet in his life's journey, too, as in that of "his" Augustine, the heart had shared the traces with the head and if, here also like Augustine, he had found a final peace where both head and heart might rest secure, he underwent no violent change of character and retained to the end his fresh, warm, spontaneous readiness to give and to receive love—a love transmuted into a wholly benevolent and unselfish goodwill, embracing all who would accept it, yet having for each the delicate individuality of a mother's love, to which indeed his biographer, writing half a century before St. Francis had made the expression familiar, did not hesitate to compare it.

St. Augustine the thinker, the preacher and the theologian, had dominated and saturated the intellectual life of the West to a degree which even now is not, perhaps, sufficiently realized; Augustine "the man," the Augustine of Monica and the *Confessions,* appears but rarely. It is the peculiar characteristic of Ailred that he was, until

Petrarch's day, almost the only one to approach his Augustine through the *Confessions,* to recognize in him a fellowship of deep feeling, and to look to him as a predecessor and a guide in his own pilgrimage. To him, as to his illustrious exemplar, the April days of his boyhood, days of shine and shower in a Northumbrian school where he had for fellow and friend the Prince Henry, son of King David of Scotland, were an abiding memory, rich in moulding influence.

When I was still a boy at school [wrote Ailred later at Rievaulx], and took great delight in the charm of the companionship of those around me, it seemed good to me to give myself up unreservedly to my heart's leading and to dedicate myself to friendship. Nothing to me seemed more delightful, more sweet, or more profitable than to love and to be loved.

As Augustine had been stung to thought by Cicero, so Ailred, reading the Roman orator's *De Amicitia,* was humiliated at the contrast between his own impulsive, dominating emotions and the calm dignity, as it seemed to him, of Cicero's judgements, and though he had none of Augustine's intellectual crises, he found at the court of King David of Scotland, where he held for a time official rank, ties of ambition and affection not dissimilar to those which had held the great African shackled. When he describes his struggle to us, he falls naturally into the very rhythm of the *Confessions,* though the sincerity of personal experience is all his own.

When once he had found his spiritual home at Rievaulx, Ailred's great and in some ways unique gifts of mind and soul found full scope. To the visitor of today, who surveys the white ruins across the lawns and foliage of their exquisite setting, the past inevitably takes shape in a vision of the hard, sparing life of Cîteaux, shut out for ever from the world. The Rievaulx of St. William, St. Waldef and St. Ailred had indeed an observant, austere and deeply spiritual life, but perhaps no greater surprise in all the varied life of the twelfth century awaits the student familiar only with feudalism, Domesday and the crusades than his first glimpse of the fermenting life at Rievaulx in its secluded dale—an overflowing household of more than a hundred monks and five hundred lay brothers, with its centre of acute intellectual debate and its interplay of eager and ardent personalities. Here indeed, far from the familiar centres of European life, is the quintessence of the humanism of the twelfth century; Ailred, the novice-master and teacher, surrounded by a small group of finely educated young minds absorbed in living debates—Ailred, the friend and guide, learning recollection and true charity from his contact with others—Ailred the abbot, in middle age and in premature old age brought on by long and sharp illness, the centre of an ever shifting gathering of his sons to whom he, with his old charm intensified by suffering and sanctity, was all things to all, now discussing the nature of the soul in a dialogue left unfinished at his death, now counselling an illiterate lay-brother with equal care, while around him the fixed life of choir and farm-work, of changeless routine and sparing diet, went on unchanged.

We his monks were around him [writes Walter Daniel of his last days on earth], now twelve in number, now twenty, now forty, now even a hundred, for he who loved us all was thus loved exceedingly by us in return . . . and he considered it his greatest happiness that he should be thus loved. No one ever said to us "Depart, be off, do not touch your abbot's bed," but stepping upon his pallet or sitting upon it we spoke with him as a child speaks with its mother.

And so he died, surrounded by his monks, lying on the sackcloth and ashes of the monastic custumal, with his eyes upon the crucifix on the wall.

The familiarity of all educated men of the age with the masterpieces of Latin literature has often been remarked upon. The mention of Héloïse touches upon another aspect of this renaissance: the share, that is, of women in the higher culture of the day. Héloïse, indeed, was something of a prodigy, but nowhere is there any suggestion that her uncle, Fulbert, was acting in an eccentric or even in an unconventional manner when he decided to give his niece a perfect education in letters. Nor did she stand wholly alone. It may not be easy to point to individual *bas bleus* in Paris or even in the convents of France in general, but in England there was no lack of them. The daughter of Margaret of Scotland, the future Queen Maud, was given a thorough literary education at Romsey; Shaftesbury, a little later, sheltered Marie de France, and Muriel of Wilton was not the only other poetess in England, as is shown by the numerous copies of Latin verses attached by the convents of women to the bead-rolls of exalted personages. These cloistered elegists, however, scarcely differ in kind from their sisters who, four hundred years before, had corresponded with St. Boniface; Héloïse, alike in her single-minded enthusiasm, in her real literary powers, and in her devoted, even pedantic reverence for her classical models, is a true predecessor of Camilla Rucellai, Margaret Roper and Lady Jane Grey; to her, as to these, Dorothea in George Eliot's novel would have looked with admiration.

Héloïse may well have outdistanced all rivals of her own sex. In deploring the lack of letters among men, however, Peter the Venerable, in his celebrated letter to the widowed abbess, is using the language of exaggeration, for no one acquainted with the literature of the age can be unaware of the wide familiarity shown by so many with Latin literature. Ailred of Rievaulx can assume a familiarity with Cicero's *De Amicitia* as a matter of course in a young Cistercian of his abbey; quotations from the poets are common in almost all the more elaborate chronicles and letters of the period; the greatest humanists, such as Hildebert of Lavardin, Abelard and John of Salisbury, quote aptly and copiously from a very wide range of Latin poetry. Rarely, perhaps, are the poets quoted solely on account of the intrinsic beauty of their words; Abelard, however, and John of Salisbury often give evidence of their appreciation of the purely poetic. For most the favourite authors are the rhetoricians and satirists of the Silver Age and the learned, artificial poets of the later Gallo-Roman culture. Though Virgil has pride of place, it may be suggested that even he may appear rhetorical to a superficial and unintuitive mind; Horace, significantly enough, is often quoted from the *Satires* and *Epistles,* rarely from the *Odes*—their beauty, it may be, was too sophisticated and too exquisite to be appreciated, their urbanity too unfamiliar, and their pagan morality and religion too obvious. For similar reasons Tibullus and Propertius rarely occur, and scarcity of manuscripts is sufficient of itself to account for unfamiliarity with Lucretius and Catullus. Juvenal, on the other hand, Lucan and the difficult Persius were, relatively speaking, more familiar to the contemporaries of Abelard than to classical scholars of today.

Nothing, perhaps, shows both the reality and the extent of the training on classical models than the facility with which numbers were able to compose sets of perfectly correct Latin verses, and that not only in hexameters and elegiacs, but in the lyric metres used by Horace and Catullus. That the inhabitants of nunneries in Wessex should have been able to write passable elegiacs, and that it should have seemed natural to a monk when composing a saint's life to break without warning or apparent reason into alcaics, hendecasyllabics and the still more elaborate iambic and trochaic metres, are phenomena of the late eleventh century to which it would be hard to find a parallel save in the late fifteenth or early sixteenth. That only a few—a Peter Damian, an Abelard, a Hildebert—should have attained real poetry in their compositions should be no occasion for wonder; the rest fail where the most felicitous versus of a Jebb, of a Calverley, and even of a Milton fail; the remarkable fact is that so many had achieved a mastery of the language and the metre without any aid from a Gradus or dictionary. Occasionally, indeed, the level of true poetry is attained, together with perfect felicity of vocabulary; Peter Damian's Sapphic hymns to St. Benedict, like the earlier hymn to the Baptist, *Ut queant laxis,* are supreme in their kind, and it would be difficult for a scholar, familiar only with ancient Latin literature, to assign their composition to the eleventh rather than to the sixth or the sixteenth century. More often, however, the nearest approach to true poetry is made in the simpler accentual metres and the lyrics that verge upon the vernacular.

The decline of this humanism, like its rise, was comparatively rapid. The phase of sentiment we are considering touched its apogee between the rise of Hildebert of Lavardin and the central years of the literary life of John of Salisbury. With Peter of Blois the decline is beginning, and though in England there was something of a time-lag, the end was reached with Walter Map, Gerald of Wales and their circle; Gerald, indeed, lived on into another world and lamented the change. By the death of King John the transformation was complete. The great figures of the early thirteenth century, whether thinkers or administrators, are all but inarticulate when not in their schools or chanceries. It is from the class of the unlettered, from a Francis of Assisi or a Joinville, that the clearest utterances come, "the earliest pipe of half-awakened birds," heralding another dawn in Europe. Literary, philosophical, scholarly humanism was dead, and it is significant that the supreme and balanced art, the Pheidian assurance and repose of the sculptures of Chartres, of Wells, of Amiens and of Rheims, was the expression of life as seen, not by a Leonardo or a Michelangelo, but by unlettered handicraftsmen living wholly in the present and wholly ignorant of the literature and culture of the past.

This is not to say that the new age owed no debt, paid no homage, to the past. In one sense the debt of no century had been heavier; for, as recent scholarship has shown, a larger and larger portion of the corpus of Aristotelian writings and numerous dialogues of Plato and Greek philosophers of the Empire were becoming familiar to the West, together with works of science, Greek and Arabian. St. Thomas rests upon Aristotle, "the Philosopher," more completely and unreservedly than does Abelard upon Augustine or Jerome or Seneca; and, as regards language, all metal is tested upon the touchstone of Cicero. Plato, Aristotle and Augustine, in their various ways, are not merely the foundations of the fabric of scholasticism; they are its *materia prima,* the very medium in which Aquinas works. Yet scholars of today who, when rightly demonstrating the traditional and wholly European character of medieval culture, emphasize the debt of the schoolmen to the ancients, may perhaps mislead those familiar only with modern history when they speak of the humanism, or of the classical tradition, of the great scholastics. The attitude of St. Thomas towards the masters of the past differs by a whole heaven from that of Abelard and Ailred, as it does from that of Erasmus and

More. The humanists, though living in times so very different from those of Greece and Rome, scrutinize the lives and emotions of the ancients, imitate their modes of expression and seek to reach the heart of their thought by long and sympathetic examination; the schoolmen revere the past no less deeply, but it is the external, visible fabric of thought, the purely intellectual, impersonal element that they absorb, and so far from submitting themselves to its moulding influence, they adapt it without hesitation to serve a wholly new system of philosophy, an utterly different *Weltanschauung*. To the schoolmen the personalities, the emotions, the external vicissitudes of the lives of Aristotle and Augustine meant nothing; the skeleton of their thought was all in all. To Ailred and to Héloïse, as to the contemporaries of Cosimo de' Medici, the joy and anguish of an Augustine or a Cornelia were a consolation and a light; they turned to them, and to the poets of the past, for guidance and sympathy. "Then 'twas the Roman, now 'tis I." So the humanists, but never the schoolmen, found strength in a community of feeling with those who, centuries before, had trodden the same path, and it is this consciousness of the unchanging mind of man that divides the culture of the first Renaissance from the more familiar culture of the later Middle Ages.

16. *Medieval Humanism*

R. W. SOUTHERN

As a general rule medieval historians do well to avoid words which end in "ism." They are words which belong to a recent period of history, and their use injects into the past the ideas of a later age. But some of these words like feudalism, romanticism, and humanism have become so closely bound up with our conception of various periods of history that it is almost impossible to write of these periods without some reference to the words which have been so often used to describe their main characteristics. They distort, but they also summarise a large assortment of facts and impressions; and we are obliged sometimes to ask what they mean and whether they correctly describe the main traits of the ages to which they have been applied.

One of the main difficulties with the word "humanism" is that it has two distinct, though related, meanings, and historians have used the word sometimes in one sense and sometimes in the other, and sometimes in a mixture of the two. This has caused a good deal of confusion. The most general meaning of the word according to the Oxford English Dictionary is "any system of thought or action which is concerned with merely human interests or with those of the human race in general." It is in this sense that this word is now in popular use, especially among those who call themselves humanists. This meaning of the word associates humanism with the extension

From R. W. Southern, *Medieval Humanism* (Cambridge: Basil Blackwell, Ltd., 1970), pp. 29–41, 48–50, 58–60. Reprinted by permission of Basil Blackwell Publisher. A revised and much enlarged version of this essay will appear in Vol. I of the author's *Schools, Scholasticism and Society in the Middle Ages* to be published by Blackwell in 1993.

of the area of human knowledge and activity, and consequently with the activity of limiting (or abolishing) the supernatural in human affairs. Its main instrument is scientific knowledge leading ultimately to a single coherent rational view of the whole of nature, including the nature of men. I shall call this the "scientific" view of humanism. I suppose that most people who support this type of humanism look on the medieval period—with its emphasis on the supernatural end of man, with its insistence on the primacy of theology among the sciences, with its predominantly clerical culture and hierarchical organization under a universal papal authority—as the embodiment of all that they most bitterly oppose.

Alongside this popular view of humanism, there is also an academic view which goes back to the Renaissance. In this view, the essential feature of humanism is the study of ancient Latin and Greek literature: hence the use of phrases like "Professor of Humanity" and "literae humaniores" in our academic jargon. These studies were regarded as pre-eminently *humane* in contrast to the formal and systematic studies of the Middle Ages in scholastic theology, canon law and logic, which were thought to have excluded humanity, destroyed style, and to have dissociated scholarship from the affairs of the world and men. I shall call this the "literary" view of humanism. On this view of the matter the Middle Ages, in the eyes of the early literary humanists, represented the enemy, not only in their comparative neglect of the literary qualities of the ancient masterpieces, but also in their supposed neglect of the human qualities which the study of these masterpieces inculcated.

The protagonists of both these types of humanism, therefore, have generally looked on the Middle Ages as hostile country. Historians indeed have protested, and on many grounds. They have pointed out that the Middle Ages cannot be lumped together in a single undifferentiated period of a thousand years, and they have singled out the Carolingian age and the twelfth century as periods of "Renaissance" and "humanism" in one sense or another; they have brought to light medieval lovers of classical literature and writers of elegant Latin prose and poetry; they have spoken of medieval science, and medieval Platonism, and medieval influences on Renaissance scholarship and so on. But there is a confusion of voices. Those who have spoken most forcibly about the humanism of the twelfth century have been inclined to admit that it was short-lived, and that there was a falling-away long before the beginning of the thirteenth century. Those who have extolled the medieval stylists and lovers of the classics have found them disconcertingly indifferent to the authors whose words they quoted so lavishly. As we watch so notable a humanist as John of Salisbury striding through the classics, heaping up each page with quotations from half a dozen authors, with sovereign indifference to the source, we are forced to ask what kind of sensitivity to ancient literature this great man possessed. Certainly it was not the sensitivity of a Petrarch.

The confusions of the subject could be discussed without end—confusions in the use of words, confusions in the views of historians, confusions in the subject itself. Instead of pursuing these shadows let me attempt to state quite simply why, and in what sense, I believe the period from about 1100 to about 1320 to have been one of the great ages of humanism in the history of Europe: perhaps the greatest of all. As a corollary of this I shall argue that, far from the humanism of the twelfth century running into the sand after about 1150 to re-emerge two centuries later, it had its fulfillment in the thirteenth and early fourteenth centuries—in the period which the humanists of the Renaissance most despised. Lastly I shall ask why the humanism of this period appeared so repellent to the humanists of a later age.

In order to discuss these questions, we must first be clear [about] what we are looking for. What are the symptoms which will establish the existence of a deep-seated humanism in the period we are to study? I take them to be these:

In the first place there can be no humanism without a strong sense of the dignity of human nature. That man is a fallen creature, that he has lost his immediate knowledge of God, that his instincts and reason are often in conflict, and that he is radically disorganized and disorientated—all this is common ground to all Christian thinkers. We must not expect a denial of these facts in the Middle Ages, or even for that matter in the Renaissance; but we may expect a humanist to assert not only that man is the noblest of God's creatures, but also that his nobility continues even in his fallen state, that it is capable of development in this world, that the instruments exist by which it can be developed, and that it should be the chief aim of human endeavour to perfect these instruments.

Along with this large view of man's natural dignity there must go a recognition of the dignity of nature itself. This second feature of humanism is a consequence of the first, for if man is by nature noble, the natural order itself, of which he forms part, must be noble. The two are linked together by indissoluble ties, and the power to recognize the grandeur and splendour of the universe is itself one of the greatest expressions of the grandeur and splendour of man. Thus man takes his place in nature; and human society is seen as part of the grand complex of the natural order bound together by laws similar to those which tie all things into one.

Finally the whole universe appears intelligible and accessible to human reason: nature is seen as an orderly system, and man—in understanding the laws of nature—understands himself as the main part, the key-stone, of nature. Without this understanding it is hard to see how men can experience that confidence in human powers which humanism implies.

When those elements of dignity, order, reason and intelligibility are prominent in human experience, we may reasonably describe as humanistic the outlook which ensues. This humanism will be much nearer to the type I have described as "scientific" than to "literary" humanism, but I believe that this must be our starting point in any study of the central period of the Middle Ages.

The starting point is important because the subject has been confused by the tendency to start with the humanism of the Renaissance. This has given the love of ancient literature and the ability to imitate the style of ancient authors an exaggerated importance in judging medieval humanism. If we start with the concepts of natural nobility and of reason and intelligible order in the universe, the whole subject takes on a different appearance.

We may at once say that there is little evidence that these concepts played an important part in medieval experience before about 1050. In the main tradition of the early Middle Ages nearly all the order and dignity in the world was closely associated with supernatural power. There was order in symbolism and ritual, and order in worship and sacrament, and both of them were very elaborate and impressive. Man's links with the supernatural gave his life a framework of order and dignity; but in the natural order the chaos was almost complete. Almost nothing was known about secondary causes in natural events. Rational procedures in law, in government, in medicine, in argument, were scarcely understood or practised even in the most elementary way. Man chiefly knew himself as a vehicle for divine activity. There was a profound sense of the littleness and sinfulness of man. Both physically and mentally human life had narrow limits: only in prayer and penance, in clinging to the saints, was there any enlargement. Man was an abject being, except when he was clad in symbolic garments, performing symbolic and sacramental acts, and holding in his hands the earthly remains of those who already belonged to the spiritual world.

That at least is how I interpret the main evidence for the period before the late eleventh century. Perhaps this awe-struck, sacramental view of man's place and powerlessness in the world gives a more satisfactory account of man's situation in the universe than the optimism of the succeeding centuries; and optimism never overcame the final impotence of man and his need for supernatural aid. But there is a sharp change of emphasis after about 1050. It is this change of emphasis that we are to examine.

We shall look first into the monasteries, for they were the great centres of supernatural influence in the early Middle Ages, and it is in them that we see the first signs of a change that had a profound effect on the religious life of Europe. Briefly, the change took the form of a greater concentration on man and on human experience as a means of knowing God. This was a significant step towards the restoration of the dignity of man, for it made the study of man an integral part of religious life. The search for God within the soul became one of the chief preoccupations of the monastic leaders of the late eleventh and twelfth centuries and this search expanded into a general demand for self-knowledge. The search took many forms and can be found in many places. For my part I find one of its most significant moments in Normandy in 1079. In this year Anselm at Bec entered into the chamber of his mind, excluded everything but the word "God," and found that suddenly the word articulated itself into a demonstration of God's existence, which he believed to be both new and true. It was new, and whether or not it was true, it was a triumph of an analytical introspective method. It seemed to show that men could find new truths of the greatest general importance simply by looking within themselves. The idea of finding something new was itself new to a generation which had believed itself to be at the end of the road; and to find the new things so close at hand, and so entirely central, was a revelation of the powers that lay within man's mind.

It was St. Bernard, a generation later, who popularized the method of introspection and made it the property of a school of monastic writers. He gave the whole exercise a new direction. He was not interested, like Anselm, in logic or analysis, but only in spiritual growth. According to Bernard, man's love of God begins with man's love of himself for himself alone. This love can be refined by reason and virtue until it gives birth to the love of one's neighbour, and this in turn to the love of God. So here too we find a programme of spiritual growth starting with man, and with a most unpromising aspect of man, his self-love. The programme is rooted in nature, and it uses the instruments of natural virtue to reach a supernatural end. From nature itself arises the necessity for turning to God.

To begin with man and nature and to find in them the road to God is very characteristic of the new age. As St. Bernard's younger contemporary, Richard of St. Victor, said:

A man raises his eyes in vain to see God who has not yet succeeded in seeing himself. Let a man first learn to understand the invisible things of himself before he presumes to stretch out to the invisible things of God . . . for unless you can understand yourself, how can you try to understand those things which are above yourself?

   This search for man was at first a monastic programme, and it was in the monasteries also that another aspect of human experience began to be appreciated—the experience of friendship. Without the cultivation of friendship there can be no true humanism. If self-knowledge if the first step in the rehabilitation of man, friendship—which is the sharing of this knowledge with someone else—is an important auxiliary. This was understood by the humanists of the Renaissance; but the discovery was made in the monasteries of the late eleventh century.
   Here again, it was St. Anselm who first in his generation groped for words to express the intensity of his feelings for his friends. But very soon in many places friendship came to appear an essential part of a full religious life. By 1160 Aelred of Rievaulx was able to sum up the results of the monastic experience of the past century in the words "Friendship is widsom," *"amicitia nihil aliud est quam sapientia,"* or even "God is friendship," *"Deus est amicitia."* He was careful to say that these phrases had to be accepted with some reserve, but they expressed the close relationship between human friendship and the nature of God. The experience of friendship lay along the road to God. Nature, said Aelred, makes man desire friendship, experience fortifies it, reason regulates it, and the religious life perfects it. So here again we start with nature and end with God. The treatise that Aelred wrote on friendship is the most beautiful example of the casting of an ancient humanistic theme into a Christian mould, and the sequence which it elaborates—nature prompting, reason regulating, experience strengthening, religion prefecting—is the basis of all religious humanism.
   Of all the forms of friendship rediscovered in the twelfth century, there was none more eagerly sought than the friendship between God and man. This may seem a commonplace theme, and one which had been debased by countless sentimentalities and trivialities. But it was once fresh, and it lifted a great weight from men's lives. In the early Middle Ages God had not appeared as a friend. By great labour and exertion, by crippling penances and gifts to the Church, by turning from the world to the monastic life, men might avert God's anger: but of God as a friend they knew little or nothing. It was terribly difficult to approach Him. Then quite suddenly the terror faded and the sun shone.
   There were many forces working in this direction. One of them

was just a new way of thinking about God. Prayers, poems, devotions of all kinds, poured forth from the twelfth century onwards, which had one predominant theme—the humanity of God. I do not forget that one of these poems—the greatest of them, of about 1250— begins with the tremendous words:

> Dies irae, dies illa,
> solvet saeclum in favilla . . .
> [That day of wrath, that dreadful day,
> Shall the whole world in ashes lay]

But it is wrong to think that this superb poem simply describes a scene of terror. Its second half mitigates the terror by an appeal to the sufferings and humanity of Christ:

> Recordare, Jesu pie
> quod sum causa tuae viae,
> ne me perdas illa die.
> Quaerens me sedisti lassus;
> redemisti, crucem passus:
> tantus labor non sit cassus.
> [Forget not what my ransom cost,
> Nor let my dear-bought soul be lost
> In storms of guilty terror tost
> Thou who for me didst feel such pain
> Whose precious blood the cross did stain
> Let not these agonies be in vain—
>   Trans. Wentworth Dillon]

This is just one of the many signs that since the days of St. Anselm the God of human sufferings and emotions had become an object of tender contemplation. The whole creation had become filled with humanity. The theme is capable of an infinite amount of illustration, but I shall quote only a few sentences from an anonymous thirteenth century treatise on the use of adversity. It shows how even this theme so redolent of sin, misery and impotence has been sweetened by the common humanity of God and man:

Tribulations illuminate the heart of man with self-knowledge, and this is the perfection of the human condition.

Just as lovers send letters to each other to refresh their memories one of another, so Christ sends tribulations to refresh our memories of him and his sufferings.

By denying us earthly satisfactions God forces us to seek those which are heavenly, just as an earthly lord who wants to sell his own wine orders the public houses to close until he has sold it.

We may object that these gentle similes cover the harsh realities of the world with sentimentality, and this may be an inevitable result of humanism in religion. But it is a form of humanism that has survived all the religious divisions of Europe, and it has made a lasting contribution to the way in which ordinary people have looked at the universe. Popular piety has never lost this sentimental familiarity.

Some may think that these religious themes, however expressed, are far from the themes of humanism. But if we are looking for a growing sense of human dignity, and for an enlargement of man's powers and place in the universe, the hymns and meditations of the twelfth and thirteenth centuries supply us with abundant evidence. Indeed these religious developments are perhaps the greatest triumph that humanism has ever achieved, for they conquered the universe for humanity, and made God so much man's friend that his actions became almost indistinguishable from our own.

The greatest triumph of medieval humanism was to make God seem human. The Ruler of the Universe, who had seemed so terrifying and remote, took on the appearance of a familiar friend. The next triumph was to make the universe itself friendly, familiar, and intelligible. This is an essential part of the heritage of western Europe which we owe to the scholars of the twelfth and thirteenth centuries. The experience of earlier centuries had suggested that so far as man could see, the universe was a scene of chaos and mystery, and that renunciation, submission to the supernatural, and a grateful acceptance of miraculous aid were the best that men could aim at. But in the late eleventh century, secular schools began to multiply which were dedicated to the task of extending the area of intelligibility and order in the world in a systematic way.

The importance of these schools for the intellectual development of Europe is very great. They provided permanent centres of learning which faced the world instead of facing away from it. The studies of the monasteries were necessarily dominated by the needs of the monastic life, but the secular schools belonged to the world. They were normally found in centres of urban life. They drew their scholars from a class of men who expected to live in the world and to make their careers in the government of church and state. The greatest of these schools became the prototypes of all modern universities. Oxford, Paris and Bologna have had a continuous history since the twelfth century: likewise our academic faculties and disciplines have had an unbroken development since that time. These schools and universities and disciplines have many achievements to their credit, but their first achievement was the foundation of all others: they brought the idea of an indefinitely expanding order and rationality into every area of human experience.

The emancipating role of the medieval schools has been obscured partly by the prejudices and misconceptions of a later age, and partly by the hardening of the arteries that afflicts all institutions in the course of time. Later scholars, who saw that the medieval secular schools existed to train tonsured clerks in sciences necessary for running ecclesiastical courts and institutions, could not understand that they had once been the great liberating force in European thought. They could not see how small was the gap that separated the clerks of these schools from the secular world. The masters and scholars wore the ecclesiastical tonsure and were subject to ecclesiastical courts, but many of them looked forward to employment in secular business. They were willing to use their skills as much to oppose ecclesiastical claims as to promote them. They had no sense of separation from secular affairs. Contemporaries criticised them for wasting the resources of the Church on studies irrelevant or hostile to the purposes of the Church, and though this was a narrow-minded criticism it was nearer the truth than the later charge of subservience to ecclesiastical interests. Certainly it would be difficult to imagine a less clerical body, in any modern sense of the word, than the unruly and undisciplined communities of the medieval universities. This was an aspect of the medieval schools hidden from the view of later critics who could only see them engaged in a long struggle to preserve a clerical monopoly in academic effort.

As for the curriculum and methods of study of the schools, they came to seem very arid to almost all thinking men. In the early days of the revival of medieval studies, no more than a century ago, the best that a deeply learned and serious observer could find to say about medieval scholastic writers was that:

those men handed down to us much precious knowledge, with much verbiage and false logic. . . . They ticketed every portion of man's moral anatomy, found a rule for every possible case of choice, a reason and a reward for every virtue, and a punishment for every conceivable crime; they turned generalizations into law, and deduced from them as laws the very facts from which they had generalized. They benefited mankind by exercising and training subtle wits, and they reduced dialectics, almost, we might say, logic itself, to absurdity. . . . In reading Thomas Aquinas one is constantly provoked to say, What could not such a mind have done if it had not been fettered by such a method?

These are in their way very judicious remarks: this is what it all came to in the end. But in the beginning, the medieval scholastic curriculum met an urgent need for order in the intellectual outlook of a Europe first rising to independent thought. At that time the only available instrument of intellectual order was a thorough command of the sciences and techniques of the Greco-Roman world so far as they had been preserved in the West. This command was achieved, and it brought intellectual order into human life in a wonderfully short space of time. No doubt it is possible to imagine better starting-points. But none other was available, and we must judge the achievement in the light of the problems and the tools that lay to hand.

I have said that there can be no humanism without a strong sense of the dignity and intelligibility of man and nature; and if God exists, the same qualities must characterize the relations of God with his creation. These phrases could almost be taken as a description of the programme of the medieval secular schools. One of the first things they did was to renew a sense of the dignity and nobility of man. These terms are rare in the eleventh century, but very common in the twelfth. They meant that man's powers of reason and will, cultivated as they can be by study, give him a splendour which survives all the effects of sin and degeneration. As a twelfth century schoolmaster, Bernard Silvestris, wrote:

> The animals express their brute creation
> By head hung low and downward looking eyes;
> But man holds high his head in contemplation
> To show his natural kinship with skies.
> He sees the stars obey God's legislation:
> *They* teach the laws by which mankind can rise.

These images were largely borrowed from Ovid, but whereas in Ovid they were a poetic fiction, for the twelfth century scholar they were a scientific fact. They provided a basis for intellectual ambition and optimism. For scholars of an earlier generation the dignity of man and nature had been lost through sin, and could only be restored by supernatural means. But the leading scholars of the secular schools, from the beginning of the twelfth century onwards, stressed the natural remedies to the ravages of sin, and saw the seven liberal arts as instruments for the mitigation of human frailties.

This view of the nature of man and his hopes for the future was based on man's apparently unlimited capacity for knowledge. It may seem strange that scholars who had so recently emerged from an extremely pessimistic view of human capacities, and who believed that man's faculties had been grievously impaired by sin, should rush to the other extreme and proclaim that everything, or almost everything, could be known. But in intellectual affairs almost all revolu-

tions are violent, and this was no exception. Scholars discovered that
there existed a scientific basis for optimism. They learnt from their
sources that man's affinity with every part of nature gives him the
power to understand everything in nature; that his elements and
humours, and the influences playing upon his birth and development, are the raw materials for the whole universe. Hence man,
being the epitome of the universe, is built to understand the universe. Despite the ravages of sin, he can still intellectually trace the
primitive perfection of the creation, and collaborate with God in its
restoration.

The instrument of this collaboration with God in the regeneration
of nature is reason. With comprehensive enthusiasm, the secular
masters of the early twelfth century began to let fall such *dicta* as
these: "The dignity of our mind is its capacity to know all things";
"We who have been endowed by nature with genius must seek
through philosophy the stature of our primeval nature"; "In the
solitude of this life the chief solace of our minds is the study of
wisdom"; "We have joined together science and letters, that from
this marriage there may come forth a free nation of philosophers."
These were ancient thoughts, but for the first time for many centuries we find men confident that all those things could be done and
that nature could be known. Hence the future seemed bright. Men
knew little as yet, but they could know everything, and already, as it
seemed to those optimistic masters, they knew more than had ever
been known before. At last, in a famous phrase of Bernard of
Chartres, they "stood on the shoulders of the giants, and could see
further than their great predecessors." They had mastered the past:

> His eagle eye could clearly see
> through each perplexed obscurity
> of all the seven liberal arts.
> He knew them well in all their parts,
> and made quite clear to everyone
> truths that for Plato dimly shone.

This was the epitaph of Thierry, one of the great masters who died
about 1150. The idea that he could see further than Plato, not
through revelation but through superior science, was surely very
bold. Thierry was only one of a large number of masters responsible
for the intellectual revival I have been describing. A surprisingly high
proportion of them died or retired in the decade before 1150; Abelard, Hugh of St. Victor, William of Conches, Thierry, Bernard Silvestris. It has seemed to many scholars that humanism died with
them. Certainly some freshness and charm died with them. But if we

look at the principles of enquiry for which they stood, the main current of their work suffered no setback. These men represented the intellectual adolescence of Europe, and it is natural to mourn the passing of youth. But we must not exaggerate their youthful achievement. What they made was partly a ground-plan and partly a castle in the air. It still remained to build on the foundation and to give reality to the vision.

• • •

No reality is ever as beautiful as the vision. When people see the elaborate structures of thirteenth century thought and compare them with the visions of the age of William of Conches they find them less interesting in detail, less liberating in their effects, and less beautiful in their expression. Consequently they are apt to think that the intention of the later thinkers was quite different and much less humane. But the main difference is that the later writers knew vastly more than their predecessors and they had to work harder to integrate their material. The lack of new material, which had threatened to bring the humanism of the early twelfth century to a halt, was abundantly made good by the flow of new translations in the century after 1150. By 1250 virtually the whole corpus of Greek science was accessible to the western world, and scholars groaned under its weight as they strove to master it all. The days had gone when two large volumes could hold all that was essential for the study of the liberal arts. There was no time for artistic presentation and literary eloquence. This was a grave loss, but the achievement was there all the same. The main ideas of the earlier masters—the dignity of man, the intelligibility of the universe, the nobility of nature—not only remained intact, but were fundamental concepts in the intellectual structures of the thirteenth century.

These concepts were so much taken for granted that they no longer seemed to call for poetic expression. They were introduced as a matter of course into the most technical discussions on the most unlikely subjects. I have in front of me a highly abstract argument about the Incarnation, written by the first great Oxford master, Robert Grosseteste, about 1230. If we compare it with Anselm's great treatise on the same subject, completed just a hundred and thirty years earlier, we see the great difference that the scientific humanism of the intervening period had made. Anselm is far superior in literary grace, but Grosseteste is inspired by a much more profound humanism. Anselm had argued that the Incarnation was necessary because man had sinned beyond the possibility of redemption by any other means, and that God necessarily became man, not because of any quality in man, but because of his otherwise total ruin. For Grosseteste the picture was quite different. He too saw God's Incarnation as necessary for man's salvation. But it was not man's sin that made it necessary: it was necessary for the completion of man's nature, and it would have happened if man had never sinned. It was therefore not a last desperate throwing of God's final reserves into a battle that was almost lost. It was a final act in the unfolding drama of creation: it made Man and Nature complete, and it bound the whole created universe together in union with God.

Whether this is good theology or good science I do not know. But it is certainly profoundly humanistic in a way that Anselm's argument is not. It is filled with a conception of a human dignity so exalted that God could not stop short of Incarnation, and of a natural order so sublime that it required to be completed by a God-perfected man. This is the final step in scientific humanism. It was not a step that was generally taken by Grosseteste's contemporaries, but a large body of the theological work of the thirteenth century displays a similar faith in man and nature. Indeed the chief objection that can be brought against scholastic theology is not its lack of humanism, but its persistent tendency to make man appear more rational, human nature more noble, the divine ordering of the universe more open to human inspection, and the whole complex of man, nature and God more fully intelligible, than we can now believe to be plausible. But—regarded simply as an effort to comprehend the structure of the universe and, in the striking image of William of Conches, to demonstrate the dignity of the human mind by showing that it can know all things—this body of thought is one of the most ambitious displays of scientific humanism ever attempted.

From this point of view, the two *Summae* of Thomas Aquinas mark the highest point of medieval humanism. . . . The reader is tempted to say as he reads: "Of course there are things man cannot yet understand—but not many; of course man is a sinner—but how wonderfully the ravages of sin have been restored by reason, and how easy, how natural, how rational the steps to salvation." The natural faculties are no longer in ruins. Reason and nature have inherited the world. The work of Thomas Aquinas is full of illustrations of the supremacy of reason and nature. His judgements nearly always give the natural man rather more than his due. He reversed the ancient opinion that the body is the ruined habitation of the soul, and held with Aristotle that it is the basis of the soul's being. Everywhere he points to the natural perfection of man, his natural rights, and the power of his natural reason. The dignity of human nature is not simply a poetic vision; it has become a central truth of philosophy.

Thomas Aquinas died in 1274, and it is probably true that man has never appeared so important a being in so well-ordered and intelligible a universe as in his works. Man was important because he was the link between the created universe and the divine intelligence. He alone in the world of nature could understand nature. He alone in nature could understand the nature of God. He alone could use and perfect nature in accordance with the will of God, and thus achieve his full nobility.

• • •

Many reasons may be given for rejecting the kind of humanism we have been considering. We may disagree with its theological basis, or its belief in the intelligibility of the universe, or the central position accorded to man, or the optimism about man's rational powers. But it is at first sight puzzling that men who had no quarrel with God or with reason, and who sought to glorify man, should have denied that the ways of thinking I have described had any claim to be called humanistic. Anyone who knew anything about the world of the eleventh century would have had to agree that the dignity of man, the intelligibility of the world and of God, and the application of reason to practical affairs had made such progress in the twelfth and thirteenth centuries that they had become the central features of all thought and experience. Why then did these two centuries come to seem in retrospect so hostile to humanistic values?

I think the main explanation to this puzzle lies in the early fourteenth century. Europe then entered a period when the optimism which had buoyed up the efforts of the previous two centuries was abruptly destroyed: the flow of new intellectual materials came to an end; the forward movement in settlement and expansion came to a halt; the area of disorder in the world was everywhere increasing; everything began to seem insecure. Until this time it had seemed that, however horrible the present might be, the future was likely to be better. It was reasonable to believe that all the new information about the universe could be fitted into one grand universal plan, and it was not unreasonable to think that the papal, or perhaps the imperial, system of universal authority would in time bring universal peace. There was very little ground for thinking that the universe and God might after all be beyond the reach of reason, and humanly speaking chaotic.

But quite quickly this whole situation changed. It does not need a dramatic disaster to change the intellectual outlook of a generation. It only needs a slight change of direction, the end of expansion, the drying up of sources of information, a series of small setbacks, a persistent sense that nothing is going well. Petrarch, who above all stood for a new kind of humanism in the mid-fourteenth century, had reason to be disillusioned with the achievements of the last two centuries. The kind of intellectual and practical order at which men had aimed suddenly seemed quite unattainable:

Turn where you will, there is no place without its tyrant; and where there is no tyrant, the people themselves supply the deficiency. When you escape the One, you fall into the hands of the Many. If you can show me a place ruled by a just and mild king, I will take myself there with all my baggage. ... I will go to India or Persia or the furthest limits of the Garamantes to find such a place and such a king. But it is useless to search for what cannot be found. Thanks to our age, which has levelled all things, the labour is unnecessary.

The hopes of the past had to be buried. But such hopes are never buried with simple quiet resignation: they have to be buried with scorn and derision and a sense of betrayal. Hence the clerical schools with their formalised procedures and legalistic distinctions came to be seen, not simply as the agents of a great failure, but as the promoters of a great enslavement.

All systems of thought have some pervasive weakness built into their structure, and the weakness is all the more ineradicable when it forms in some sense the strength of the system. The characteristic weakness of medieval scientific thought was its dependence on *auctoritates* and *sententiae.* These were the bricks from which the system was formed; they provided the material for argument and the foundations for the most daring conclusions. But they also defined limits beyond which the system could not develop. So the moment of stasis was bound to come sooner or later. This is not a phenomenon peculiar to medieval thought or to scholastic processes of argument; it is a universal phenomenon in the development of every system; but the moment arrived in the Middle Ages with a peculiarly paralysing effect because it arrived without warning.

As soon as men lost confidence in the system and its aims, the details all appeared intensely repellent. No books have ever been written that give less invitation to study by their physical appearance than the manuscripts of the medieval schools; their illegible script, crabbed abbreviations, and margins filled with comments even less legible than the text, invite derision. As soon as men lost confidence in the end toward which this whole apparatus of learning moved, the adjuncts were bound to seem barbarous and inhumane. They had no beauty of style or vivacity of wit to support them.

Hence, as the residuary legatee of the scientific and systematic humanism of the twelfth and thirteenth centuries, a new kind of humanism came into existence. It was the product of disillusion with the great projects of the recent past. When the hope of universal order faded, the cultivation of sensibility and personal virtue, and the nostalgic vision of an ancient utopia revealed in classical literature, remained as the chief supports of humane values. Instead of the confident and progressive humanism of the central Middle Ages, the new humanism retreated into the individual and the past; it saw the aristocracy rather than the clergy as the guardians of culture; its sought inspiration in literature rather than theology and science; its ideal was a group of friends rather than a universal system; and the nobility of man was expressed in his struggle with an unintelligible world rather than in his capacity to know all things. When this happened the humanism of the central Middle Ages came to be mistaken for formalism and hostility to human experience.

17. Renaissance or Proto-Renaissance?

EVA MATTHEWS SANFORD

There are two phases of our problem: what do we mean by a renaissance, and does the twelfth century conform to this definition sufficiently to justify giving it the name? Since the term was first applied to the humanism of the Italian *Quattrocento* and to the appropriation of the antique in combination with direct observation of man and nature in its art, its original connotations were in the fields of classical scholarship and of literature and art. The humanists' reaction against their own concept of mediaevalism, as a period of dull stagnation dominated by blind acceptance of authority, and limited by indifference to the material world, gave rise to the idea of "rebirth" or *renaissance,* and to Michelet's classic phrase, "the rediscovery of the world and of man." Few scholars would now insist on the literal meaning of the word "Renaissance," with its suggestion of a preceding state of coma, if not of actual death, though it is difficult to wean undergraduates from this prejudiced view of the Middle Ages. If we substitute the criterion of intensified interest and vitality for rebirth and rediscovery, we still have to reckon with the Renaissance factors of individualism, secularism, skeptical criticism of traditional authority, and the creation of new standards and techniques in scholarship, literature and the arts, based in part on the interworking of classical and contemporary factors. We have also to consider the conspicuous influence on humanistic scholars and artists, and on Renaissance thought in general, of the "notion of belonging to a

From Eva Matthews Sanford, "The Twelfth Century—Renaissance or Proto-Renaissance?" *Speculum,* Vol. 26 (1951), pp. 635–641. Reprinted by permission of the Mediaeval Academy of America.

new time" and of the historical definition of the Renaissance as the transition from the mediaeval to the modern world.

In a recent paper Professor Wallace Ferguson has discussed our need of a new synthesis of the Renaissance as "an age of moral, religious, intellectual and aesthetic crisis, closely interrelated with acute economic, political and social crisis." He considers the revival of antiquity as a great, but secondary, causative force in this age. He notes decisive changes in all countries of western Europe from the beginning of the fourteenth century, and therefore proposes that the Renaissance, as the transition from mediaeval to modern culture, should be dated from about 1300 to 1600. This proposal embodies a most comprehensive view of the Renaissance. It accents the principle of crisis as a determinant, an extension of the "new age" emphasis, and it reminds us of a chronological problem. If we consider the twelfth century, according to Professor Haskins' chronology, as extending to about 1250, when "the signature of the thirteenth century" became clearly recognizable in literature, art, and thought, the period between a Renaissance of the twelfth century and the inauguration of the major Renaissance would be only fifty years long. This may lead us to a fruitful application of the obvious differences between the organic phenomena of the two periods, the one representing the height of mediaeval culture, and the other a decidedly transitional phase, but both contributing directly in their different ways to the emergence of the modern world.

As far as literature and art are concerned, Erwin Panofsky, in his brilliant essay on "Renaissance and Renascences," proposed the terms "proto-humanism" and "proto-Renaissance" for the twelfth century, on the ground that (1) the appropriation of the antique in this period, however notable in its immediate results, was subjective and fragmentary, as contrasted with the focussed perspective and comprehensive interests of the true Renaissance, and (2) it was limited both by the strong sense of continuity with antiquity and by Christian antagonism to pagan culture. He held that the elements taken over from antiquity were so fully assimilated into the mediaeval patterns that they did not inspire further progress, whereas the Italian Renaissance, though academic, was permanent, because of the changes it created in the minds of men. I find the specific illustrations by which he supports this thesis more convincing in art than in literature. But he brings out an essential difference between the two periods in their attitude toward the classical models that both used so much in their various ways. Writers and artists of the twelfth century did not recognize a cultural break between antiquity and their own time, whereas those of the fifteenth century not only recognized but emphasized it. The distinction between the twelfth century and the later Renaissance in regard to direct stimulus provided for further development, however, does not hold good in all the fields that interest historians.

Professor McIlwain has demonstrated the fallacy of contrasting the political theories and institutions of the twelfth century with those of the Renaissance in this respect. In "Mediaeval Institutions in the Modern World" he wrote: "In the field of political institutions and ideas, I venture to think that what Professor Haskins has termed 'the Renaissance of the Twelfth Century' marks a more fundamental change than the later developments to which we usually attach the word 'Renaissance'; that the constitutionalism of the modern world owes as much, if not even more, to the twelfth and thirteenth centuries than to any later period of comparable length until the seventeenth." He cited especially the mediaeval limitations of governmental authority by private rights, the development of parliamentary institutions, and the gradual assimilation of Roman constitutionalism. The slow process of assimilation of Roman law was speeded up in twelfth-century Italy by the rivalries of empire, papacy, and north Italian communes, which in this period developed the autonomous institutions that contributed so much to their leadership in fifteenth century culture. The University of Bologna and the work of the great glossators show that in the field of Roman law the twelfth and thirteenth centuries left no opportunity for fundamental "discovery" but only for continued study and application of foundations already well and truly laid.

In the field of the natural sciences, we are increasingly aware that the basis for the phenomenal progress of the sixteenth and seventeenth centuries was established before the Renaissance, and that the translations of Greek and Arabic scientific works in the twelfth and thirteenth centuries provided the initial stimulus for such significant research in scientific theory and techniques as that carried on at Padua from about 1300. It is now generally recognized that Roger Bacon, as his own words testify, was not the first mediaeval scholar to set a high value on experimental science, and to formulate sound criteria for it. The net results of mediaeval science, in comparison with the achievements of the sixteenth century, are small indeed, yet the period of incubation began here rather than in the fifteenth century. In the latter period, although many humanists tended to scorn the natural sciences in favor of classical learning (as some have been known to do even in later times), the careful reexamination of mediaeval scientific works together with those of the Greeks and Romans, and the increasing interchange of ideas and techniques between scholars, artists, and craftsmen, prepared the way more fully for the dynamic scientific achievements of the sixteenth century. It would seem that in the scientific as well as in the political field the twelfth century exerted a sufficiently direct influence on later developments to make its definition as a "proto-Renaissance" untenable.

Unqualified insistence on a twelfth-century Renaissance, however, involves the risk of emphasizing the Renaissance characteristics of the period at the expense of its essentially mediaeval qualities. In many respects, like all periods of dynamic activity, it was an age of transition, but the factors of change, significant though they were, still operated to extend and enrich the traditional pattern of a unified Christian culture, with its closely knit communities and personal ties, rather than to destroy them. There were many crises in the twelfth century, but there was not, it seems to me, the over-all motivation in terms of crisis that Professor Ferguson attributes to the later Renaissance. For all the new phases of economic, political, social, aesthetic and intellectual life in the twelfth century, I have not found in it that prevalent consciousness of a new age, or the determination of ideas by the sense of newness, that is so conspicuous in the fifteenth century.

The conviction of continuity with the ancient world is one controlling factor here. We see it in the "Christian synthesis" of Hebrew, Greek, Hellenistic, and Roman with Christian history, and in the historical pattern of the four empires, ending with the Roman, which was expected to endure till the end of the created world. Mediaeval historians, even those who fully recognized that the imperial power in the west had been transferred from Roman to Frankish and German rulers, often echoed the old statement, "The last age is the Roman, in which we now live." They did not look back to the ideas and achievements of antiquity for fresh inspiration from a distant source, but as a direct inheritance and a native possession. This conviction of the unity of history made them unconscious of anachronism and blocked of many approaches to historical criticism, but it also saved the ancient world from the aspect of unreality that it has had for many students in later ages. With the great increase in historical writing in the twelfth century, the theme of *renovatio* appears, as it does also in the political theories of the imperial partisans. Peter of Blois' famous defence of the study of ancient history may serve to illustrate this "Renaissance" attitude, which appears frequently in the works of the chief twelfth-century writers, but, as in this case, within the framework of the mediaeval pattern of world history: "However dogs may bark at me, and pigs grunt, I shall always imitate the writings of the ancients: these shall be my study, nor, while my strength lasts, shall the sun find me idle. We are like dwarfs on the shoulders of giants, by whose grace we see farther than they. Our study of the works of the ancients enables us to give fresh life to their finer ideas, and rescue them from time's oblivion and man's neglect." Here is no blind reverence for ancient authority, but a dignified, though not unmodest assumption that a twelfth-century scholar could and should see farther than the giants of the past. Here, also, is one of many possible answers to the common charge that mediaeval scholars in general feared and distrusted the influence of pagan ideas. The strictures of Bernard of Clairvaux and other ascetic Christians represent a significant but by no means a universal mediaeval attitude. They were often occasioned by the genuine devotion to classical literature displayed by contemporary humanists. Not only the intimate knowledge that twelfth-century writers exhibit of the works of Virgil, Ovid, Horace, and other Latin authors, but the frequent occurrence, even in theological works, of pagan *exempla virtutis* and the wide range of mediaeval quotations from classical authors, show that the classics were commonly read and used for their own value, and not merely to assail pagan corruption or to despoil the Egyptians. The extensive use of classical citations, chiefly for ethical purposes, in Petrus Cantor's *Abbreviated Word,* is one striking example of this. Another significant clue to mediaeval attitudes toward the classics is afforded by marked passages in manuscripts of the authors most read, which indicate the sentiments that the scribe, or some mediaeval reader, found particularly valuable. In the case of Juvenal, for example, one of the pagan writers classified as an *auctor ethicus,* the passages marked in many manuscripts that I have examined show clearly that he was read as a source of ethical precepts, and not merely, as some modern critics state, for evidence of pagan vice.

To those Renaissance historians who broke away from the mediaeval scheme of history, antiquity was an age long past, separated by a thousand years from their own time, and hence studies more objectively, for its possible contributions to their new and rapidly changing world. In the twelfth century, the sense of continuity with the past is conspicuous in the leading cultural centers of northern France, England, the Rhineland and the upper Danube, where the Latin language and literature were not native to the same degree that they were in southern France and Italy. Though Latin was no longer a mother tongue, even in the latter areas, it was in many respects a living language, flexibly handled by educated men, without the artificial restrictions on style and vocabulary that extreme Ciceronians later imposed on it. The hymns and lyric and narrative poems of the twelfth and thirteenth centuries testify that poets found in Latin a natural medium for the expression of their ideas and emotions. The occurrence of both Latin and vernacular versions of the same themes, and the evidences of cross-fertilization between Latin and vernacular literature, deserve serious consideration in this connection. Greek literature, however, remained unknown, aside from the arid and prosaic Latin epitomes of Homer, and such works as had been earlier incorporated in the Latin tradition by the great translators of the Roman period, or by the popular versions of Aesop's fables and the romance of Apollonius of Tyre, for example. The names of Greek authors were known from histories of literature; the scholars who diligently sought out and translated Aristotle's books on logic and natural science might presumably have recovered literary texts also, if they had wished, but they left this important phase of the appropriation of the antique for a later time.

Secularism, individualism, and criticism of established authority are much stressed as distinguishing characteristics of the Renaissance. How far should our appraisal of the twelfth century be influenced by the ecclesiastical character of its culture as contrasted with later secularism? Professor Boyce has wisely pointed out that the terms "secular" and "ecclesiastical" are not mutually exclusive in the Middle Ages. When education was provided chiefly by monastic and cathedral schools, and private tutors were usually monks or priests, when there were few non-clerical careers for intellectual men, and students, however worldly, could claim benefit of clergy, when all society, except for the small minority of Jews and avowed heretics, was united in one Christian fellowship, there could be no clear line of demarcation between the religious and the secular except that drawn by extremists. Not all priests and bishops, monks and friars were insulated from the world by an ecclesiastical ivory tower. Those whose undue worldliness aroused the righteous indignation of contemporary reformers were sometimes, though not always, among the intellectual leaders of their day, and some very secular works were dedicated to ecclesiastical patrons. The learning and literature of the courts of Henry II, Eleanor of Aquitaine, and the Norman rulers of Sicily remind us that patronage was not entirely clerical, though there were fewer wealthy lay patrons—as indeed, there were fewer wealthy men—than in the fifteenth century. Professor Thompson and others have taught us that not all the laity were illiterate; the twelfth century saw a marked increase in the reading public, and the desire of the new readers for edification and entertainment from books met with a notable response on the part of both Latin and vernacular writers. Honorius Augustodunensis, a priest and monk who chose the extremely unworldly life of an "inclusus," shows in his varied works a lively appreciation of the variety and beauties of the natural world, and a keen understanding of the material problems of the congregations for whom he composed his sermons. His writings deal not only with theological and ethical questions, but with secular history, geography, political theory, and the liberal arts. He considered this life a pilgrimage, but he made every effort to help the pilgrim live a well-rounded life during the journey of his soul to God, though he himself had narrowly restricted his own physical activities. He defined man as "a rational soul, clothed with a body," and he provided appropriate nourishment for all three elements.

The most notable buildings that afforded opportunity for the development of architecture and the decorative arts were churches, but in their decoration secular motifs were blithely introduced with apparent unconsciousness of incongruity. Though the traditional symbolism of many of these motifs is well established, the naturalism and freshness with which they are often presented make them no less convincing evidence that details of the physical world were recognized as belonging in the religious context. As the church was the unifying factor in society, its interests embraced many secular elements which later ages associate with the body politic and social rather than with the communion of saints. Obviously, however, the ecclesiastical side of the scales was more heavily weighted than the secular, whereas the next few generations were to change the balance. Here there is a fundamental difference between twelfth-century and Renaissance culture, though the contrast is relative rather than absolute.

The question of individualism is also a relative one. We no longer identify outstanding individuals in the Middle Ages as forerunners of the Renaissance, but recognize Abelard, for example, as a natural product of his time, albeit an exceptional one. In what age would Abelard not have been exceptional? The personal tone of much lyric and satirical poetry is pertinent here. Anonymity was not always due to the Christian subordination of individual claims to creative talent in favor of the Creator. Sometimes, as in Honorius' case, it was expressly attributed to fear of malicious opponents, and sometimes, as in the case of the most popular treatise on education, the Pseudo-Boethius, *De disciplina scholarium,* to the desire to gain a wider public by fathering one's book on a noted ancient authority. Again there is a marked difference in proportion between the two periods; individualism is by no means exceptional in the twelfth century, but it runs rampant in the fifteenth.

Outspoken criticism of traditional authority was not unknown in the twelfth century, when the range of ecclesiastical questions open to dispute was somewhat wider than it was on the eve of the Reformation. The risk of a trial for heresy was not always a deterrent to scholars convinced of their own sound judgment. Skepticism and the spirit of objective inquiry did not always provoke condemnation, and Abelard's critical method survived numerous attacks before his works were incorporated in the curriculum of the University of Paris. His rational thesis, "By doubting we are led to inquire, and by inquiry we perceive the truth," represents the constructive theological approach of the period better than the attacks it provoked from the more intellectually inert of his contemporaries. Bishop Otto of Freising stated the case of the imperial party against the Donations of Constantine in a brief and matter of fact fashion without the elaborate display of learning that was to make Lorenzo Valla's treatise on the same subject a landmark of the critical spirit of the Renaissance. While he left the case open, as a problem not within the province of his *Chronicle* to decide, his presentation leaves no doubt as to his own point of view. Honorius openly attacked the performance for unworthy motives of such "good works" as pilgrimages and crusades, without any inhibitions about criticizing activities sponsored by the church.

For the Age of Faith assumed the exercise of reason, within the bounds of its clearly defined and finite world, which still provided ample range for speculative and critical thought. In his memorable Harvard Tercentenary lecture on Mediaeval Universalism, Etienne Gilson pointed out the intellectual obligations imposed by the mediaeval conviction of universal truth as valid for all men at all times and places. In the twelfth century a unified society with a common meaning for all its members still transcended local differences; its culture was still non-national and non-racial, though there was an increasing consciousness of local and national distinctions. Changes were being wrought by the expansion of commerce and industry with their new contacts, implements and techniques, and their new types of communities and opportunities. Many political and social adjustments were required by these changes and by the concomitant increase in population and production. In their later stages these changes were to create a new world and in so doing, break down the unity of the old, but they had not as yet destroyed the equilibrium.

As we look back at the twelfth century, it is difficult to remember that feudal and agrarian institutions were still actively developing, with more conscious definition of their functions and principles than before, and were still being furthered rather than weakened by the expanding horizons of the age.

To sum up: the designation of the twelfth century as a proto-Renaissance seems both misleading and inadequate. But if we describe it, without considerable qualifications, as a Renaissance period, do we not risk underestimating and even distorting its real character? Can we use this term without implying more identity than the twelfth century really had with the later Renaissance, with its atmosphere of crisis and its consciousness of a new age, in which the secular motivation of political, social, economic and intellectual life replaced the universalism that still directed and inspired the thought and action of the twelfth century? I must confess that I have found the idea of a twelfth-century Renaissance very useful in teaching undergraduates mediaeval history, and I have not really questioned its validity before I wrote this paper. Now I am not so sure. If the men of the Renaissance had not put mediaevalists on the defensive by insistence on their rescue of the world and man from mediaeval ignorance and oblivion, should we feel the need of defining the earlier period as a renaissance? Should we not rather be satisfied to let the twelfth century stand on its own merits as a dynamic period of mediaeval culture, which made fruitful contributions to the development of modern man and the modern world without forfeiting its own essentially mediaeval character?

WOMEN AND FAMILY

IN THE PAST medieval historians used to study the position of women in medieval life and thought principally from two points of view. Many writers were fascinated by the aristocratic literature on courtly love that emerged in the twelfth century. Others investigated the influence of medieval religion on attitudes toward women. (In this sphere they had to consider the cult of the Virgin and the actual role of women in medieval religious life.) Eileen Power, a fine economic historian, discussed the two usual approaches in her pioneering essay, "The Position of Women," and then went beyond them to delineate the actual day-to-day activities of medieval women belonging to various social classes. In the next selection C. S. Lewis reminds us of the striking originality and enduring influence of medieval courtly love. Caroline Bynum's essay presents a more recent approach to women's history; here it is not just a question of how the church treated women but of how some distinctive spiritual experiences of medieval women reacted on the whole religious culture of the age. In the last reading Robert Fossier explores the relationships between wives, husbands, and children in the peasant families that formed the great bulk of the medieval population.

18.   The Position of Women

EILEEN POWER

The position of women has been called the test point by which the
civilization of a country or of an age may be judged, and although
this is in many respects true, the test remains one which it is extraor-
dinarily difficult to apply, because of the difficulty of determining
what it is that constitutes the position of women. Their position in
theory and in law is one thing, their practical position in everyday
life another. These react upon one another, but they never entirely
coincide, and the true position of women at any particular moment
is an insidious blend of both. In the Middle Ages the proper sphere
of women was the subject of innumerable didactic treatises addressed to them, or written about them, and their merits and defects
were an evergreen literary theme, which sometimes gave rise to controversies in which the whole fashionable literary world of the day
was engaged, such as the debate which raged round Jean de Meun's
section of the *Roman de la Rose* and Alan Chartier's poem *La Belle
Dame sans Merci* at the beginning of the fifteenth century.

The characteristic medieval theory about women, thus laid down
and debated, was the creation of two forces, the Church and the
Aristocracy, and it was extremely inconsistent. The Church and the
Aristocracy were not only often at loggerheads with each other, but
each was at loggerheads with itself, and both taught the most contradictory doctrines, so that women found themselves perpetually
oscillating between a pit and a pedestal. Had the Church, indeed,

From Eileen Power, "The Position of Women," in *The Legacy of the Middle Ages*, G. C.
Crump and E. F. Jacob, eds. (Oxford: Clarendon Press, 1926), pp. 401–407,
410–421. Reprinted by permission of Oxford University Press.

been consistent in its attitude towards them in the early days of its predominance, their position might have been much better or much worse. But it was remarkably inattentive to the biblical injunction against halting between two opinions. Janus-faced it looked at woman out of every pulpit, every law book and every treatise, and she never knew which face was turned upon her. Was she Eve, the wife of Adam, or was she Mary, the mother of Christ? "Between Adam and God in Paradise," says Jacques de Vitry (d. 1240), "there was but one woman; yet she had no rest until she had succeeded in banishing her husband from the garden of delights and in condemning Christ to the torment of the cross." On the other hand, "Woman," says a manuscript in the University of Cambridge, "is to be preferred to man, to wit: in material, because Adam was made from clay and Eve from the side of Adam; in place, because Adam was made outside paradise and Eve within; in conception, because a woman conceived God, which a man could not do; in apparition, because Christ appeared to a woman after the Resurrection, to wit, the Magdalen; in exaltation, because a woman is exalted above the choirs of angels, to wit, the Blessed Mary." It is extremely curious to follow the working of these two ideas upon the medieval mind. The view of woman as an instrument of the Devil, a thing at once inferior and evil, found expression very early in the history of the Church, and it was the creation of the Church; for while Rome knew the tutelage of woman, and barbarism also placed her in man's *mund,* both were distinguished by an essential respect for her. As the ascetic ideal rose and flourished and monasticism became the refuge of many of the finest minds and most ardent spirits who drew breath in the turmoil of the dying Empire and the invasions, there came into being as an inevitable consequence a conception of woman as the supreme temptress, "ianua diaboli," the most dangerous of all obstacles in the way of salvation. It is unnecessary to enter fully into the ramifications of this attitude. Its importance is that it established a point of view about woman which survived long after the secular conditions which created it had passed away. In practice it had little influence upon men's daily lives; they continued marrying and giving in marriage and invoked the blessing of the Church upon their unions. But opinion may change irrespective of practice and the monastic point of view slowly permeated society. Tertullian and St. Jerome took their place beside Ovid in that "book of wikked wyves," which the Wife of Bath's fifth husband was wont to read aloud nightly, with such startling results. The clergy, who preached the ascetic ideal, were for many centuries the only educated and hence the only articulate section of the community, and it is not surprising that the fundamental theory about women should have been a theory of their essential inferiority.

This theory was accepted by the ordinary layman, but only up to a point. Outside the ranks of monastic writers and the more extreme members of a celibate priesthood, no one, save professional misogynists like the notorious Matheolous, took the evil nature of women very seriously, and most men would probably have agreed with the Wife of Bath's diagnosis,

> For trusteth wel, it is an impossible
> That any clerk wol speke good of wyves,—
> But if it be of hooly Seintes lyves,—
> Ne of noon oother womman never the mo.

What they did accept was the subjection of women. The ideal of marriage which inspires the majority of the didactic works addressed to women in the course of the Middle Ages is founded upon this idea and demands the most implicit obedience. It is set forth in the stories of Patient Griselda and the Nut-Brown Maid, and the possessive attitude towards women is nowhere more clearly marked than in the remarks made upon feminine honour by Philippe de Novaire (d. 1270) in his treatise *Des quatre tens d'aage d'ome.* "Women," he says, "have a great advantage in one thing; they can easily preserve their honour if they wish to be held virtuous, by one thing only. But for a man many are needful, if he wish to be esteemed virtuous, for it behoves him to be courteous and generous, brave and wise. And for a woman, if she be a worthy woman of her body, all her other faults are covered and she can go with a high head wheresoever she will; and therefore it is in no way needful to teach as many things to girls as to boys."

The subjection of women was thus one side of medieval theory, accepted both by the Church and by the Aristocracy. On the other hand, it was they also who developed with no apparent sense of incongruity the counter-doctrine of the superiority of women, that adoration (*Frauendienst*) which gathered round the persons of the Virgin in heaven and the lady upon earth, and which handed down to the modern world the ideal of chivalry. The cult of the Virgin and the cult of chivalry grew together, and continually reacted upon one another; they were both, perhaps, the expression of the same deep-rooted instinct, that craving for romance which rises to the surface again and again in the history of mankind; and just as in the nineteenth century the romantic movement followed upon the age of common sense, so in the Middle Ages the turmoil and pessimism of the Dark Ages were followed by the age of chivalry and of the Virgin. The cult of the Virgin is the most characteristic flower of medieval religion and nothing is more striking than the rapidity with which it spread and the dimensions which it assumed. She was already supreme by the eleventh century, and supreme she remained until the end of the Middle Ages. Great pilgrimages grew up to her shrines and magnificent cathedrals were reared and decorated in her honour, while in almost every church not specifically her own she had a lady chapel. In the thirteenth century—about the same time that Philippe de Novaire was deciding that girls must not be taught to read—Albertus Magnus debated the scholastic question whether the Virgin Mary possessed perfectly the seven liberal arts and resolved it in her favour. Her miracles were on every lip, her name was sown in wild flowers over the fields, and the very fall of humanity became a matter for congratulation, since without it mankind would not have seen her enthroned in heaven.

> Ne hadde the appil take ben,
>   The appil taken ben,
> Ne hadde never our lady
>   A ben hevene quene.
> Blessed be the time
>   That appil take was.
> Therefore we moun singen
>   'Deo gracias'.

The cult of the lady was the mundane counterpart of the cult of the Virgin and it was the invention of the medieval aristocracy. In chivalry the romantic worship of a woman was as necessary a quality of the perfect knight as was the worship of God. As Gibbon puts it, with more wit than amiability, "The knight was the champion of God and the ladies—I blush to unite such discordant terms," and the idea finds clear expression in the refrain of a French *ballade* of the fourteenth century, "En ciel un dieu, en terre une déesse." One of its most interesting manifestations was the development of a theory of "courtly love," strangely platonic in conception though in many ways as artificial as contemporary scholasticism, which inspired some of the finest poetry of the age, from the Troubadours and Minnesingers of France and Germany to the singers of the "dolce stil nuovo" and Dante himself in Italy. It is obvious that a theory which regarded the worship of a lady as next to that of God and conceived her as the mainspring of brave deeds, a creature half romantic, half divine, must have done something to counterbalance the dogma of subjection. The process of placing women upon a pedestal had begun, and whatever we may think of the ultimate value of such an elevation (for few human beings are suited to the part of Stylites, whether ascetic or romantic) it was at least better than placing them, as the Fathers of the Church had inclined to do, in the bottomless pit. Nevertheless, as a factor in raising the position of women too much importance must not be attributed to the ideal of chivalry. Just as asceticism was the limited ideal of a small clerical caste, so chivalry was the limited ideal of a small aristocratic caste, and those who were outside that caste had little part in any refining influence which it possessed. Even in the class in which it was promulgated and prac- tised, it is impossible not to feel that it was little more than a veneer. Not only in the great *chansons de geste,* but in the book which the fourteenth-century knight of La Tour Landry wrote for the edifica- tion of his daughters, gentlemen in a rage not infrequently strike their wives to the ground, and the corporal chastisement of a wife was specifically permitted by canon law. The ideal of *l'amour courtois,* too, rapidly degenerated and its social was far less than its literary importance. It had a civilizing effect upon manners, but the funda- mental sensuality and triviality beneath the superficial polish is to be seen clearly enough in the many thirteenth-century books of de- portment for ladies, which were modelled upon Ovid's *Ars Amatoria,* so severely condemned by Christine de Pisan. It is probable that the idea of chivalry has had more influence upon later ages than it had upon contemporaries. As a legacy it has certainly affected the posi- tion of women in modern times, for whatever its effect upon medi- eval practice, it was one of the most powerful ideas evolved by the Middle Ages, and though it owed something to Arab influences, it was substantially an original idea.

Such, then, was the medieval theory as to the position of woman, an inconsistent and contradictory thing, as any generalization about a sex must be, teaching simultaneously her superiority and her inferiority.

• • •

But the theory about women, inconsistent and the work of a small articulate minority as it was, was only one factor in determining their position and it was the least important factor. The fact that it received a voluminous and often striking literary expression has given it a somewhat disproportionate weight, and to arrive at the real position of women it is necessary constantly to equate it with daily life, as revealed in more homely records. The result is very much what com- mon sense would indicate, for in daily life the position occupied by woman was one neither of inferiority nor of superiority, but of a certain rough-and-ready equality. This equality was as marked in the feudal as in the working classes; indeed it allowed the lady of the upper classes considerably more scope than she sometimes enjoyed at a much later period, for example, in the eighteenth and early nineteenth centuries. In order to estimate it, we may with advantage turn from theories to real life and endeavour, if possible, to disentangle some of the chief characteristics of the existence led by three typical women, the feudal lady, the bourgeoise, and the peasant. The typical woman must be taken to be the wife and more generally the housewife, but it must not be imagined that marriage was the lot of every woman and that the Middle Ages were not as familiar as our own day with the independent spinster. Then as now the total number of adult women was in excess of that of men. Reliable statistics are sadly to seek, but here and there poll-tax and hearth-tax lists afford interesting information. In the fourteenth and fifteenth centuries certain of the German towns took censuses, from which it appears that for every 1,000 men there were 1,100 women in Frankfort in 1385, 1,207 women in Nuremberg in 1449, and 1,246 women in Basel in 1454; the number of women was, it is true, swelled in these towns, because it was customary for widows from the country round to retire there, but a disproportion between the two sexes certainly existed. It is, indeed, to be expected on account of the greater mortality of men in the constant crusades, wars and town and family factions, and the discrepancy was aggravated by the fact that the celibacy of the clergy removed a very large body of men from marriage.

Medieval records are, indeed, full of these independent women. A glance at any manorial 'extent' will show women villeins and cotters living upon their little holdings and rendering the same services for them as men; some of these are widows, but many of them are obviously unmarried. The unmarried daughters of villeins could always find work to do upon their father's acres, and could hire out their strong arms for a wage to weed and hoe and help with the harvest. Women performed almost every kind of agricultural labour, with the exception of the heavy business of ploughing. They often acted as thatcher's assistants, and on many manors they did the greater part of the sheep-shearing, while the care of the dairy and of the small poultry was always in their hands. Similarly, in the towns women carried on a great variety of trades. Of the five hundred crafts scheduled in Étienne Boileau's *Livre des Métiers* in medieval Paris, at least five were their monopoly, and in a large number of others women were employed as well as men. Two industries in particular were mainly in their hands, because they could with ease be carried on as by-industries in the home. The ale, drunk by every one who could not afford wine, in those days when only the most poverty-striken fell back upon water, was almost invariably prepared by

women, and every student of English manorial court rolls will remember the regular appearance at the leet of most of the village
alewives, to be fined for breaking the Assize of Ale. Similarly, in all
the great cloth-working districts, Florence, the Netherlands, England, women are to be found carrying out the preliminary processes
of the manufacture. Spinning was, indeed, the regular occupation
of all women and the "spinster's" habitual means of support; God,
as the Wife of Bath observes, has given three weapons to women,
deceit, weeping, and spinning! Other food-producing and textile
industries were also largely practised by them, and domestic service
provided a career for many. It must, of course, be remembered that
married as well as single women practised all these occupations, but
it is clear that they offered a solution to the problem of the "superfluous" women of the lower classes. Nevertheless, this equality of
men and women in the labour market was a limited one. Many craft
regulations exclude female labour, some because the work was considered too heavy, but most for the reason, with which we are familiar, that the competition of women undercut the men. Then, as now,
women's wages were lower than those of men, even for the same
work, and the author of a treatise on *Husbandry* was enunciating a
general principle when, after describing the duties of the daye or
dairywoman, he added: "If this is a manor where there is no dairy,
it is always good to have a woman there at a much less cost than a
man."

The problem of the unmarried girl of the upper class was more
difficult, for in feudal society there was no place for women who did
not marry and marry young. It was the Church which came to their
rescue, by putting within their reach as brides of Christ a dignity
greater than that which they would have attained as brides of men.
The nunnery was essentially a class institution. It absorbed only
women belonging to the nobility, the gentry, and (in the later
Middle Ages) the bourgeoisie, and in practice (though not in strict
canon law) it demanded a dowry, though a smaller dowry than an
earthly husband might have required. But the spinsters of the working class were absorbed by industry and the land and did not need
it. To unmarried gentlewomen monasticism gave scope for abilities
which might otherwise have run to waste, assuring them both self-
respect and the respect of society. It made use of their powers of
organization in the government of a community, and in the management of household and estates; it allowed nuns an education
which was for long better than that enjoyed by men and women alike
outside the cloister; and it opened up for them, when they were
capable of rising to such heights, the supreme experiences of the
contemplative life. Of what it was capable at its best great monastic

saints and notable monastic housewives have left ample record to testify. Even if it suffered decline and sheltered the idle with the industrious and the black sheep with the white, it was still an honourable profession and fulfilled a useful function for the gentlewomen of the Middle Ages. In the towns, and for a somewhat lower social class, various lay sisterhoods, grouped in their *Béguinages, Samenungen, Gotteshäuser,* offered the same opportunities.

But what of the well-born girl who was not destined for a nunnery? Of her it may be said that she married, she married young and she married the man selected for her by her father. The careful father would expect to arrange for his daughter's marriage and often to marry her before she was fourteen, and if he found himself dying while she was still a child he would be at great pains to leave her a suitable dowry *ad maritagium suum* in his will. A girl insufficiently dowered might have to suffer that disparagement in marriage which was so much dreaded and so carefully guarded against, and even in the lowest ranks of society the bride was expected to bring something with her besides her person when she entered her husband's house. The dowering of poor girls was one of the recognized forms of medieval charity and, like the mending of bad roads, a very sound one. The system, of course, had its bad side. Modern civilization has steadily extended the duration of childhood, and to-day there seems something tragic in the spectacle of these children, taking so soon upon their young shoulders the responsibilities of marriage and motherhood. Similarly, since marriage is to-day most frequently a matter of free choice between its participants, the indifference sometimes shown to human personality in feudal marriages of the highest rank appears shocking. They were often dictated solely by the interests of the land. "Let me not to the marriage of true fiefs admit impediments" may be said to have been the dominating motive of a great lord with a son or daughter or ward to marry, and weddings were often arranged and sometimes solemnized when children were in their cradles.

Medieval thinkers showed some consciousness of these disadvantages themselves. The fact that all feudal marriages were *mariages de convenance* accounts for the fundamental dogma of *l'amour courtois,* so startling to modern ideas, that whatever the respect and affection binding married people, the sentiment of love could not exist between them, being in its essence freely sought and freely given and must therefore be sought outside marriage. "Causa coniugii ab amore non est excusatio."* Langland, again, inveighs against the "modern" habit of marrying for money and counsels other consid-

*"Marriage does not excuse from loving."—Ed.

erations; "and loke that loue be more the cause than lond other [or] nobles."

It is more rarely that the woman's view of a loveless marriage finds expression, but once at least, in the later Middle Ages, the voice of a woman passes judgement upon it, and with it upon the loneliness, the *accidia* (as monastic writers would have called it) of that life which medieval literature decks in all the panoply of romance. The Saxon reformer, Johann Busch, has preserved in his *Liber de reformatione monasteriorum* (1470–5) a poignant dialogue between himself and the dying Duchess of Brunswick.

"When her confession, with absolution and penance was ended," he writes, "I said to her, 'Think you, lady, that you will pass to the kingdom of heaven when you die?' She replied, 'This believe I firmly.' Said I, 'That would be a marvel. You were born in a fortress and bred in castles and for many years now you have lived with your husband, the Lord Duke, ever in the midst of manifold delights, with wine and ale, with meat and venison both roast and boiled; and yet you expect to fly away (*evolare*) to heaven directly you die.' She answered: 'Beloved father, why should I not now go to heaven? I have lived here in this castle like an anchoress in a cell. What delights or pleasures have I enjoyed here, save that I have made shift to show a happy face to my servants and to my maidens? I have a hard husband, as you know, who has scarce any care or inclination towards women. Have I not been in this castle even as it were in a cell?' I said to her, 'You think, then, that as soon as you are dead God will send his angels to your bed to bear your soul away to Paradise and to the heavenly kindom of God?' and she replied, 'This believe I firmly.' Then said I, 'May God confirm you in your faith and give you what you believe.' "

But it is unnecessary to suppose that the majority of feudal marriages turned out badly. The father is not human who does not wish to do his best for his daugther, and it was only in the most exalted rank that worldly could entirely outweigh personal considerations. Moreover, the fact that most wedded couples began life together while they were both very young was in their favour. Human nature is extremely adaptable, and they came to each other with no strongly marked ideas or prejudices and grew up together. The medieval attitude towards child marriages was that to which Christine de Pisan gave such touching expression when she recalled her own happy life with the husband whom she married before she was fifteen and who left her at twenty-five an inconsolable widow with three children. . . .

Certainly medieval records as a whole show a cameraderie between husband and wife which contrasts remarkably both with the picture of woman in subjection which the Church delighted to draw and with that of the worshipped lady of chivalry. An obscure Flemish weaver of the sixteenth century, writing to his wife from England, signs himself with the charming phrase "your married friend," and of medieval wives as a whole it may be said with truth, that while literature is full of Griseldas and *belles dames sans merci,* life is full of married friends. The mothers, wives, and daughters of the barons and knights of feudalism are sturdy witnesses to the truth of Mrs. Poyser's immortal dictum, "God Almighty made 'em to match the men." If feudal marriages submitted them completely to their fiefs, they could inherit and hold land, honours, and offices like men, and are to be found fighting for their rights like men, while widows, in their own right or as guardians of infant sons, often enjoyed great power. Blanche of Champagne waged war for fourteen years (1213–27) on behalf of her minor son, and Blanche of Castile governed a kingdom as regent for the boy Louis IX. Indeed, the history of the early thirteenth century is strongly impressed with the character of those two masterful and energetic sisters, in beauty, talent, and iron strength of purpose the worthy granddaughters of "the eagle," Eleanor of Aquitaine, Blanche, the mother of Saint Louis of France, and Berengaria, the mother of Saint Frederick of Castile.

Throughout the Middle Ages, too, the social and physical conditions of life, the constant wars, and above all the slow communications, inevitably threw a great deal of responsibility upon wives as the representatives of their absent husbands. It has been asserted in all ages that the sphere of woman is the home, but it has not always been acknowledged that that sphere may vary greatly in circumference, and that in some periods and circumstances it has given a much wider scope to women than in others. In the Middle Ages it was, for a variety of reasons, a very wide sphere, partly because of this constantly recurring necessity for the wife to take the husband's place. While her lord was away on military expeditions, on pilgrimages, at court, or on business, it was she who became the natural guardian of the fief or manager of the manor, and Europe was full of competent ladies, not spending all their time in hawking and flirting, spinning and playing chess, but running estates, fighting lawsuits, and even standing sieges for their absent lords. When the nobility of Europe went forth upon a crusade it was their wives who managed their affairs at home, superintended the farming, interviewed the tenants, and saved up money for the next assault. When the lord was taken prisoner it was his wife who collected his ransom, squeezing every penny from the estate, bothering bishops for indulgences, selling her jewels and the family plate. Once more it was these extremely practical persons and not the Griseldas, or the

store of Ladies whose bright eies
Rain influence and judge the prise,

who were the typical feudal women. . . .

But it was not only on exceptional occasions and in the absence of her husband that the lady found a weight of responsibility upon her shoulders. It is true that her duties as a mother were in some ways less arduous than might have been supposed. Large families were general, and the death-rate among children was high (as may be guessed from many a medieval tombstone, in which little shrouded corpses are ranged with living children behind their kneeling parents), but the new-born child, in the upper classes at least, was commonly handed over to a wet nurse and it is sometimes mentioned as a sign of special affection in a mother that she should have fed her own children at the breast. Again, the training of the young squire often took him at an early age from his mother's society, and it was customary to send both boys and girls away to the households of great persons to learn breeding, although no doubt they often remained at home. In any case the early marriages of the day meant short childhoods. Books of deportment are singularly silent, as a whole, on the subject of maternal duties; they were (as might be inferred from the shocking behaviour of Griselda) overshadowed by those of the wife. But if the nursery was not a great burden, housekeeping in the Middle Ages, and indeed in all ages prior to the Industrial Revolution, was a much more complicated business than it is to-day, except for the fact that domestic servants were cheap, plentiful, and unexacting. It was no small feat to clothe and feed a family when households were large, guests frequent, and when much of what is to-day made in factories and brought in shops had to be prepared at home. The butter and cheese were made in the dairy and the beer in the brewhouse, the candles were made up and the winter's meat salted down in the larder, and some at least of the cloth and linen used by the household was spun at home. The lady of the house had to supervise all these operations, as well as to make, at fair and market or in the nearest town, the necessary purchases of wine and foodstuffs and materials which could not be prepared on the manor.

The country housewife, too, was expected to look after the bodies of her household in sickness as well as in health, and it was necessary for her to have a certain skill in physic and surgery. Life was far less professionalized in the Middle Ages; a doctor was not to be found round every corner, and though the great lady in her town house or the wealthy bourgeoise might find a physician from Oxford or Paris or Salerno within reach, someone had to be ready to deal with emergencies on the lonely manors. Old French and English metrical romances are full of ladies physicking and patching up their knights, and household remedies were handed down with recipes for puddings and perfumes from mother to daughter; such knowledge was expected of them, as it was expected of the "wise woman," who mingled it with charms and spells.

19. *Courtly Love*

C. S. LEWIS

Every one has heard of courtly love, and every one knows that it appears quite suddenly at the end of the eleventh century in Languedoc. The characteristics of the Troubadour poetry have been repeatedly described. With the form, which is lyrical, and the style, which is sophisticated and often 'aureate' or deliberately enigmatic, we need not concern ourselves. The sentiment, of course, is love, but love of a highly specialized sort, whose characteristics may be enumerated as Humility, Courtesy, Adultery, and the Religion of Love. The lover is always abject. Obedience to his lady's lightest wish, however whimsical, and silent acquiescence in her rebukes, however unjust, are the only virtues he dares to claim. There is a service of love closely modelled on the service which a feudal vassal owes to his lord. The lover is the lady's "man." He addresses her as *midons,* which etymologically represents not "my lady" but "my lord." The whole attitude has been rightly described as "a feudalisation of love." This solemn amatory ritual is felt to be part and parcel of the courtly life. It is possible only to those who are, in the old sense of the word, polite. It thus becomes, from one point of view the flower, from another the seed, of all those noble usages which distinguish the gentle from the vilein: only the courteous can love, but it is love that makes them courteous. Yet this love, though neither playful nor licentious in its expression, is always what the nineteenth century called "dishonourable" love. The poet normally addresses another

From C. S. Lewis, *The Allegory of Love* (Oxford: Oxford University Press, 1936), pp. 2–12. Reprinted by permission of Oxford University Press.

man's wife, and the situation is so carelessly accepted that he seldom concerns himself much with her husband: his real enemy is the rival. But if he is ethically careless, he is no light-hearted gallant: his love is represented as a despairing and tragical emotion—or almost despairing, for he is saved from complete wan-hope by his faith in the God of Love who never betrays his faithful worshippers and who can subjugate the cruellest beauties.

The characteristics of this sentiment, and its systematic coherence throughout the love poetry of the Troubadours as a whole, are so striking that they easily lead to a fatal misunderstanding. We are tempted to treat "courtly love" as a mere episode in literary history—an episode that we have finished with as we have finished with the peculiarities of Skaldic verse or Euphuistic prose. In fact, however, an unmistakable continuity connects the Provencal love song with the love poetry of the later Middle Ages, and thence, through Petrarch and many others, with that of the present day. If the thing at first escapes our notice, this is because we are so familiar with the erotic tradition of modern Europe that we mistake it for something natural and universal and therefore do not inquire into its origins. It seems to us natural that love should be the commonest theme of serious imaginative literature: but a glance at classical antiquity or at the Dark Ages at once shows us that what we took for "nature" is really a special state of affairs, which will probably have an end, and which certainly had a beginning in eleventh-century Provence. It seems—or it seemed to us till lately—a natural thing that love (under certain conditions) should be regarded as a noble and ennobling passion: it is only if we imagine ourselves trying to explain this doctrine to Aristotle, Virgil, St. Paul, or the author of *Beowulf,* that we become aware how far from natural it is. Even our code of etiquette, with its rule that women always have precedence, is a legacy from courtly love, and is felt to be far from natural in modern Japan or India. Many of the features of this sentiment, as it was known to the Troubadours, have indeed disappeared; but this must not blind us to the fact that the most momentous and the most revolutionary elements in it have made the background of European literature for eight hundred years. French poets, in the eleventh century, discovered or invented, or were the first to express, that romantic species of passion which English poets were still writing about in the nineteenth. They effected a change which has left no corner of our ethics, our imagination, or our daily life untouched, and they erected impassable barriers between us and the classical past or the Oriental present. Compared with this revolution the Renaissance is a mere ripple on the surface of literature.

There can be no mistake about the novelty of romantic love: our only difficulty is to imagine in all its bareness the mental world that existed before its coming—to wipe out of our minds, for a moment, nearly all that makes the food both of modern sentimentality and modern cynicism. We must conceive a world emptied of that ideal of "happiness"—a happiness grounded on successful romantic love—which still supplied the motive of our popular fiction. In ancient literature love seldom rises above the levels of merry sensuality or domestic comfort, except to be treated as a tragic madness, [a folly] which plunges otherwise sane people (usually women) into crime and disgrace. Such is the love of Medea, of Phaedra, of Dido; and such the love from which maidens pray that the gods may protect them. At the other end of the scale we find the comfort and utility of a good wife acknowledged: Odysseus loves Penelope as he loves the rest of his home and possessions, and Aristotle rather grudgingly admits that the conjugal relation may now and then rise to the same level as the virtuous friendship between good men. But this has plainly very little to do with "love" in the modern or medieval sense; and if we turn to ancient love-poetry proper, we shall be even more disappointed. We shall find the poets loud in their praises of love, no doubt. . . . "What is life without love, tra-la-la?" as the later song has it. But this is no more to be taken seriously than the countless panegyrics both ancient and modern on the all-consoling virtues of the bottle. If Catullus and Propertius vary the strain with cries of rage and misery, this is not so much because they are romantics as because they are exhibitionists. In their anger or their suffering they care not who knows the pass to which love has brought them. They are in the grip of the [folly]. They do not expect their obsession to be regarded as a noble sorrow—they have no "silks and fine array."

Plato will not be reckoned an exception by those who have read him with care. In the *Symposium*, no doubt, we find the conception of a ladder whereby the soul may ascend from human love to divine. But this is a ladder in the strictest sense; you reach the higher rungs by leaving the lower ones behind. The original object of human love—who, incidentally, is not a woman—has simply fallen out of sight before the soul arrives at the spiritual object. The very first step upwards would have made a courtly lover blush, since it consists in passing on from the worship of the beloved's beauty to that of the same beauty in others. Those who call themselves Platonists at the Renaissance may imagine a love which reaches the divine without abandoning the human and becomes spiritual while remaining also carnal; but they do not find this in Plato. If they read it into him, this is because they are living, like ourselves, in the tradition which began in the eleventh century.

Perhaps the most characteristic of the ancient writers on love, and certainly the most influential in the Middle Ages, is Ovid. In the piping times of the early empire—when Julia was still unbanished and the dark figure of Tiberius had not yet crossed the stage—Ovid sat down to compose for the amusement of a society which well understood him an ironically didactic poem on the art of seduction. The very design of his *Art of Love* presupposes an audience to whom love is one of the minor peccadilloes of life, and the joke consists in treating it seriously—in writing a treatise, with rules and examples *en règle* for the nice conduct of illicit loves. It is funny, as the ritual solemnity of old gentlemen over their wine is funny. Food, drink, and sex are the oldest jokes in the world; and one familiar form of the joke is to be very serious about them. . . .

The fall of the old civilization and the coming of Christianity did not result in any deepening or idealizing of the conception of love. The fact is important, because it refutes two theories which trace the great change in our sentiments respectively to the Germanic temperament and to the Christian religion—especially to the cult of the Blessed Virgin. The latter view touches on a real and very complex relationship; but as its true nature will become apparent in what follows, I will here content myself with a brief and dogmatic statement. That Christianity in a very general sense, by its insistence on compassion and on the sanctity of the human body, had a tendency to soften or abash the more extreme brutalities and flippancies of the ancient world in all departments of human life, and therefore also in sexual matters, may be taken as obvious. But there is no evidence that the quasi-religious tone of medieval love poetry has been transferred from the worship of the Blessed Virgin: it is just as likely—it is even more likely—that the colouring of certain hymns to the Virgin has been borrowed from the love poetry. Nor is it true in any unequivocal sense that the medieval church encouraged reverence for women at all: while it is a ludicrous error (as we shall presently see) to suppose that she regarded sexual passion, under any conditions or after any possible process of refinement, as a noble emotion. The other theory turns on a supposedly innate characteristic in the Germanic races, noted by Tacitus. But what Tacitus describes is a primitive awe of women as uncanny and probably prophetic beings, which is as remote from our comprehension as the primitive reverence for lunacy or the primitive horror of twins; and because it is thus remote, we cannot judge how probably it might have developed into the medieval *Frauendienst*, the service of ladies. What is certain is that where a Germanic race reached its maturity untouched by the Latin spirit, as in Iceland, we find nothing at all like courtly love. The position of women in the Sagas is, indeed, higher than that which they enjoy in classical literature; but it is based on a purely commonsensible and unemphasized respect for the courage or prudence which some women, like some men, happen to possess. The Norsemen, in fact, treat their women not primarily as women but as people. It is an attitude which may lead in the fullness of time to an equal franchise or a Married Women's Property Act, but it has very little to do with romantic love. The final answer to both theories, however, lies in the fact that the Christian and Germanic period had existed for several centuries before the new feeling appeared. "Love," in our sense of the word, is as absent from the literature of the Dark Ages as from that of classical antiquity. Their favourite stories were not, like ours, stories of how a man married, or failed to marry, a woman. They preferred to hear how a holy man went to heaven or how a brave man went to battle. We are mistaken if we think that the poet in the Song of Roland shows restraint in disposing so briefly of Alde, Roland's betrothed. Rather by bringing her in at all, he is doing the opposite: he is expatiating, filling up chinks, dragging in for our delectation the most marginal interests after those of primary importance have had their due. Roland does not think about Alde on the battle-field: he thinks of his praise in pleasant France. The figure of the betrothed is shadowy compared with that of the friend, Oliver. The deepest of worldly emotions in this period is the love of man for man, the mutual love of warriors who die together fighting against odds, and the affection between vassal and lord. . . . Germanic and Celtic legend, no doubt, had bequeathed to the barbarians some stories of tragic love between man and woman—love "star-crossed" and closely analogous to that of Dido or Phaedra. But the theme claims no preeminence, and when it is treated the interest turns at least as much on the resulting male tragedy, the disturbance of vassalage or sworn brotherhood, as on the female influence which produced it. Ovid, too, was known to the learned; and there was a plentiful literature on sexual irregularities for the use of confessors. Of romance, of reverence for women, of the idealizing imagination exercised about sex, there is hardly a hint. The centre of gravity is elsewhere—in the hopes and fears of religion, or in the clean and happy fidelities of the feudal hall. But, as we have seen, these male affections—though wholly free from the taint that hangs about "friendship" in the ancient world—were themselves lover-like; in their intensity, their wilful exclusion of other values, and their uncertainty, they provided an exercise of the spirit not wholly unlike that which later ages have found in "love." The fact is, of course, significant. Like the formula "Ovid misunderstood," it is inadequate to explain the appearance of the new sentiment; but it goes far to explain why that sentiment, having appeared, should make haste to become a "feudalization" of love. What is new usually wins its way by disguising itself as the old.

The new thing itself, I do not pretend to explain. Real changes in human sentiment are very rare—there are perhaps three or four on record—but I believe that they occur, and that this is one of them. I am not sure that they have "causes," if by a cause we mean something which would wholly account for the new state of affairs, and so explain away what seemed its novelty. It is, at any rate, certain that the efforts of scholars have so far failed to find an origin for the content of Provencal love poetry. Celtic, Byzantine, and even Arabic influence have been suspected; but it has not been made clear that these, if granted, could account for the results we see. A more promising theory attempts to trace the whole thing to Ovid; but this view— apart from the inadequacy which I suggested above—finds itself with the fatal difficulty that the evidence points to a much stronger Ovidian influence in the north of France than in the south. Something can be extracted from a study of the social conditions in which the new poetry arose, but not so much as we might hope. We know that the crusading armies thought the Provencals milk-sops, but this will seem relevant only to a very hardened enemy of *Frauendienst*. We know that this period in the south of France had witnessed what seemed to contemporaries a signal degeneracy from the simplicity of ancient manners and an alarming increase of luxury. But what age, what land, by the same testimony, has not? Much more important is the fact that landless knighthood—knighthood without a place in the territorial hierarchy of feudalism—seems to have been possible in Provence. The unattached knight, as we meet him in the romances, respectable only by his own valour, amiable only by his own courtesy, predestined lover of other mens' wives, was therefore a reality; but this does not explain why he loved in such a new way. If courtly love necessitates adultery, adultery hardly necessitates courtly love. We come much nearer to the secret if we can accept the picture of a typical Provencal court drawn many years ago by an English writer, and since approved by the greatest living authority on the subject. We must picture a castle which is a little island of comparative leisure and luxury, and therefore at least of possible refinement, in a barbarous country-side. There are many men in it, and very few women—the lady, and her damsels. Around these throng the whole male *meiny,* the inferior nobles, the landless knights, the squires, and the pages—haughty creatures enough in relation to the peasantry beyond the wall, but feudally inferior to the lady as to her lord—her "men" as feudal language had it. Whatever "courtesy" is in the place flows from her: all female charm from her and her damsels. There is no question of marriage for most of the court. All these circumstances together come very near to being a "cause"; but they do not explain why very similar conditions elsewhere had to wait for Provencal example before they produced like results. Some part of the mystery remains inviolate.

20. Fast, Feast, and Flesh: The Religious Significance of Food to Medieval Women

CAROLINE WALKER BYNUM

In reading the lives of the [ancients] our lukewarm blood curdles at the thought of their austerities, but we remain strangely unimpressed by the essential point, namely, their determination to do God's will in all things, painful or pleasant.

—Henry Suso
German mystic of the fourteenth century

Strange to say, the ability to live on the eucharist and to resist starvation by diabolical power died out in the Middle Ages and was replaced by "fasting girls" who still continue to amuse us with their vagaries.

—William Hammond
Nineteenth-century American physician and founder
of the New York Neurological Society

Scholars have recently devoted much attention to the spirituality of the thirteenth, fourteenth, and fifteenth centuries. In studying late medieval spirituality they have concentrated on the ideals of chastity and poverty—that is, on the renunciation, for religious reasons, of sex and family, money and property. It may be, however, that modern scholarship has focused so tenaciously on sex and money because sex and money are such crucial symbols and sources of power in our own culture. Whatever the motives, modern scholars have ignored a religious symbol that had tremendous force in the lives of medieval Christians. They have ignored the religious significance of food. Yet, when we look at what medieval people themselves wrote,

From Caroline Walker Bynum, "Fast, Feast, and Flesh: The Religious Significance of Food to Medieval Women," © 1985 by the Regents of the University of California. Reprinted from *Representations*, Vol. 11 (Summer 1985), pp. 1–6, 8–16.

we find that they often spoke of gluttony as the major form of lust, of fasting as the most painful renunciation, and of eating as the most basic and literal way of encountering God. Theologians and spiritual directors from the early church to the sixteenth century reminded penitents that sin had entered the world when Eve ate the forbidden fruit and that salvation comes when Christians eat their God in the ritual of the communion table.

In the Europe of the late thirteenth and fourteenth centuries, famine was on the increase again, after several centuries of agricultural growth and relative plenty. Vicious stories of food hoarding, of cannibalism, of infanticide, or of ill adolescents left to die when they could no longer do agricultural labor sometimes survive in the sources, suggesting a world in which hunger and even starvation were not uncommon experiences. The possibility of overeating and of giving away food to the unfortunate was a mark of privilege, of aristocratic or patrician status—a particularly visible form of what we call conspicuous consumption, what medieval people called magnanimity or largesse. Small wonder then that gorging and vomiting, luxuriating in food until food and body were almost synonymous, became in folk literature an image of unbridled sensual pleasure; that magic vessels which forever brim over with food and drink were staples of European folktales; that one of the most common charities enjoined on religious orders was to feed the poor and ill; or that sharing one's own meager food with a stranger (who might turn out to be an angel, a fairy, or Christ himself) was, in hagiography and folk story alike, a standard indication of heroic or saintly generosity. Small wonder too that voluntary starvation, deliberate and extreme renunciation of food and drink, seemed to medieval people the most basic asceticism, requiring the kind of courage and holy foolishness that marked the saints.

Food was not only a fundamental material concern to medieval people; food practices—fasting and feasting—were at the very heart of the Christian tradition. A Christian in the thirteenth and fourteenth centuries was required by church law to fast on certain days and to receive communion at least once a year. Thus the behavior that defined a Christian was food-related behavior. This point is clearly illustrated in a twelfth-century story of a young man (of the house of Ardres) who returned from the crusades claiming that he had become a Saracen in the East; he was, however, accepted back by his family, and no one paid much attention to his claim until he insisted on eating meat on Friday. The full impact of his apostasy was then brought home, and his family kicked him out.

Food was, moreover, a central metaphor and symbol in Christian poetry, devotional literature, and theology because a meal (the eucharist) was the central Christian ritual, the most direct way of encountering God. And we should note that this meal was a frugal repast, not a banquet but simply the two basic foodstuffs of the Mediterranean world: bread and wine. Although older Mediterranean traditions of religious feasting did come, in a peripheral way, into Christianity, indeed lasting right through the Middle Ages in various kinds of carnival, the central religious meal was reception of the two basic supports of human life. Indeed Christians believed it *was* human life. Already hundreds of years before transubstantiation was defined as doctrine, most Christians thought that they quite literally ate Christ's body and blood in the sacrament. Medieval people themselves knew how strange this all might sound. A fourteenth-century preacher, Johann Tauler, wrote:

St. Bernard compared this sacrament [the eucharist] with the human processes of eating when he used the similes of chewing, swallowing, assimilation and digestion. To some people this will seem crude, but let such refined persons beware of pride, which comes from the devil: a humble spirit will not take offense at simple things.

Thus food, as practice and as symbol, was crucial in medieval spirituality. But in the period from 1200 to 1500 it was more prominent in the piety of women than in that of men. Although it is difficult and risky to make any quantitative arguments about the Middle Ages, so much work has been done on saints' lives, miracle stories, and vision literature that certain conclusions are possible about the relative popularity of various practices and symbols. Recent work by André Vauchez, Richard Kieckhefer, Donald Weinstein, and Rudolph M. Bell demonstrates that, although women were only about 18 percent of those canonized or revered as saints between 1000 and 1700, they were 30 percent of those in whose lives extreme austerities were a central aspect of holiness and over 50 percent of those in whose lives illness (often brought on by fasting and other penitential practices) was the major factor in reputation for sanctity. In addition, Vauchez has shown that most males who were revered for fasting fit into one model of sanctity—the hermit saint (usually a layman)— and this was hardly the most popular male model, whereas fasting characterized female saints generally. Between late antiquity and the fifteenth century there are at least thirty cases of women who were reputed to eat nothing at all except the eucharist, but I have been able to find only one or possibly two male examples of such behavior before the well-publicized fifteenth-century case of the hermit Nicholas of Flüe. Moreover, miracles in which food is miraculously multiplied are told at least as frequently of women as of men, and giving away food is so common a theme in the lives of holy women that it is very difficult to find a story in which this particular charitable activity does not occur. The story of a woman's basket of bread for the poor turning into roses when her husband (or father) protests her almsgiving was attached by hagiographers to at least five different women saints.

If we look specifically at practices connected with Christianity's holy meal, we find that eucharistic visions and miracles occurred far more frequently to women, particularly certain types of miracles in which the quality of the eucharist as food is underlined. It is far more common, for example, for the wafer to turn into honey or meat in the mouth of a woman. Miracles in which an unconsecrated host is vomited out or in which the recipient can tell by tasting the wafer that the priest who consecrated it is immoral happen almost exclusively to women. Of fifty-five people from the later Middle Ages who supposedly received the holy food directly from Christ's hand in a vision, forty-five are women. In contrast, the only two types of eucharistic miracle that occur primarily to men are miracles that underline not the fact that the wafer is food but the power of the priest. Moreover, when we study medieval miracles, we note that miraculous abstinence and extravagant eucharistic visions tend to occur together and are frequently accompanied by miraculous bodily changes. Such changes are found almost exclusively in women. Miraculous elongation of parts of the body, the appearance on the body of marks imitating the various wounds of Christ (called stigmata), and the exuding of wondrous fluids (which smell sweet and heal and sometimes *are* food—for example, manna or milk) are usually female miracles.

If we consider a different kind of evidence—the *exempla* or moral tales that preachers used to educate their audiences, both monastic and lay—we find that, according to Frederic Tubach's index, only about 10 percent of such stories are about women. But when we look at those stories that treat specifically fasting, abstinence, and reception of the eucharist, 30 to 50 percent are about women. The only type of religious literature in which food is more frequently associated with men is the genre of satires on monastic life, in which there is some suggestion that monks are more prone to greed. But this pattern probably reflects the fact that monasteries for men were in general wealthier than women's houses and therefore more capable of mounting elaborate banquets and tempting palates with delicacies.

Taken together, this evidence demonstrates two things. First, food practices were more central in women's piety than in men's. Second, both men and women associated food—especially fasting and the eucharist—with women. There are, however, a number of problems with this sort of evidence. In addition to the obvious problems of the paucity of material and of the nature of hagiographical accounts—problems to which scholars since the seventeenth century have devoted much sophisticated discussion—there is the problem inherent in quantifying data. In order to count phenomena the historian must divide them up, put them into categories. Yet the most telling argument for the prominence of food in women's spirituality is the way in which food motifs interweave in women's lives and writings until even phenomena not normally thought of as eating, feeding, or fasting seem to become food-related. In other words, food becomes such a pervasive concern that it provides both a literary and a psychological unity to the woman's way of seeing the world. And this cannot be demonstrated by statistics. Let me therefore tell in some detail one of the many stories from the later Middle Ages in which food becomes a leitmotif of stunning complexity and power. It is the story of Lidwina of the town of Schiedam in the Netherlands, who died in 1433 at the age of 53.

Several hagiographical accounts of Lidwina exist, incorporating information provided by her confessors; moreover, the town officials of Schiedam, who had her watched for three months, promulgated a testimonial that suggests that Lidwina's miraculous abstinence attracted more public attention than any other aspect of her life. The document solemnly attests to her complete lack of food and sleep and to the sweet odor given off by the bits of skin she supposedly shed.

The accounts of Lidwina's life suggest that there may have been early conflict between mother and daughter. When her terrible illness put a burden on her family's resources and patience, it took a miracle to convince her mother of her sanctity. One of the few incidents that survives from her childhood shows her mother annoyed with her childish dawdling. Lidwina was required to carry food to her brothers at school, and on the way home she slipped into church to say a prayer to the Virgin. The incident shows how girlish piety could provide a respite from household tasks—in this case, as in so many cases, the task of feeding men. We also learn that Lidwina was upset to discover that she was pretty, that she threatened to pray for a deformity when plans were broached for her marriage, and that, after an illness at age fifteen, she grew weak and did not want to get up from her sickbed. The accounts thus suggest that she may have been cultivating illness—perhaps even rejecting food—before the skating accident some weeks later that produced severe internal injuries. In any event, Lidwina never recovered from her fall on the ice. Her hagiographers report that she was paralyzed except for her left hand. She burned with fever and vomited convulsively. Her body putrified so that great pieces fell off. From mouth, ears, and nose, she poured blood. And she stopped eating.

Lidwina's hagiographers go into considerable detail about her abstinence. At first she supposedly ate a little piece of apple each day, although bread dipped into liquid caused her much pain. Then she reduced her intake to a bit of date and watered wine flavored with spices and sugar; later she survived on watered wine alone—only half a pint a week—and she preferred it when the water came from the river and was contaminated with salt from the tides. When she ceased to take any solid food, she also ceased to sleep. And finally she ceased to swallow anything at all. Although Lidwina's biographers present her abstinence as evidence of saintliness, she was suspected by some during her lifetime of being possessed by a devil instead; she herself appears to have claimed that her fasting was natural. When people accused her of hypocrisy, she replied that it is no sin to eat and therefore no glory to be incapable of eating.

Fasting and illness were thus a single phenomenon to Lidwina. And since she perceived them as redemptive suffering, she urged both on others. We are told that a certain Gerard from Cologne, at her urging, became a hermit and lived in a tree, fed only on manna sent from God. We are also told that Lidwina prayed for her twelve-year-old nephew to be afflicted with an illness so that he would be reminded of God's mercy. Not surprisingly, the illness itself then came from miraculous feeding. The nephew became sick by drinking several drops from a pitcher of unnaturally sweet beer on a table by Lidwina's bedside.

Like the bodies of many other women saints, Lidwina's body was closed to ordinary intake and excreting but produced extraordinary effluvia. The authenticating document from the town officials of Schiedam testifies that her body shed skin, bones, and even portions of intestines, which her parents kept in a vase; and these gave off a sweet odor until Lidwina, worried by the gossip that they excited, insisted that her mother bury them. Moreover, Lidwina's effluvia cured others. A man in England sent for her wash water to cure his ill leg. The sweet smell from her left hand led one of her confessors to confess his own sins. And Lidwina actually nursed others in an act that she herself explicitly saw as a parallel to the Virgin's nursing of Christ.

• • •

Lidwina did not write herself, but some pious women did. And many of these women not only lived lives in which miraculous abstinence, charitable feeding of others, wondrous bodily changes, and eucharistic devotion were central; they also elaborated in prose and poetry a spirituality in which hungering, feeding, and eating were central metaphors for suffering, for service, and for encounter with God. For example, the great Italian theorist of purgatory, Catherine of Genoa (d. 1510)—whose extreme abstinence began in response to an unhappy marriage and who eventually persuaded her husband to join her in a life of continence and charitable feeding of the poor and sick—said that the annihilation of ordinary food by a devouring body is the best metaphor for the annihilation of the soul by God in mystical ecstasy. She also wrote that, although no simile can adequately convey the joy in God that is the goal of all souls, nonetheless the image that comes most readily to mind is to describe God as the only bread available in a world of the starving. Another Italian Catherine, Catherine of Siena (d. 1380), in whose saintly reputation fasting, food miracles, eucharistic devotion, and (invisible) stigmata were central, regularly chose to describe Christian duty as "eating at the table of the cross the food of the honor of God and the salvation of souls." To Catherine, "to eat" and "to hunger" have the same fundamental meaning, for one eats but is never full, desires but is never satiated. "Eating" and "hungering" are active, not passive, images. They stress pain more than joy. They mean most basically to suffer and to serve—to suffer because in hunger one joins with Christ's suffering on the cross; to serve because to hunger is to expiate the sins of the world. Catherine wrote:

And then the soul becomes drunk. And after it . . . has reached the place [of the teaching of the crucified Christ] and drunk to the full, it tastes the food of patience, the odor of virtue, and such a desire to bear the cross that it does not seem that it could ever be satiated. . . . And then the soul becomes like a drunken man; the more he drinks the more he wants to drink; the more it bears the cross the more it wants to bear it. And the pains are its refreshment and the tears which it has shed for the memory of the blood are its drink. And the sighs are its food.

And again:

Dearest mother and sisters in sweet Jesus Christ, I, Catherine, slave of the slaves of Jesus Christ, write to you in his precious blood, with the desire to see you confirmed in true and perfect charity so that you be true nurses of your souls. For we cannot nourish others if first we do not nourish our own souls with true and real virtues. . . . Do as the child does who, wanting to take milk, takes the mother's breast and places it in his mouth and draws to himself the milk by means of the flesh. So . . . we must attach ourselves to the breast of the crucified Christ, in whom we find the mother of charity, and draw from there by means of his flesh (that is, the humanity) the milk that nourishes our soul. . . . For it is Christ's humanity that suffered, not his divinity; and, without suffering, we cannot nourish ourselves with this milk which we draw from charity.

To the stories and writings of Lidwina and the two Catherines—with their insistent and complex food motifs—I could add dozens of others. Among the most obvious examples would be the beguine Mary of Oignies (d. 1213) from the Low Countries, the princess Elisabeth of Hungary (d. 1231), the famous reformer of French and Flemish religious houses Colette of Corbie (d. 1447), and the thirteenth-century poets Hadewijch and Mechtild of Magdeburg. But if we look closely at the lives and writings of those men from the period whose spirituality is in general closest to women's and who were deeply influenced by women—for example, Francis of Assisi in Italy, Henry Suso and Johann Tauler in the Rhineland, Jan van Ruysbroeck of Flanders, or the English hermit Richard Rolle—we find that even to these men food asceticism is not the central ascetic practice. Nor are food metaphors central in their poetry and prose. Food then is much more important to women than to men as a religious symbol. The question is why?

Modern scholars who have noticed the phenomena I have just described have sometimes suggested in an offhand way that miraculous abstinence and eucharistic frenzy are simply "eating disorders." The implication of such remarks is usually that food disorders are characteristic of women rather than men, perhaps for biological reasons, and that these medieval eating disorders are different from nineteenth-and twentieth-century ones only because medieval people "theologized" what we today "medicalize." While I cannot deal here with all the implications of such analysis, I want to point to two problems with it. First, the evidence we have indicates that extended abstinence was almost exclusively a male phenomenon in early Christianity and a female phenomenon in the high Middle Ages. The cause of such a distribution of cases cannot be primarily biological. Second, medieval people did not treat all refusal to eat as a sign of holiness. They sometimes treated it as demonic possession, but they sometimes also treated it as illness. Interestingly enough, some of the holy women whose fasting was taken as miraculous (for example, Colette of Corbie) functioned as healers of ordinary individuals, both male and female, who could not eat. Thus, for most of the Middle Ages, it was only in the case of some unusually devout women that not-eating was both supposedly total and religiously significant. Such behavior must have a cultural explanation.

On one level, the cultural explanation is obvious. Food was important to women religiously because it was important socially. In medieval Europe (as in many countries today) women were associated with food preparation and distribution *rather than* food consumption. The culture suggested that women cook and serve, men eat. Chronicle accounts of medieval banquets, for example, indicate that the sexes were often segregated and that women were sometimes relegated to watching from the balconies while gorgeous foods were rolled out to please the eyes as well as the palates of men. Indeed men were rather afraid of women's control of food. Canon lawyers suggested, in the codes they drew up, that a major danger posed by women was their manipulation of male virility by charms and potions added to food. Moreover, food was not merely *a* resource women controlled; it was *the* resource women controlled. Economic resources were controlled by husbands, fathers, uncles, or brothers. In an obvious sense, therefore, fasting and charitable food distribution (and their miraculous counterparts) were natural religious activities for women. In fasting and charity women renounced and distributed the one resource that was theirs. Several scholars have pointed out that late twelfth- and early thirteenth-century women who wished to follow the new ideal of poverty and begging (for example, Clare of Assisi and Mary of Oignies) were simply not permitted either by their families or by religious authorities to do so. They substituted fasting for other ways of stripping the self of support. Indeed a thirteenth-century hagiographer commented explicitly that one holy woman gave up food because she had nothing else to give up. Between the thirteenth and fifteenth centuries, many devout laywomen who resided in the homes of fathers or spouses were able to renounce the world in the midst of abundance because they did not eat or drink the food that was paid for by family wealth. Moreover, women's almsgiving and abstinence appeared culturally acceptable forms of asceticism because what women ordinarily did, as housewives, mothers, or mistresses of great castles, was to prepare and serve food rather than to eat it.

The issue of control is, however, more basic than this analysis suggests. Food-related behavior was central to women socially and religiously not only because food was a resource women controlled but also because, by means of food, women controlled themselves and their world.

First and most obviously, women controlled their bodies by fasting. Although a negative or dualist concept of body does not seem to have been the most fundamental notion of body to either women or men, some sense that body was to be disciplined, defeated, occasionally even destroyed, in order to release or protect spirit is present in women's piety. Some holy women seem to have developed an extravagant fear of any bodily contact. Clare of Montefalco

(d. 1308), for example, said she would rather spend days in hell than be touched by a man. Lutgard of Aywières panicked at an abbot's insistence on giving her the kiss of peace, and Jesus had to interpose his hand in a vision so that she was not reached by the abbot's lips. She even asked to have her own gift of healing by touch taken away. Christina of Stommeln (d. 1312), who fell into a latrine while in a trance, was furious at the laybrothers who rescued her because they touched her in order to do so.

Many women were profoundly fearful of the sensations of their bodies, especially hunger and thirst. Mary of Oignies, for example, was so afraid of taking pleasure in food that Christ had to make her unable to taste. From the late twelfth century comes a sad story of a dreadfully sick girl named Alpaïs who sent away the few morsels of pork given her to suck, because she feared that any enjoyment of eating might mushroom madly into gluttony or lust. Women like Ida of Louvain (d. perhaps 1300), Elsbeth Achler of Reute (d. 1420), Catherine of Genoa, or Columba of Rieti (d. 1501), who sometimes snatched up food and ate without knowing what they were doing, focused their hunger on the eucharist partly because it was an acceptable object of craving and partly because it was a self-limiting food. Some of women's asceticism was clearly directed toward destroying bodily needs, before which women felt vulnerable.

Some fasting may have had as a goal other sorts of bodily control. There is some suggestion in the accounts of hagiographers that fasting women were admired for suppressing excretory functions. Several biographers comment with approval that holy women who do not eat cease also to excrete, and several point out explicitly that the menstruation of saintly women ceases. Medieval theology—profoundly ambivalent about body as physicality—was ambivalent about menstruation also, seeing it both as the polluting "curse of Eve" and as a natural function that, like all natural functions, was redeemed in the humanity of Christ. Theologians even debated whether or not the Virgin Mary menstruated. But natural philosophers and theologians were aware that, in fact, fasting suppresses menstruation. Albert the Great noted that some holy women ceased to menstruate because of their fasts and austerities and commented that their health did not appear to suffer as a consequence.

Moreover, in controlling eating and hunger, medieval women were also explicitly controlling sexuality. Ever since Tertullian and Jerome, male writers had warned religious women that food was dangerous because it excited lust. Although there is reason to suspect that male biographers exaggerated women's sexual temptations, some women themselves connected food abstinence with chastity and greed with sexual desire.

Women's heightened reaction to food, however, controlled far more than their physicality. It also controlled their social environment. As the story of Lidwina of Schiedam makes clear, women often coerced both families and religious authorities through fasting and through feeding. To an aristocratic or rising merchant family of late medieval Europe, the self-starvation of a daughter or spouse could be deeply perplexing and humiliating. It could therefore be an effective means of manipulating, educating, or converting family members. In one of the most charming passages of Margery Kempe's autobiography, for example, Christ and Margery consult together about her asceticism and decide that, although she wishes to practice both food abstention and sexual continence, she should perhaps offer to trade one behavior for the other. Her husband, who had married Margery in an effort to rise socially in the town of Lynn and who was obviously ashamed of her queer penitential clothes and food practices, finally agreed to grant her sexual abstinence in private if she would return to normal cooking and eating in front of the neighbors. Catherine of Siena's sister, Bonaventura, and the Italian saint Rita of Cascia (d. 1456) both reacted to profligate young husbands by wasting away and managed thereby to tame disorderly male behavior. Columba of Rieti and Catherine of Siena expressed what was clearly adolescent conflict with their mothers and riveted family attention on their every move by their refusal to eat. Since fasting so successfully manipulated and embarrassed families, it is not surprising that self-starvation often originated or escalated at puberty, the moment at which families usually began negotiations for husbands for their daughters. Both Catherine and Columba, for example, established themselves as unpromising marital material by their extreme food and sleep deprivation, their frenetic giving away of paternal resources, and their compulsive service of family members in what were not necessarily welcome ways. (Catherine insisted on doing the family laundry in the middle of the night.)

Fasting was not only a useful weapon in the battle of adolescent girls to change their families' plans for them. It also provided for both wives and daughters an excuse for neglecting food preparation and family responsibilities. Dorothy of Montau, for example, made elementary mistakes of cookery (like forgetting to scale the fish before frying them) or forgot entirely to cook and shop while she was in ecstasy. Margaret of Cortona refused to cook for her illegitimate son (about whom she felt agonizing ambivalence) because, she said, it would distract her from prayer.

Moreover, women clearly both influenced and rejected their families' values by food distribution. Ida of Louvain, Catherine of Siena, and Elisabeth of Hungary, each in her own way, expressed distaste for family wealth and coopted the entire household into Christian charity by giving away family resources, sometimes surreptitiously or even at night. Elisabeth, who gave away her husband's property, refused to eat any food except that paid for by her own dowry because the wealth of her husband's family came, she said, from exploiting the poor.

Food-related behavior—charity, fasting, eucharistic devotion, and miracles—manipulated religious authorities as well. Women's eucharistic miracles—especially the ability to identify unconsecrated hosts or unchaste priests—functioned to expose and castigate clerical corruption. The Viennese woman Agnes Blannbekin, knowing that her priest was not chaste, prayed that he be deprived of the host, which then flew away from him and into her own mouth. Margaret of Cortona saw the hands of an unchaste priest turn black when he held the host. Saints' lives and chronicles contain many stories, like that told of Lidwina of Schiedam, of women who vomited out unconsecrated wafers, sometimes to the considerable discomfiture of local authorities.

The intimate and direct relationship that holy women claimed to the eucharist was often a way of bypassing ecclesiastical control. Late medieval confessors and theologians attempted to inculcate awe as well as craving for the eucharist; and women not only received ambiguous advice about frequent communion, they were also sometimes barred from receiving it at exactly the point at which their fasting and hunger reached fever pitch. In such circumstances many women simply received in vision what the celebrant or confessor withheld. Imelda Lambertini, denied communion because she was too young, and Ida of Léau, denied because she was subject to "fits," were given the host by Christ. And some women received, again in visions, either Christ's blood, which they were regularly denied because of their lay status, or the power to consecrate and distribute, which they were denied because of their gender. Angela of Foligno and Mechtild of Hackeborn were each, in a vision, given the chalice to distribute. Catherine of Siena received blood in her mouth when she ate the wafer.

It is thus apparent that women's concentration on food enabled them to control and manipulate both their bodies and their environment. We must not underestimate the effectiveness of such manipulation in a world where it was often extraordinarily difficult for women to avoid marriage or to choose a religious vocation. But such a conclusion concentrates on the function of fasting and feasting, and function is not meaning. Food did not "mean" to medieval women the control it provided. It is time, finally, to consider explicitly what it meant.

As the behavior of Lidwina of Schiedam or the theological insights of Catherine of Siena suggest, fasting, eating, and feeding all meant suffering, and suffering meant redemption. These complex meanings were embedded in and engendered by the theological doctrine of the Incarnation. Late medieval theology, as is well known, located the saving moment of Christian history less in Christ's resurrection than in his crucifixion. Although some ambivalence about physicality, some sharp and agonized dualism, was present, no other period in the history of Christian spirituality has placed so positive a value on Christ's humanity as physicality. Fasting was thus flight not so much *from* as *into* physicality. Communion was consuming—i.e., becoming—a God who saved the world through physical, human agony. Food to medieval women meant flesh and suffering and, through suffering, salvation: salvation of self and salvation of neighbor. Although all thirteenth and fourteenth-century Christians emphasized Christ as suffering and Christ's suffering body as food, women were especially drawn to such a devotional emphasis. The reason seems to lie in the way in which late medieval culture understood "the female."

Drawing on traditions that went back even before the origins of Christianity, both men and women in the later Middle Ages argued that "woman is to man as matter is to spirit." Thus "woman" or "the feminine" was seen as symbolizing the physical part of human nature, whereas man symbolized the spiritual or rational. Male theologians and biographers of women frequently used this idea to comment on female weakness. They also inverted the image and saw "woman" as not merely below but also above reason. Thus they somewhat sentimentally saw Mary's love for souls and her mercy toward even the wicked as an apotheosis of female unreason and weakness, and they frequently used female images to describe themselves in their dependence on God. Women writers, equally aware of the male/female dichotomy, saw it somewhat differently. They tended to use the notion of "the female" as "flesh" to associate Christ's humanity with "the female" and therefore to suggest that women imitate Christ through physicality.

Women theologians saw "woman" as the symbol of humanity, where humanity was understood as including bodiliness. To the twelfth-century prophet, Elisabeth of Schönau, the humanity of Christ appeared in a vision as a female virgin. To Hildegard of Bingen (d. 1179), "woman" was the symbol of humankind, fallen in Eve, restored in Mary and church. She stated explicitly: "Man signifies the divinity of the Son of God and woman his humanity." Moreover, to a number of women writers, Mary was the source and container of Christ's physicality; the flesh Christ put on was in some sense female, because it was his mother's. Indeed whatever physio-logical theory of reproduction a medieval theologian held, Christ (who had no human father) had to be seen as taking his physicality from his mother. Mechtild of Magdeburg went further and implied that Mary was a kind of preexistent humanity of Christ as the Logos was his preexistent divinity. Marguerite of Oingt, like Hildegard of Bingen, wrote that Mary was the *tunica humanitatis,* the clothing of humanity, that Christ puts on. And to Julian of Norwich, God himself was a mother exactly in that our humanity in its full physicality was not merely loved and saved but even given being by and from him. Julian wrote:

For in the same time that God joined himself to our body in the maiden's womb, he took our soul, which is sensual, and in taking it, having enclosed us all in himself, he united it to our substance. . . . So our Lady is our mother, in whom we are all enclosed and born of her in Christ, for she who is mother of our saviour is mother of all who are saved in our saviour; and our saviour is our true mother, in whom we are endlessly born and out of whom we shall never come.

Although male writers were apt to see God's motherhood in his nurs-ing and loving rather than in the fact of creation, they too associated the flesh of Christ with Mary and therefore with woman.

Not only did medieval people associate humanity as body with woman; they also associated woman's body with food. Woman was food because breast milk was the human being's first nourishment— the one food essential for survival. Late medieval culture was extraor-dinarily concerned with milk as symbol. Writers and artists were fond of the theme, borrowed from antiquity, of lactation offered to a father or other adult male as an act of filial piety. The cult of the Virgin's milk was one of the most extensive cults in late medieval Europe. A favorite motif in art was the lactating Virgin. Even the bodies of evil women were seen as food. Witches were supposed to have queer marks on their bodies (sort of supernumerary breasts) from which they nursed incubi.

Quite naturally, male and female writers used nursing imagery in somewhat different ways. Men were more likely to use images of being nursed, women metaphors of nursing. Thus when male writers spoke of God's motherhood, they focused more narrowly on the soul being nursed at Christ's breast, whereas women were apt to associate mothering with punishing, educating, or giving birth as well. Most visions of drinking from the breast of Mary were received by men. In contrast, women (like Lidwina) often identified with Mary as she nursed Jesus or received visions of taking the Christchild to their own breasts. Both men and women, however, drank from the breast of Christ, in vision and image. Both men and women wove together—from Pauline references to milk and meat and from the rich breast and food images of the Song of Songs—a complex sense of Christ's blood as the nourishment and intoxication of the soul. Both men and women therefore saw the body on the cross, which in dying fed the world, as in some sense female. Again, physiological theory reinforced image. For, to medieval natural philosophers, breast milk was transmuted blood, and a human mother (like the pelican that also symbolized Christ) fed her children from the fluid of life that coursed through her veins.

Since Christ's body itself was a body that nursed the hungry, both men and women naturally assimilated the ordinary female body to it. A number of stories are told of female saints who exuded holy fluid from breasts or fingertips, either during life or after death. These fluids often cured the sick. The union of mouth to mouth, which many women gained with Christ, became also a way of feeding. Lutgard's saliva cured the ill; Lukardis of Oberweimar (d. 1309) blew the eucharist into another nun's mouth; Colette of Corbie regularly cured others with crumbs she chewed. Indeed one suspects that stigmata—so overwhelmingly a female phenomenon—appeared on women's bodies because they (like the marks on the bodies of witches and the wounds in the body of Christ) were not merely wounds but also breasts.

Thus many assumptions in the theology and the culture of late medieval Europe associated woman with flesh and with food. But the same theology also taught that the redemption of all humanity lay in the fact that Christ was flesh and food. A God who fed his children from his own body, a God whose humanity *was* his children's humanity, was a God with whom women found it easy to identify. In mystical ecstasy as in communion, women ate and became a God who was food and flesh. And in eating a God whose flesh was holy food, women both transcended and became more fully the flesh and the food their own bodies were.

Eucharist and mystical union were, for women, both reversals and continuations of all the culture saw them to be. In one sense, the roles of priest and lay recipient reversed normal social roles. The priest became the food preparer, the generator and server of food. The woman recipient ate a holy food she did not exude or prepare. Woman's jubilant, vision-inducing, inebriated eating of God was the opposite of the ordinary female acts of food preparation or of bearing and nursing children. But in another and, I think, deeper sense, the eating was not a reversal at all. Women became, in mystical eating, a fuller version of the food and the flesh they were assumed by their culture to be. In union with Christ, woman became a fully fleshly and feeding self—at one with the generative suffering of God.

Symbol does not determine behavior. Women's imitation of Christ, their assimilation to the suffering and feeding body on the cross, was not uniform. Although most religious women seem to have understood their devotional practice as in some sense serving as well as suffering, they acted in very different ways. Some, like Catherine of Genoa and Elisabeth of Hungary, expressed their piety in feeding and caring for the poor. Some, like Alpaïs, lay rapt in mystical contemplation as their own bodies decayed in disease or in self-induced starvation that was offered for the salvation of others. Many, like Lidwina of Schiedam and Catherine of Siena, did both. Some of these women are, to our modern eyes, pathological and pathetic. Others seem to us, as they did to their contemporaries, magnificent. But they all dealt, in feast and fast, with certain fundamental realities for which all cultures must find symbols—the realities of suffering and the realities of service and generativity.

21. Peasant Families and Popular Religion

ROBERT FOSSIER

Hearts and Minds

I have referred continually to "man" and "men" as if the population consisted solely of one confused mass or, worse still, of a single sex; but I trust my meaning is clear despite this stylistic device. But now we must look into the seething mass that confronts the medievalist and examine the individual grains of sand. It is couples that then immediately stand out on this broader canvas of individual particles; and I have no hesitation whatsoever in stating that this pattern is clearer in the cottage than the castle and in the country rather than the town.

HEARTH AND HOME
This is the case primarily because the relevant sources refer more frequently than others to the union of the two sexes, whether in property documents, conciliar canons or *fabliaux*. Here male superiority—so distinct in the military and political spheres—appears blurred, and is certainly challenged by woman's control of household management and of food supplies. The castle resounds with the cries of men, the clash of arms and the thud of horses' hooves; in the town the artisan is prominent, merchants and civic officials dominate the stage; in the village the man is in the fields or the woods: everything else is in the woman's hands and it is impossible

From Robert Fossier, "Families and Popular Religion," *Peasant Life in the Medieval West* (Oxford: Basil Blackwell Ltd., 1988), pp. 17–33, 39–43. Reprinted by permission of Basil Blackwell Ltd.

to ignore this fact. One has only to read the *exempla*, collections of model sermons written in the thirteenth century for the use of preachers short of inspiration and the speciality of Dominicans like Etienne de Bourbon: women easily occupy first place, as they do too in *fabliaux*, lyric poetry or *chansons de toile*. The superhuman exploits of Roland or Lancelot appealed only to a tiny masculine audience. And there is an overwhelming preponderance of objects of female use amongst archaeological finds from rural sites. As I have said, it is not until the end of the thirteenth century that our texts provide adequate statistical information and officials or notaries used the terms "hearth" or "household" as if the grouping round the hearth or in the house was the primary unit. These terms have been the subject of heated debate for far too long, with some historians insisting that the domanial or financial official saw individuals only in terms of small household units of certain size. They have advanced theories as to their possible size—all with excellent and incontrovertible supporting evidence but at odds with that provided by other researchers—which has been estimated variously at 3, 3.5, conceivably 4, or (at the other extreme) as much as 6 or 7.

It is inevitable that differences of period, place and social class, and even the context of research, will result in variations and make it futile to search for a universally applicable solution. It is not a case of "asking the wrong question"—the easy way of dropping a tedious subject—but a genuinely insoluble problem. I shall only add one observation (and that a very tentative one) to the general disagreement, that since a number of cases in the thirteenth century suggest that between 25 and 30 per cent of households and individuals were without surviving issue, at least three children were generally required to maintain the population level, in which case the "hearth" of a married couple would consist of at least five individuals—a figure which I hasten to stress is purely hypothetical.

On the other hand, I think it is much more interesting that the official's knowledge went no further than the average unit, although there might have been an elderly widow living alone in one household and a couple with eight children in another. For him, as it should be for us, the primary unit of productivity consisted of those who lived together under one roof (*à feu et à pot*, sharing the same fire and food, as the later saying went) and, if they were man and wife, in *mesnie* or *ménage* (household). Thus it was that the sixteenth century formulated the legal tag, "*manger et dormir ensemble, c'est mariage, ce me semble* (eating and sleeping together constitutes marriage)." We are now very familiar with this definition of marriage, whether defined by the Church at the end of a long period of evolution, or stemming from the accumulation of rites and formulae connected with earlier societies and constituting the *mos patriae,* common practice, which scarcely impinged on the Christian world.

Let us concentrate on essentials. Amongst the aristocracy and the urban patriciate endogamous marriage was necessary to preserve the family's high connections and to keep the estate intact. This was an in-bred union after negotiations of an almost commercial character between the two fathers, to which the children's agreement and mutual affection (*dilectio*) were entirely irrelevant. This concept hardly impinged on the great majority of peasants, who were unaffected both by the young people's feelings and by any fear of incest. (In the period before 1215 the Church had gone so far as to forbid unions of the seventh degree, that is between the descendants of four successive generations.) It was in fact precisely in rural society that endogamy (marriage within the confines of the extended family), with its attendant risks of illegal incest, was most likely to occur: the serfs did not have the resources to pay a tax for the privilege of finding a wife outside their lord's domain (a practice known as *formariage*) and the isolated populations of mountains, islands or newly reclaimed regions undoubtedly resorted to marrying their cousins. In about 1170 Pope Alexander III realized that these prohibitions were in fact encouraging concubinage and adultery; his successors at the Fourth Lateran Council agreed to annul them. Again, it might sometimes be in the interests of two well-off peasant families to conclude a formal alliance by means of a marriage of convenience, decided upon by its older and wiser members; the brilliance of peasant weddings has not yet been completely dulled and these occasions are perhaps a mute echo of the celebrations open to all-comers at which each family tried to outdo the other in munificence.

Nevertheless, I believe that in the great majority of cases, rural marriage was a much simpler affair: mutual attraction, with close relations doubtless keeping an eye on the courtship to ensure there was no disaster in material or moral terms. In other words both *dilectio* and *consensus* (affection and consent) were present. The ceremony itself required witnesses, possibly a notary in the south, the exchange of promises, followed by the exchange of rings and gifts—a relic of the protohistoric custom of mutual gift-giving. The intervention of a priest (which seems to have become standard after 1275 or 1300) made no real difference, for the Church admitted that it was the exchange of promises and not the blessing by the priest which constituted the sacrament accepted by the two spouses. This kind of union was generally accompanied by village festivities—a meal, dancing and bawdy entertainments, even true *saturnalia* in the form of the *charivari,* when the local youth disapproved of the match. But the material aspect should not be neglected, for the country dwellers did not need to realize that they were following the precepts of Justinian's *Novella* (of which they had never heard) in order to appreciate the contractual aspect of the *mise en ménage* (setting up home), a term still sometimes used in French. In the ordinary course of events marriage was preceded by *sponsalia,* incorrectly rendered *épousailles* (espousal) in modern French, whereas this was in fact a formal agreement which involved the reciprocal settlement of revenue, the dowry brought by the girl on the one hand and the gift on the occasion of the wedding which the husband agreed his wife should have from his goods on the other. This was called the *donatio propter nuptias, sponsalium* or *maritagium* and might vary from a third to a tenth of their total value. This *douaire* (dower), as it was later called, was essentially a guarantee of income for the woman in the event of widowhood, while the dowry, or what remained of it, returned to the wife's family should she die before her husband.

THE "JOYS OF MARRIAGE"

Legal terminology still held sway even when the parties present understood no Latin at all and it brings us face-to-face with peasant life for a married couple. We should be sceptical—as those rural households undoubtedly were—of homilies exhorting chastity, continence and moderation, not to mention virginity. Sexual relations, the *copula carnalis* of the lawyers, were the inevitable corollary of cohabitation. Nevertheless, before attempting any scrutiny of an essentially private subject, a few preliminary remarks about differences from twentieth-century practices are in order.

First of all, it would only be at a fairly late date, in my estimation, that the couple would have a room of their own inside a peasant house and that the matrimonial bed replaced collective sleeping arrangements. In other words (and without dwelling on the temptations and satisfactions which are the same whatever the period and whose details are irrelevant to our present subject) the intimacy between man and wife bore no resemblance to that of our own time. But more than the practical arrangements of married life, the moral climate differed from our own. Perhaps less forcibly than the artisan living in the town, where everything was expensive, or the noble who had to wait for his inheritance before he might seek a wife, the peasant had nevertheless to experience the same enforced delay in marriage whose causes and effects were both of fundamental importance. When the girl was of marriageable age, perhaps about 15 years old, she was put on the marriage market, while a boy had to wait, employed as his older brother's stable-hand until he had an "estate," that is the wherewithal to provide a dower for the girl he wanted to marry; he could of course look for a rich widow, but at the risk of a *charivari* that would ridicule and humiliate him; or he could borrow or hire himself out. The man was generally at least 25 or 27 years old when he took to wife a girl of 16. During the period before his marriage it is unlikely that he paid much attention to clerical exhortations and probably sought sexual satisfaction either in ancillary concubinage, which is well documented, or in prostitution, of which by contrast virtually nothing is known in the countryside apart from the reference of St. Bernard in the mid-twelfth century to the "women of ill repute" offering their services to young men waiting their turn outside the miller's door, which suggests a traditional commerce that was inevitably tolerated.

The essential problem, but one so distant and so elusive, is that of emotional attachment. What did this man in his thirties, labouring in the fields, expect on his return from a 20-year old wife, almost constantly pregnant, whose place was at home with the children she had borne? His authority was inevitably brutal because it could be exerted only occasionally; he was happy that they no longer lived *sub iugo patris,* that is in the house of an older relative and under his sway. There has been much interest in the role played from the twelfth century onwards by wet nurses, women whose still-born children left them with milk with which they could suckle others'. Historians have detected in this practice a conscious wish to increase the birth-rate, since, as the paid wet nurse suckled the baby, the mother's own lactation soon ceased and she could become pregnant again more quickly. Whatever the case, there is little evidence of such practices in the country: all the iconographical evidence tends to show the peasant woman with a child at her breast. But in terms of the effect on society, the result was identical: by very lengthy breast-feeding (18 months, or even 22 for boys) the woman was able to space out her pregnancies, but they continued without a break, nonetheless, binding her to motherhood throughout most of her young life. When the surplus of women in the population after 1160 or 1170 caused the Church to look more favourably on second marriages, with the supposed aim of protecting the attractive young widow from the lust of young men in search of adventure, even this condition no longer procured her freedom.

What conclusions should we draw? That deprived of the distractions of the courtly life and knowing nothing of the contraceptives of which a townswoman might avail herself, the peasant woman was bound to a considerably older spouse, constantly preoccupied with the provision of food for husband and children and could not have experienced any of the "fifteen joys" of marriage listed in the fourteenth-century satire? How are we to pierce the thick veil of fabliaux, where the husband is held up to ridicule, and reconcile sermons, in which the wife is all but a martyr, with legal texts multiplying her legal rights with remarkable emphasis? Perhaps simply by drawing attention to various scattered observations, which underline the same trend: the number of documents in which the husband who has had to make inroads into the woman's dower takes pains to re-endow her with lands elsewhere (in the presence of a notary in Italy), providing a good income and concerning which action is taken *similiter et insimul,* as equals and together; the cemeteries where, with none of the effigies of the noble classes, the bodies lie close together; and the terms of endearment which husbands lavish in wills upon their future widows. And even in our society, which is based upon an approximate equality of age between spouses, there are occasional marriages between a young girl and a man in his fifties whose feelings are sometimes more than usually passionate. Why then should we deny to these people the possibility of an intense love for one another even when the match was arranged by their fathers? It is easy to overlook the brief duration of the union which may have made the flame burn more brightly: their marriage would probably last between eight and, at the very most, 20 years, terminated by the premature death of the husband, or of the wife, worn out by difficult pregnancies.

Literary evidence for the life of a peasant couple is too often of urban origin to carry much weight. But there are *pastourelles,* short pieces written in the thirteenth century for singing and dancing, a form sometimes adopted by authors famous for other works such as the poet-minstrel from Arras Adam de la Halle (*fl.* 1250–87) or his prolific contemporary Rutebeuf. These were very traditional compositions generally intended for an exclusively noble audience in which a knight makes advances to a shepherdess, who either rejects or accepts them. But behind the very generalized canvas of so much of Adam de la Halle's *Robin et Marion* (composed for the soldiers of Count Robert II of Artois campaigning in southern Italy) a picture of love in the country does emerge—distorted, but familiar to the members of the lord's household, themselves countrydwellers, who might listen to the piece. Certain characteristics occur repeatedly and there is every probability that they are accurate: pre-occupation with custom and propriety; fear of the reproaches of their older relatives, the notion of a contract broken on peril of damnation; the many "attentions" which the young people bestowed on one another—and if nobles laughed at the spectacle of Robin bringing Marion a cheese which she hid in her bodice, it should give historians food for thought. In the miniatures of country dances with which Books of Hours and moral treatises were decorated the couples form a continuous chain, hand in hand, defying all sexual discrimination.

FATHERS AND SONS
The condition of children in the Middle Ages has been the subject of many studies and opinion has long been divided as to whether these unformed creatures, most of whom would meet an early death, were the object if not of scorn, at least of persistent adult indifference; or whether economic factors made it imperative that the parents should bring up an individual who would be self-supporting as soon as possible. Supporters of the first theory point to the representation of children in the visual arts, where there is no attempt to indicate age or sex, if indeed they are portrayed at all, while written sources are silent on the subject or, should they have to narrate the death of a child, do so with cool detachment. The other school emphasizes that from the moment of his birth until death was no longer a daily threat, the *puer* was educated by the example of his elders and, from six or seven years old, "on the job," so that when he was 12 or 14 he could be an apprentice, squire or stable boy. Once again it is archaeology that has provided a fuller picture of the child in his home environment, justifying in the process individual features of both theories. Excavations of settlements from the Frankish and Saxon periods onwards have revealed fragments of little toys, miniature crockery, lead soldiers, wax dolls, knuckle bones, tops and dummies, demonstrating an interest in children's toys quite comparable to our own. No cradles or baby seats have survived (probably because they were made of wood and have consequently perished), but grooves close to the fireplace are evidence of the regular rocking of new-born babies. The discovery of skeletons of foetuses, or very small babies buried in the actual floor of the house bears witness to the peasant superstition that credited them with a special bond with the spirits of their ancestors.

Although visual representations are traditional and unconvincing, they provide a wealth of detail about the behaviour of the *infans:* Jesus is swaddled tightly in his crib and strapped to his bed to prevent him from falling out; scarcely able to move and grotesque in a miniature version of adult clothing, he plays on the ground in the middle of the shavings that have fallen from Joseph's work-bench; or Mary kisses his hand tenderly, or hugs him close to her. Portrayed like a little angel he plays with his mother's hair, as a peasant child she feeds him and spins at the same time; a little older he follows his mother about, clinging to her skirts. There is nothing exceptional in these timeless activities of a small child. Nor is there anything very revealing in the depictions of an angry father's blows, or the accompanying text. The father had authority over the child by law: in Sweden he could still put it up for sale or adoption in the twelfth century and markets for the sale of children are documented in Barcelona at a slightly earlier date.

So there are two contrasting faces in the short period between weaning at about 18 months and being put to work at 10 or 12 years: in the first (the "night" which St. Augustine said he did not wish to experience again for anything in the whole world) the mother undoubtedly played the principal role; the man (the *baron*, as men even of peasant status were called in Normandy after 1250) was master of the household, custodian and protector and dispenser of punishments. Now all child-specialists know that an individual's character is formed during this first phase, when the dominant influence in our period was entirely female. Apart from the signs of affection we have already noted there is virtually no evidence for relations between parents and children. E. Coleman recently suggested that small girls were more at risk than boys because they were more neglected and weaned relatively soon and that this explains the higher incidence of female mortality at this period, since the supposedly "weaker" sex usually has greater resistance to disease. But during these early years young children played a role which seems incomprehensible today: they were intermediaries between the other world and this: it was through their words and actions and in the guise of their desires that the dead were to be recognized and spoke to those who had outlived them. It was as if the child were the temple of memory and his (or her) innocence protected him from adult temptations. The importance of this role (above all in areas where it held a more prominent place in country superstition) explains both the protection which children undoubtedly enjoyed until they were eight or 10 years old and the *enfances*—stereotyped and somewhat improbable accounts of the childhood of an individual destined for an exceptionally saintly or heroic existence and whose first years were steeped in the supernatural.

When this stage of childhood had passed the father took over the child's education at the approach of adolescence; he set the boy to gleaning and the girl to look after his flock; he taught the tricks of his trade, the receipts and rules of life on the land; the mother had only hastily to teach the girls some needlework before they were married. However, it should not be forgotten that the basic precepts of social life, such as conviviality or thrift, were instilled at a much earlier stage, under the mother's influence. It may have been then, too, that the bond between maternal uncle and his nephews and nieces was established, the "nepotism" well known in noble circles, when the difference in age between husband and wife would account for the presence of her younger brother, from whom the children grew to expect a more protective attitude than from a father whose presence was synonymous with instruction or punishment. Moreover the child would have had virtually no-one else to turn to: there were no grandparents who might intervene between father and son. Since life expectancy was relatively short (50 or 60 years, with rare exceptions) they were already dead before they could have any influence; or, alternatively, the new household that had stemmed from theirs was henceforth independent and its members led their own lives. At any rate the child would have known nothing of the buffer role which is so readily thrust upon older relatives today. Many a young man must have waited impatiently for his encumbrance of a father to die. For although he might legally lead an independent life at the age of 15—witness Bracton in about 1270 and the *coutumiers* of Champagne and elsewhere—this was still too young an age to hope that the youth might have the wherewithal to live of his own.

THE LIVING DEAD

As a child, married or widowed, even alone in his house and without friends and relations, the peasant never escaped the company of the dead. This was perhaps the essential difference between the medieval peasant and even the most credulous twentieth-century villager. Until the very end of the Middle Ages, even beyond it, the age-old tyranny of the dead caused the living considerable suffering. It was not a question of fear conjuring up a picture of suffering and putrefaction: death was too familiar to these people surrounded by illness, hunger and violence; they spoke of it often and without emotion, in contrast to our silent fear. Simply because, whether they were truly Christians or simply deists without realizing it—the distinctions would have been lost on them—they saw death or "passage," as they called it, as the entry into life itself, or rather the period of waiting for the judgement that would determine their destiny for ever. Perhaps the celebrations with music and feasting that accompanied a death were less a consolation for the survivors or a last present for the dead man or woman, than an outburst of unalloyed joy at the knowledge that one of their number had at last entered the final phase of existence. Even after 1350, when death's embrace became more intense and was represented in increasingly gruesome forms in both the visual arts, the written word and sermons, the living never conceived of death as a hopeless condition that was hideous and terrifying. Jacques Le Goff has recently shown how, in addition, the increasingly widespread belief in Purgatory after 1180 or 1200 (a middle way that offered hope) made the passage into the other world a simpler and perhaps a sweeter affair for even the worst of men.

For the living, the dead were interlocutors with the supernatural far more than the memory of what they had said or done whilst they were alive. Until the sound of the Last Trumpet they wandered without repose, asexual and joyless, where they had lived, round the church where they had been baptized and where (often in the bare earth) they had been buried. At night a lantern shone in the church tower to keep demons at bay and gather together the spirits of the dead; with the exception of the Jews (buried elsewhere) and the still-born buried in their homes they were like a double village community. There they made themselves known only to women, whilst in the daytime they spoke through the mouths of children or idiots in their former houses. Moreover, as in classical times, they had their altar close by the fire which the women tended. They cast spells or foretold the future; several times a year, the young girls, widows and mothers all went in procession to asperge their tombs, burn an offering of incense or corn, even to put lard by their tombs on the eve of Lent. Can we report that the Church protested, threatened and sermonized? It seems unlikely: from the councils of the fifth century to the Dominicans in the thirteenth there is a continuous series of complaints about female credulity, abuse by demons, and the laxness of the men who allowed it to continue. These protests were all to no avail.

What could be more desirable than intermediaries and fortune-tellers in one's own home? When a member of the family group died, the hair and nails continued to grow and were cut and kept by his relatives, incontrovertible proof that death did not mark the end either of the person who had died or their family. And, as I said earlier, the corpse of a still-born child was buried under the threshold, fixed to the ground by a stake so that the devil could not remove the earthly remains of this creature that had not become truly human. Unlike their master in his castle peasants very rarely had the wherewithal to build a chapel in which everyone was buried and the family clan preserved even in death. This dynastic concern, what the Germans call *Sippenbewusstsein* was the preserve of the nobles, who believed (or wished to believe) in a descent that was of Carolingian, if not of supernatural origin. In the peasant's cottage the dead man lived on in a more modest form: his example was cited to the children and embellished the tales told round the fire by the *diseur* or story-teller, perhaps a cousin with a reputation for conversing with the dead, or simply the father of the family. These stories were not likely to be about exploits in battle or prestigious duties in his master's service, but the purchase of a rich meadow, the discovery of treasure or a surprising marriage. Today these byways have been obliterated in an almost exclusive concentration on the genealogy of noble families, and our only access is by means of a surname or first name, acquired and then transferred from generation to generation. It is striking that women as well as men could introduce an enduring name of this kind into the family group. Soubriquets of this kind first appear amongst men-at-arms between 1050 and 1100 and are found several generations later in lists of villagers witnessing a document or of tax-payers who have discharged their obligations. They sometimes recall the qualities attributed to a totem—wolf, bear, eagle, boar—but more frequently a physical characteristic, a trade or an exploit, such as *le fort* (the brave), *le fèvre* (the smith), *d'outremers* (from overseas). It is unclear whether these names were transmitted systematically before the thirteenth century; when this did occur, it was an indication that the family group had found an ancestor whose protection should be sought. It was at this juncture (1050–1100) that the nobility on the other hand opted for the name of a fief or their own land, that is the toponymic usage which until then had been more common amongst peasants. The same concern for links with the dead is reflected in the adoption of their name at baptism by peasants and nobles alike; fashion certainly played a part, witness the sudden eruption of Jean, Hans and John (according to geographical situation) after 1160 or 1170, but so did the practice of using more noble names, faithfully transmitted from generation to generation, above all royal names like Charles, Louis, Conrad, Heinrich and Edward, that had long been taboo. What peasant in his modest dwelling would not consider his life enhanced by such protection?

The Family Group

The growing body of historians of the family are well aware that this structure was the primary unit of production and mutual assistance. The salient characteristic of the medieval economy was its reliance on these individual constituents and it really does not matter whether we call the system "feudalism" or "seigneurial exploitation," or refer to it by any other term, medieval or modern, so long as the principle of working within the family unit is understood. The combined efforts of these productive individuals supported the system which, as is well known, involved a heavy and sometimes excessive tax on the goods produced or finished by the worker in the fields or in his workshop, indeed on all sorts of services, in return for the supposed exercise of justice and the protection of the individual which the state, the *Res publica*—regardless of the ruler—was in no position to provide. Our picture has to be fitted into this social structure, which was established in about 950 or 1000 and gradually declined in the period 1250–1300.

THE INDIVISIBILITY OF WORK

The *ménage* (household) which I have just described, based on the couple and unmarried children living under the same roof, was of course the dynamic force behind production. As long as there were sufficient sons or daughters working at home (in the *domus,* or, in Languedoc, the *ostal*), the group clearly operated in an almost exclusively domestic context, without the option of seeking outside assistance, in contrast to the lord whose ample resources allowed him to do so. Seigneurial dues undoubtedly meant that the peasant had to work harder than if he had only to be self-sufficient. He did not have the means to do more than meet the immediate, practical needs of food, clothes and implements: the notion of accumulating capital with a view to profit or new investment was quite foreign to such a system. It was in fact the progressive introduction of precisely this concept which undermined the system. But initially peasant farming was simple and the peasant knew nothing of specialized labour with a specific end in mind, nor did he see the possible advantages of greater effort, since the general level of needs and expectations remained low. The limitations and weaknesses of such a system are very apparent: on the one hand, the greater the importance of the household group, the less stress was laid on individual effort—hence, no doubt, what to our eyes seem a surprising number of hours for rest, feast days and siestas which punctuated the working day. (It has been calculated that scarcely 250 days were worked in a year.) On the other hand the peremptory financial demands of the lord or a chance combination of circumstances, climatic or otherwise, destabilized a system that had no reserves to fall back upon and no contact with neighbouring areas. The consequences are more comprehensible in these circumstances, both the periods in which groups either grew closer together or, alternatively—but as a result of the same causes— the violent outbursts that occurred if it transpired that the crisis did not impinge equally on all sections of society.

This concept of the peasant as no more than a tiny grain of sand— the *paysan granulé* as E. Le Roy Ladurie has called him—explains a certain fragility in the social structure as a whole to which I shall return. First of all we must provide some details. As no-one could do anything until they had been shown how to do it by an older man, such as a father or older brother, there is a clear concentration of effort, not in respect of age (for children were soon assimilated into adult life in this scheme of things, even if it meant sparing them the heavier physical tasks) but in respect of sex. And here we are once more confronted with the problems posed by the rural female population.

I shall deliberately pass over the misogynist tirades of a supposedly "popular" literary genre that is almost exclusively masculine and urban in origin, and which draws to the full on the reservoir of feminine faults and weaknesses. We clearly lack its counterpart on the egoism, vanity and idleness of men, whose damaging effect on rural production one would have no difficulty in documenting. On the other hand, I would emphasize in the strongest terms that it is a facile excuse for the twentieth-century historian to accuse his contemporaries or his predecessors of the last two centuries of a total failure to understand domestic tasks. I have already said how much archaeology has contributed in this area to the restoration of the image of the "mistress" of the household. If one adds the exclusive care—and for very good reasons—of children under seven or eight, it must, I hope, be agreed that in a society founded on the triple pillars of subsistence, education and procreation, the women who ensured the provision of the labour force had a position of prime importance. The bourgeois spirit of the nineteenth century has been primarily responsible for grouping these duties with all that was demeaning in the life of a peasant couple and we must stop thinking of them as servile and degrading, especially in a rural context. Moreover, although contemporary literature (with a few honourable exceptions such as St. Bernard, Rupert of Deutz and, later, Christine de Pisan or the Knight of La Tour-Landry) referred scornfully or with hypocritical pity to women at home, iconographical representations are clearer and more charitable. Women appear sporadically at first, then with increasing frequency in the course of the fourteenth century, in the calendar scenes in Books of Hours, but it is above all in illustrations from the Bible that women are shown distributing alms or food and as the source of good counsel.

That said, I must return to my earlier remarks, firstly about the unimportance of age and also the physical disadvantages of repeated pregnancies and subsequent breast-feeding which affected the wife and placed her in a state that was morally and physically inferior to that of her husband. Moreover, as a result, he would only carry more responsibility for work in the fields or the woods in preference to household tasks; and it was undoubtedly the husband who dug and tilled, sowed the seed, reaped, dressed the vines and performed the labour and carrying services demanded by the lord. The wife, if her physical state permitted, was responsible for haymaking, milking, sheep-shearing and sometimes the grape harvest. The tasteless country saying about this division of labour—the land to the man who fertilizes and the fruits to the fertile woman—has been quoted in this context, perhaps with some justification. It was even more true in the case of an old maid, for countrydwellers did not have the money to secure her a place in a convent and there was nothing for her to do but grow old and wizened before the fire, amongst her brothers and sisters-in-law, maid of all work, but good for nothing. But, even pregnant or fitting these tasks in between feeds, the woman was responsible for the provision of water—a worrying necessity we can hardly conceive of—for looking after the fire, preparing gruel, seeing to the milling of corn and the baking of bread if the lord had not made milling and baking at the communal mill and oven compulsory: even then it was often the woman who went there and although St. Bernard railed against the loose women who tempted young men there, St. Dominic advised his friars to go and preach there to the village gossips, who would be forced to listen or lose their place in the queue. Then we should also remember the opportunities to meet afforded by carrying laundry to the river, mutual delousing and the communal spreading of dung and household wastes on the kitchen-gardens which surrounded the village.

Historians have looked for signs of evolution in this conservative and unbalanced structure. These have been observed in the employment of domestic servants and the introduction of technical improvements and in both cases the remedy seems to have been worse than the original ill: servants were undoubtedly either members of the wage-earning class and thus a contributory factor in the deteriorating system of domestic labour, or they constituted part of an expensive system of subsidy if it was a case of a relative in need. As for the introduction of the spinning wheel into the cottage in the thirteenth century, it undoubtedly saved the women invaluable time, compared with spinning with a simple spindle, but the contraption also immobilized the woman in the home, for there was no means of taking it about with her to spin in the fields, an activity documented in twelfth-century iconography. The old maids were certainly bound to it for life; indeed the English word 'spinster' originally meant no more than 'one who spins'.

• • •

Knowledge and Belief

This is an ambitious title to which we all know it is impossible to give a satisfactory answer. Even in the modern period any understanding of rural attitudes is hampered by irrelevant assumptions. These people could not write and speak to us only through clerics and nobles who presented them as absurd caricatures. Iconography continued, unperturbed, to reproduce the classical and Carolingian *topoi* of men working the land. As we shall see, it is only their fantasies which have reached us untouched, because the Church tracked them down in its fight against witchcraft and heresy and they are sometimes illuminated by accusations in trial proceedings. But for the anonymous poets of *Aucassin et Nicolette* and *Le Charroi de Nîmes* and for Chrétien de Troyes these deformed beings, dressed in rags with squashed features and filthy mops of hair, black hands and yellow teeth, verged on the bestial. Thought was beyond them!

BELIEFS RATHER THAN A FAITH

All preachers were unanimous and all the conciliar canons in agreement on one issue: that peasant worship was irregular, their knowledge and understanding of dogma scanty in the extreme. St Bernard in the twelfth century and Jacques de Vitry 100 years later both deplored the misconceptions on which heresy thrived; Dominicans like Hugues de Romans or Etienne de Bourbon, prelates like Eudes Rigaut, archbishop of Rouen, who scoured their dioceses, documented poor attendance at mass, ignorance of the Creed and even the Lord's Prayer, the infrequent practice of confession and even more of communion; the men were in the tavern, the women doing their laundry together: behind the lord and his household at mass there was a handful of children, widows and spinsters. Moreover, they had no knowledge of Latin, an ignorance sometimes shared by their priest, and there was no question of learning to write. At first sight, although the church dominated the village with its sheer size and served as a meeting-place and defensive retreat, it was little more than a communal building whose bells marked the hours of work and rest. It made little difference if the fields and houses were owned by a monastery, or whether they were one of the restitutions of patronage usurped by the laity and very, very slowly surrendered to the monasteries between 1050 and 1225–50.

This miserable picture, a little brighter in the thirteenth than in the eleventh century, distressed Rome at the time and affects too many historians of the Church today. This is undoubtedly to misunderstand peasant spirituality; in our largely urban and mechanized world we take too little account of the effect on the peasant soul of the forest encircling the village, the heath or marsh covered by sudden mists, thunderstorms and capricious rains. Where were God and the Incarnation to be found in these experiences? This was why the practice of the Christian faith remained at the level of what was useful, visible and probable, mingling the Christian message with the phantasms of protohistory. Of the sacraments proclaimed by the hierarchy of the Church only baptism was universal, for that was a rite of passage, a ceremony of introduction to the world in which they were to find their place and there were difficulties in persuading the villagers to proceed with it at the earliest opportunity. In their eyes this rite should accompany the dawn of the child's full consciousness when he was six or seven years old. The Last Rites were also in demand, but bore a strange resemblance to the pagan departure for the other world. Moreover, well into the thirteenth century there are descriptions of strange ceremonies performed by women in which new-born children were exposed on the edge of the forest, immersed in water, passed nine times between the branches of a tree or lighted tapers: "Puerile superstition!" exclaimed Etienne de Bourbon, who knew nothing of anthropology and had no comprehension of the rites of separation, purification and retrieval which freed the new-born child from the powers of evil and made him truly his mother's son. For supreme power was seen to reside in Nature who was to be flattered and entreated. This was why women were intermediaries with the irrational: preachers saw this as the consequence of the Fall from grace in Eden, also brought about by a woman, without realizing that Earth, Moon and Water were also female. Only women could avert or precipitate sterility by the enchantments they practised at night in the *escrennes* in the wood or the land round the hut where they spun and wove. Only they could concoct philtres of mandrake, deadly nightshade or mint which served as contraceptives or abortifacients; only they could turn into witches and fairies to mislead credulous males or spoil the crops. Think of Yvain, Perceval or Tristan, ridiculed by wandering Melusines, goddesses of death and misfortune. The forest remained the favoured place for manifestations of this kind and of beings, good or evil, like elves, or the werewolves that have since metamorphosed into the child-eating wolves of fairytales.

Throughout this period the Church did not attempt to forbid—although little inclined to indulgence, like St Bernard, many priests made a real effort to understand—but it did attempt to regain control of these agrarian, sexual or initiation rites. When fertile rains had to be induced in late spring, the village priest placed himself at the head of the Rogationtide procession (on the Sunday before Ascension Day) and sprinkled the fields with holy water; after the harvest, when the earth had set an example of fecundity, boys and girls danced or coupled on the threshing floor to beat the grain; afterwards purificatory fires were organized in the name of St John, who could do nothing whatever about it; similarly, in May, the priests led torch-lit processions to plant a new tree or decked the girls who were to be married with garlands. Lent, too, was happily placed at the moment when the granaries were empty, transforming grudging penury into voluntary sacrifice; there was the sacrificial Paschal lamb of the Bible from whose blood the God was reborn and also the sacrifice of the pig fattened during the autumn and killed at Christmas, not—as once upon a time—to celebrate the winter solstice, but the presumed birth of Jesus.

Our list will stop there. The "conversion" of the European peasantry was not complete at the beginning of the fourteenth century; it could be maintained that the process was not finished until after the Council of Trent. But this distorted faith was based on essential beliefs rooted in centuries of agrarian life: the bonds between the living and the dead, the belief in salvation, the concept of good and evil and the certainty that there would be a Judgement when the indistinct Godhead who ruled the world willed it. This Godhead was so indistinct that the workers in the fields required an intermediary to make themselves understood: if men did not consult a wizard or a hermit in the forest, it would be the Virgin or a patron saint—a terribly human Virgin with a child in her arms, a saint still more so, because they kept a relic such as a piece of bone or clothing.

Overall during this period the peasant gave the Church all his not inconsiderable tokens of acceptance and obedience: the "Hail Mary" was easily introduced and became widespread at the time when statues of the mother of God were also appearing in church portals; the priest was virtually everywhere and it was he, even more than the blacksmith, who went up to the castle and talked to the lord of the manor; the wealthier man was prepared to make a bequest to the neighbouring monastery on his deathbed; peasants were willing to fast and to receive the body and blood of Christ once a year. The peasant accepted the Christian faith because in it he found the roots of simple belief—rustic in the full sense of the word— which gave a regular pattern to his daily earthly life. As for the future of the world and eschatological hopes and fears, if he gave way to moments of exaltation and terror, it was always because an impassioned preacher had led him to join a wandering band searching for a better existence. There were feverish outbursts of millenariarism at intervals throughout this period: around the years 1000, 1033 (millennium of the passion of Christ), 1095 (when the fall of Jerusalem was believed to have defiled the city), but it also broke out around 1107 and 1120, then again in 1170–80, in the middle of the thirteenth century and at its close. But in each case religious desire for purification was mingled with a specific upheaval of a different kind—oppression by the lord, famine, the threat of an epidemic, a desire to re-establish peace or to save the king.

SPIRITUAL AND TEMPORAL POWER

DURING THE MIDDLE Ages the church was not regarded as a private association within the state. Medieval thinkers instead set out from the idea of one Christian people ruled over by two hierarchies of government. The ecclesiastical hierarchy directed spiritual and religious affairs; the temporal hierarchy directed secular and mundane affairs. There always existed a possibility that the two hierarchies might come into conflict with one another. In that case, which had the higher claim on a Christian's allegiance? The attempt to work out the right relationship between the two powers provides one of the main themes of medieval history.

In the eleventh century, kings were regarded as sacred figures. They controlled the appointment of bishops and regulated most aspects of church affairs. This system was radically challenged by Pope Gregory VII (1073–1085). He claimed to be fighting for the "freedom of the church," but in fact asserted a dominant role for the papacy. In its most extreme form papal ideology came to assert that secular rulers derived their authority from the church or, specifically, from the pope. The basic argument in favor of this position was simple and, to some medieval minds, compelling. The pope was God's representative on earth. All power flowed from God. Therefore all power on earth flowed from the pope. But papal claims did not rest solely on abstract theology. As a matter of historical fact, ever since the days of Charlemagne popes had crowned emperors. It could be argued that, in receiving a crown from the Roman pontiff, the emperor acknowledged the pope as the source of his authority.

The first two readings below discuss these questions further. Walter Ullmann explores the underlying ideology of papal power. Harold Berman argues that Gregory VII initiated one of the great revolutions of Western history and that, paradoxically, one effect of his policies was to stimulate the growth of the secular state.

The last reading discusses another aspect of medieval religious life. As the authority of the church increased in the twelfth and thirteenth centuries, savage outbreaks of anti-Jewish violence occurred. To explain why this happened is a major problem for historians. Was it because of the church's teachings or in spite of them? Was the underlying cause religious animosity? Economic grievances? Dawning nationalism? Jeremy Cohen's review of some recent literature indicates the complexity of the theme.

22.   *The Hierocratic Doctrine*

WALTER ULLMANN

It may be helpful to state here the essence of the hierocratic ideology, according to which the pope as successor of St. Peter was entitled and bound to lead the community of the faithful, the Church. The means for the pope to do so were the laws issued by him in his supreme jurisdictional function, which claimed universal validity, and concerned themselves with everything that affected the vital interests and structural fabric of the Christian community. Obviously, from this hierocratic point of view, the judge of what was in the interests of that community, what facts, circumstances, actions, or situations touched its vital concerns, was the pope. He was the "judge ordinary" and claimed to possess the specific knowledge of when legislation was required. The function of the pope was that of a true monarch, governing the community that was entrusted to him. A further essential feature of this theory was the hierarchical gradation of offices, which ensured what was called order and smooth working of the whole community. This order was said to be maintained if everyone remained within his functions which were assigned to him. Bishops had their special functions, and so had kings. If either king or bishop intervened in, or rather interfered with, the other's functions, order would suffer and disorder would follow. The limitation of functional action was the hallmark of the hierocratic thesis, or, in other words, the principle of division of labour was a vital structural element of the thesis. Supreme directive control, the supreme

From Walter Ullmann, *A History of Political Thought: The Middle Ages* (London: Penguin Books, 1965), pp. 100–106, 110–111. Copyright © 1965 by Walter Ullman. Reprinted by permission of the publisher.

authority (sovereignty), remained with the pope, who, standing as he did outside and above the community of the faithful, issued his directions as a "steersman," as a *gubernator.*

While considering the theory, the allegorical manner of expressing the relationship between priesthood and laity deserves consideration. The metaphor constantly used was that of the soul and body. The *anima-corpus* allegory was adduced a hundredfold to show the inferiority of the laity and the superiority of the clergy, to show that, just as the soul ruled the body, in the same manner the clergy ruled the laity, with the consequence that, as for instance Cardinal Humbert in the mid-eleventh century stated, the kings were the strong arms of the clergy, for the clergy were the eyes of the whole Church who knew what was to be done. In interpreting this antithesis one should not be misled by pure allegory. What the metaphorical use of soul and body attempted to express was that, because faith in Christ was the cementing bond of the whole Church and the exposition of the faith the business of the clergy, the law itself as the external regulator of society was to be based upon the faith. Faith and law stood to each other in the relation of cause and effect. The "soul" in this allegory was no more and no less than the pure idea of right and law, the uncontaminated Christian idea of the right way of living. What legal or legislative action faith required could be discerned only by those who had the eyes to see, the clergy. Differently expressed, since every law was to embody the idea of justice, and since justice was an essential ingredient of the Christian faith, the "soul" in this allegory meant the Christian idea of justice. There can be little doubt that this thesis was the medieval idea of the "rule of law," manifested the idea of the supremacy of the law. For the body of the faithful could, so it was said, be held together only by the law based on (Christian) justice, which on the one hand externalized the faith and on the other hand reflected the teleological thesis, for the law was considered the appropriate vehicle by which the body of the faithful was enabled to achieve its end. In short, the law was the soul which ruled the body corporate of the Christians. The legalism of the Middle Ages and quite especially of the hierocratic form of government found its ready explanation. It was said often enough that only through the law could a public body live, develop, and reach its end. Within the hierocratic thesis the king was subjected to sacerdotal rulings, the basic idea being that the king was not qualified enough to lay down the law in those matters which touched the essential fabric of Christian society. Fundamentally, this thesis of soul and body expressed simply the idea of governing a body public and corporate by means of the law.

As a consequence, the hierocratic ideology which emerged in its full maturity from the pontificate of Gregory VII onwards (1073–85) also laid particular stress upon the law. In fact, this pope went so far as to state dogmatically that it was "legal discipline" that had led kings onto the path of salvation. After all, they were distinguished by divinity to be the trustees of their kingdoms and had therefore all the more grounds for showing themselves "lovers of justice" (*amatores justitiae*), and justice, as an ingredient of the Christian faith, could be expounded only by the Roman Church, which was consequently called the "seat of justice." The king's duty was obedience to papal commands: he was a subject of the pope, to whom all Christians in any case were subjects. The teleological argumentation received its precision, notably by reference to the accumulated body of knowledge and learning as well as to the interpretation of the coronation orders: the purpose of God granting power to the king in the public sphere was to repress evil. If there had been no evil, there would have been no need for the power of the physical sword. Hence the pope claimed to exercise a "universal government" (*regimen universale*) by means of the law which made no distinction between matters or persons. The Petrine powers were comprehensive, exempting no one and nothing from the pope's jurisdiction. With exemplary unambiguity for instance Gregory VII declared:

If the holy see has the right to judge spiritual things, why then not secular things as well?

On another occasion he stated:

For if the see of St. Peter decides and judges celestial things, how much more does it decide and judge the earthly and secular.

From the papal standpoint it was true to say that the pope bore a very heavy burden, not only of spiritual tasks, but also of secular business, for he considered himself responsible for the direction of the body of the faithful under his control and in his charge. Obviously, the governmental power of the popes referred specifically to kings, because they disposed of the means of executing papal orders and decrees. Moreover, the king, for the reason already stated, was an "ecclesiastical person," whose office concerned itself with the repression of evil. Both the kingdom and the king's soul were, as the popes repeatedly declared, in their power. But the developed hierocratic programme did make the qualification that the pope considered papal jurisdiction to come into play only when the basic and vital interests of the body of the faithful called for his intervention. None expressed this principle better than Innocent III

(1198–1216) in his usual concise language. He stated that feudal matters as such were of no concern to the pope's jurisdiction, which came into full operation however when sin was involved. *Ratione peccati* (by reason of sin) was the technical expression to denote the overriding papal jurisdiction. Evidently, the judge of when sin was involved was the pope himself.

The process of monopolizing the Bible had meanwhile made great strides. The popes applied to themselves the passage in Jeremiah i, 10: "I have set thee over the nations and kingdoms . . . ," because this was, according to Innocent III, a "prerogative" (the term occurs here for the first time) of the pope: this was nothing but the explicit expression of the monarchic principle. The same Innocent III declared that he was less than God but more than man, a statement that brings into clearest possible relief the very essence of the papal thesis, namely the superior status of the pope, his sovereignty, standing outside and above the community of the faithful. And it was precisely by virtue of his "superior" status that the papal Ruler gave the law. The development in the twelfth century leading to the concept of the pope as the vicar of Christ only underlined this point of view. The papal vicariate of Christ in itself changed nothing in the papal function. It attributed no more powers to him than he already had. What the concept of the vicariate of Christ focused attention on were the vicarious powers which Peter was said to have been given by Christ: it was these which, by way of succession, came to be wielded by the pope. The concept considerably clarified the function of the pope, with the consequence that a number of biblical passages which referred to Christ were now directly applied to the pope, so, for instance, the Matthean passage: "All power is given unto me. . . ." The vicariate of Christ in the pope demonstrated the pope as the point of intersection between heaven and earth. Hence it was that Innocent III said that what he had decreed was decreed by Christ Himself. And Innocent IV (1245–54) stated that the pope figured as Christ's "corporal presence." It was quite in keeping with this theory that the government of the pope was considered to be a true *monarchatus*, because, as the canon lawyers taught, in his hands the "keys of the kingdom of heaven" had changed into the "keys of the law." This monarchic theory was succinctly expressed by Gregory IX (1227–41) thus:

When Christ ascended into heaven, He left one vicar on earth, and hence it was necessary that all who wished to be Christians were to be subjected to the government of the vicar.

By the virtue of the thesis that God was the creator of everything on earth, the claim was raised by Innocent IV that every human creature (and not merely Christians) were subjects of the pope (who in the doctrine of the canon lawyers was *de jure,* but not *de facto,* the universal monarch). Indeed, the pope possessed—or at least claimed to possess—supreme overlordship over both bodies and souls of all men, as the same Gregory IX asserted. And before him a similar theory was expressed by Innocent III who held that the princes of the world had power over the body only, whilst the priests had power on earth as well as in heaven and over the souls also.

Because the pope functioned as the monarch of the body of the faithful, he claimed that his laws had reference to anyone and anything. Wherever the line of distinction between spiritual and temporal matters might have been drawn, for papal governmental ideology the distinction had no operational value. Since the end of the body of the faithful governed by the pope lay in the other world, anything that might be called temporal was subjected to that spiritual end. St. Paul had often enough declared the superiority of the spiritual over and above the mundane, the visible, the corporeal, or the secular. And by the process of monopolization the papacy made these Pauline views its own. Some statements of Gregory VII have already been quoted, but there were dozens of similar views expressed by other popes in the twelfth and thirteenth centuries. There was also the actual government of the popes who intervened in what might well have appeared, to the less sophisticated contemporaries, purely temporal matters. In the final resort the papal standpoint was based on the view that Christianity seized the whole of man and the whole of his activities without splitting them up into different compartments, which view led to the "totalitarian" system of government. If, indeed—and as we shall see, it was the royal opposition which argued in this way—the temporal was to be exempt from papal jurisdiction, this would not only have contradicted the all-embracing character of the Petrine powers of binding and loosing, but also the very essence of Christianity, at least as the papacy saw it. Neither things temporal nor the temporal Ruler could have had an autonomous, independent, autogenous standing in the papal scheme of government. Each was a means to an end. The pope, as monarchic sovereign, stood indeed outside and above the body of the faithful, a body that was one—"we are one body in Christ" according to St. Paul—and which suffered no division. In brief, unity of the body demanded unity of government, which manifested itself in the monarchy of the pope as the "overseer" (*speculator*) over all matters of basic concern to the well-being of the body.

• • •

Innocent III's thesis owed a good deal to St. Bernard of Clairvaux who, a generation before, had introduced the hierocratically orientated Two-Sword theory into the discussion, a theory that was alleged to have had its origin in Luke xxii, 38, and which had been used in a different sense already by Charlemagne's adviser, Alcuin, as well as by Henry IV. But, according to the doctrine of St. Bernard the pope possessed both swords, that is, the spiritual and the temporal (material), the one signifying the pope's priestly coercive power, the other the regal coercive power. During the coronation the pope gave the latter to the emperor, who was then said to wield the sword at the bidding of the pope (*ad nutum*). This Two-Sword theory was to signify that the actual physical power the emperor possessed was derived from the pope, or rather from God through the mediating organ of the pope. The ancient Isidorian doctrine was given its allegorical clothing. Gregory IX explicitly stated that the Lord had given the pope both swords, one of which the pope retained and wielded, the other he gave away. Or, as his successor Innocent IV stressed, the power of the material sword belonged potentially to the pope, but actually to the emperor. This Two-Sword allegory had reference to the emperor only. What therefore at the end of the thirteenth century Boniface VIII asserted in his *Unam sanctam* could barely be squared with the actual development, for he applied the allegory also to the kings who had never been crowned, nor had ever expressed an intention to be crowned, as emperors: a characteristic extension of a suggestive allegory. What, however, is significant is that the relevant decrees of the popes, especially Innocent III and IV and Gregory IX, were appropriately enough incorporated in the official canon law books under the title "Of majority and obedience," which seems very important in view of the (medieval) meaning of "majority," that is, sovereignty and the corresponding obedience on the part of the subjects.

23.   The Papal Revolution

HAROLD BERMAN

The Revolutionary Character of the Papal Revolution

The term revolution, as applied to the great revolutions of European history, has four main characteristics which, taken together, distinguish it from reform or evolution, on the one hand, and from mere rebellions, coups d'etat, and counterrevolutions and dictatorships, on the other. These are its *totality,* that is, its character as a total transformation in which political, religious, economic, legal, cultural, linguistic, artistic, philosophical, and other basic categories of social change are interlocked; its *rapidity,* that is, the speed or suddenness with which drastic changes take place from day to day, year to year, decade to decade as the revolution runs its course; its *violence,* which takes the form not only of a class struggle and civil war but also of foreign wars of expansion; and its *duration* over two or three generations, during which the underlying principles of the revolution are reconfirmed and reestablished in the face of necessary compromises with its initial utopianism, until the grandchildren of the founding fathers themselves acknowledge devotion to their grandparents' cause. Then evolution can take place at its own pace, without fear of either counterrevolution from the right or the radicalism of a new left.

From Harold J. Berman, *Law and Revolution* (Cambridge, Mass.: Harvard University Press, 1983), pp. 99–109, 112–115, 118–119. Reprinted by permission of the publisher from *Law and Revolution* by Harold J. Berman, Cambridge, Mass.: Harvard University Press. Copyright © 1983 by the President and Fellows of Harvard College.

THE TOTALITY OF THE PAPAL REVOLUTION

The search for a basic cause of historical change, and the very division of causes into basic causes and secondary causes, may obscure the fact that great revolutions do not occur without the coincidence of a great many different factors. The classification of these factors into political, economic, cultural, and other categories is a matter of convenience of exposition. To give a true picture, however, the exposition must show the necessary interconnections among the factors. Otherwise, the most important point is missed, namely, that such revolutions are experienced as total events.

Thus the Papal Revolution may be viewed in political terms, as a massive shift in power and authority both within the church and in the relations between the church and the secular polities; also it was accompanied by decisive political changes in the relations between western Europe and neighboring powers. The Papal Revolution may also be viewed in socioeconomic terms as both a response and a stimulus to an enormous expansion of production and of trade and to the emergence of thousands of new cities and towns. From a cultural and intellectual perspective, the Papal Revolution may be viewed as a motive force in the creation of the first European universities, in the emergence of theology and jurisprudence and philosophy as systematic disciplines, in the creation of new literary and artistic styles, and in the development of a new social consciousness. These diverse political, economic, and cultural movements may be analyzed separately; yet they must also be shown to have been linked with one another, for it was the linking of them all that constituted the revolutionary element in the situation.

Political Changes. The major political shifts in power and authority within the church and in its relations with secular rulers have been described in preceding pages. It is necessary here, however, to state briefly some of the political changes that took place at the same time in relations between western Europe and neighboring powers.

For centuries there had been constant military incursions into Europe from the north and west by the Norsemen, from the south by the Arabs, and from the east by the Slavs and Magyars. The whole of Western Christendom "was a beleaguered citadel which only survived because its greatest enemy, Islam, had reached the end of its lines of communication, and its lesser enemies (the Slavs, the Hungarians, and the Vikings) were organized only for raids and for plunder." It was the role of the emperor to mobilize soldiers, especially knights, from among the various peoples of the empire, to resist by military force these pressures from the outside. He also had enemies within—to the west the French kings were not always friendly, and across the Alps the princes of northern Italy were openly hostile. Thus Europe was turned in upon itself, with its main axis running from north to south. At the end of the eleventh century, however, the papacy, which for at least two decades had been urging secular rulers to liberate Byzantium from the infidels, finally succeeded in organizing the First Crusade (1096–1099). A second crusade was launched in 1147 and a third crusade in 1189. These first crusades were the foreign wars of the Papal Revolution. They not only increased the power and authority of the papacy but also opened a new axis eastward to the outside world and turned the Mediterranean Sea from a natural defensive barrier against invasion from without into a route for western Europe's own military and commercial expansion.

• • •

Cultural and Intellectual Changes.   In the late eleventh and the twelfth centuries western Europe experienced not only political and economic explosions but also a cultural and intellectual explosion. This was the time when the first universities were created, when the scholastic method (as it later came to be called) was first developed, when theology and jurisprudence and philosophy were first subjected to rigorous systematization. This period marked the beginning of modern scientific thought.

It was also the period of transition first to Romanesque and then to Gothic architecture; it was the age when the first great European cathedrals were started—St. Denis and Notre Dame de Paris, Canterbury and Durham.

This was the age when Latin as a scholarly language was modernized and when vernacular languages and literature began to take their modern form. It was the period of great epic poetry (the *Song of Roland,* the Arthurian epics) and of courtly lyrics and romances (the writings of Bernard de Ventadour). It was a time of remarkable growth of literacy among the laity, and of the earliest development of national cultural sentiments in most of the countries of western Europe.

Three other basic changes in social consciousness contributed to the transformation of the cultural and intellectual life of the peoples of western Europe in the late eleventh and the twelfth centuries: first, the growth of the sense of corporate identity of the clergy, its self-consciousness as a group, and the sharp opposition, for the first time, between the clergy and the laity; second, the change to a dynamic concept of the responsibility of the church (considered primarily as the clergy) to reform the world, the *saeculum* (considered primarily as the lay world); and third, the development of a new sense of historical time, including the concepts of modernity and progress.

THE RAPIDITY AND VIOLENCE OF THE PAPAL REVOLUTION

In trying to comprehend the full dimensions of the changes that took place during the eleventh and twelfth centuries, one may lose sight of the cataclysmic character of the events that were at the heart of the Papal Revolution. These events may be explained, ultimately, only by the totality of the transformation; but they must be seen initially as the immediate consequence of the effort to achieve a political purpose, namely, what the papal party called "the freedom of the church"—the liberation of the clergy from imperial, royal, and feudal domination and their unification under papal authority. By placing that political purpose, and the events that followed immediately from the effort to realize it, in the context of the total transformation, one can see that what was involved was far more than a struggle for power. It was an apocalyptic struggle for a new order of things, for "a new heaven and a new earth." But at the same time, the political manifestation of that struggle, where power and conviction, the material and the spiritual, coincided, is what gave it its tempo and its passion.

Rapidity is, of course, a relative matter. It may seem that a transformation which began in the middle of the eleventh century and was not secured until the latter part of the twelfth century, or possibly the early part of the thirteenth century, should be called gradual. However, the length of time which it takes a revolution to run its course is not necessarily the measure of its rapidity. The concept of rapid change refers to the pace at which drastic changes occur from day to day or year to year or decade to decade. In a revolution of the magnitude of the Papal Revolution, life is speeded up; things happen very quickly; great changes take place overnight. First, at the start of the revolution—in the *Dictatus Papae* of 1075—the previous political and legal order was declared to be abolished. Emperors were to kiss the feet of popes. The pope was to be "the sole judge of all" and to have the sole power "to make new laws to meet the needs of the times." The fact that many of the features of the old society persisted and refused to disappear did not change the suddenness of the effort to abolish them or the shock produced by that effort. Second, new institutions and policies were introduced almost as suddenly as old ones were abolished. The fact that it took a long time—several generations—for the revolution to establish its goals did not make the process a gradual one.

• • •

It is doubtful that the rapidity of the Papal Revolution can be separated from its violence. This is not to say that if the struggle could have been carried on without civil war—if Henry IV could have been persuaded not to resist Gregory by armed force, or Gregory not to summon his Norman allies in defense—the events would have lost their rapid tempo. Nevertheless, in the Papal Revolution, as in the great revolutions of Western history that succeeded it, the resort to violence was closely related to the speed with which changes were pressed as well as to their total or fundamental character. It was partly because of the rapidity of the changes and partly because of their totality that the preexisting order was unwilling and unable to make room for them; and so force, in Karl Marx's words, became "the necessary midwife" of the new era.

Force, however, could not give a final victory either to the revolutionary party or to its opponents. The Papal Revolution ended in compromise between the new and the old. If force was the midwife, law was the teacher that ultimately brought the child to maturity. Gregory VII died in exile. Henry IV was deposed. The eventual settlement in Germany, France, England, and elsewhere was reached by hard negotiations in which all sides renounced their most radical claims. What can be said for force is that it took the experience of civil war in Europe to produce the willingness of both sides to compromise. The balance was struck, ultimately, by law.

The Duration of the Papal Revolution

The totality of the transformation of Western Christendom in the late eleventh and the twelfth centuries, its rapidity, and its violence would not in themselves justify its characterization as the first of the great revolutions of Western history, if the revolutionary movement had not endured for several generations.

At first, the long duration of a revolution may seem to contradict its speed and violence; in fact, however, it is partly because of the speed and violence of the changes, as well as their totality, that their underlying principles must be reconfirmed and reestablished by successive generations. Moreover, the basic goals of the revolution must be preserved in the face of necessary compromises with its initial utopianism. Just as the totality of the transformation distinguishes a revolution from reform, and just as the rapidity and violence distinguish it from evolution, so the transgenerational character of the great revolutions of Western history distinguishes them from mere rebellions, coups d'état, and shifts in policy, as well as from counterrevolutions and military dictatorships.

The Papal Revolution was the first transgenerational movement of a programmatic character in Western history. It took almost a generation, from about 1050 to 1075, for the papal party to proclaim the program to be a reality. Then followed forty-seven years of struggle before another pope could reach an agreement with another emperor on the single question of papal versus imperial investiture of bishops and abbots. It took even longer for the respective criminal and civil jurisdictions of the ecclesiastical and secular powers within each of the major western European kingdoms to be defined. In England it was not until 1170, the year of Becket's martyrdom—ninety-five years after Gregory's *Dictatus* and sixty-three years after Henry I, the English king, had yielded on the investiture issue—that the Crown finally renounced its pretension to be the supreme ruler of the English clergy. Ultimately compromises were reached on a whole range of issues involving not only the interrelationship of church and state but also the interrelationship of communities within the secular order—the manorial system, the lord-vassal unit, the merchant guilds, the chartered cities and towns, the territorial duchies and kingdoms, the secularized empire. The children and grandchildren of the revolution enacted its underlying principles into governmental and legal institutions. Only then was it more or less secure for succeeding centuries. Indeed, it was never wholly secure; there were always disputes at the boundaries of the ecclesiastical and secular powers.

Social-Psychological Causes and Consequences of the Papal Revolution

Mention has been made of three aspects of the new social consciousness that emerged during the eleventh and twelfth centuries—a new sense of corporate identity on the part of the clergy, a new sense of the responsibility of the clergy for the reformation of the secular world, and a new sense of historical time, including the concepts of modernity and progress. These all had a strong influence on the development of the Western legal tradition.

The first aspect, the corporate self-consciousness of the clergy (it would be called *class* consciousness today) was essential to the revolution, both as cause and as consequence. Of course, the clergy had always had some sense of their own group identity; yet it was at best a sense of spiritual unity, a unity of belief and of calling, and not a sense of political or legal unity. Politically and legally, the clergy prior to the eleventh century had been dispersed locally, with very few links to central ecclesiastical authorities. Even the sense of spiritual unity was flawed by the sharp division between the "regular" clergy and the "secular" clergy; the regular clergy were the "religious" ones, the monks and nuns, who having died to "this world," lived out their membership in the Eternal City; the secular clergy were the priests and bishops, who were almost wholly involved in the political, economic, and social life of the localities where they lived.

More than any other single factor, the Cluniac Reform laid the foundation for the new sense of corporate political unity among the clergy of Western Christendom. The zeal of the reformers helped to give a new consciousness of common historical destiny to both the regular and the secular clergy. In addition, Cluny provided a model for uniting the clergy in a single translocal organization, since all Cluniac houses were subject to the jurisdiction of the central abbey.

In adopting the principal aims of the Cluniac Reform, including the celibacy of the priesthood and the elimination of the purchase and sale of church offices, the papal party in the 1050s and 1060s appropriated the moral capital of the earlier movement, including the clerical class consciousness that it had helped to develop. To those older aims was joined the new cry for "the freedom of the church"—that is, its freedom from control by "the laity." This was both an appeal to clerical class consciousness and a stimulation of it. Moreover, by the very act of denouncing imperial control of the church, Gregory shattered the old Carolingian ideal. The clergy were confronted with a choice between political unity under the papacy and political disunity among new national churches, which would have inevitably arisen in the various polities of Europe if the papacy had lost the battle. The investiture struggle made that clear. Ultimately the question of investiture was settled by separate negotiations between each of the principal secular rulers, representing his secular polity, and the papacy, representing the entire clergy of Western Christendom. The Papal Revolution itself thus helped to establish the clerical class consciousness on which it was based.

The clergy became the first translocal, transtribal, transfeudal, transnational class in Europe to achieve political and legal unity. It became so by demonstrating that it was able to stand up against, and defeat, the one preexisting universal authority, the emperor. The emperor had no such universal class to support him. From the twelfth century to the sixteenth the unity of the clerical hierarchy in the West could only be broken by a few powerful kings. Even the Norman kings of Sicily, who in the twelfth and thirteenth centuries were able to exclude papal control over a clergy nominally subordinate to Rome, agreed to submit to the pope any disputed elections of bishops.

The term "class" has been used here to describe the clergy partly to emphasize that the Papal Revolution, like the German (Protestant) Revolution, the English Revolution, the French and American revolutions, and the Russian Revolution, involved the interactions not only of individuals or elites but also of large social groups that performed major functions in the society. The validity of the Marxian insight that a revolution involves class struggle, and the rise of a new ruling class, need not commit one to the narrow Marxian definition of class in terms of its relation to the means of production of economic wealth. The clergy in western Europe in the late eleventh and twelfth centuries did, in fact, play an important role in the production of economic wealth, since the church owned between one-fourth and one-third of the land; bishops and abbots were lords of manors with the same economic interests as their nonecclesiastical counterparts; the struggle against lay investiture was in part a struggle to wrest economic power from lay lords and to transfer it to the church. However, it was not primarily the economic interests of the clergy that gave them their class character. It was, rather, their role as producers of spiritual goods—as father confessors, as performers of marriage ceremonies, as baptizers of infants, as ministers of last rites, as preachers of sermons, and also as expounders not only of the theology of Western society but also of its basic political and legal doctrines.

The growth of the class consciousness of the clergy was associated with the second aspect of the new social consciousness of the eleventh and twelfth centuries—the development of a new sense of the clergy's mission to reform the secular world. On the one hand, the new tendency to identify the church primarily with the clergy, the "hierarchy," led to a sharp distinction between the clergy and the laity. On the other hand, this distinction carried the implication that the clergy were not only superior to, but also responsible for, the laity. In other words, the class consciousness of the clergy was at the same time a social consciousness in the modern sense, a conscientiousness with respect to the future of society.

• • •

Closely related to both the clergy's sense of corporate identity and its sense of mission to reform the world was a third aspect of the new social consciousness that emerged in the eleventh and twelfth centuries, namely, a new sense of historical time, including the concepts of modernity and of progress. This, too, was both a cause and a consequence of the Papal Revolution.

A new sense of time was implicit in the shift in the meaning of *saeculum* and in the new sense of mission to reform the world. A relatively static view of political society was replaced by a more dynamic view; there was a new concern with the future of social institutions. But there was also a fundamental revaluation of history, a new orientation toward the past as well as the future, and a new sense of the relationship of the future to the past. The distinction between "ancient" and "modern" times, which had occasionally been made in previous centuries, became common in the literature of the papal party. In the twelfth century there appeared the first European historians who saw the history of the West as moving from the past, through stages, into a new future—men such as Hugo of St. Victor, Otto of Freising, Anselm of Havelberg, Joachim of Floris, and others. These men saw history as moving forward in stages, culminating in their own time, which some referred to as modern times or modernity (*modernitas*). Joachim of Floris and his disciples considered that a new age of the Holy Spirit was about to replace the age of the Son, which had come to an end. Otto of Freising wrote that secular history had entered into sacred history and was intertwined with it.

Like the English Revolution of the seventeenth century, the Papal Revolution pretended to be not a revolution but a restoration. Gregory VII, like Cromwell, claimed that he was not innovating, but restoring ancient freedoms that had been abrogated in the immediately preceding centuries. As the English Puritans and their successors found precedents in the common law of the thirteenth and fourteenth centuries, largely passing over the century or more of Tudor-Stuart absolutism, so the Gregorian reformers found precedents in the patristic writings of the early centuries of the church, largely passing over the Carolingian and post-Carolingian era in the West. The ideological emphasis was on tradition, but the tradition could only be established by suppressing the immediate past and returning to an earlier one. Writings of leading Frankish and German canonists and theologians of the ninth and tenth centuries were simply ignored. In addition, the patristic writings were interpreted to conform to the political program of the papal party, and when particular patristic texts stood in the way of that program they were rejected. Faced with an obnoxious custom, the Gregorian reformers would appeal over it to truth, quoting the aphorism of Tertullian and St. Cyprian, "Christ said, 'I am the truth.' He did not say 'I am the custom.' " Gregory VII quoted this against Emperor Henry IV. Becket quoted it against King Henry II. It had special force at a time when almost all the prevailing law was customary law.

It is the hallmark of the great revolutions of Western history, starting with the Papal Revolution, that they clothe their vision of the radically new in the garments of a remote past, whether those of ancient legal authorities (as in the case of the Papal Revolution), or of an ancient religious text, the Bible (as in the case of the German Reformation), or of an ancient civilization, classical Greece (as in

the case of the French Revolution), or of a prehistoric classless society (as in the case of the Russian Revolution). In all of these great
upheavals the idea of a restoration—a return, and in that sense a
revolution, to an earlier starting point—was connected with a dynamic concept of the future.

It is easy enough to criticize the historiography of the revolutions
as politically biased and, indeed, purely ideological. This, however,
is to impose on revolutionaries the standards of objectivity asserted
by modern historical scholarship, which is itself a product of its times
and has its own biases. Moreover, it is important to recognize that
the revolutionaries were perfectly aware that they were reinterpret-
ing the past and adapting historical memories to new circumstances.
What is significant is that at the most crucial turning points of Western history a projection into the distant past has been needed to
match the projection into the distant future. Both the past and the
future have been summoned, so to speak, to fight against the evils
of the present.

The Rise of the Modern State

The Papal Revolution gave birth to the modern Western state—the
first example of which, paradoxically, was the church itself.

As Maitland said a century ago, it is impossible to frame any acceptable definition of the state which would not include the medieval church. By that he meant the church after Pope Gregory VII,
since before his reign the church had been merged with the secular
society and had lacked the concepts of sovereignty and of independent lawmaking power which are fundamental to modern state-
hood. After Gregory VII, however, the church took on most of the
distinctive characteristics of the modern state. It claimed to be an
independent, hierarchical, public authority. Its head, the pope, had
the right to legislate, and in fact Pope Gregory's successors issued a
steady stream of new laws, sometimes by their own authority, sometimes with the aid of church councils summoned by them. The
church also executed its laws through an administrative hierarchy,
through which the pope ruled as a modern sovereign rules through
his or her representatives. Further, the church interpreted its laws,
and applied them, through a judicial hierarchy culminating in the
papal curia in Rome. Thus the church exercised the legislative, administrative, and judicial powers of a modern state. In addition, it
adhered to a rational system of jurisprudence, the canon law. It imposed taxes on its subjects in the form of tithes and other levies.
Through baptismal and death certificates it kept what was in effect
a kind of civil register. Baptism conferred a kind of citizenship, which

was further maintained by the requirement—formalized in 1215—that every Christian confess his or her sins and take Holy Communion at least once a year at Easter. One could be deprived of citizenship, in effect, by excommunication. Occasionally, the church even raised armies.

Yet it is a paradox to call the church a modern state, since the principal feature by which the modern state is distinguished from the ancient state, as well as from the Germanic or Frankish state, is its secular character. The ancient state and the Germanic-Frankish state were religious states, in which the supreme political ruler was also responsible for maintaining the religious dogmas as well as the religious rites and was often himself considered to be a divine or semidivine figure. The elimination of the religious function and character of the supreme political authority was one of the principal objectives of the Papal Revolution. Thereafter, emperors and kings were considered—by those who followed Roman Catholic doctrine—to be laymen, and hence wholly without competence in spiritual matters. According to papal theory, only the clergy, headed by the pope, had competence in spiritual matters. Nevertheless, for several reasons this was not a "separation of church and state" in the modern sense.

First, the state in the full modern sense—that is, the secular state existing in a system of secular states—had not yet come into being, although a few countries (especially the Norman Kingdom of Sicily and Norman England) were beginning to create modern political and legal institutions. Instead, there were various types of secular power, including feudal lordships and autonomous municipal governments as well as emerging national territorial states, and their interrelationships were strongly affected by the fact that all of their members, including their rulers, were also subject in many respects to an overarching ecclesiastical state.

Second, although emperor, kings, and other lay rulers were deprived of their ecclesiastical authority, they nevertheless continued to play a very important part—through the dual system of investiture—in the appointment of bishops, abbots, and other clerics and, indeed, in church politics generally. And conversely, members of the clergy continued to play an important part in secular politics, serving as advisers to secular rulers and also often as high secular officials. The Chancellor of England, for example, who was second in importance to the King, was virtually always a high ecclesiastic—often the Archbishop of Canterbury or of York—until the sixteenth century.

Third, the church retained important secular powers. Bishops continued to be lords of their feudal vassals and serfs and to be managers of their estates. Beyond that, the papacy asserted its power to influence secular politics in all countries; indeed, the pope claimed the supremacy of the spiritual sword over the temporal, although he only claimed to exercise temporal supremacy indirectly, chiefly through secular rulers.

Thus the statement that the church was the first modern Western state must be qualified. The Papal Revolution did lay the foundation for the subsequent emergence of the modern secular state by withdrawing from emperors and kings the spiritual competence which they had previously exercised. Moreover, when the secular state did emerge, it had a constitution similar to that of the papal church—minus, however, the church's spiritual function as a community of souls concerned with eternal life. The church had the paradoxical character of a church-state, a *Kirchenstaat*: it was a spiritual community which also exercised temporal functions and whose constitution was in the form of a modern state. The secular state, on the other hand, had the paradoxical character of a state without ecclesiastical functions, a secular polity, all of whose subjects also constituted a spiritual community living under a separate spiritual authority.

• • •

The most important consequence of the Papal Revolution was that it introduced into Western history the experience of revolution itself. In contrast to the older view of secular history as a process of decay, there was introduced a dynamic quality, a sense of progress in time, a belief in the reformation of the world. No longer was it assumed that "temporal life" must inevitably deteriorate until the Last Judgment. On the contrary, it was now assumed—for the first time—that progress could be made in this world toward achieving some of the preconditions for salvation in the next.

Perhaps the most dramatic illustration of the new sense of time, and of the future, was provided by the new Gothic architecture. The great cathedrals expressed, in their soaring spires and flying buttresses and elongated vaulted arches, a dynamic spirit of movement upward, a sense of achieving, of incarnation of ultimate values. It is also noteworthy that they were often planned to be built over generations and centuries.

Less dramatic but even more significant as a symbol of the new belief in progress toward salvation were the great legal monuments that were built in the same period. In contrast not only to the earlier Western folklaw but also to Roman law both before and after Justinian, law in the West in the late eleventh and twelfth centuries, and thereafter, was conceived to be an organically developing system, an ongoing, growing body of principles and procedures, constructed—like the cathedrals—over generations and centuries.

24.   The Decline of European Jewry

JEREMY COHEN

The Catholic church in western Europe first took official note of the
Jewish community in its midst at one of its earliest episcopal synods,
the Council of Elvira held at the beginning of the fourth century.
Even before the Roman Empire had chosen to tolerate Christianity,
Spanish prelates must have viewed the Jews as a sufficiently significant element in society to warrant legislation against excessive social
intercourse with them.[1] Throughout the Midddle Ages, the Jews constituted the only nonbelieving group consistently allowed to live in
Latin Christendom on any regular and prosperous basis. Nevertheless, by the middle of the sixteenth century few Jews remained in
western Europe. Expelled from England in 1290, France in 1394,
Spain and Sicily in 1492, Portugal in 1497, and the Kingdom of
Naples in 1541, European Jews could then live only in portions of
Germany and Italy. Most of those who remained found themselves
subject to increasingly harsh and humiliating forms of discrimination, ranging from ghettoization and exclusion from respectable occupations to excessive taxation and the public degradation of their
religion.

How ought one to account for the dramatic downfall of European
Jewry—a community which had once stood at the forefront of Jewish
economic and cultural productivity—during the closing centuries of

the medieval period? Historians have grappled incessantly with this question since the rise of critical Judaic scholarship in nineteenth-century Germany, and the subject has still not been exhausted. Virtually every authority on the period has had something new to add to the discussion, so that the pertinent historiography now abounds and itself demands recognition as a primary source for more recent intellectual history. . . .

The church's role in the decline of medieval European Jewry constitutes a complex question, whose difficulty is underscored by the decisiveness with which some historians have discounted it. The church did not contribute to the downfall of the medieval Jewish community, Gavin Langmuir and Kenneth Stow have argued, because medieval popes themselves never abandoned the patristic doctrine, first formulated as an institutional policy by Pope Gregory the Great, that the Jews had a rightful place in Christian society. *Sicut Iudeis*, the title of the papal edict of protection for the Jews issued repeatedly during the High Middle Ages, faithfully captured the spirit of ecclesiastical Jewish policy: "Just as license ought not to be granted the Jews to presume to do . . . more than the law permits them, just so ought they not to suffer curtailment in those [privileges] which have been conceded them."[2] Christian theology, to be sure, generated often virulent anti-Judaism in medieval society, but, in Kenneth Stow's words, "as the formal executive and legislative—and theological—center of the Church, it was the papacy which established what, for want of a better word, may be called the official policy toward the Jews. And it was to the papacy that Jews, from all the countries of Latin Europe, turned in time of crisis and tried to secure guarantees against attacks."[3]

Ought our discussion to end here? Should we reformulate our concern as the *religious component* in (rather than the ecclesiastical causes of) late medieval anti-Judaism, or may we recall that the medieval church viewed itself as embodying not only the papacy but all of Christian society? Semantic considerations aside, distinctions between the upper echelons of the ecclesiastical hierarchy, particular clerics or clerical factions, and the masses of the European laity acting on religious impulse deserve mention in any treatment of the church and the Jews.[4] And just as expressions of popular Christian piety often failed to comport with "official" church policy, so too did that policy at times develop for reasons having little to do with theology and doctrine, the anti-Jewish legislation of late medieval popes, for example, was seldom enforced thoroughly in the Papal States.[5] Moreover, since most would agree that medieval Jewry declined for a variety of interrelated reasons, how ought one to isolate and calculate the responsibility of the church? If anti-Jewish teachings permeated Christian theology when the Jews prospered as well as when they suffered, can one fairly deem them the cause of Jewish misfortune? Lacking extensive physical control over the life of the late medieval layman, does the church deserve blame for his actions undertaken in the name of its God? These and other questions have moved scholars to differentiate between "origins" and "causes" in evaluating the responsibility of the church for medieval anti-Judaism.[6] ...

Against this background, we may proceed to classify the noteworthy scholarly literature, characterized by two opposing schools of thought. On the one hand stand those interpretations which ascribe a major role in the decline and virtual disappearance of medieval Jewry to theological factors—reflected in official church policy or popular piety and belief, expressed in a substantive shift in Christian ideology, or manifested simply in the diligent application of hitherto unenforced doctrinal principles. The most popular tendency among such opinions, first evidenced clearly over a century ago by Otto Stobbe, views 1096 and the anti-Jewish violence which accompanied the Crusades as a decisive turning point, after which the status of the Jew declined steadily. The massacres of Franco-German Jewish communities in the name of Catholic piety revealed the inadequacy of existing legal safeguards for the person and property of the Jews. . . . The blood of the Jews had, as it were, been made free for the Christian masses. In respect to legal formulations, security and possibilities of livelihood, the First Crusade inaugurated a new and harsh epoch for Jews in Christian lands."[12] This outlook is reflected in the periodization which underlies major works of recent Judaic scholarship, despite a disinclination to view the crusading period as a "watershed" in general or Christian historiography.[13] Insightful variations on this theme include the argument of Hans Liebeschütz, that the ideas of Cluniac and Gregorian reform turned Christendom against the Jews even before the Council of Clermont in 1095. Amos Funkenstein has noted a new conception of medieval Jews as irrational and even heretical in the polemical writings of twelfth-century theologians. Lester Little, moreover, has argued that in the wake of the Crusades, European society first projected onto the Jews, who had played a dominant role in early medieval trade and commerce, the guilt derived from its own emergent "profit" economy. Christendom subsequently dispensed with the Jews altogether once new types of spirituality had mollified such pangs of conscience, and the presence of the Jews with their investment capital was no longer essential.[14] Nevertheless, the continuing prosperity of the western European Jewish community during the 150 years after 1096 has led other writers to discern religious causes for its decline only after the early Crusades. Heinrich Graetz, Moritz Güdemann, George Caro, and above all Solomon Grayzel have located such developments in the anti-Jewish legislation of Innocent III and his papal successors.[15] . . . And I have stressed the ideas and activities of the new mendicant friars, who called for the exclusion of the Jews from Europe on theological grounds, just as the thirteenth-century *Ecclesia* was attempting to regiment all of Western society into a perfectly integrated Christian commonwealth, often conceived organically as the mystical body of Christ. Scrutinizing the Talmud and other works of postbiblical Judaism, Dominican and Franciscan friars claimed that medieval Jews had forsaken their Old Testament heritage for a heretical, rabbinic perversion thereof and had thereby forfeited their privilege of inclusion in a properly ordered Christendom. Instead of the blind witnesses to the Christological truth of biblical prophecy whom church fathers like Augustine had perceived in the Jews, the friars now depicted them as deliberate unbelievers, ones who had killed the divine messiah intentionally and whose books and traditions could serve the church no constructive purpose.[16]

On the other hand, various scholars minimize the significance of religious factors in explaining the changing plight of medieval European Jewry. "Expansion and contraction of West-European Jewry," Salo Baron asserts categorically, "coincided with the great rise and decline in the temporal power of the Roman Church."[17] Only as the power and political influence of the papacy waned did the rulers of Europe expel their Jews. To explain this, Wilhelm Roscher contended in 1875 that the commercial jealousies of a nascent Christian bourgeoisie turned late medieval rulers against the Jewish community, which had virtually monopolized European commerce before the Crusades but by the thirteenth and fourteenth centuries could no longer be deemed indispensable. . . .

Despite the probable affinity between Roscher's views and German anti-Semitism of the late nineteenth century which Toni Oelsner has identified and vehemently condemned, many scholars, Jewish as well as Christian, have accepted this idea at face value and assumed it to be valid.[18] Others have suggested that the socioeconomic impact of Jewish moneylending, or perhaps even the emptiness of royal treasuries, caused the downfall of Jewish communities and the confiscation of their assets.[19] True to his theory that the Jews throughout history have fared worst in Gentile states of single nationalities, Baron himself explains that incipient medieval nationalism underlay the expulsions from England, France, Spain, and Portugal. Baron thus accounts for the survival of Jews in portions of early modern Italy and Germany, which failed to coalesce into national policies before the nineteenth century.[20] Yet another school of thought has stressed the changing configurations of political alliances involving king, aristocracy, and bourgeoisie, in which the Jews were not directly involved but from whose volatility they often had most to lose.[21]

From this spectrum of interpretations, three stand out as especially helpful in illuminating and clarifying the complexities of our subject. In a lengthy article titled "The Jews and the Archives of Angevin England: Reflections on Medieval Anti-Semitism," Gavin Langmuir grapples with the question through his analysis of H. G. Richardson's *English Jewry under the Angevin Kings* and exemplifies the tendency to disregard almost completely the role of the church in the decline of medieval Jewry. Criticizing "an archival perspective in medieval studies . . . whose horizon is limited by a concern to establish as much detailed information on a given topic as the state of the archives will permit . . . but the level of [whose] insight into the implication of the facts so discovered tends to be low,"[22] Langmuir demonstrates the extensive ramifications of medieval anti-Judaism as a historical and historiographical problem. Popular prejudices both medieval and modern join with the complex legal, socioeconomic, and theological status of the Jews so as to require of the historian an imaginative and discerning disposition as well as a scientific one. As for the church's contribution to the persecution and eventual expulsion of English Jews in the thirteenth century, assumed by Richardson to be significant, Langmuir proceeds to the opposite extreme. Not only must one distinguish between ecclesiastical policies properly implemented by clerical authorities and unlicensed actions of individual churchmen, but one must also look beyond the reason why the Jews in particular suffered during the Middle Ages and consider European society's need for a scapegoat in the first place. Although the church had always condemned Judaism, it consistently called for toleration; and "what is remarkable in the Middle Ages is not that the doctrine on the Jews was emphasized, but that it underwent so little change."[23] Such constancy in Christian doctrine was hardly duplicated in the actual treatment of the Jews—hence "the existence of the doctrine is a very insufficient explanation" for their downfall, especially in view of the simultaneously waning influence of the church over European kings. Instead, Langmuir calls for further research into the effects "of a new social, political, and economic order" on late medieval Jewry, and into the changing nature of irrational popular attitudes toward the Jews between 1096 and 1400.[24]

Writing only two years after Langmuir, Lea Dasberg presents a sound case that religious ideas did contribute heavily to the anti-

Jewish persecutions of the High and late Middle Ages, beginning with the massacres accompanying the Crusades.[25] Dasberg argues effectively against attributing these hostilities to commercial rivalries, still a popular scholarly tendency. The Jews did not dominate European commerce to the extent that many have assumed, nor was it the Christian merchant who typically turned against them.[26] Although sympathetic with Kisch's view of 1236 as the commencement of Jewish serfdom in Germanic law, Dasberg's argument demonstrates the gap so characteristic of the relationship between imperial policy and lawbook. In this case, "Jewry law" lagged far behind important changes in "Jewish policy," which in turn emerged from a new religious orientation two centuries in its development. For the changing conceptions of the Jews evident in the massacres of 1096 derived from the spirit of Cluniac reform in the tenth century, a new idealism vis-à-vis worldly issues which within several generations had influenced the policies of the papacy. While the church endeavored to raise the esteem of the simple man and transformed basically economic issues into religious-ethical ones, it also began to pose itself against the established political-economic power held responsible for such social injustice—the secular princes and, by extension, the Jews under their protection. Dasberg treats the Investiture Controversy and the anti-Jewish violence of the Crusades as two stages of the same conflict, that of reformers versus the simoniacal establishment, and even classifies the respective reactions of burghers, princes, and bishops to the violence according to their stance in the papal-imperial conflict. Coupled with a surge of apocalyptic fervor calling for the conversion of the infidel, the piety which sustained the Crusade understandably precipitated the persecution of the Jews.

In a brief but penetrating essay published [in 1978], Israeli historian Maurice Kriegel proposes a qualitatively new "organic" model to account for the expulsion of Jews from England, France, and Spain (and even from portions of Germany)—a theory which in many ways balances the opposing viewpoints of Langmuir and Dasberg.[27] This interpretation properly considers each of the traditional explanations—theological, socioeconomic, or political—unsatisfactory on its own, either because it fails to account for the complexity of the process which culminated in the expulsions or because the events of the specific expulsions simply fail to substantiate it. Instead, Kriegel argues, decrees of banishment in fact derived from royal attempts to integrate and mobilize previously fragmented societies, through the consolidation of territorial domains, the strengthening of urban power centers, the institution of a governmental bureaucracy—in a word, through the construction of a state. Realization of these goals depended in large measure on the successful manipulation of public opinion to engender a unity of spirit among diverse elements of the population. Here Kriegel's thesis departs from the nationalistic interpretation of Salo Baron. For the goal of unity induced Edward I of England, Philip IV of France, and Ferdinand and Isabella of Spain to exploit the traditional religious sentiments of their subjects, seeking to characterize their monarchies as sacred, heavenly kingdoms. Appeal to popular religious belief and custom allowed these monarchs to rally their constituencies around policies which often lacked theological derivation, without impinging upon their ability to generate and pursue such policies autocratically. . . . Desire for political and economic gain did not preclude the sincerity of their piety; such was "le paradoxe de la double présence de la religiosité et de la convoitise."[28] Sociopolitical mobilization and modernization built upon age-old Christian beliefs and institutions, and the need for valuable unanimity in religious ideology outweighed any benefits which accrued from the Jewish presence. Curiously, concludes Kriegel, the emergence of the modern state united with traditional religious fervor to induce the expulsion of the Jews, *ad maiorem Dei gloriam.*

Each of the three scholars mentioned here signals progress achieved in recent historiography as well as directions in which research into this question must still advance. The problematic relationship between popular piety and official ecclesiastical doctrine notwithstanding, the teachings and policies of the medieval church clearly played a part in the downfall of the European Jewish community together with numerous other factors. These require careful identification and definition, while their interaction with Christian theology and popular prejudice demands analysis. We need to know precisely how religious ideas were brought to bear upon political policy and socioeconomic reality. The arguments of Langmuir, Dasberg, and Kriegel have shown that the answer is far from simple. Any convincing interpretation of the demise of medieval Jewry must consider factors which ultimately had little to do with the Jews and Judaism—Cluniac or Gregorian reform, the development of popular superstition and prejudice, and the drive toward sociopolitical integration on a national scale. In much the same way as John Boswell has shown how the general penchant for order and uniformity in twelfth-century Christendom triggered the persecution of homosexuals, who previously had enjoyed toleration, historians of the Jews must integrate their particular concerns with the larger tendencies and processes of medieval European history in general.[29] Moving in this direction, Langmuir, Dasberg, and Kriegel succeed in discrediting traditional and simplistic interpretations of earlier historians, but the full value of their respective theories has not yet been appreciated. Their speculative suggestions have yet to be tested thoroughly, and the applicability of their explanatory models must be shown to transcend medieval political boundaries, in order to do justice to our historical puzzle.

NOTES

1. Mansi, 2:8 (16), 14 (49–50), 18 (78). See also my "Roman Imperial Policy toward the Jews from Constantine until the End of the Palestinian Patriarchate (ca. 429)," *Byzantine Studies* 3 (1976): 3ff.

2. Kenneth R. Stow, *Catholic Thought and Papal Jewry Policy, 1555–1593,* Moreshet: Studies in Jewish History, Literature and Thought 5 (New York, 1977), pp. xi–xxviii; Gavin I. Langmuir, "The Jews and the Archives of Angevin England: Reflections on Medieval Anti-Semitism," *Traditio* 19 (1963): 183–244. The text and a translation of *Sicut Iudeis* appear in Solomon Grayzel, *The Church and the Jews in the XIIIth Century* (1933; reprint New York, 1966), pp. 92–95. See also Solomon Katz, "Pope Gregory the Great and the Jews," *Jewish Quarterly Review,* n.s. 24 (1933–34): 113–36; and Grayzel, "The Papal Bull *Sicut Judaeis,*" in *Studies and Essays in Honor of Abraham A. Neuman,* ed. Meir Ben-Horin et al. (Leiden, 1962), pp. 243–80.

3. Stow, *Catholic Thought,* p. xix. Stow has since developed, refined, and strengthened his thesis in "Hatred of the Jews, or Love of the Church: Papal Policy toward the Jews [in Hebrew]," in *Antisemitism through the Ages,* ed. S. Almog (Jerusalem, 1980), pp. 91–111; and in *The "1007 Anonymous" and Papal Sovereignty: Jewish Perceptions of the Papacy and Papal Policy in the High Middle Ages,* Hebrew Union College Annual Supplements 4 (Cincinnati, 1984).

4. Among many others, see in this regard Peter Browe, "Die Judenbekämpfung im Mittelalter," *Zeitschrift für katholische Theologie* 62 (1938): 197–231, 349–84, "Die religiöse Duldung der Juden im Mittelalter," *Archiv für katholisches Kirchenrecht* 118 (1938): 3–76, and *Die Judenmission im Mittelalter und die Päpste,* Miscellanca historiae pontificiae 6 (Rome, 1942); and Joshua Trachtenberg, *The Devil and the Jews: The Medieval Conception of the Jew in Its Relation to Modern Antisemitism* (New Haven, 1943), esp. chaps. 11ff.

5. Moritz Güdemann, *Geschichte des Erziehungswesens und der Cultur des abendländischen Juden während des Mittelalters und der neueren Zeit,* 3 vols. (1880–88; reprint Amsterdam, 1966); 2:74ff.; Solomon Grayzel, "The Avignon Popes and the Jews," *Historia Judaica* 2 (1940): 1–12; and Salo Wittmayer Baron, *A Social and Religious History of the Jews,* 2d ed., 17 vols. (New York, 1952–80), 9:44–50—among others.

6. Langmuir, "Jews," p. 230.

12. Otto Stobbe, *Die Juden in Deutschland während des Mittelalters in politischer, socialer and rechtlicher Beziehung* (1866, reprint Amsterdam, 1966), pp. 15, 103ff., 163–93; Haim Hillel Ben-Sasson et al., *A History of the Jewish People*, trans. George Weidenfeld (Cambridge, Mass., 1976), p. 414. Cf. also Simon Dubnow, *Weltgeschichte des jüdischen Volkes*, 10 vols. (Berlin, 1925–30), 4:269ff.; Browe, "Judenbekämpfung im Mittelalter," pp. 198, 211–23; Parkes, *Jew*, pp. 81ff.; George LaPiana, "The Church and the Jews," *Historia Judaica* 11 (1949): 117–44; Trachtenberg, *Devil*, p. 167; and Leon Poliakov, *The History of Anti-Semitism*, vol. 1, trans. Richard Howard and Natalie Gerardi (New York, 1965), pt. 2.

13. For examples of the tendency in Jewish historiography, see Benzion Dinur, *Israel in the Diaspora, II: From the Persecutions of 1096 until the Black Death* (in Hebrew), 2d ed., vol. 1 (Tel Aviv, 1965), esp. pp. 1–6; Blumenkranz, *Juifs et Chrétiens*; Cecil Roth, ed., *The Dark Ages: Jews in Christian Europe, 711–1096*, World History of the Jewish People 11 (New Brunswick, N.J., 1966); and the original Hebrew of Ben-Sasson, *History of the Jewish People*, vol. 2, *The Middle Ages* (in Hebrew) (Tel Aviv, 1969), pp. 21, 83. Robert Chazan's *European Jewry and the First Crusade* (Berkeley, 1986) did not appear in time for consideration in this essay.

14. Hans Liebeschütz, "The Crusading Movement in Its Bearing on the Christian Attitude towards Jewry," *Journal of Jewish Studies* 10 (1959): 97–111; Amos Funkenstein, "Changes in the Patterns of Christian Anti-Jewish Polemic in the Twelfth Century" (in Hebrew), *Zion*, n.s. 33 (1968): 125–44, and idem, "Basic Types of Christian Anti-Jewish Polemics in the Later Middle Ages," *Viator* 2 (1971): 373–82; Lester K. Little, *Religious Poverty and the Profit Economy in Medieval Europe* (Ithaca, N.Y., 1978), pp. 42–57, 216.

15. Graetz, *Geschichte*, 6:226f., and ibid., vol. 7, 3d ed. (Leipzig, 1894), pp. 3–18; Güdemann, *Geschichte*, 2:84ff.; Georg Caro, *Sozial- und Wirtschaftsgeschichte der Juden im Mittelalter und der Neuzeit* (1908–18; reprint Hildesheim, 1964), 1:228–453; and of the many works of Solomon Grayzel, see, above all, *Church and the Jews*, esp. pp. 1–82; "The Beginning of Exclusion," *Jewish Quarterly Review*, n.s. 61 (1970); 15–26 (quotation on p. 15), and "Popes, Jews, and the Inquisition from 'Sicut' to 'Turbato,' " in *Essays on the Occasion of the Seventieth Anniversary of Dropsie University*, ed. Abraham I. Katsch and Leon Nemoy (Philadelphia, 1979), pp. 151–88. Cf. also Louis I. Rabinowitz, *The Social Life of the Jews of Northern France in the XII–XIV Centuries as Reflected in the Rabbinical Literature of the Period* (1938; reprint New York, 1972), p. 18.

16. See my *The Friars and the Jews: The Evolution of Medieval Anti-Judaism* (Ithaca, N.Y., 1982), "The Jews as the Killers of Christ in the Latin Tradition, from Augustine to the Friars," *Traditio* 39 (1983): 1–27, and "Scholarship and Intolerance in the Medieval Academy: The Study and Valuation of Judaism in European Christendom," *American Historical Review* 91 (1986): 592–613.

17. Baron, *History*, 9:3, 5.

18. Wilhelm Roscher, "Die Stellung der Juden im Mittelalter, betrachtet

vom Standpunkte der allgemeinen Handelspolitik," *Zeitschrift für die gesamte Staatswissenschaft* 31 (1875): 503–26, the relevant portion of which has been translated by Solomon Grayzel as "The Status of the Jews in the Middle Ages Considered from the Standpoint of Commercial Policy," *Historia Judaica* 6 (1944): 13–26 (quotation on p. 20). The nature and influence of Roscher's views have been discussed by Guido Kisch, "The Jews' Function in the Medieval Evolution of Economic Life," *Historia Judaica* 6 (1944): 1–12; and Toni Oelsner, "Wilhelm Roscher's Theory and the Economic and Social Position of the Jews in the Middle Ages: A Critical Examination," *Yivo Annual of Jewish Social Science* 12 (1958–59): 176–95, and idem "The Place of the Jews in Economic History as Viewed by German Scholars," *Yearbook of the Leo Baeck Institute* 7 (1962): 188–91. Subsequent advocates of Roscher's approach to our question have included Karl Gottfried Hugelmann, "Studien zum Recht der Nationalitäten un deutschen Mittelalter," *Historisches Jahrbuch* 48 (1928): 578–81; Raphael Straus, "The Jews in the Economic Evolution of Central Europe," *Jewish Social Studies* 3 (1941): 15–40; Karl W. Deutsch, "Anti-Semitic Ideas in the Middle Ages," *Journal of the History of Ideas* 6 (1945): 248, 250; and Abraham Leon, *The Jewish Question: A Marxist Interpretation* (New York, 1970).

19. P. Elman, "The Economic Causes of the Expulsion of the Jews in 1290," *Economic History Review*, 1st ser. 7 (1936–37): 145–54; Parkes, *Jew,* chap. 10; Trachtenberg, *Devil,* chap. 13; Simon Schwarzfuchs, "The Expulsion of the Jews from France (1306)," in *Seventy-fifth Anniversary Volume of the Jewish Quarterly Review,* ed. Abraham A. Neuman and Solomon Zeitlin (Philadelphia, 1967), pp. 482–89.

20. Salo Wittmayer Baron, "Nationalism and Intolerance," *Menorah Journal* 16 (1929): 503–15 (quotation on p. 504), 17 (1929): 148–58; idem, *History* 10:116–17, 11:118–283, 12:3–4.

21. Benzion Netanyahu, *Don Isaac Abravanel, Statesman and Philosopher,* 3d ed. (Philadelphia, 1972), chaps. 1–2, passim; Barnett D. Ovrut, "Edward I and the Expulsion of the Jews," *Jewish Quarterly Review,* n.s. 67 (1977): 224–35.

22. Langmuir, "Jews," p. 185; H. G. Richardson, *English Jewry under the Angevin Kings* (London, 1960).

23. Langmuir, "Jews," p. 235. On attitudes to Jewish history in modern historiography, see also idem, "Majority History and Post-Biblical Jews," *Journal of the History of Ideas* 27 (1966): 343–64.

24. Langmuir, "Jews," pp. 235–44. In "L'absence d'accusation de meurtre rituel à l'ouest du Rhône," in *Juifs et judaisme de Languedoc: XIIIe siècle-début XIVe siècle,* ed. Marie-Humbert Vicaire and Bernhard Blumenkranz, Collection Franco-Judaica 6/Cahiers de Fanjeaux 12 (Toulouse, 1977), pp. 235–49, Langmuir subsequently applied his perspective to the popularity of the ritual murder accusation in northern Europe of the later Middle Ages and its virtual absence in southern Europe. Socioeconomic and psychological factors, not the doctrine of the church, underlay the realia of anti-Jewish persecutions. In the south, Langmuir explains (pp. 245–46),

"l'hostilité populaire existait, bien sûr, mais elle fut bien moindre qu'en Europe du Nord, peut-être parce que, en Europe du Sud, le developpement précoce du commerce et du crédit chrétien avait rendu les Juifs moins distincts; y contribuaient également le pluralisme culturel, l'instruction générale, et la complexité de l'organisation sociale. De plus, 'il semble que les croyances religieuses aient joué un rôle plus circonscrit dans cette vielle société bien romanisée."

25. Lea Dasberg, *Untersuchungen über die Entwertung des Judenstatus im II. Jahrhundert* (Paris, 1965).

27. Maurice Kriegel, "Mobilisation politique et modernisation organique: Les expulsions de Juifs au bas Moyen Age," *Archives de sciences sociales des religions* 46 (1978): 5–20. Kriegel has developed his interpretation of the expulsion from Spain more extensively in "La prise d'une décision: L'expulsion des Juifs d'Espagne en 1492," *Revue historique* 260 (1978): 49–90. Cf. also his *Les Juifs à la fin due Moyen Age dans l'Europe.*

28. Kriegel, "Mobilisation," p. 17.

29. John Boswell, *Christianity, Social Tolerance, and Homosexuality: Gay People in Europe from the Beginning of the Christian Era to the Fourteenth Century* (Chicago, 1980), pt. 4. See also my *Friars*, esp. chap. 10, which seeks to establish a similar basis for the anti-Judaism of thirteenth- and fourteenth-century Dominicans and Franciscans.

THE MEDIEVAL STATE: SOVER-EIGNTY, LAW, CONSTITUTIONALISM

THE PROBLEM OF periodization connected with the idea of a
"twelfth-century Renaissance" arises in an especially interesting
form when we turn to problems concerning political theory and the
growth of governmental institutions.

Some historians have seen the political practices and political
theories of the medieval period as the essential sources of modern
constitutionalism. Others insist on a radical discontinuity between
medieval and modern forms of government. The first group points
to the existence of representative assemblies in the Middle Ages and

to the widely held ideal of "government under the law." The second group argues that the very idea of the state was lacking in the Middle Ages and was created only in the sixteenth century with Machiavelli's "ragione dello stato" and Bodin's theory of sovereignty.

This second point of view is presented in the first two readings of this section. The current criticisms of it are based in large part on recent studies in medieval Roman and canon law. Even if the earlier Middle Ages had no conception of the state or legislative sovereignty, it is argued, this situation began to change with growth of legal studies in the twelfth century. Gaines Post maintains that medieval jurists derived sophisticated concepts of sovereignty, public utility, and "reason of state" from their studies of Roman law. The next reading explores some sources of the Western constitutional tradition. Finally, the reading from G. L. Haskins complements these theoretical discussions with a description of a fourteenth-century parliament in action.

25. On the Lack of a State and Legislative Power in the Middle Ages

A. The Lack of a State

NEVILLE FIGGIS

When all is said (and in studying this subject one is at times inclined to deny that political doctrines ever began at all) there remains a great gulf fixed between medieval and modern thought. We in the twentieth century think of the State as essentially one, irresistible in theory and practice, with a uniform system of law and a secure government. Rights of personal liberty, of the security of property, of general protection, of legal equality, and religious liberty, are so generally recognized that however difficult it may be to agree upon an abstract basis we take them for granted and they have become a part of the furniture of our minds. In our view the world of politics is composed of certain communities entirely independent, territorially omnipotent, and to some extent morally responsible. A set of rules founded upon an insecure basis of custom, convenience, humanity, or natural reason admittedly exists, to which under the name of international law they pay a nominal, reluctant, and none too regular obedience—which is however more regular and less reluctant than was the obedience six centuries ago paid to the common law by any decently placed medieval feudatory.

From Neville Figgis, *Studies of Political Thought from Gerson to Grotius*, 2nd ed., (Cambridge: Cambridge University Press, 1916), pp. 12–15. Reprinted by permission of the publisher.

Again, the theocratic and still more the juristic conception of political right has gone from the educated world. Providence, doubtless, has to do with politics as with other human affairs, and all
Theists must allow that political associations have some divine sanction. But most are now agreed to relegate the part of Providence to
that of final cause. There has been a revolution in political thought,
not dissimilar to the substitution of efficient for final causes as an
account of natural phenomena. I do not of course mean that all
hold the same ethical theory, but that institutions and all alleged
rights must be able to show some practical utility if their existence
is to be maintained. All arguments but those of public policy are to
a great extent laughed out of court. Now in the Middle Ages political
argument went on the basis of alleged private rights, whether divine
or purely human in origin. Arguments from convenience are sometimes found; at no time can institutions maintain themselves for
which some form of utility cannot be argued. We have passed the
defence of rights to the realisation of right and it is not at all clear
that we have gained. Perhaps it would be most accurate to say, that
in the Middle Ages human welfare and even religion was conceived
under the form of legality, while in the modern world this has given
place to utility.

In the Middle Ages the omnipotent territorial State, treated as a
person and the coëqual of other states, was non-existent. It might
be a dream, or even a prophecy, it was nowhere a fact. What we call
the State was a loosely compacted union with "rights of property
and sovereignty everywhere shading into one another" and the central power struggling for existence. Neither Normandy nor Burgundy, neither the dominions of Henry the Lion nor those of a Duke
of Aquitaine, formed a State in the modern sense, yet how far can
their rulers be regarded as in any real sense subjects? At last indeed,
with the growth of federalism in idea and fact and in our own possessions beyond the seas, we are going back to a state of things in
some ways analogous to the medieval. But the modern post-Refor-
mation State *par excellence* is unitary, omnipotent, and irresistible, and
is found in perfection not in England, but in France or the German
States of the *ancien régime*. Joseph II dotted the i's of Luther's handwriting.

Yet even granting that the King of France or Germany was a
true sovereign in his temporal dominions, the power of the Church
and the orders was a vast inroad on governmental authority. It is to
be noted that Suarez and others developed a doctrine of extra-
territoriality out of rights preserved by the universities and the monastic orders of the Church. There was one really universal order in
Western Christendom and its right name was the Church. True, the

Canonists never got all that they wanted, yet as has been said "no one dreams that the King can alter the Common Law of the Catholic Church," and that Common Law included a great deal of what is really civil law. Nowadays it is to be decided on grounds of public policy how far the State shall permit the freedom of religious bodies, although our own views of policy may be that interference is inexpedient because it is wrong. But at that time it was the State which existed on sufferance, or rather the secular authority, for the very term State is an anachronism. It would be an interesting point to determine accurately the casues which have led to the substitution in general use of the term State for Commonwealth or republic. I think that Italy and Machiavelli are important factors. The object of the civil power, the wielder of the temporal sword, *within* the Church-State was not attack, but defence against a claim to universal dominion. The Holy Roman Empire, the most characteristic of all medieval institutions, did indeed attempt to realise the idea of an all powerful State, but that State was the Church. The ideal was realised only very partially and then as a rule only by the undue predominance of the ecclesiastical element. Innocent III was a more truly universal power than most of the successors of Charles the Great. The conflict with the Popes which prevented the Emperors realising this idea was also an assistance to the gradual growth of national States, and the break-up of Christendom. That word is now merely a geographical expression. It was a fact in the Middle Ages. The real State of the Middle Ages in the modern sense—if the words are not a paradox—is the Church.

B. The Lack of Legislative Power

FRITZ KERN

For us law needs only one attribute in order to give it validity; it must, directly or indirectly, be sanctioned by the State. But in the Middle Ages, different attributes altogether were essential; mediaeval law must be "old" law and must be "good" law. Mediaeval law could dispense with the sanction of the State, but not with the two qualities of Age and Goodness, which, as we shall see, were considered to be one and the same thing. If law were not old and good law, it was not law at all, even though it were formally enacted by the State.

From Fritz Kern, *Kingship and Law in the Middle Ages,* S. B. Chrimes, trans. (Oxford: Basil Blackwell, 1956), pp. 149–151. Reprinted by permission of the publisher.

I. Law Is Old

Age has at all times been important for subjective rights, especially for rights of possession, and in certain circumstances, prescription can have the force of law. But for the validity of objective law, Age, in the present era of enacted law, is of no account. For us, law, from the time of its promulgation to that of its repeal, is neither old nor new, but simply exists. In the Middle Ages, it was a different matter altogether; Age was then the most important quality even of objective law. *Law was in fact custom.* Immemorial usage, testified to by the memory of the oldest and most credible people; the *leges patrum,* sometimes but not necessarily proven by external aids to memory, such as charters, boundaries, law-books, or anything else that out-lived human beings: this was objective law. And if any particular sub-jective right was in dispute, the fact that it was in harmony with an ancient custom had much the same importance as would be given to-day to the fact that it was derived from a valid law of the State.

It is true that for law to be law, it had to be not only old, but also "good." The controversy among modern jurists, as to whether great age creates or merely reveals the binding force of customary law, would have been meaningless to mediaeval minds. For age cannot create law, and long-usage does not prove a practice to be rightful. On the contrary, "a hundred years of wrong make not one hour of right," and Eike of Repgow in the *Sachsenspiegel,* for example, em-phasized that slavery, which originated in force and unjust power, and was a custom so ancient that "it is now held for law," was only an "unlawful custom." The existence of an unlawful or "evil" cus-tom for so long a time shows that usage or age cannot make or reveal law. In Eike's estimation, slavery, though ancient, was a modern abuse as compared with the universal liberty which prevailed "when man first established law." Prior to the centuries of abuse, there were a thousand years of law, perhaps even an eternal and imprescriptible law. It was through the notion of imprescriptibility that ecclesiastical ideas entered into Germanic concepts of law. The law of nature of the Golden Age, in the ultimate analysis, stamped as unlawful every legal system resting upon the inequality of man. Even if in this ex-ample the popular legal ideas of the Middle Ages (with which we are alone concerned in this study) are coloured by learned jurisprud-ence, the fact remains that the law's inflexible resistance to institu-tions justified solely by long usage is characteristic of mediaeval legal thought as a whole.

Not the State, but "God is the source of all law." Law is a part of the world-order; it is unchangeable. It can be twisted anf falsified, but then it restores itself, and at last confounds the evil-doer who meddled with it. If anyone, a member of the folk, or even the highest authority in the State, made a "law" which conflicted with a good old custom, and this custom were proved beyond doubt by the evidence of venerable witnesses or by the production of a royal charter, then the newly-made law was no law, but a wrong; not *usus*, but *abusus*. In such a case, it was the duty of every lawful man, of those in authority as well as the common man, to restore the good old law. The common man as well as the constituted authority is under obligation to the law, and required to help restore it. The law being sacred, both ruler and subject, State and citizen, are equally authorized to preserve it. These facts lead to extremely important conclusions in the constitutional sphere; but we shall also see that ideas as wide in scope and as ill-defined as the mediaeval idea of law, gave rise to great confusion in practical life.

But let us first throw more light upon the peculiar consequences that followed from the fact that Age was a necessary attribute of law.

When a case arises, for which no valid law can be adduced, then the lawful men or doomsmen will make new law in the belief that what they are making is good old law, not indeed expressly handed-down, but tacitly existent. They do not, therefore, create the law; they "discover it." Any particular judgment in court, which we regard as a particular inference from a general established legal rule, was to the mediaeval mind in no way distinguishable from the legislative activity of the community; in both cases a law hidden but already existing is discovered, not created. There is, in the Middle Ages, no such thing as "the first application of a legal rule." Law is old; new law is a contradiction in terms; for either new law is derived explicitly or implicitly from the old, or it conflicts with the old, in which case it is not lawful. The fundamental idea remains the same: the old law is the true law, and true law is the old law. According to mediaeval ideas, therefore, the enactment of new law is not possible at all; and all legislation and legal reform is conceived of as the restoration of the good old law which has been violated.

26. The Emergence of the State

GAINES POST

Almost forty years ago Charles Homer Haskins applied the word renaissance to the twelfth century. Whether or not it was a renaissance the twelfth century was in fact a period of great creative activity. The revival of political, economic, and social life, along with the appearance of new learning, new schools, and new literature and styles of art and architecture, signified the beginnings, in the West, of modern European civilization. In the thirteenth century what had begun in the twelfth arrived at such maturity that it is safe to say that early modern Europe was coming into being.

Among the institutions and fields of knowledge created by medieval men, the university and the State and the legal science that aided in the creation of both were, as much as the rise of an active economy and the organization of towns, important manifestations of the new age. While accepting and respecting tradition and believing in the unchanging higher law of nature that came from God, kings, statesmen, and men of learning confidently applied reason and skill to the work of introducing order into society and societies, into feudal kingdoms, Italian communes, and lesser communities of the clergy and laity. Long before the recovery of Aristotle's *Politics,* the naturalness of living in politically and legally organized communities of corporate guilds, chapters, towns, and States was recognized both in practice and in legal thought. Nature itself sanctioned the use of human reason and art to create new laws for the social

From Gaines Post, *Studies in Medieval Legal Thought* (Princeton, NJ: Princeton University Press, 1964), pp. 3–4, 7–9, 12–16, 23–24, 248–249. Reprinted by permission of Princeton University Press.

and political life on earth—provided always, of course, that the new laws did not violate the will of God.

At the very time when merchants, artisans, townsmen, and school-men were forming their associations for mutual aid and protection, the study of the Roman and Canon law at Bologna introduced law-yers, jurists, and secular and ecclesiastical authorities to the legal thought of Rome on corporations. When kings were trying to over-come the anarchy of feudalism, the new legal science furnished those principles of public law that helped them convert their realms into States.

• • •

For the present purpose, it is sufficient to observe that Hans Kel-sen, one of the greatest authorities on the modern State and the public law, defined the State as a juristic entity, a personification of the national legal order, a politically organized society, and a subject of rights and duties. Its rights are largely public rights, asserted in terms of the public welfare and the common utility. And the public law, let me add, is not only the law that deals with the public authority and the public welfare; it is at times the government, the constitu-tional order, without which the State is nothing. At any rate, we can understand that when the "public welfare clause" is invoked in con-nection with the building of highways or with necessary preparations for war, private rights inevitably must yield. The public interest, sometimes tyrannically, demands it. Evidently the "public welfare clause" is connected with the "right of State"; and the State, what-ever it is, is thus superior to all individuals and individual rights. The State is above the law of the land which protects private rights. In times of grave crisis, of a national emergency, of necessity, it is certain that the government of the United States can do extraordinary things which normally the law of the land does not permit. And yet even then the public "right of State" must have some regard for the rights of private citizens.

In Germany and Italy we have seen the extreme logical application of the idea that the State is above the law—and normally rather than in emergencies. The State of Nazi Germany and Fascist Italy was the culmination of that amoral necessity or "reason of State" which, some historians claim, first appeared in the Italian Renaissance. In 1914 Bethmann-Hollweg asserted the principle in the words "Ne-cessity knows no law" in order to justify the German violation of the neutrality of Belgium.

All of these expressions—"public" or "common utility" or "wel-fare," "emergency," "necessity," "necessity knows no law," and "reason of the *status* or public welfare"—are to be found in the twelfth and thirteenth centuries. The purpose of this study is to point to their origin in the Roman law, to show how the legists and canonists used them to develop the early modern theory of public law and the State; and to observe how kings, emperors, and popes were employing the new terminology to justify their claim to an authority that represented the public and common welfare and the *status* (state) of Realm or Church and was therefore above human if not natural law.

• • •

The legists started building their theories, naturally, on the foundation of Roman law, although Aristotle was of some influence by the end of the thirteenth century. They started with Ulpian's famous statement (D.1, 1, 1, 2; also *Inst.* 1, 1): "Public law pertains to the *status rei Romanae* [state of the Roman republic*]; private, to the utility of individuals. Public law relates to religion, priests, and magistrates." On this, as early as 1228, a glossator even seemed to personify *status*, saying that public law exists "to preserve the state, lest it perish." But probably, like others, he meant the public welfare of the Empire. For Odofredo a little later asserted that the public law pertains chiefly to the *status* of the whole Empire, and the glossators in Accursius' *Glossa ordinaria* related *status* to the public utility. Like Azo, they held that if private law pertains primarily to the utility of individuals, it pertains secondarily to the public utility, since it interests the *Respublica* (the State) that no one should misuse his property. Contrariwise, what is primarily public, secondarily pertains to the utility of individuals. Accursius added that it is for the utility or welfare of individuals that the Republic be preserved unharmed—an approach to the frequently expressed idea that the common utility is essentially the safety of all collectively and individually. Odofredo said, in adding to the thought of the glossators, that one of the concerns of the Republic is that its subjects be rich, even though property belongs to private law.

The public law, then, dealt with the public or common utility and safety, with the *status* of the State. In the sense that the public utility was generally a higher good than private (this was also the opinion of the scholastic philosophers, particularly of St. Thomas Aquinas— the salvation of one's soul is the only private right that is superior to the public utility, except in the case of a bishop, who cannot, said Pope Innocent III, resign his office to save his own soul if he is

---

*The medieval word *status* was used in phrases like "state of the Church" and "state of the republic" to mean the general condition or public welfare of a community. Such usages led to the modern, more abstract concept of "the State."—Ed.

needed to help others to salvation), in this sense the State, the true bearer of the public utility, was superior to its subjects considered individually and collectively.

It follows that public law must deal more specifically with the means of assuring the *status* of the *Respublica*. The concept of public law was attached to the public authority, the government, which existed to administer the State for the common utility, good, and safety of all, which interpreted the public law and the common welfare, and which therefore had a certain prerogative that made it superior, in an emergency or necessity, to the private law and private rights. Therefore, as Odofredo put it, summing up Azo and the glossators, it was of public interest to have *sacra,* churches and priests to save people from their sins, and to protect priests from injury; and to have magistrates, for laws would be of no value without men to administer justice. Public law, then, dealt with the Church and the clergy, and with the office of magistrates. The *Glossa ordinaria* added the *fiscus* and fiscal law to the realm of public law.

. . .

In their treatment of public law, therefore, the legists included the right of the public authority to tax for the *status* or public utility of the community. This power of taxation was not an outgrowth of the right of expropriation by the public authority, because it was not confiscation, and the consent of those taxed was more clearly involved. If the power to tax came under the scope of public law, so the power to legislate. This is not the place to discuss the medieval theory of legislation as law-finding rather than law-making. But in the thirteenth century the legists certainly held that the right to make statutes, general laws for the common utility, belonged to the public authority by public law, even though the consent of prelates and nobles (or, in the Italian republic, the consent of the leading citizens) was necessary. The power to legislate belonged to the ruler as the public authority, and general laws were made for the *status* or public utility of empire, kingdom, or city state. Moreover, the power of jurisdiction, as we have seen, was a part of the public law on magistracy, and jurisdiction in the Middle Ages was not clearly distinguished from legislation as law-finding. But all the same, there was a theory of law-making in the antique-modern sense. This theory derived in part from passages in *Code* and *Digest* on legislation by the Roman emperor for emergencies not covered by the old body of law, and on the making of new laws for new matters not decided by the old law, if "evident utility" exists. The legists interpreted "evident utility" as the common utility of all subjects and as a case of necessity. By doing so they showed that the public authority existed to meet emergencies, new situations, in order to maintain the common welfare or *status*, in the field of legislation as in that of taxation.

• • •

On the foundation of the two laws and of the rise of feudal monarchies, the theory, and some practice, of public law and the State thus arose in the twelfth and thirteenth centuries. Private rights and privileges remained powerful and enjoyed a recrudescence in localism and privileged orders in the fourteenth century and later. At times, in periods of war and civil dissension, they weakened the public authority of kings and threatened the very survival of the State. But the ideas and ideal of the State and public order, of a public and constitutional law, were constantly at hand to remind statesmen of their right to reconstitute the State. . . .

The objection is often raised, however, that medieval kingdoms were not States because (1) they accepted the spiritual authority of the pope and the universal Church, (2) king and realm were under God and the law of nature, and (3) the royal government was poorly centralized. As for the first argument, it might be raised against the use of the term "State" for Eire and Spain today. Yet we assume that these two countries are States even though they are essentially Catholic and in some fashion recognize the spiritual authority of the Roman Church. With respect to other ideals of universalism, the United States and Italy, not to mention other nations, are sovereign States, while belonging to the United Nations. As for the second argument, on subjection to God and a moral law, it must be replied that the official motto of the United States is "In God We Trust," and Americans take an oath of loyalty to "one nation indivisible under God." Furthermore, the sovereignty of the American people and their State is surely limited in fact by a moral law that belongs to the Judaeo-Christian tradition: it is not likely that the representatives of the people in Congress will ever think of making laws that violate the Ten Commandments, nor that the Supreme Court will approve them. It is therefore not absurd to call medieval kingdoms States despite limitations within which derived from the ideal of law and justice, and despite limitations from without (also within) from the universalism of Christianity and the Church. Papal arbitration of "international" disputes in the thirteenth century interfered with the sovereign right of kings to go to war (always the "just war" in defense of the *patria* and the *status regni*) no more and no less than international organizations do in the twentieth century. And "world opinion" was respected as much or as little.

In reply to the third argument, regarding the amount of centralization, one must ask, what degree of centralization is necessary for a State to exist? If the central government must be absolute in power, then the United States might not qualify, since a great many powers remain in the fifty states within. And did France become a State only with the more thorough centralization that resulted from the Revolution? Logically we might conclude that only a totalitarian State is a true State.

27. Religion and Constitutional Thought

BRIAN TIERNEY

The growth of a distinctive medieval tradition of constitutional thought was a complicated, difficult process. That is not surprising. Western constitutionalism itself is an unusual phenomenon in the general history of human government. In the past, when primitive peoples emerged from tribalism to form a civilization and a state, they most commonly turned to theocratic absolutism as the only effective way of maintaining order and unity in a complex society—to the rule of a sacred monarch, a priest-king, a divine emperor. So too, during our present era, the new "third-world" nations, which everywhere began with brave dreams of democracy, have almost everywhere found it necessary to accept some form of charismatic dictatorship in order to survive. The classical age provides examples of city-states that learned to practice self-government within the framework of a small-scale society; but the Greek cities were eventually assimilated into a Roman state that moved from avowed republicanism to military dictatorship to overt theocracy. Humans find it consoling to imagine that the order imposed by their rulers reflects a divine ordering of the universe; most of the time, as Bernard Shaw observed, "The art of government is the organization of idolatry." (The great advance of the twentieth century has been our discovery that it is possible to combine all the advantages of theocracy with all the conveniences of atheism.) I do not suggest that this is an inevitable outcome of human affairs—merely a statistical probability. The

From Brian Tierney, *Religion, Law, and the Growth of Constitutional Thought* (New York: Cambridge University Press, 1982), pp. 8–13. Reprinted by permission of the publisher.

historical problem of how constitutional theories and practices could first emerge and persist is a fascinating one partly because the practical problem of whether constitutionalism can survive and expand in the modern world remains so delicately poised.

Aspects of Medieval Society

In Western Europe, from the twelfth and thirteenth centuries onward, events took an unusual turn. Nations turned aside from anarchy without stumbling into absolutism and began to build structures of constitutional government—and structures of thought—some elements of which have persisted into the modern world. The perception by modern historians that new constitutional ideas were growing up (especially among the jurists) at the same time that new institutions of government were emerging helps to make the situation more understandable; we need not suppose that institutional development was taking place in an intellectual void. But the emergence of the new ideas themselves calls for some explanation. They were related to the whole configuration of medieval society, and in the final analysis nothing less than the whole configuration will serve to explain their development; but, since we are dealing with such an uncommon set of ideas, it seems reasonable that the first question we might ask is: What was unusual about the society?

The question leads us necessarily to the religious aspects of medieval civilization. For, after all, there was nothing very unusual about the early substructure of Teutonic folkways that scholars used to find so fascinating. Ancient notions of customary law and of popular participation in local assemblies did persist throughout the Middle Ages and did continue to influence medieval ways of thought. But such practices are in no way peculiar to the Germanic peoples of Western Europe. They are found in primitive societies in many parts of the world; and such societies, as we have said, do not normally evolve into constitutional states. It is the same with the later growth of medieval feudalism. We can find rather close analogues for Western feudal institutions in other parts of the world, especially in Japan, but feudal practices elsewhere did not lead on to the distinctive forms of experimentation in the art of government that occurred in the medieval West. One could hardly exaggerate the importance of feudal attitudes in stimulating local hostilities to centralizing absolutisms throughout our period; but the preconceptions of a feudal society, taken by themselves and carried to all their logical conclusions, do not lead on to a doctrine of the constitutional state simply because they lack the basic concepts of the state itself—ordered public authority, rational jurisprudence, legislation regarded as a delib-

erate product of reason and will. In any feudal society tensions between central and local authorities will exist, and such tensions have
to be resolved if an effective centralized government is to emerge;
but the usual solution is a sacral monarchy, not a constitutional state.

It is only when we turn to the religious aspects of medieval civilization that we find situations which are extremely abnormal by the
standards of other societies. Otto Hintze saw the significance of this.
In studying representative institutions, he wrote, "one faces a phenomenon that is characteristic only of the Christian West."[1] This
remark seems to me true and important but by no means self-ex-
planatory. Obviously, the different forms of Western Christianity
have co-existed happily enough with a variety of absolutisms at different times and places. If things turned out differently in the Middle
Ages, it could not have been simply because of the presence of Christianity; rather we have to consider the exceptional role of the Christian church in the organization of medieval society.

The most obviously distinctive feature of that society was an unusual duality of structure. In the first great struggle of medieval empire and papacy, the Investiture Contest of around 1100, neither side
was able to make good its more extreme theocratic pretensions.
From then onward a duality persisted. There was never just one structure of government, presided over by an unchallenged theocratic
head, but always two structures, ecclesiastical and secular, always jealous of each other's authority, always preventing medieval society
from congealing into a single monolithic theocracy. Ecclesiastical
criticism diminished the aura of divine right surrounding kingship;
royal power opposed the temporal claims of the papacy. Each hierarchy limited the authority of the other. It is not difficult to see that
such a situation could be conducive to a growth of human freedom,
and the fact has often been pointed out. Lord Acton long ago wrote,
"To that conflict of four hundred years we owe the rise of civil
liberty."

Moreover, internal tensions existed within each hierarchy. In the
thirteenth century feudal barons resisted royal centralization in the
secular world while feudally minded bishops resisted papal centralization in the ecclesiastical sphere. The barons had more real power,
but the bishops had a whole ancient theology of the church to draw
on in defending their position and so were able to give to their
arguments a more sophisticated and enduring formulation.

If we were to ask now, in a merely negative sense, why medieval
society did not develop into a simple, theocratic absolutism, it might
be sufficient to point to these various tensions within it and leave the
matter at that. But if we ask a more positive question—not merely
why absolutism was avoided but how constitutional theories and

practices grew into existence—another aspect of medieval church-state relations becomes important. The institutional structures that we have described as being often in conflict were also in a state of constant interaction, mutually influencing one another. Frequent interchanges of personnel occurred between the two spheres of government; a medieval king's "clerks" were also "clerics," often holders of ecclesiastical benefices. The career of Thomas Becket, alternating between service to king and church, was unusual only in its dénouement. This situation facilitated an exchange of ideas and practices between the two spheres. Kings were anointed like bishops, and popes were crowned like kings. Papal sovereignty was defined according to rules derived from civil law, and imperial elections were conducted according to rules derived from canon law. One could give endless such examples. The interchanges become especially important for constitutional thought when ideas concerning representation and consent are involved. Such ideas often emerged first in the academic writings of the medieval canonists; but the canonistic doctrines themselves grew from a fusion of secular and religious ideas, and trained canonists staffed the chanceries of kings as well as the bureaucracy of the church. (G. P. Cuttino once investigated the careers of 135 middle-ranking administrators in the government of King Edward I of England; he found that most of them had studied canon law.)

In discussing the "configuration" of medieval society there is one more complexity to be considered. Growing up within each hierarchy, ecclesiastical and secular, were innumerable new corporate groups—monasteries, cathedral chapters, collegiate churches, confraternities, universities, guilds, communes. Their growth was stimulated both by movements of reform in the church that emphasized the apostolic way of life, a life lived in common, as an ideal to be emulated, and by the commercial revival of the twelfth century, which encouraged craftsmen and merchants to band together for mutual support. Even in the earliest hard-to-trace origins of such groups we can find evidence of interplay between religious and secular institutions. Often bishops, as lord of cities, were in conflict with the newly emerging communes; but sometimes, it seems, the communes originally grew out of diocesan peace associations. In the little French town of Agde, according to Foreville, the canons of the cathedral church first formed themselves into a corporate body, and then the citizens created a commune modeled on the example of the chapter of canons. A typical medieval guild displayed a fusion of secular and religious functions that would be hard to parallel in any modern institution.

Medieval jurists wrote extensively about the various kinds of corporative association, using the Roman law term *universitas* as a generic word to describe them all. A modern social scientist has observed that all societies contain elements of hierarchy and of collegiality; and this is most obviously true of the medieval world. By the 1250s even the barons of England could think of themselves, not only as members of a feudal hierarchy, but as a corporate entity, the *universitas regni,* the corporate body of the realm. Virtually all the medieval thinkers I shall mention were accustomed to day-to-day participation in the life of corporate groups, either as masters in universities or as members of cathedral chapters or religious orders. The everyday reality exercised a pervasive influence on their ways of thinking about the structure of human societies in general, including political societies.

The aspects of medieval life that we have considered so far—the existence of two hierarchies of government, the tensions within each hierarchy, the growth of corporative associations—all these things help to explain the content of medieval constitutional thought; there can be no understanding of the thought without a knowledge of the society. But there is a limit to how far social analysis can take us even if we were to press the argument in much finer detail. When considering medieval culture we cannot in the end simply dissolve intellectual history into social history—we cannot treat the history of ideas as merely a subdivision of the history of society—if only because social reality was not the only source of medieval ideas.

In twelfth-century civilization there was a sort of double duality, not only a duality between church and state but, also, so to speak, a duality between past and present. Claude Lévi-Strauss, in his well-known inaugural lecture of 1960, distinguished between a "synchronic" and a "diachronic" approach to the study of societies; the first approach considers only present-day realities, the second explores the whole life of a society in time. Lévi-Strauss, I think, was using his technical language here to make a simple point; some societies display anomalous characteristics that can be explained only as atavisms. But medieval culture was more complex than this. We have to deal, not only with atavisms (though they existed abundantly), but also with conscious revivals of ancient thought—first Roman law, then Aristotelian philosophy. To use the current jargon for once, we might say that, if the synchronic aspect of medieval constitutional thought seems complex, that is because its diachronic structure is quite unusually intricate. Medieval intellectuals approached the problems of their society with ideas formed in the earlier, sophisticated civilizations of Greece and Rome. But they did not merely repeat those ideas, parrot-like. They blended the ancient ways of thought with their own Christian world-view; they used classical concepts to rethink the political experience of their own society; and in doing these things they created much of the substructure of later constitutional thought.

The "political experience" of the Middle Ages included experience with church structures; and this, as we have seen, gave rise to complicated relationships. A fine Renaissance scholar, Garrett Mattingly, has observed that it is "intelligible ... that the medieval church should foreshadow and as it were recapitulate in advance the development of the modern state."[2] The process is intelligible, but it is not easy to understand; and it would not be intelligible at all if we simply supposed that the medieval church somehow, mysteriously, spun constitutional theories out of its own inner Christian consciousness, and that the state then simply copied them as if by a duplicating operation. Rather there existed always the tension and interchange between the two spheres that I have mentioned. The church borrowed secular ideas just as the state borrowed ecclesiastical ones; the church had to become half a state before the state could become half a church. Moreover, some of the secular ideas that the church assimilated were not taken from the contemporary medieval world but from ancient classical civilization. It is these areas of interaction that we need to study—the interplay between religious and secular ideas and, more subtly, the interplay betwen medieval present and classical past—if we want to understand why the Western tradition of constitutional thought developed in its unique way, differently from that of China, say, or ancient Peru, or Japan, or the lands of Islam.

NOTES

1. O. Hintze, 'Weltgeschichtliche Bedingungen der Repräsentativverfassung', *Historische Zeitschrift*, 143 (1930), 1–47 (p. 4).

2. G. Mattingly, 'Introduction' to Figgis, *Political Thought from Gerson to Grotius*, p. xii.

28.   A Fourteenth-Century Parliament

GEORGE L. HASKINS

Most people, when they think of parliament or the house of commons, conjure up to the mind's eye the spectacle of the stately neo-Gothic Houses of Parliament on the Embankment of the Thames. But it is not with buildings such as these that the medieval parliament was associated, for they date only from the second quarter of the nineteenth century. Shadowed by those Houses, and by the towering Abbey of Westminster, lies the long bulk of gray-black stone known as Westminster Hall. No one edifice typifies so well the continuity of the English government; few places have been so intimately associated with its history. Its dark roof has rung with the acclamations that hailed many an heir to the throne; its somber flags have known the tread of throngs who sought to pay last homage to a sovereign king. It was here that the royal courts of justice had their first beginnings. Here the king's High Court of Parliament was convened; here, until the eighteenth century, the great trials for high treason were held. "The Great Hall of William Rufus," exclaims Macaulay in his famed description of the trial of Warren Hastings.[1] A great hall it is, and a masterpiece of early English architecture—in length all of two hundred and forty feet, in height nearly one hundred. In the proud boast of its builder, the Red King, son and heir of William the Conqueror, it was but a bedchamber in comparison with the building he intended to put up.[2]

From George L. Haskins, *The Growth of English Representative Government* (Philadelphia: University of Pennsylvania Press, 1948), pp. 4–17. Reprinted by permission.

Could we turn back the centuries in the glass of time, it would be a very different spectacle we should see at Westminster on a winter's morning in the opening years of the fourteenth century. No more than tapering pinnacles and crockets of neo-Gothic, nor the massive grays of Whitehall: instead, low-lying marshes and pasture land, flooded by a swollen Thames, sullenly resenting the massive walls and bulwarks of the royal palace on the Isle of Thorns. It is a wide and muddy Thames that runs with the salt tide by the palace, by the long staple of the wool merchants, and by the gleaming white of the sumptuous Abbey church hard by. A slow river, with many a small fishing craft and much river traffic, running by the orchards of the Strand, past the river Fleet down to London City, with its red roofs, its lead-clad steeples, its hostels, its monasteries, its great cathedral church of St. Paul.

It is not to London City that we shall look on this early morning, but to the bustle and activity about the royal palace and the Great Hall at Westminster. It is Sunday, and the bells and chimes cannot be stilled; for King Edward I has returned from the North to consult with his magnates and the princes of the Church from all England, summoned by royal writ to attend his parliament at Westminster.

Edward, by the Grace of God, King of England, Lord of Ireland and Duke of Aquitaine, Greeting. Inasmuch as we wish to hold a special consultation with you and the other lords of this realm, touching certain establishments to be made concerning our land of Scotland, we strictly enjoin you, by the love and fidelity by which you are bound to us, and command that you shall put aside all other business and appear before us at our palace of Westminster on the Sunday after the Feast of St. Matthew the Apostle next ensuing, personally there to treat with us on these matters, in order that we may weigh your counsel.[3]

Parliament is a very solemn affair to which all the great of the kingdom must come. It is the great council of the realm, wherein appointments must be made, difficult cases discussed, and important matters of policy considered. For more than two hundred years now the kings of England have been following a practice, current throughout the kingdoms of Europe, of summoning to their courts at the great festivals of the Christian year their vassals, tenants-in-chief, and the princes of the Church, in order that they may hold "deep speech" with them. Yet the English kings are more than feudal lords. Of late, now, King Edward has stretched out his powerful administrative arm into the private feudal jurisdictions of the kingdom, questioning closely by what warrant they are held. His royal courts have multiplied, and his enemies declare that the land is wearied by excess of justice, by the constant questioning of royal justices, as they move from county to county, enquiring into the misdeeds of local officers and all manner of crime and malfeasance. King Edward is a powerful king, the "English Justinian" he will be called in time to come. He has opened his courts to the poorest and humblest subject, and step by step he is destroying local franchises and customs and building up a great body of uniform, national law. His parliament has thus become a great court of justice, wherein, as a contemporary lawyer describes it, "judicial doubts are determined, and new remedies are established for new wrongs, and justice is done to every one according to his deserts."[4] In his parliaments, held usually three times a year, the king is surrounded by lawyers from the courts, by jurists from the great Universities of Paris and Bologna, experts in the civil and canon law. Parliament is indeed a very solemn affair.

Besides counsel and justice, the king has found still another use for his parliaments. His elaborate administration requires many servants who must be paid; and he cannot give away his justice for nothing. His ordinary revenues do not suffice, for there is as yet no general taxation. He can ask a gracious aid from his barons and from the Church; but that again will not suffice. And so, following a precedent of recent years, writs have gone out to the sheriffs of every county in England, phrased in these words:

> To the sheriff, greeting:
> We firmly enjoin you to see to it that from your county two knights are elected without delay; and from each town or city in your county, two of the more discreet burgesses or citizens, capable of work. And they are to be made to appear before us at Westminster on the Sunday following the Feast of St. Matthew next ensuing. And these knights, citizens and burgesses are to have full and sufficient power for themselves and their respective communities to do and consent to those things which in our parliament shall be ordained, lest for lack of this power these matters should remain unaccomplished.[5]

It has become clear that there are many persons of property and wealth who are not actually among the magnates of the realm, particularly that there are many rich merchants in the towns and cities. And so two hundred of the townsfolk of England and seventy-four knights of the shire will respond to the summons; they have no choice. Altogether the numbers attending the king's parliament will be very nearly seven hundred: upwards of one hundred great prelates of the Church, one hundred and fifty representatives or proctors of the lower clergy, more than one hundred barons and earls, besides fifty or so of the king's official staff.

Such is the parliament the king has summoned. Of late it has been to the royal palace of Westminster that he has called his assembly, although there is no prescription by law or custom that he may not call it elsewhere. Although but a straggling village among the marshes, many sentiments of the people are crystallized about Westminster. Since before the coming of the Normans, it has been the recognized home of the king. The Conqueror was wont to hold his summer courts here, and for long the work of government and justice has centered about the royal palace. The pious Edward the Confessor, last of the Saxon kings, lived here and died here, and the Abbey church has in the course of time become the scene of royal coronations. "The crown, the grave, the palace, the festival . . . all illustrate the perpetuity of a national sentiment typifying the continuity of the national life."[6]

It is easy to understand that the summoning of a parliament means an enormous increase of activity about Westminster. Some days before this parliament was to meet, orders went out to the sheriffs of Surrey, Sussex, Kent, and London to purchase some three thousand bushels of wheat, much livestock, and over one hundred tuns of ale; wooden dishes, brazen pots, and copper in mass were to be supplied.[7] There were to be many mouths to feed, for the king's household is large. And a week before, a grave and important-looking personage, called Master in Chancery, had stood forth in the Great Hall and silenced the noisy courts of law there assembled. Scroll in hand, he had read out his "crye," that the king was to gather his great council of the realm on the Sunday next ensuing. Continuing, he pronounced:

All who wish to bring forward petitions at this next parliament should deliver them day by day between now and the first Sunday in Lent, at the latest, to Sir John Kirkby, and Master John Bush, or to one of these. And they are assigned to receive them between now and the first Sunday in Lent.[8]

The same proclamation he had read publicly in the West Cheap, by St. Paul's in London, and also in the ancient Guildhall close by. And everywhere it had been greeted with applause, as the king thus proffered his readiness to hear any complaint. People had come to associate the relief of private grievances with the meeting of the king's parliament; and somewhere in their minds would echo the famed promise in the Great Charter of nearly a century ago, "to no one will we sell, to no one will we deny or delay right or justice."[9]

To others the holding of this parliament meant something very different. To most of the great tenants-in-chief, to most, that is, who were not perpetually attendant on the king's person, it meant a long

and wearisome journey in the flood season from some remote corner of England, restless nights in smoke-clouded inns, with the
dreary creaking of a loose blind outside, and the splash of rain in
the mire-filled roads. It meant leaving the hunting, the comfort of
the castle or the big manor house; it meant a dreary three weeks in
London at one's own expense, with a wearying attention to details
of the king's affairs with Philip of France, or his dispute about the
investiture of the new archbishop. The king would ask for money;
and he would have new statutes to enact, currently described as
amendments to the customary law, but in reality a fresh and insolent
excuse to invade some local immunity or prerogative. Undoubtedly,
the baron reflects, one of his own men will have the face to bring
up some trifling case of injustice to the king's highest tribunal, and
he, the lord, will be amerced or fined. The tedious journey to Westminster would entail little pleasure. Yet if he disobeys the summons,
one of the ubiquitous royal officers will carry off a part of his goods
until a fine has been paid.

To the lesser nobility, if we may use this term of the knights of the
shire, the king's summons is equally irksome. Though closely connected by blood ties and other interests with the earls and barons,
the elected knights are made to feel distinctly unimportant at the
king's parliament. True, the knight senses he is vastly superior to the
uncouth burgess representative from the town; and he has been
elected to parliament because he is a prominent man in county affairs. The king may want official information as to the doings of royal
officers, the bailiffs and sheriffs; the allegations of a petitioner may
want corroboration. Unofficial testimony may be wanted, as to "what
men are saying in remote parts of England, . . . and the possibilities
of future taxation have to be considered."[10] None the less it is no
privilege to come to Westminster, and the wages which his county
will pay him, four shillings a day, will hardly balance his disburse-
ments. He has had to find pledges, men who will guarantee his appearance in parliament, or perhaps four of his best oxen have been
"bound over" by the sheriff, lest he try to escape the duty imposed
by the king's summons.

Many of the elected knights have been before to the king's parliament.[11] They know what to expect. If, like John de Pabenham, knight
of the shire for Bedford County in this parliament, there are any
who were at the Michaelmas Parliament in 1297, they will recall the
king's wrath when the knights and nobles in one body refused the
king a grant of money until he had redressed their grievances about
the forest laws.[12] Then, of an earlier day, one or two may recall that
the knights and lords had promised the king a levy of a fifteenth on
all their movable property, on condition that he would expel every

Jew from England.[13] That was, they could reflect, a masterful stroke of genius. Oh yes, it was money the old king wanted, and when it had been promised he would bid them all go quietly and quickly, prepared to come again when they were needed. Why else had he thought to summon the vulgar townspeople, who spent their days dicing and drinking in an unsavory room at the Sign of the Rose, listening to vagrant student songs on an untuned lute?

After this fashion the baron or the knight might well be thinking as he crowds into the king's Great Hall beside the palace. Close on seven hundred persons are there, and the morning mists hang heavy about the old roof. Bay upon bay the stout chestnut of Normandy and the black oak of Ireland stretch on into the gloom to where at the end, surrounded by torches, sits King Edward I. His lined face and graying beard bear witness to relentless campaigns against the Scot and the turbulent Welsh, to ceaseless energies in building up his great administrative machine in the face of the tyranny of feudal franchises. Now he sits in his capacity as lawgiver, the English Justinian, holding his full court before the communities of the realm.

On his right is the Archbishop of Canterbury; on his left the Chancellor, William de Hamilton; below, some thirty members of the king's small council—his ministers and permanent official advisers. For reasons of comfort as well as in token of their dignity they sit upon great wool-sacks, brought in from the neighboring Woolstaple. Close at hand are the justices of the Common Pleas, the Exchequer, and the King's Bench; their advice will be needed during the session to frame any statutes the king may propose. Among them are the great lawyers of the day, Bereford and Ralph Hengham, whose learning and common sense have forged powerful links in the relentless chain of the king's justice.

Sitting apart are the ninety-five prelates of the realm, together with all manner of archdeacons and deans from the cathedral chapters. The king's business is not their business, they feel; even though they are ranked as an estate of the realm. But they know that if they do not attend parliament, in all likelihood there will be little left of their lands and property, which the barons and earls will almost certainly vote to tax. And at this moment there is grave fear that the king means to take action against the exporting of gold and other tribute to the Holy See in Rome.

Beyond stand the barons, earls, and other magnates of the realm, clothed in stamped velvets of blue, red, or yellow, with cloaks of silk and cloth of Tars. Their arms and weapons they have been forbidden to bear in time of parliament by an ordinance of the king, whose special peace, protecting all coming to parliament, he means to enforce.[14] It is not so long since the treasurer and other retainers of the Earl of Cornwall were murdered in the streets in broad daylight when on their way to parliament at Westminster.[15] And some can still remember how a jealous Archbishop of Canterbury set armed men upon the retainers of the Archbishop of York, broke his cross, and committed other outrages upon the prelate as he was making his way to parliament.[16]

Toward the back of the hall, mingled with the barons, are the knights of the shire, clad in velvet doublets, well lined with rich furs; and beyond, awkward and uncertain in a group of nearly two hundred, the citizens and burgesses elected by the towns. Two or three, like Gilbert de Rokesle, the great wool merchant and master of the exchange, seem to know their business and form the center of groups who talk about the grant of money that the king is sure to demand.

Suddenly the Bishop of London, clad in purple and scarlet, arises, and the talking ceases as he opens with a prayer. The Archbishop of Canterbury follows with a sermon on the text, "How shall a court correct the ills of the whole realm, unless it shall first be itself corrected." What is in store is now clear enough to many; and there are mutterings as the sermon comes to a close. How, they think, can the king reform his realm when his subjects in parliament are reluctant to grant him money? This is the plain meaning of what the Archbishop has been saying. Enough of this reform, it is in the mouths of many to cry. Let the king live of his own; let him mind his own affairs and leave other people alone to mind theirs. And many will instinctively pluck their purses from their sleeves and draw the strings together more closely.

Then silence again, as the Chancellor, the dignified Dean of York, William de Hamilton, addresses the assembled parliament. The purport of the summons to parliament is reiterated: the Archbishop, bishops, earls, barons, knights, and burgesses elected by the communities of the shires and towns have been called together in the king's parliament to discuss certain weighty affairs touching the safety of the realm and in particular the land of Scotland. The king wishes to urge that those who have petitions to present or grievances to be redressed are to bring their complaints to those of the king's council commissioned to receive them. Lastly he emphasizes that the king has incurred heavy expenses in connection with his wars, and especially because of the rebellion of Robert Bruce and others in the North. It is therefore of the utmost importance that the assembled communities should grant a gracious aid to the king for the better ordering of peace and quiet in the kingdom. He earnestly requests that the several estates should deliberate on the matter among themselves and report their decision to the council. Meanwhile, the hour being late—toward ten in the morning—the assembly is adjourned for the day.

The king, followed by his ministers and his council, leaves by the upper end of the hall into St. Stephen's Chapel; the clergy, the lay lords, and the knights remain to discuss the subsidy; the town representatives move off in disorderly groups across the Palace Yard and Dirty Lane toward the refectory of the Abbey, there to deliberate the share which they will grant the king. When these various orders have decided on the grant, as they will do very shortly, their work at the king's parliament is nearly ended.

It is, however, elsewhere than at the Great Hall that the main business of parliament will be accomplished; and it is by others than the great barons, the clergy, the elected knights and burgesses that that work will be done. Should we follow the day-by-day activities of the parliament after the opening of the session, it would be to the council chamber on the south side of the Old Palace Yard that we should repair.[17] Here we should soon understand that the king's parliament in the opening days of the fourteenth century is more in the nature of a high court of justice than a deliberative or legislative assembly. For it is the council, with the king as presiding officer, which is the heart and core of the medieval parliament—a council of ministers, judges, and experts in the law. In the great chamber beyond St. Stephen's Chapel, its roof thickly sown with golden stars on a background of azure, the council has its meeting place. In time to come this room will be known as the Star Chamber, and a mighty and powerful tribunal will take its name from the room. Now it is the center of all the work of consultation of a medieval parliament. Here, from early morning until nearly noon, the council will sit. Their work is confined to the early hours of the day, for, as Sir Henry Spelman shrewdly observes, "Our Ancestours and other the Northern Nations being more prone to distemper and excess of diet used the Forenoon only, lest repletion [in food and drink] should bring upon them drowsiness and oppression of spirit. . . . To confess the truth, our Saxons were immeasurably given to drunkenness."[18]

Before the council knights of the shire will be called and appointed to administrative posts in their shires, and prominent burgesses will be summoned to find out what future customs can be imposed on the wool export. Before the council a deputation of prelates, barons, and knights will come at this parliament we have been describing to offer the king an aid of one-thirtieth to be assessed on their movable property. Before the council the burgesses will decide on a tax of one-twentieth to be levied on their goods.

Finally, it is before the council that petitions for the redress of grievances will be presented, and before the council that the petitioner
must appear, if he is wanted, to prosecute his case.

Before the representatives at this parliament return home, a group
of townsfolk, representing their constituencies and perhaps feeling
they should not return empty handed, will essay to make complaint
that juries are corrupted by the rich and that ecclesiastical judges
are meddling in temporal suits.[19] But the king and council will decide that the complaint has not sufficient foundation, and the petition will be dismissed. To this extent will the future house of commons attempt to participate in the king's parliament. It is not very
difficult to see that the king and council are all-powerful, that the
burgesses, even the knights of the shire, are no very essential part of
parliament. There is something not a little ironical in the phrase of
the summons which enjoins them to come to do what shall be ordained.

For when they have made their grant, when they have been given
such instructions as the king sees fit, there will be another speech in
the Great hall to the assembled parliament of seven hundred. The
king then addresses the estates in words preserved for us in a contemporary record:

> Bishops and other prelates, counts, barons, knights of the counties, citi-
> zens and burgesses and other people of the community who have come to
> this parliament at the bidding of the lord king: greatly the king thanks you
> for your coming and wishes that you will return at once again to your home,
> so that you may come again quickly and without delay at whatever hour
> you shall be needed. But the bishops, counts, barons, judges, justices and
> other members of the lord king's council shall not go without special leave
> of the king. Those, too, who have business to transact before the council
> may remain and pursue their business.
>
> And the knights of the shire who have come on behalf of the counties,
> and the others who have come on behalf of the cities and towns, are to go
> to Sir John Kirkby, who will make out writs for the payment of the expenses
> of their coming.[20]

The purpose for which the lessor barons the elected knights and
burgesses have been summoned is answered. The seventy councilors,
together with their clerks and assistants, will remain; and the high
court of parliament will still be considered in full session, even
though the representatives and many magnates have gone home. It
will remain in session for as much as three or four weeks, transacting
the important business which has waited to come before the king's
parliament.

There is much business. Nicholas Segrave has been accused of high treason in the Scottish campaign and must be indicted before the king in council. Now that the war is over, a settled form of government must be provided for Scotland—a task that will demand long debates. The Bishop of Glasgow, the Earl of Carrick, and John Mowbray will be called before the council to say how Scotland should be represented at the king's Midsummer parliament in the same year.[21] There will be discussion of policy to be pursued in the lately recovered province of Aquitaine; vast quantities of writs will have to be issued for payments in arrears, and there will be important appointments to be made there, from the seneschal downwards.[22]

The greatest activity of the king and council involves the despatching of hundreds of petitions which have come in from all over the kingdom, as well as from Scotland, Ireland, and Gascony. Four-fifths of the records which this parliament will leave behind are concerned with those petitions and the action consequent upon them. Committees will have been appointed to deal with them, and no suitor will be turned away. The citizens of Lincoln will protest against the abuse of a local franchise in prejudice to their rights.[23] The University of Cambridge will ask leave to found a college.[24] The citizens of Norwich will ask for the grant of a special aid for murage for the safety of the city.[25] Simon le Parker will plead by petition that he has not received justice before the king's judges and is being held on suspicion of murder in the gaol at Canterbury.[26]

Oftentimes the courts of common law, even though sufficiently honest, were not sufficiently strong to do justice in cases where a powerful magnate interfered. The power of granting relief lay in the king, and extraordinary jurisdiction could be, and was, exerted in behalf of an otherwise helpless suitor.[27] And so the idea of relief of private grievances fast became an essential characteristic of the king's parliament. It came to be a court placed over all other courts, for the purpose, as the contemporary lawyer reminds us, of resolving doubtful judgments, providing new remedial measures for newly emergent wrongs and meting out justice to all according to their deserving.[28]

NOTES

1. T. B. Macaulay, "Warren Hastings," *Literary and Historical Essays* (Oxford, 1923), p. 618.

2. J. Stow, *A Survey of the Cities of London and Westminster* (ed. Kingford: Oxford, 1908), ii. 113.

3. Cf. *The Parliamentary Writs and Writs of Military Summons* (ed. Palgrave: London, 1827), i. 138.

4. *Fleta* (London, 1647), p. 66.

5. Cf. *Parliamentary Writs,* i. 115, 140.

6. W. Stubbs, *The Constitutional History of England* (Oxford, 1896), iii. 395.

7. *Parliamentary Writs,* i. 407.

8. *Ibid.,* i. 155.

9. C. 40.

10. *Records of the Parliament Holden at Westminster, 1305* (ed. Maitland, Rolls Series: London, 1893), lxxv.

11. Figures on the number of knights who were reëlected to Parliament at this time may be found in J. G. Edwards, "Personnel of the Commons in the Parliaments of Edward I and Edward II," *Essays in Medieval History Presented to T. F. Tout* (Manchester, 1925).

12. *Chronicon Walteri de Hemingburgh* (ed. Hamilton: London, 1848–1849), ii. 148.

13. *Annales Monastici* (ed. Luard, Rolls Series: London, 1866), iii. 362.

14. Cf. *Statutes of the Realm* (Record Commissioners: London, 1810), i. 170.

15. *Calendar of the Patent Rolls, 1281–1292,* pp. 489, 517.

16. *Historical Papers and Letters from the Northern Registers* (ed. Raine, Rolls Series: London, 1873), pp. 59–63.

17. In 1293 and in 1305 the council was assembled in the house of the Archbishop of York, which stood where the White Hall of later years was to stand. See *Rotuli Parliamentorum,* i. 91, 178.

18. H. Spelman, *Posthumous Works* (Oxford, 1698), p. 89.

19. *Records of the Parliament of 1305,* p. 305, number 472.

20. *Parliamentary Writs,* i. 155.

21. *Records of the Parliament of 1305,* pp. 14–16.

22. *Ibid.,* pp. 328–38.

23. *Ibid.,* pp. 305–6, number 473.

24. *Ibid.,* p. 33, number 50.

25. *Ibid.,* p. 11, number 10.

26. *Ibid.,* p. 11, number 10.

27. *The Collected Historical Works of Sir Francis Palgrave* (ed. Thompson: Cambridge, 1922), viii, 114.

28. Above, note 4.

GOD, NATURE, AND ART

ONE ASPECT OF the rise of medieval civilization in the twelfth and thirteenth centuries was the growth of a more confident attitude concerning man's relationship with the natural world. In combating the Cathar heresy—which held that material creation was intrinsically evil—medieval Christians remembered the teaching of Genesis that, in the beginning, God made the whole universe and "saw that it was good." On a practical level, the extension of agricultural land around existing villages and the planting of new settlements in former wasteland brought more and more of the natural environment under human control. The intellectual life of the universities in the thirteenth century was characterized by an enormous confidence in natural human reason; theologians thought that they could combine all the natural science of Aristotle with the sacred truths of Christian revelation into great, new works of synthesis.

The following readings suggest that ways of perceiving nature could influence spheres as diverse as the practice of agriculture, the art of the great cathedrals, and the speculations of leading theologians. Lynn White offers a provocative thesis on the relationship between traditional Christianity and modern ecological problems. Emile Mâle discusses the medieval view of the universe as a symbol of divine wisdom and power in relation to Gothic art. Finally, Etienne Gilson explains how Thomas Aquinas transformed the remote, impersonal "first cause" of Aristotle's natural philosophy into the living, active God of Jewish and Christian revelation.

29. The Historical Roots of Our Ecological Crisis

LYNN WHITE, JR.

A conversation with Aldous Huxley not infrequently puts one at the receiving end of an unforgettable monologue. About a year before his lamented death he was discoursing on a favorite topic: Man's unnatural treatment of nature and its sad results. To illustrate his point he told how, during the previous summer, he had returned to a little valley in England where he had spent many happy months as a child. Once it had been composed of delightful grassy glades; now it was becoming overgrown with unsightly brush because the rabbits that formerly kept such growth under control had largely suc-cumbed to a disease, myxomatosis, that was deliberately introduced by the local farmers to reduce the rabbits' destruction of crops. Being something of a Philistine, I could be silent no longer, even in the interests of great rhetoric. I interrupted to point out that the rabbit itself had been brought as a domestic animal to England in 1176, presumably to improve the protein diet of the peasantry.

All forms of life modify their contexts. The most spectacular and benign instance is doubtless the coral polyp. By serving its own ends, it has created a vast undersea world favorable to thousands of other kinds of animals and plants. Ever since man became a numerous species he has affected his environment notably. The hypothesis that his fire-drive method of hunting created the world's great grasslands and helped to exterminate the monster mammals of the Pleistocene from much of the globe is plausible, if not proved. For 6 millennia

From Lynn White, Jr., "The Historical Roots of Our Ecological Crisis," *Science*, Vol. 155 (1967), pp. 1203–1207. Copyright 1967 by the American Association for the Advancement of Science.

at least, the banks of the lower Nile have been a human artifact rather than the swampy African jungle which nature, apart from man, would have made it. The Aswan Dam, flooding 5000 square miles, is only the latest stage in a long process. In many regions terracing or irrigation, overgrazing, the cutting of forests by Romans to build ships to fight Carthaginians or by Crusaders to solve the logistics problems of their expeditions, have profoundly changed some ecologies. Observations that the French landscape falls into two basic types, the open fields of the north and the *bocage* of the south and west, inspired Marc Bloch to undertake his classic study of medieval agricultural methods. Quite unintentionally, changes in human ways often affect nonhuman nature. It has been noted, for example, that the advent of the automobile eliminated huge flocks of sparrows that once fed on the horse manure littering every street.

The history of ecologic change is still so rudimentary that we know little about what really happened, or what the results were. The extinction of the European aurochs as late as 1627 would seem to have been a simple case of overenthusiastic hunting. On more intricate matters it often is impossible to find solid information. For a thousand years or more the Frisians and Hollanders have been pushing back the North Sea, and the process is culminating in our own time in the reclamation of the Zuider Zee. What, if any, species of animals, birds, fish, shore life, or plants have died out in the process? In their epic combat with Neptune have the Netherlanders overlooked ecological values in such a way that the quality of human life in the Netherlands has suffered? I cannot discover that the questions have ever been asked, much less answered.

People, then, have often been a dynamic element in their own environment, but in the present state of historical scholarship we usually do not know exactly when, where, or with what effects man-induced changes came. As we enter the last third of the 20th century, however, concern for the problem of ecologic backlash is mounting feverishly. Natural science, conceived as the effort to understand the nature of things, had flourished in several eras and among several peoples. Similarly there had been an age-old accumulation of technological skills, sometimes growing rapidly, sometimes slowly. But it was not until about four generations ago that Western Europe and North America arranged a marriage between science and technology, a union of the theoretical and the empirical approaches to our natural environment. The emergence in widespread practice of the Baconian creed that scientific knowledge means technological power over nature can scarcely be dated before about 1850, save in the chemical industries, where it is anticipated in the 18th century.

Its acceptance as a normal pattern of action may mark the greatest event in human history since the invention of agriculture, and perhaps in nonhuman terrestrial history as well.

Almost at once the new situation forced the crystallization of the novel concept of ecology; indeed, the word *ecology* first appeared in the English language in 1871. Today, less than a century later, the impact of our race upon the environment has so increased in force that it has changed in essence. When the first cannons were fired, in the early 14th century, they affected ecology by sending workers scrambling to the forests and mountains for more potash, sulfur, iron ore, and charcoal, with some resulting erosion and deforestation. Hydrogen bombs are of a different order: a war fought with them might alter the genetics of all life on this planet. By 1285 London had a smog problem arising from the burning of soft coal, but our present combustion of fossil fuels threatens to change the chemistry of the globe's atmosphere as a whole, with consequences which we are only beginning to guess. With the population explosion, the carcinoma of planless urbanism, the now geological deposits of sewage and garbage, surely no creature other than man has ever managed to foul its nest in such short order.

There are many calls to action, but specific proposals, however worthy as individual items, seem too partial, palliative, negative: ban the bomb, tear down the billboards, give the Hindus contraceptives and tell them to eat their sacred cows. The simplest solution to any suspect change is, of course, to stop it, or, better yet, to revert to a romanticized past: make those ugly gasoline stations look like Anne Hathaway's cottage or (in the Far West) like ghost-town saloons. The "wilderness area" mentality invariably advocates deep-freezing an ecology, whether San Gimignano or the High Sierra, as it was before the first Kleenex was dropped. But neither atavism nor prettification will cope with the ecologic crisis of our time.

What shall we do? No one yet knows. Unless we think about fundamentals, our specific measures may produce new backlashes more serious than those they are designed to remedy.

As a beginning we should try to clarify our thinking by looking, in some historical depth, at the presuppositions that underlie modern technology and science. Science was traditionally aristocratic, speculative, intellectual in intent; technology was lower-class, empirical, action-oriented. The quite sudden fusion of these two, towards the middle of the 19th century, is surely related to the slightly prior and contemporary democratic revolutions which, by reducing social barriers, tended to assert a functional unity of brain and hand. Our ecologic crisis is the product of an emerging, entirely novel, democratic culture. The issue is whether a democratized world can survive its own implications. Presumably we cannot unless we rethink our axioms.

The Western Traditions of Technology and Science

One thing is so certain that it seems stupid to verbalize it: both modern technology and modern science are distinctly *Occidental.* Our technology has absorbed elements from all over the world, notably from China; yet everywhere today, whether in Japan or in Nigeria, successful technology is Western. Our science is the heir to all the sciences of the past, especially perhaps to the work of the great Islamic scientists of the Middle Ages, who so often outdid the ancient Greeks in skill and perspicacity: al-Rāzi in medicine, for example; or ibn-al-Haytham in optics; or Omar Khay-yám in mathematics. Indeed, not a few works of such geniuses seem to have vanished in the original Arabic and to survive only in medieval Latin translations that helped to lay the foundations for later Western developments. Today, around the globe, all significant science is Western in style and method, whatever the pigmentation or language of the scientists.

A second pair of facts is less well recognized because they result from quite recent historical scholarship. The leadership of the West, both in technology and in science, is far older than the so-called Scientific Revolution of the 17th century or the so-called Industrial Revolution of the 18th century. These terms are in fact outmoded and obscure the true nature of what they try to describe—significant stages in two long and separate developments. By A.D. 1000 at the latest—and perhaps, feebly, as much as 200 years earlier—the West began to apply water power to industrial processes other than milling grain. This was followed in the late 12th century by the harnessing of wind power. From simple beginnings, but with remarkable consistency of style, the West rapidly expanded its skills in the development of power machinery, labor-saving devices, and automation. Those who doubt should contemplate that most monumental achievement in the history of automation: the weight-driven mechanical clock, which appeared in two forms in the early 14th century. Not in craftsmanship but in basic technological capacity, the Latin West of the later Middle Ages far outstripped its elaborate, sophisticated, and esthetically magnificent sister cultures, Byzantium and Islam. In 1444 a great Greek ecclesiastic, Bessarion, who had gone to Italy, wrote a letter to a prince in Greece. He is amazed by the superiority of Western ships, arms, textiles, glass. But above all he is astonished by the spectacle of waterwheels sawing timbers and pumping the bellows of blast furnaces. Clearly, he had seen nothing of the sort in the Near East.

By the end of the 15th century the technological superiority of Europe was such that its small, mutually hostile nations could spill out over all the rest of the world, conquering, looting, and coloniz- ing. The symbol of this technological superiority is the fact that Por- tugal, one of the weakest states of the Occident, was able to become, and to remain for a century, mistress of the East Indies. And we must remember that the technology of Vasco da Gama and Albuquerque was built by pure empiricism, drawing remarkably little support or inspiration from science.

In the present-day vernacular understanding, modern science is supposed to have begun in 1543, when both Copernicus and Vesalius published their great works. It is no derogation of their accomplish- ments, however, to point out that such structures as the *Fabrica* and the *De revolutionibus* do not appear overnight. The distinctive West- ern tradition of science, in fact, began in the late 11th century with a massive movement of translation of Arabic and Greek scientific works into Latin. A few notable books—Theophrastus, for exam- ple—escaped the West's avid new appetite for science, but within less than 200 years effectively the entire corpus of Greek and Muslim science was available in Latin, and was being eagerly read and criti- cized in the new European universities. Out of criticism arose new observation, speculation, and increasing distrust of ancient author- ities. By the late 13th century Europe had seized global scientific leadership from the faltering hands of Islam. It would be as absurd to deny the profound originality of Newton, Galileo, or Copernicus as to deny that of the 14th century scholastic scientists like Buridan or Oresme on whose work they built. Before the 11th century, sci- ence scarcely existed in the Latin West, even in Roman times. From the 11th century onward, the scientific sector of Occidental culture has increased in a steady crescendo.

Since both our technological and our scientific movements got their start, acquired their character, and achieved world dominance in the Middle Ages, it would seem that we cannot understand their nature or their present impact upon ecology without examining fun- damental medieval assumptions and developments.

Medieval View of Man and Nature

Until recently, agriculture has been the chief occupation even in "advanced" societies; hence, any change in methods of tillage has much importance. Early plows, drawn by two oxen, did not normally turn the sod but merely scratched it. Thus, cross-plowing was needed and fields tended to be squarish. In the fairly light soils and semiarid climates of the Near East and Mediterranean, this worked well. But such a plow was inappropriate to the wet climate and often sticky soils of northern Europe. By the latter part of the 7th century after Christ, however, following obscure beginnings, certain northern peasants were using an entirely new kind of plow, equipped with a vertical knife to cut the line of the furrow, a horizontal share to slice under the sod, and a moldboard to turn it over. The friction of this plow with the soil was so great that it normally required not two but eight oxen. It attacked the land with such violence that cross-plowing was not needed, and fields tended to be shaped in long strips.

In the days of the scratch-plow, fields were distributed generally in units capable of supporting a single family. Subsistence farming was the presupposition. But no peasant owned eight oxen: to use the new and more efficient plow, peasants pooled their oxen to form large plow-teams, originally receiving (it would appear) plowed strips in proportion to their contribution. Thus, distribution of land was based no longer on the needs of a family but, rather, on the capacity of a power machine to till the earth. Man's relation to the soil was profoundly changed. Formerly man had been part of nature; now he was the exploiter of nature. Nowhere else in the world did farmers develop any analogous agricultural implement. Is it coincidence that modern technology, with its ruthlessness toward nature, has so largely been produced by descendants of these peasants of northern Europe?

This same exploitive attitude appears slightly before A.D. 830 in Western illustrated calendars. In older calendars the months were shown as passive personifications. The new Frankish calendars, which set the style for the Middle Ages, are very different: they show men coercing the world around them—plowing, harvesting, chopping trees, butchering pigs. Man and nature are two things, and man is master.

These novelties seem to be in harmony with larger intellectual patterns. What people do about their ecology depends on what they think about themselves in relation to things around them. Human ecology is deeply conditioned by beliefs about our nature and destiny—that is by religion. To Western eyes this is very evident in, say, India or Ceylon. It is equally true of ourselves and of our medieval ancestors.

The victory of Christianity over paganism was the greatest psychic revolution in the history of our culture. It has become fashionable today to say that, for better or worse, we live in "the post-Christian age." Certainly the forms of our thinking and language have largely ceased to be Christian, but to my eye the substance often remains amazingly akin to that of the past. Our daily habits of action, for example, are dominated by an implicit faith in perpetual progress which was unknown either to Greco-Roman antiquity or to the Orient. It is rooted in, and is indefensible apart from, Judeo-Christian teleology. The fact that Communists share it merely helps to show what can be demonstrated on many other grounds: that Marxism, like Islam, is a Judeo-Christian heresy. We continue today to live, as we have lived for about 1700 years, very largely in a context of Christian axioms.

What did Christianity tell people about their relations with the environment?

While many of the world's mythologies provide stories of creation, Greco-Roman mythology was singularly incoherent in this respect. Like Aristotle, the intellectuals of the ancient West denied that the visible world had had a beginning. Indeed, the idea of a beginning was impossible in the framework of their cyclical notion of time. In sharp contrast, Christianity inherited from Judaism not only a concept of time as nonrepetitive and linear but also a striking story of creation. By gradual stages a loving and all-powerful God had created light and darkness, the heavenly bodies, the earth and all its plants, animals, birds, and fishes. Finally, God had created Adam and, as an after-thought, Eve to keep man from being lonely. Man named all the animals, thus establishing his dominance over them. God planned all of this explicitly for man's benefit and rule: no item in the physical creation had any purpose save to serve man's purposes. And, although man's body is made of clay, he is not simply part of nature: he is made in God's image.

Especially in its Western form, Christianity is the most anthropocentric religion the world has seen. As early as the 2nd century both Tertullian and Saint Irenaeus of Lyons were insisting that when God shaped Adam he was foreshadowing the image of the incarnate Christ, the Second Adam. Man shares, in great measure, God's transcendence of nature. Christianity, in absolute contrast to ancient paganism and Asia's religions (except, perhaps, Zoroastrianism), not only established a dualism of man and nature but also insisted that it is God's will that man exploit nature for his proper ends.

At the level of the common people this worked out in an interesting way. In Antiquity every tree, every spring, every stream, every hill had its own *genius loci*, its guardian spirit. These spirits were accessible to men, but were very unlike men; centaurs, fauns, and mermaids show their ambivalence. Before one cut a tree, mined a mountain, or dammed a brook, it was important to placate the spirit in charge of that particular situation, and to keep it placated. By destroying pagan animism, Christianity made it possible to exploit nature in a mood of indifference to the feelings of natural objects.

It is often said that for animism the Church substituted the cult of saints. True: but the cult of saints is functionally quite different from animism. The saint is not *in* natural objects: he may have special shrines, but his citizenship is in heaven. Moreover, a saint is entirely a man: he can be approached in human terms. In addition to saints, Christianity of course also had angels and demons inherited from Judaism and perhaps, at one remove, from Zoroastrianism. But these were all as mobile as the saints themselves. The spirits *in* natural objects, which formerly had protected nature from man, evaporated. Man's effective monopoly on spirit in this world was confirmed, and the old inhibitions to the exploitation of nature crumbled.

When one speaks in such sweeping terms, a note of caution is in order. Christianity is a complex faith, and its consequences differ in differing contexts. What I have said may well apply to the medieval West, where in fact technology made spectacular advances. But the Greek East, a highly civilized realm of equal Christian devotion, seems to have produced no marked technological innovation after the late 7th century, when Greek fire was invented. The key to the contrast may perhaps be found in a difference in the tonality of piety and thought which students of comparative theology find between the Greek and the Latin Churches. The Greeks believed that sin was intellectual blindness, and that salvation was found in illumination, orthodoxy—that is, clear thinking. The Latins, on the other hand, felt that sin was moral evil, and that salvation was to be found in right conduct.

Eastern theology has been intellectualist. Western theology has been voluntarist. The Greek saint contemplates; the Western saint acts. The implications of Christianity for the conquest of nature would emerge more easily in the Western atmosphere.

The Christian dogma of creation, which is found in the first clause of all the Creeds, has another meaning for our comprehension of today's ecologic crisis. By revelation, God had given man the Bible, the Book of Scripture. But since God had made nature, nature also must reveal the divine mentality. The religious study of nature for the better understanding of God was known as natural theology. In the early Church, and always in the Greek East, nature was conceived primarily as a symbolic system through which God speaks to men: the ant is a sermon to sluggards; rising flames are the symbol of the soul's aspiration. This view of nature was essentially artistic rather than scientific. While Byzantium preserved and copied great numbers of ancient Greek scientific texts, science as we conceive it could scarcely flourish in such an ambience.

However, in the Latin West by the early 13th century natural theology was following a very different bent. It was ceasing to be the decoding of the physical symbols of God's communication with man and was becoming the effort to understand God's mind by discovering how his creation operates. The rainbow was no longer simply a symbol of hope first sent to Noah after the Deluge: Robert Grosseteste, Friar Roger Bacon, and Theodoric of Freiberg produced startlingly sophisticated work on the optics of the rainbow, but they did it as a venture in religious understanding. From the 13th century onward, up to and including Leibnitz and Newton, every major scientist, in effect, explained his motivations in religious terms. Indeed, if Galileo had not been so expert an amateur theologian he would have got into far less trouble: the professionals resented his intrusion. And Newton seems to have regarded himself more as a theologian than as a scientist. It was not until the late 18th century that the hypothesis of God became unnecessary to many scientists.

It is often hard for the historian to judge, when men explain why they are doing what they want to do, whether they are offering real reasons or merely culturally acceptable reasons. The consistency with which scientists during the long formative centuries of Western science said that the task and the reward of the scientist was "to think God's thoughts after him" leads one to believe that this was their real motivation. If so, then modern Western science was cast in a matrix of Christian theology. The dynamism of religious devotion, shaped by the Judeo-Christian dogma of creation, gave it impetus.

An Alternative Christian View

We would seem to be headed toward conclusions unpalatable to many Christians. Since both *science* and *technology* are blessed words in our contemporary vocabulary, some may be happy at the notions, first, that, viewed historically, modern science is an extrapolation of natural theology and, second, that modern technology is at least partly to be explained as an Occidental, voluntarist realization of the Christian dogma of man's transcendence of, and rightful mastery over, nature. But, as we now recognize, somewhat over a century ago science and technology—hitherto quite separate activities—joined to give mankind powers which, to judge by many of the ecologic effects, are out of control. If so, Christianity bears a huge burden of guilt.

I personally doubt that disastrous ecologic backlash can be avoided simply by applying to our problems more science and more technology. Our science and technology have grown out of Christian attitudes toward man's relation to nature which are almost universally held not only by Christians and neo-Christians but also by those who fondly regard themselves as post-Christians. Despite Copernicus, all the cosmos rotates around our little globe. Despite Darwin, we are *not*, in our hearts, part of the natural process. We are superior to nature, contemptuous of it, willing to use it for our slightest whim. The newly elected Governor of California, like myself a churchman but less troubled than I, spoke for the Christian tradition when he said (as alleged), "when you've seen one redwood tree, you've seen them all." To a Christian a tree can be no more than a physical fact. The whole concept of the sacred grove is alien to Christianity and to the ethos of the West. For nearly 2 millennia Christian missionaries have been chopping down sacred groves, which are idolatrous because they assume spirit in nature.

What we do about ecology depends on our ideas of the man-nature relationship. More science and more technology are not going to get us out of the present ecologic crisis until we find a new religion, or rethink our old one. The beatniks, who are the basic revolutionaries of our time, show a sound instinct in their affinity for Zen Buddhism, which conceives of the man-nature relationship as very nearly the mirror image of the Christian view. Zen, however, is as deeply conditioned by Asian history as Christianity is by the experience of the West, and I am dubious of its viability among us.

Possibly we should ponder the greatest radical in Christian history since Christ: Saint Francis of Assisi. The prime miracle of Saint Francis is the fact that he did not end at the stake, as many of his left-wing followers did. He was so clearly heretical that a General of the Franciscan Order, Saint Bonaventura, a great and perceptive Christian, tried to suppress the early account of Franciscanism. The key to an understanding of Francis is his belief in the virtue of humility—not merely for the individual but for man as a species. Francis tried to depose man from his monarchy over creation and set up a democracy of all God's creatures. With him the ant is no longer simply a homily for the lazy, flames a sign of the thrust of the soul toward union with God; now they are Brother Ant and Sister Fire, praising the Creator in their own ways as Brother Man does in his.

Later commentators have said that Francis preached to the birds as a rebuke to men who would not listen. The records do not read so: he urged the little birds to praise God, and in spiritual ecstasy they flapped their wings and chirped rejoicing. Legends of saints, especially the Irish saints, had long told of their dealings with animals but always, I believe, to show their human dominance over creatures. With Francis it is different. The land around Gubbio in the Apennines was being ravaged by a fierce wolf. Saint Francis, says the legend, talked to the wolf and persuaded him of the error of his ways.

The wolf repented, died in the odor of sanctity, and was buried in consecrated ground.

What Sir Steven Runciman calls "the Franciscan doctrine of the animal soul" was quickly stamped out. Quite possibly it was in part inspired, consciously or unconsciously, by the belief in reincarnation held by the Cathar heretics who at that time teemed in Italy and southern France, and who presumably had got it originally from India. It is significant that at just the same moment, about 1200, traces of metempsychosis are found also in western Judaism, in the Provençal *Cabbala*. But Francis held neither to transmigration of souls nor to pantheism. His view of nature and of man rested on a unique sort of pan-psychism of all things animate and inanimate, designed for the glorification of their transcendent Creator, who, in the ultimate gesture of cosmic humility, assumed flesh, lay helpless in a manger, and hung dying on a scaffold.

I am not suggesting that many contemporary Americans who are concerned about our ecologic crisis will be either able or willing to counsel with wolves or exhort birds. However, the present increasing disruption of the global environment is the product of a dynamic technology and science which were originating in the Western medieval world against which Saint Francis was rebelling in so original a way. Their growth cannot be understood historically apart from distinctive attitudes toward nature which are deeply grounded in Christian dogma. The fact that most people do not think of these attitudes as Christian is irrelevant. No new set of basic values has been accepted in our society to displace those of Christianity. Hence we shall continue to have a worsening ecologic crisis until we reject the Christian axiom that nature has no reason for existence save to serve man.

The greatest spiritual revolutionary in Western history, Saint Francis, proposed what he thought was an alternative Christian view of nature and man's relation to it: he tried to substitute the idea of the equality of all creatures, including man, for the idea of man's limitless rule of creation. He failed. Both our present science and our present technology are so tinctured with orthodox Christian arrogance toward nature that no solution for our ecologic crisis can be expected from them alone. Since the roots of our trouble are so largely religious, the remedy must also be essentially religious, whether we call it that or not. We must rethink and refeel our nature and destiny. The profoundly religious, but heretical, sense of the primitive Franciscans for the spiritual autonomy of all parts of nature may point a direction. I propose Francis as a patron saint for ecologists.*

*On April 6, 1980, Pope John Paul II named Francis patron saint of ecology.—Ed.

30. The Mirror of Nature

EMILE MÂLE

The Mirror of Nature is carved in brief on the façades of most of the French cathedrals. We find it at Chartres, at Laon, at Auxerre, Bourges and Lyons, treated in a restrained and conventional way. At Chartres a lion, a sheep, a goat and a heifer stand for the animal world, a fig tree and three plants of indeterminate character represent the vegetable kingdom; there is an element of greatness in this summing up of the universe in some five or six bas-reliefs. Some naïve details are full of charm. In the representation at Laon the Creator sits in deep reflection before dividing the darkness from the light, and counts on His fingers the number of days needed to finish His work. Later in the series, when His task is accomplished, He sits down to rest like a good workman at the end of a well-spent day, and leaning on His staff he falls asleep.

One might well feel that these few typical forms were inadequate representations of the wealth of the universe, and might accuse the thirteenth-century craftsmen of timidity and want of power, did the animal and vegetable worlds really occupy no further place in the cathedral scheme. But a glance upward shows us vines, raspberries heavy with fruit and long trails of the wild rose clinging to the archivolts, birds singing among the oak leaves or perching on the pillars. Beasts from far-off lands side by side with homely creatures of the countryside—lions, elephants and camels, squirrels, hens and

From *The Gothic Image*, by Emile Mâle, trans. Dora Nussey, (New York: E. P. Dutton, 1913), pp. 27–32. Used by permission of the publisher, Dutton, an imprint of New American Library, a division of Penguin Books USA Inc., and J. M. Dent & Sons, Ltd.

rabbits—enliven the basement of the porch, while monsters securely fastened by their heavy stone wings bark fiercely at us from above. How little do these old masters with their unequalled, if naive love of nature deserve the reproach of lack of power or invention. Their cathedrals are all life and movement. The Church to them was the ark to which every creature was made welcome, and then—as if the works of God were not sufficient for them—they invented a whole world more of terrible beings, creatures so real that they surely must have lived in the childhood of the world.

In this way the chapters of the Mirror of Nature are inscribed everywhere—on pinnacle and balustrade as on the smallest capital. What is the meaning of all the plants, animals, monsters? Are they due to caprice or have they significance, and do they teach some great and mysterious truth? May one not suppose that they too are symbols, clothing some thought like the statues and bas-reliefs which we shall have occasion to study later?

In order to answer such questions some attempt must be made to understand the mediæval view of the world and of nature. What is the visible world? What is the meaning of the myriad forms of life? What did the monk dreaming in his cell, or the doctor meditating in the cathedral cloister before the hour of his lecture think of it all? Is it merely appearance or is it reality? The Middle Ages were unanimous in their reply—the world is a symbol. As the idea of his work is in the mind of the artist, so the universe was in the thought of God from the beginning. God created, but He created through His Word, that is, through His Son. The thought of the Father was realised in the Son through whom it passed from potentiality to act, and thus the Son is the true creator. The artists of the Middle Ages, imbued with his doctrine, almost invariably represent the Creator in the likeness of Jesus Christ. The absence in the churches of any likeness of God the Father filled Didron with needless amazement and Michelet with mistaken indignation. For, according to the theologians, God the Father created *in principio,* which is to say *in verbo,* that is by His Son. Jesus Christ is at once Creator and Redeemer.

The world therefore may be defined as "a thought of God realised through the Word." If this be so then in each being is hidden a divine thought; the world is a book written by the hand of God in which every creature is a word charged with meaning. The ignorant see the forms—the mysterious letters—understanding nothing of their meaning, but the wise pass from the visible to the invisible, and in reading nature read the thoughts of God. True knowledge, then, consists not in the study of things in themselves—the outward forms—but in penetrating to the inner meaning intended by God for our instruction, for in the words of Honorius of Autun, "every

creature is a shadow of truth and life." All being holds in its depths
the reflection of the sacrifice of Christ, an image of the Church and
of the virtues and vices. The material and the spiritual worlds are
one.

How mystical were the thoughts which arose in the minds of the
mediæval doctors in the presence of nature. We read how in the
refectory of the monastery Adam of St. Victor, holding a nut in his
hand, reflects—"What is a nut if not the image of Jesus Christ? The
green and fleshy sheath is His flesh, His humanity. The wood of the
shell is the wood of the Cross on which that flesh suffered. But the
kernel of the nut from which men gain nourishment is His hidden
divinity."

Peter of Mora, cardinal and bishop of Capua, contemplates the
roses in his garden. Their natural beauty does not move him, for he
is intent on thoughts which are unfolding within. "The rose," he
says, "is the choir of martyrs, or yet again the choir of virgins. When
red it is the blood of those who died for the faith, when white it is
spotless purity. It opens among thorns as the martyr grows up in the
midst of heretics and persecutors, or as the pure virgin blooms ra-
diant in the midst of iniquity."

Hugh of St. Victor looking at a dove thinks of the Church. "The
dove has two wings even as the Christian has two ways of life, the
active and the contemplative. The blue feathers of the wings are
thoughts of heaven; the uncertain shades of the body, the changing
colours that recall an unquiet sea, symbolise the ocean of human
passions in which the Church is sailing. Why are the dove's eyes this
beautiful golden colour? Because yellow, the colour of ripe fruit, is
the colour too of experience and maturity, and the yellow eyes of
the dove are the looks full of wisdom which the Church casts on the
future. The dove, moreover, has red feet, for the Church moves
through the world with her feet in the blood of the martyrs."

Marbodus, bishop of Rennes, ponders on precious stones and dis-
covers a mystic consonance between their colours and things of the
spirit. The beryl shines like sunlit water and warms the hand that
holds it. Is this not an image of the Christian life warmed and illuminated to its depths by Christ the sun? The red amethyst seems to
send out fire. Here is an image of the martyrs, who as their blood is
shed send up ardent prayers for their persecutors.

The whole world is a symbol. The sun, the stars, the seasons, day
and night, all speak in solemn accents. Of what were the Middle
Ages thinking in the winter time when the days were shortening sadly
and the darkness seemed to be triumphing for ever over the light?
They thought of the long centuries of twilight that preceded the
coming of Christ, and they understood that in the divine drama both

light and darkness have their place. They gave the name of Advent (*Adventus*) to those weeks of December, when by means of the liturgy and lessons from Scripture they expressed the long waiting of the ancient world. It was at the winter solstice, at the time when light begins to reappear and the days to lengthen, that the Son of God was born. Even the round of the year shadows forth man's course upon earth, and recounts the drama of life and death. Spring, which gives new life to the world, is the symbol of baptism which renews the spirit of man at his entrance into life. Summer too is a type, for its burning heat and light are reminders of the light of another world and of the ardent love of the eternal life. Autumn, season of harvest and vintage, is the dread symbol of the last Judgment—that great Day on which men will reap as they have sown. Winter is a shadow of that death which awaits mankind and the universe. Thus the thinker moved in a world of symbols, thronged by forms pregnant with spiritual meaning.

Are these the interpretations of individuals, mystical fancies born of the exaltation of cloistered life, or are we in the presence of an ordered system, an ancient tradition? The answer is found in the most cursory reading of the works of the Fathers and the mediæval doctors. Never was doctrine more closely knit or more universally accepted. It dates back to the beginning of the Church, and is founded on the words of the Bible itself. In the Scriptures, indeed, as interpreted by the Fathers, the material world is a constant image of the spiritual world. In each word of God both the visible and the invisible are contained. The flowers whose scent overpowered the lover in the Song of Songs, the jewels which adorned the breastplate of the high priest, the beasts of the desert which passed before Job are at once realities and symbols. The juniper tree, the terebinth, and the snowy peaks of Lebanon are alike thoughts of God. To interpret the Bible is to apprehend the harmony which God has established between the soul and the universe, and the key to the scriptures is the key to the two worlds.

31. Thomas Aquinas: Reason and Revelation

ETIENNE GILSON

... [Thomas's] intention was not to make theology still more learned than Albert the Great had already made it. It was first to eliminate from it all learning irrelevant to the exposition and intellection of the saving truth, then to integrate in theology the relevant learning even if, in order to do so, it was necessary to reform certain commonly held positions and to reinterpret certain philosophical principles. Insofar as Christian faith itself was concerned, Thomas Aquinas never intended to touch it. The magnificent elaboration of Christian dogma left by Augustine to his successors was likewise taken up by Thomas Aquinas and integrated by him in his new synthesis. On the contrary, always with a pious respect for his great predecessor, yet fearlessly, Thomas felt free to reinterpret and, wherever it was necessary, to replace with a truer philosophy the purely philosophical elements integrated by Augustine in his own theological synthesis. His reason for doing so was simple. Philosophy is not necessary for human salvation; it is not even necessary for theology to resort to philosophy, but, if it does, the philosophy it uses should be the true philosophy. When a theologian has good reasons to think that Augustine did not make use of the best possible philosophy, he should not hesitate to change it.

Because Thomas Aquinas did so, his reformation of theology entailed a reformation of philosophy. There is no reason not to call it an Aristotelian reformation, for indeed, on many points, Thomas

From *History of Christian Philosophy in the Middle Ages* by Etienne Gilson (New York: Random House, 1955), pp. 364–372. Copyright © 1955 by Etienne Gilson. Reprinted by permission of Random House, Inc. and Sheed and Ward.

Aquinas substituted for the doctrines borrowed from Plotinus by Augustine, other doctrines which he himself was borrowing from Aristotle. Two points, however, should be kept in mind. First, the philosophical reformation achieved by Thomas Aquinas is a moment in the history of theology before being one in the history of metaphysics. Secondly, even on the level of pure philosophy, his doctrine cannot be understood as a further stage in the progressive discovery of Aristotle by the Latins. Thomism was not the upshot of a better understanding of Aristotle. It did not come out of Aristotelianism by way of evolution, but of revolution. Thomas uses the language of Aristotle everywhere to make the Philosopher say that there is only one God, the pure Act of Being, Creator of the world, infinite and omnipotent, a providence for all that which is, intimately present to every one of his creatures, especially to men, every one of whom is endowed with a personally immortal soul naturally able to survive the death of its body. The best way to make Aristotle say so many things he never said was not to show that, had he understood himself better than he did, he could have said them. For indeed Aristotle seems to have understood himself pretty well. He has said what he had to say, given the meaning which he himself attributed to the principles of his own philosophy. Even the dialectical acumen of Saint Thomas Aquinas could not have extracted from the principles of Aristotle more than what they could possibly yield. The true reason why his conclusions were different from those of Aristotle was that his own principles themselves were different. As will be seen, in order to metamorphose the doctrine of Aristotle, Thomas has ascribed a new meaning to the principles of Aristotle. As a philosophy, Thomasism is essentially a metaphysics. It is a revolution in the history of the metaphysical interpretation of the first principle, which is "being."

We are living in times so different from those of Thomas Aquinas that it is difficult for us to understand how philosophy can become theology and yet gain in rationality. This, however, is exactly what happened to philosophy in the *Summa Theologiae,* when Thomas changed the water of philosophy to the wine of theology. Thomas always considered himself a theologian. Up to the last years of his life he kept faith with the teaching of Augustine forcefully restated in the injunction of Gregory IX to the theologians of the University of Paris. In his own view, he was not only a theologian, but a monk who had no right to indulge in philosophical activities except in the spirit of his religious vocation. "The philosophers," Thomas says, "made profession of studying Letters in view of acquiring secular learning, but what chiefly befits a religious is to study those Letters that pertain to the learning that is *according to godliness,* as is written

in the Epistle to Titus, i, I. As to the other branches of learning, they
are not suitable objects of study for a religious whose whole life is
dedicated to the divine service, except insofar as their study is related
to sacred learning." Whereupon Thomas immediately quotes Augustine in support of his assertion. Thomas intended to do exactly
the same thing as all the other theologians of his time, only he did
it differently. Then, naturally, the question arises: since he was a
theologian, and such a strict one, how could he have anything to do
with philosophy? His own notion of the nature of theology will be
the answer to this difficulty.

• • •

The true nature of the distinction there is between philosophy
and theology is a matter to be settled between philosophers and
theologians. All that a historian can say is that, in the mind of
Thomas Aquinas himself, their distinction was not as simple as it is
sometimes supposed to be. With all theologians, Thomas affirms
that, supposing the free will of God to save mankind as a whole, it
was necessary that the knowledge required for human salvation
should be revealed to men. This is evident in the case of those saving
truths which escape the grasp of natural human reason. But even
when it was within the grasp of natural human reason, saving truth
had to be revealed because, otherwise, most men would have remained ignorant of it. Few men are gifted for metaphysical or ethical
studies; even those who have the necessary gifts have to wait up to
the later part of their life before reaching conclusions in these lofty
matters, and who knows at what age he will die? Above all, even those
philosophers who live long enough to reach these conclusions, never
or seldom do it without some admixture of error.

A first consequence follows from these facts. To the extent that it
pertains to the sacred teaching imparted to man through revelation
(*sacra doctrina*) theology must deal with some philosophically knowable truths, namely, those whose knowledge is required for the salvation of any man; for instance, God exists, he is one, he is incor-
poreal, etc. Since they have been in fact revealed to men, these truths
were revealable, but the formal reason of the "revealable" extends
even beyond the limits of the actually revealed; it includes the whole
body of human natural knowledge inasmuch as it can be considered
by the theologian in the light of revelation and used by him in view
of its end, which is the salvation of man in general. This leaves intact,
within theology, the formal distinction between natural knowledge
and supernatural knowledge, but it includes them both under a still
wider formal reason since "revealables" comprise the whole body
of natural cognitions considered as being at the disposal of the theo-

logian in view of his own theological end which is the salvation of man.

If this be true, the unity of theology is that of an organic whole whose parts are united under one single formal reason. Naturally, it first includes what God has actually revealed (whether it be naturally knowable or not). It also includes what the theologian deduces, as a necessary consequence, from the actually revealed truth (theologians often call this the "virtually" revealed). Moreover, it includes all the material provided by logic, the sciences of nature and metaphysics, to the extent that it is taken up by the theologian and incorporated by him into his work. He alone is judge of this extent. Just as it is the soul that builds itself a body, so also theology builds itself the philosophical body which it needs in order to promote the saving work of the sacred teaching.

• • •

Like all theologies the doctrine of Saint Thomas is dominated by his own notion of God. Like all Christian theologians, he knew that the proper name of God was I AM WHO AM, or HE WHO IS (Exod. 3, 14), but even for men who agreed on the truth of this divine name, there remained a problem of interpretation. Modern philology has a right to investigate the question; naturally, it will find in this text what can be found in any text by means of grammars and dictionaries alone. This is not negligible but, philosophically speaking, it seldom amounts to much. Even with such a limited aim in mind, the grammarians have already achieved amazingly different results. What we are concerned with is very different. Our own problem is to know what meaning the Christian masters have attributed to this famous text. Most of them agreed that it meant: I am Being. But what is being? To Augustine, "who was imbued with the doctrines of the Platonists," being was eternal immutability. To John Damascene, absolute being was an "infinite ocean of entity." To Saint Anselm, it was that whose very nature it is to be: *natura essendi*. In all these cases, the dominating notion was that of "entity" (*essentia*). In the mind of Thomas Aquinas, the notion of being underwent a remarkable transformation; from now on, and so long as we will be dealing with Thomas Aquinas, the deepest meaning of the word "being" will be the act pointed out by the verb "to be." Since, in common human experience, to be is to exist, it can be said that, in the doctrine of Thomas Aquinas, being has received the fullness of its existential meaning. In order to avoid all possible confusions with some modern uses of the word "existence," let us add that, in every being, "to be," or *esse*, is not to become; it is not any kind of projection from the present into the future. On the contrary, because it is act, "to be" is something fixed and at rest in being: *esse est aliquid fixum et quietum in ente.* In short, this act is the very core of all that is, inasmuch precisely as what is, is a being.

As Thomas Aquinas understands him, God is the being whose whole nature it is to be such an existential act. This is the reason why his most proper name is, HE IS. After saying this, any addition would be a subtraction. To say that God "is this," or that he "is that," would be to restrict his being to the essence of what "this" and "that" are. God "is," absolutely. Because "what" a thing is usually receives the name of "essence," or of "quiddity" (its "whatness"), some say that since he is "being only" (*esse tantum*), God has no essence or quiddity. Thomas Aquinas does not seem to have favored this way of expressing the purity of the divine act of being. He prefers to say that the essence of God is his *esse.* In other words, God is the being of which it can be said that, what in other beings is their essence, is in it what we call "to be." All the attributes of God are either deducible from this true meaning of his name, or qualified by it.

In our human experience, a "being" is "something that is," or exists. Since, in God, there is no something to which existence could be attributed, his own *esse* is precisely that which God is. To us, such a being is strictly beyond all possible representation. We can establish *that* God is, we cannot know *what* he is because, in him, there is no what; and since our whole experience is about things that *have* existence, we cannot figure out what it is to be a being whose only essence is "to be." For this reason, we can prove the truth of the proposition "God is," but, in this unique case, we cannot know the meaning of the verb "is." Such is the Thomistic meaning of the classical doctrine of the ineffability of God.

Unknowable to himself, at least to us and in this life, God can be known by man imperfectly, from the consideration of his creatures. Two things at least are known of him in this way: first, that he is entirely unlike any one of his creatures; secondly, that he is in himself at least what he has to be in order to be their cause. For this reason, our knowledge of God is said to be "analogical"; we know that God is, with respect to the universe, in a relation similar to that which obtains, in our human experience, between causes and their effects. Such a cognition is not purely negative, since it enables us to say something true about God; it is not wholly positive, and far from it, since not a single one of our concepts, not even that of existence, properly applies to God; we call it "analogical" precisely because it bears upon resemblances between relations, that is, upon proportions.

This notion of God as the absolute act of being flows from the demonstrations of his existence. To demonstrate it is both possible and necessary. It is necessary because the existence of God is not immediately evident; self-evidence would only be possible in this matter if we had an adequate notion of the divine essence; the essence of God would then appear to be one with his existence. But God is an infinite being and, as it has no concept of him, our finite mind cannot see existence as necessarily implied in his infinity; we therefore have to conclude, by way of reasoning, that existence which we cannot intuit. Thus the direct way apparently opened by Saint Anselm's ontological argument is closed to us; but the indirect way which Aristotle has pointed out remains open. Let us therefore seek in sensible things, whose nature is proportioned to our intellect, the starting point of our way to God.

All the Thomistic proofs bring two distinct elements into play: (1) the existence of a sensible reality whose existence requires a cause; (2) the demonstration of the fact that its existence requires a finite series of causes, and consequently a Prime Cause, which is what we call God. Because movement is immediately perceptible to sense knowledge, let us start from the fact that movement exists. The only superiority of this "way" with respect to the other ones, is that its point of departure is the easiest to grasp. All movement has a cause, and that cause must be other than the very being that is in motion; when a thing seems to be self-moving, a certain part of it is moving the rest. Now, whatever it is, the mover itself must be moved by another, and that other by still another. It must therefore be admitted, either that the series of causes is infinite and has no origin, but then nothing explains that there is movement, or else that the series is finite and that there is a primary cause, and this primary cause is precisely what everyone understands to be God.

Just as there is motion in sensible things, there are causes and effects. Now what has just been said of the causes of movement can also be said of causes in general. Nothing can be its own efficient cause, for in order to produce itself, it would have to be anterior, as cause, to itself as effect. Every efficient cause therefore presupposes another, which in turn presupposes another. Now, in this order of causes, in which each higher one is the cause of the lower, it is impossible to go on to infinity, otherwise, there would be neither a first efficient cause, nor intermediate causes, and the effects whose existence we perceive could not possibly exist. There must therefore be a first efficient cause of the series, in order that there may be a middle and a last one, and that first efficient cause is what everyone calls God.

Now let us consider beings themselves. As we know them, they are ceaselessly becoming. Since some of them are being generated, while others are passing away, it is possible for them to be or not to be. Their existence then is not necessary. Now the necessary needs no cause in order to exist; precisely because it is necessary, it exists of itself. But the possible cannot account for its own existence, and if there were absolutely nothing but possibility in things, there would be nothing. This is to say that, since there is something, there must be some being whose existence is necessary. If there are several necessary beings, their series must be finite for the same reason as above. There is therefore a first necessary being, to whose necessity all possible beings owe their existence, and this is what all men call God.

A fourth way goes through the hierarchical degrees of perfection observed in things. There are degrees in goodness, truth, nobility and other perfections of being. Now, more or less are always said with reference to a term of comparison which is absolute. There is therefore a true and a good in itself, that is to say, in the last resort, a being in itself which is the cause of all the other beings and this we call God.

The fifth way rests upon the order of things. All natural bodies, even those which lack knowledge, act for an end. The regularity with which, by and large, they achieve their end, is a safe indication that they do not arrive at it by chance and that this regularity can only be intentional and willed. Since they themselves are without knowledge, someone has to know for them. This primary Intelligent Being, cause of the purpose there is in natural things, is the being we call God.

Since God is first from all points of view and with respect to all the rest, he cannot enter into composition with anything else. The cause of all other beings can enter into composition with none of them. Consequently, God is simple. His simplicity itself has many consequences. Because corporeal bodies are in potency with respect to both motion and being, they are not simple; hence God cannot be corporeal. For the same reason, since he is pure act, God is not composed of matter and form. He is not even a subject endowed with its own form, essence or nature. Divinity is something that God *is*, not that he *has*. But what is such a being which *is* all that he can be said to be, and *has* nothing? He is WHO IS. Since God *is* what other beings only *have*, there is in him no distinct essence to unite with the act of being. This unique being, the only one whose whole essence it is "to be," is so perfectly simple that it is its own being.

If this direct argument seems too abstract to satisfy the intellect, let us remember the conclusions of each one of the five "ways." All particular beings owe their existence to the Prime Cause. Consequently, they receive existence. In other words, what they are (i.e., their essence) receives from God the existence which it has. On the contrary, since the Prime Efficient Cause does not receive its own existence (otherwise it would not be prime) there is no sense in which it can be said to be distinct from it. If there were such a thing as a pure and absolute "fire," it would not *have* the nature of fire, it would *be* it. Similarly, God is not really "being"; he is the very act of what we call "to be." He does not share in it, he is it. Naturally, since we have no experience of this unique being, our mind is unable to conceive it and our language has no perfectly fitting words to express it. From the very first moment we attempt to say what God is, we must content ourselves with saying that he is not in the same way as other things are. As has already been said, we do not know what it is for God "to be"; we only know that it is true to say that God is.

The metaphysician thus joins, by reason alone, the philosophical truth hidden in the name that God himself has revealed to man: I AM WHO AM (Exod. 3, 14). God is the pure act of existing, that is, not some essence or other, such as the One, or the Good, or Thought, to which might be attributed existence in addition; not even a certain eminent way of existing, like Eternity, Immutability or Necessity, that could be attributed to his being as characteristic of the divine reality; but Existing itself (*ipsum esse*) in itself and without any addition whatever, since all that could be added to it would limit it in determining it. If he is pure Existing, God is by that very fact the absolute Plenitude of being; he is therefore infinite. If he is infinite Being, he can lack nothing that he should acquire; no change is conceivable in him; he is therefore sovereignly immutable and eternal, and so with other perfections that can be fittingly attributed to him. Now, it is fitting to attribute all of them to him, for, if the absolute act of existing is infinite, it is so in the order of being; it is therefore perfect.

Such is the cause of the many deficiencies of the language in which we express him. This God whose existence we affirm, does not allow us to fathom what he is; he is infinite, and our minds are finite; we must therefore take as many exterior views of him as we can, without ever claiming to exhaust the subject. A first way of proceeding consists in denying everything about the divine essence that could not belong to it. By successively removing from the idea of God movement, change, passivity, composition, we end by positing him as an immobile, immovable being, perfectly in act and absolutely simple; this is the way of negation. But one can take a second way and try to name God according to the analogies obtaining between him and things. There is necessarily a connection, and consequently a resemblance, between cause and effect. When the cause is infinite and the effect finite, it obviously cannot be said that the properties of the effect are found in it such as they are in the cause, but what exists in effects must also be pre-existent in their cause, whatever its manner of existing. In this sense, we attribute to God all the perfections of which we have found some shadow in the creature, but we carry them to the infinite. Thus we say that God is perfect, supremely good, unique, intelligent, omniscient, voluntary, free, and all-powerful, each of these attributes being reduced, in the last analysis, to an aspect of the infinite and perfectly single perfection of the pure act that God is.

PROBLEMS OF LATE MEDIEVAL SOCIETY

T HE APPARENTLY SERENE, harmonious civilization of the thirteenth century did not endure for long. The history of the fourteenth century is a catalogue of disasters. In the later Middle Ages
European society had to endure famine, plague, war, rebellions in
many lands, and schism in the church. Some of the troubles of the
age arose from fortuitous natural disasters, e.g., a series of bad harvests in 1315–1317 and the devastating Black Death in the middle
years of the century. But many of them grew out of tensions inherent
in earlier medieval civilization.

The problems that emerged concerned both economic and religious life. All the achievements of the twelfth and thirteenth centuries had been based on a steady increase of population and of real wealth. By 1300 the growing population was beginning to press on the available economic resources. In the first group of readings below, Emmanuel Le Roy Ladurie discusses the rearing of children as a way of maintaining family prosperity in a peasant society; M. M. Postan deals with the overall economic impact of population growth; A. P. Lewis considers the strains and stresses of overpopulation in terms of the familiar "frontier thesis"; and Edith Ennen describes some aspects of urban social life in the century after the onset of the plague.

In the realm of religious life the Black Death produced some pathological results, including the renewed persecution of the Jews discussed by Philip Ziegler. (On earlier outbreaks of anti-Jewish sentiment, see Jeremy Cohen's "The Decline of European Jewry," which appears above as Reading 24.) Within the Christian church, dissident apocalyptic movements grew up which looked forward to a revolutionary transformation of society in a coming new age. In the final reading Norman Cohn compares such movements with the totalitarian ideologies of the twentieth century.

One has to add finally that these problems did not lead to a general collapse of civilization comparable to the "fall of the Roman empire." The Black Death produced new kinds of economic dislocation, but it ended for centuries the pressure of overpopulation in Europe. The fifteenth and sixteenth centuries brought further change and new problems, but there was no sharp break in the continuity of Western civilization.

32. *Family and Population*

A. Parents and Children

EMMANUEL LE ROY LADURIE*

As was normal under the *ancien régime,* the peasant family in Montaillou was a large one. Mengarde and Pons Clergue had four sons and at least two daughters known to us. Guillemette Belot had four sons and two daughters. Guillaume and Guillemette Benet had at least two sons and three daughters. Raymond Baille had four sons, but no daughter is mentioned. Pierre and Mengarde Maurs had four sons and one daughter. There were four Marty brothers. Alazaïs and Raymond Maury had six sons and at least two daughters.

There were smaller families. Bernard and Gauzia Clergue had only two known children, a son and a daughter. Two couples, Guillemette and Raymond Maurs and Bernard and Guillemette Maurs, had two sons each, as well, probably, as daughters unknown to us in name or number. From the information available, eighteen couples emerge who were in the process of completing, or had completed, their family in the demographic period 1280–1324, the time roughly covered by the Fournier Register. These eighteen families, complete

---

*Between 1318 and 1325 Bishop Jacques Fournier investigated the whole population of the little village of Montaillou in southern France on suspicion of heresy. The detailed records of the interrogations survive, and from them Emmanuel Le Roy Ladurie was able to construct a brilliant picture of the social and religious life of the village. The pages given here are a fragment of this account. Figures interpolated in the text refer to Fournier's register.—Ed.

From Emmanuel Le Roy Ladurie, *Montaillou* (New York: George Braziller, Inc., 1978), pp. 204, 207, 210–213. Reprinted by permission.

and incomplete, gave birth to a minimum of forty-two boys and twenty girls. The number of girls is clearly under-estimated or under-recorded. The figure for boys certainly does not take into account losses from infant mortality, the deaths which occurred between birth and the end of the first year of life. It also leaves out an indeterminable fraction of juvenile mortality, especially between one and five years of age. Even so, this gives us a mean of 2.3 boys per couple. So, taking into account various imponderables, it is reasonable to assume 4.5 legitimate births, including boys and girls, per family, complete or incomplete,[1] a fertility rate equal to that of the prolific inhabitants of Beauvaisis in modern times. The illegitimacy rate in Montaillou was higher.

One explanation of the size of Montaillou families is the early age at which girls married. Moreover our figures are chiefly concerned with the Cathar and endogamous group of big farming families, allied among themselves, which dominated Montaillou around 1300. For reasons which are perhaps fortuitous, the few Catholic families in the village, for example the Azémas, recorded fewer children and fewer marriages than the heretics.

There were limits to this fecundity. The richest family, the Clergues, in Pierre and Bernard's generation, seem to have practised certain kinds of birth control (magical herbs, or perhaps *coitus interruptus*). Pons Clergue's many sons left several bastards but no legitimate child, though there were other Clergues in the village to carry on the name. As for the lower ranks, the shepherds tended not to get married. More generally, the last generation with which we are concerned, that which married between the round-up of 1308 and the interrogations of 1320–25, was greatly disturbed. Many people were put in prison and the circumstances may have led some couples to practise abstinence or contraception. At all levels, during the decade beginning in 1310, which was also economically unpropitious, fertility in Montaillou seems to have declined.

Between 1280 and 1305, however, there was in Montaillou, as elsewhere, a baby boom. Large groups of two brothers or even four all living together were very common (i.193, 203). A high birth rate was taken for granted. If you lost one child and were not too old, it was very likely that you would have more and these, according to a far-fetched Cathar interpretation of metempsychosis, might be the means of restoring to a mother the souls of her previously lost children (i.203).

My fellow-sponsor, Alazaïs Munier, says Guillaume Austatz, *bayle* of Ornolac, *was sad; in a short time she had lost all her four sons. Seeing her desolate, I asked her the cause.*

'*How could I be other than unhappy,*' she asked, '*after having lost four fine children in so short a time?*'

'*Don't be upset,*' I said to her, '*you will get them back again.*'

'*Yes, in Paradise!*'

'*No, you will get them back again in this world. For you are still young. You will be pregnant again. The soul of one of your dead children will enter into the new foetus. And so on!*'

We see that Guillaume Austatz did not think it strange that a woman should have eight pregnancies in all.

The countrymen of this period were well aware of the population pressure of the 1300s, resulting from, among other things, the high fertility rates discussed above. *Where*, it was asked (i.191), *would there be room to put all the souls of all the men who are dead and of all those who are still alive? At that rate the world would be full of souls! The entire space between the city of Toulouse and the Merens Pass would not be enough to hold them all!* Fortunately, explained Guillaume Austatz, God had found a simple remedy. Every soul was used several times. *It emerged from a human body which had just died, and entered almost immediately into another. And so on.*

In theory, the Cathar dogma professed by many of the people of Montaillou, though little known to them in detail, was hostile to marriage and procreation. The most sophisticated Cathar peasants, and *parfaits* or pseudo-*parfaits* like Bélibaste, were acquainted with this point. Bélibaste himself (ii.48), who wanted *through virginity to transport the seed of this world into the next,* would not have *any man join himself carnally to a woman; nor would I have sons or daughters born of them. For if people would hold to barrenness, all God's creatures would soon be gathered together* [in heaven]. *That is what I should like.* Similarly, we have seen Pierre Clergue of Montaillou making use of contraception, perhaps magical. But how many people in the village of the yellow cross were capable of such refinements? In any case, the duty of barrenness was incumbent only on the goodmen, not on mere 'believers'. So the peasants of Montaillou, even when they were sympathetic to heresy, continued to produce numerous children. There was enough land, especially pasture, to provide them with employment when they grew up. Moreover, Catalonia, which as Bélibaste said (ii.42) *lacked neither pastures nor mountains for the sheep,* welcomed surplus youth from Montaillou with open arms. They easily found jobs there as shepherds and muleteers. In these circumstances, why worry? A *domus* rich in children was a *domus* rich in manpower; in other words, rich, pure and simple. This explains the large number of sons produced by the big farming families of Montaillou—the Belots, the Maurys, the Martys and so on. On the last generation of

Clergues, wealthy enough not to have to descend to manual labour, were not interested in producing a large number of workers. So, both in theory and in practice, they could afford views favourable to contraception and hostile to marriage.

• • •

There are many examples in upper Ariège of the sorrow of country parents at the death of their offspring. It is true that within the framework of the *domus* system, love for children was not, in the last resort, entirely disinterested. Bélibaste suggested as much when exhorting Pierre Maury against remaining a bachelor (iii.188). Alazaïs Azéma was more precise still, reporting on the feelings of Guillaume Benet, a farmer of Montaillou, on the loss of his son (i.321). *When Raymond Benet, son of Guillaume Benet, died, I went after a fortnight to Guillaume Benet's house. I found him in tears.*

'Alazaïs,' he said, 'I have lost all I had through the death of my son Raymond. I have no one left to work for me.'

All Alazaïs could say was: *'Cheer up; there's nothing we can do about it.'*

But if a male child meant a strong right arm to Guillaume Benet, he also meant much more. Guillaume loved Raymond for himself. And he was somewhat consoled to think that Guillaume Authié had hereticated his son before he died. So the son was in fact happier than his father, left behind in this vale of tears: *'I hope,'* said Guillaume, *'that my son is in a better place than I am now.'*

When Guillemette Benet of Montaillou lost a daughter and was weeping for her, Alazaïs Azéma tried to console her (i.320). *'Cheer up, you still have some daughters left; and anyhow you can't get the one that is dead back again.'*

To which Guillemette replied: *'I would mourn even more than I do for the death of my daughter; but,* Deo gratias, *I have had the consolation of seeing her hereticated on the night before her death by Guillaume Authié, who hurried here in a blizzard.'*

Sincere as all this affection was, it was also ritualized, socialized and shared. So were the condolences offered to a bereaved parent by friends and neighbours. The difference there might be between a father's and a mother's love is shown in the story of the Pierre family, an episode which has the additional interest of dealing with a little girl less than one year old. Despite the infant's extreme youth, it was undoubtedly the object of emotion. Raymond Pierre was a sheep-farmer in the village of Arques, a terminus on the migration route used by the people of Montaillou. He had one daughter, Jacotte, by Sybille his wife (iii.414–15). Jacotte, not yet a year old, was seriously ill, and her parents decided, so much did they love the child, against all the rules of heresy, to have her hereticated before she died. In theory it was not right to hereticate anyone so young: Jacotte *did not have the understanding of good.* But Prades Tavernier, the *parfait* who undertook the ceremony, was laxer than the Authiés and thought there was nothing to be lost by it.[2] So he started to administer the *consolamentum: He performed a lot of bows and elevations,* and placed that rare object, a book, on the child's head. Once these rites were accomplished, Raymond Pierre could say to his wife, *'If Jacotte dies, she will be an angel of God. Neither you nor I, wife, could give our daughter as much as this heretic has given.'*

Full of joy and disinterested love, Raymond Pierre left the house to see Prades Tavernier on his way. Before going, the *parfait* told Sybille not to give the baby any milk or meat. If Jacotte lived, all she was to have was fish and vegetables (ii.414). For a child of that age, and in the dietetic conditions of the period, this was risky. In fact, what it amounted to was that after the father and the *parfait* left, Jacotte would be doomed to imminent death by a process similar to the *endura,* or final fast.

But there was a hitch. Sybille Pierre's love for her little girl was essentially warm and physical, not spiritual and sublime like that of Raymond. So, relates Sybille, *when my husband and Prades Tavernier had left the house, I could not bear it any longer. I couldn't let my daughter die before my very eyes. So I put her to the breast. When my husband came back, I told him I had fed my daughter. He was very grieved and troubled, and lamented. Pierre Maury* [Raymond Pierre's shepherd] *tried to console his master. He said to my husband, 'It is not your fault.'*

And Pierre said to my baby, 'You have a wicked mother.'

And he said to me, 'You are a wicked mother. Women are demons.'

My husband wept. He insulted and threatened me. After this scene, he stopped loving [diligere] *the child; and he also stopped loving me for a long while, until later, when he admitted that he had been wrong.* (Raymond Pierre's change of heart occurred at the same time as all the inhabitants of Arques decided collectively to renounce Catharism.) *My daughter Jacotte,* Sybille concluded (ii.415), *survived this episode for a year; and then she died.*

All this shows that there was not such an enormous gap, as has sometimes been claimed, between our attitude to children and the attitude of the people in fourteenth-century Montaillou and upper Ariège. Another example is the case of Raymond Benet's new-born son, who was not expected to live. Perhaps his mother was already dead. Guillemette Benet, who lived in the same village as her brother, tells the story (i.264). *Raymond Benet of Ornalac had a new-*

born son who was dying. He sent for me when I was going to the woods to gather firewood, so that I could hold the dying child in my arms. So I did hold it from morning until evening, when it died.

There are, of course, some differences between our attitude to our children and the affection felt by the peasants and especially the women of Montaillou towards their offspring. But they probably loved their children just as intensely as we do, and perhaps even spoiled them too.[3] Of course, parental love had to be divided up among a greater number of children than today. It also had to adapt itself to a higher rate of infant mortality. Lastly, many couples seemed to be comparatively indifferent to very young infants.[4] But this indifference was less marked than has recently been claimed.[5]

NOTES

1. The couples in question here are: Pons Clergue and Mengarde (four boys, two girls: Guillaume, Bernard, Pierre, Raymond, Esclarmonde, Guillemette); a couple whose head, unreferred to elsewhere, was called Bar (three sons and two daughters: Pierre, Raymond, Guillaume, Mengarde, Guillemette; see i.418); Bernard Rives and Alazaïs (one son, two daughters: Pons, Raymonde and Guillemette, who married one of the Clergues); Pons Azéma and Alazaïs (one son: Raymond); Pierre Azèma and Guillemette (one son: Raymond); Bernard Clergue (the *bayle's* namesake) and Gauzia (one boy, one girl: Raymond, Esclarmonde); Bernad Clergue, *bayle* of Montaillou, and Raymonde (no children); Belot senior (Christian name unknown) and Guillemette (four sons, two daughters: Raymond, Guillaume, Bernad, Arnaud, Raymonde and, according to i.371, Alazaïs); Guillaume Benet and Guillemette (two sons, four daughters: Raymond, Bernard, Alazaïs, Montagne; and, according to i.400, Gaillarde and Esclarmonde); Raymond Baille and X (four sons: Pierre, Jacques, Raymond, Arnaud); Vital Baille and Esclarmonde (one son: Jacques); Pierre Maurs and Mengarde (four sons and one daughter: Arnaud, Guillaume, Raymond, Pierre, Guillemette); Raymond Maurs and Guillemette (two sons: Pierre and Bernard); Bernard Maurs and Guillemette (two sons: Raymond and Pierre); the four Marty brothers, the name of whose mother and father are unknown: Guillaume, Arnaud, Bernard and Jean; X Testanière and Alazaïs (one son and one daughter: Prades and Vuissane); Raymond Maury and Alazaïs (six sons and two daughters: Guillaume, Pierre, Jean, Arnaud, Raymond, Bernard, Guillemette and Raymonde); Jean Guilhabert and Allemande (one son and three daughters: Guillaume, Alazaïs, Sybille and Guillemette, according to i.403, ii.256 and ii.482 and 484). I have left out the very old groups, like those of Pons and Guillaume Clergue, which were already decimated by death, not only among infants and children but also among adults and elderly people. I have also left out very young couples only a small part of

whose procreative life fell within the last years of the Fournier Register; moreover, these were greatly disturbed by the Inquisition. Finally, I have left out the wives who were widowed early and took refuge in Catalonia. It goes without saying that the records we are dealing with have only a very indirect and unintended demographic value.

2. iii.144. In fact, Prades Tavernier, a villager by origin, not a bourgeois like the Authiés, was influenced by the pressure of Catholic behaviour, and administered the *consolamentum* to a baby in just the same way as a Roman priest would administer baptism in the same circumstances.

3. I think I have said enough to counter the point of view expounded by Madame B. Vourzay, who writes that 'children were of little account' for the people of Montaillou. (Vourzay (1969), p. 91). It is true, as she rightly says, that grown-ups in upper Ariège were afraid that children might betray them to the Inquisition. But in my view this did not affect the general feeling towards children.

4. There is little mention of the death of infants in Montaillou itself, though such losses must have been frequent.

5. There is not enough information available for us to go into the question of the attitude of grandparents. But to take a few examples, Beatrice de Planissoles was an attentive grandmother (i.249) and a dead grandmother came back as a ghost to embrace her grandchildren in bed (i.135). The Fournier Register tells us nothing about grandfathers: men were much less likely to live long enough to become grandparents. But see iii.305 for the interest taken by Raymond Authié (namesake of the *parfait*) in a suggestion of marriage concerning his granddaughter, Guillemette Cortil.

B. Land and Population

M. M. POSTAN

. . . The most obvious even if indirect sign of continued population growth will be found in the continuous expansion of land settlement and reclamation throughout the seven or eight centuries separating the Anglo-Saxon conquest from the beginning of the fourteenth century. We have seen that, to begin with, the area occupied by agricultural settlers was very small, not much greater than it had been under Roman occupation, and that the greater part of the English plain was reclaimed in later centuries. It is of course impossible to assign a precise enumerator to the total additions made to the occupied land before 1300, but we can be certain that it had grown manifold.

From M. M. Postan, *The Medieval Economy and Society* (Berkeley and Los Angeles: University of California Press, 1972), pp. 31–34. Copyright 1972 by M. M. Postan. Reprinted by permission of Weidenfeld & Nicholson Ltd.

Our demographic deduction from this fact is that population must also have grown by at least the same rate. In theory it is possible to assume that an agricultural population, even a wholly settled one, would try to expand the acreage of its land and continue to do so indefinitely merely in response to the insatiable desire of individual peasants to add and to go on adding to their holdings. This is not, however, what in fact took place in most of the rural societies in the past, and it is certainly not what happened in medieval England. On the contrary, such evidence as we possess—and it will be recalled again later—makes it quite clear that the average size of family holdings between the eleventh century and the fourteenth declined. If so, the population must have increased at a rate even faster than the areas reclaimed for arable and improved pasture. . . .

By the end of the thirteenth century the land hunger revealed itself in innumerable ways. One of its signs was the long and lengthening queues of men seeking land. In some places the queues had become so long as to disrupt the traditional routine of succession from father to son on the former's death. So valuable was the land, and so numerous were the men willing to take it up, that sitting holders were frequently tempted to sell long before they died. Purchase was becoming a common method of acquiring land. On the Glastonbury estates in the second half of the thirteenth century more than a third of the sitting tenants had acquired their holdings by various forms of open or disguised purchase, and sometimes over the heads of the legal heirs whom they frequently bought out. Another, and increasingly common, means of acquiring land was to marry well-endowed women, more especially widows with land. What made widows especially attractive was that in most villages the spouses of customary holders were allowed to keep the whole of their deceased husbands' tenements. On some manors, such as Taunton, men marrying widows with land could retain the land on the wives' death and were thus able to contract second marriages destined to produce later a further crop of marriageable widows.

The transmission of land by purchase or by marriage, and the declining proportion of transmission by ordinary inheritance, was merely one of the signs of the increasing land hunger. This hunger was the most obvious consequence of an overgrown population, and its principal economic penalty. Society was paying for its growing numbers by moving ever nearer to the margin of subsistence. It is because the margin was so close and getting closer that the death rates were high and may have been getting higher.

Needless to say, in some years the high death rate resulted from severe epidemics or bouts of severe weather. But it is highly revealing to find how frequently death rates rose in years of bad harvest. The bad harvests themselves may have become more frequent because the quality of the land was declining. But even if we make full allowances for possible deterioration of the weather (the catastrophically bad harvests of 1290 and 1315–17 were obviously due to unusually wet seasons), the high mortality in years when crops failed would not have been as high as it was had not the population been especially sensitive to bad harvests. Its sensitivity manifests itself in our documents in various ways. In years of very bad harvests we find manorial bailiffs pleading an inability to carry out this or that operation, or justifying the high cost of the operation by the dearth of labourers (*caristia operariorum*) caused by bad crops. In other words, when harvests were very bad labourers died off and were scarce. In a more general way the steeply increasing death rates in years of bad harvest are revealed by the upsurge in heriots, the manorial death duties. Moreover, on the estates on which these records of heriots are abundant and are capable of being correlated with the total number of tenants, they frequently bring out not only the connection between harvests and deaths, but also that between death rates from starvation and impoverishment. For on these estates poorer sections of the population were the ones to succumb most frequently to privations following the failures of crops. It is obvious that large and growing sections of the population had been reduced to a condition in which they could keep body and soul together only in years of moderately good harvests.

The dynamics of medieval population before the first half of the fourteenth century is thus unmistakable. Population grew but could not have gone on growing for ever. By the beginning of the fourteenth century, and perhaps even earlier, the relative overpopulation was so great as to push the death rates to a punishing height. In theory over-population could also have brought the birth rates down, by reducing the ability of the young men to set up households and to marry. Our sources being what they are, this theoretical possibility cannot be convincingly demonstrated; but even if, for lack of evidence, the changes in marriage rates and ages of marriage were disregarded, the behaviour of the death rates would by itself have been sufficient sooner or later to prevent the population from continuing its growth.

33.　The Closing of the Medieval Frontier

ARCHIBALD R. LEWIS

Historians whose field of study is American history have long found the concept of the frontier useful and meaningful in explaining the American past. In a recent important book an American historian, Walter Prescott Webb, has extended this concept to include the entire Western European world during the period from 1500 to the present. On the whole, however, historians whose interest is the Middle Ages have made little use of a frontier thesis to explain developments in Europe during the mediaeval period, except in regard to the German advance into Slavic Europe beyond the Elbe. This is a surprising fact, for few periods can be better understood in the light of a frontier concept than Western Europe between 800 and 1500 A.D. This article is then an attempt to open up what appears to be a fruitful field for historical speculation by examining a crucial period of Western European history in the light of a frontier thesis.

We must begin this examination by briefly noting that from the eleventh to the mid-thirteenth century Western Europe followed an almost classical frontier development. Indeed in some respects one might carry the beginnings of this development back to the Carolingian era of the ninth century. For our purposes, however, this is not necessary. We can begin our survey with that impetus to expansion and growth which started again after the stimulus of the Carolingian Empire and Viking expansion had ended and a new growth had begun about the year 1000 A.D. Starting about this period then what were the frontier bases of the newly emerging Western Europe for the next two and half centuries?

From Archibald R. Lewis, "The Closing of the Medieval Frontier, 1250–1350." *Speculum,* Vol. 33 (1958), pp. 475–483. Reprinted by permission of the Mediaeval Academy of America.

First let us examine Western Europe's frontiers themselves. Early in the eleventh century Western Europeans began to advance their frontiers South into the Mediterranean into regions where Carolingian and Ottonian efforts had been successful. In the next two centuries this resulted in most of Spain being successfully wrested from Moorish control, in an occupation of the Balearics, Sardinia, Corsica, and in a Norman conquest of Southern Italy and Sicily, which were lost by Byzantium and Islam. Nor did this advance stop there. The early Crusades added Cyprus, Palestine, and Syria to Western European control, and after 1204, Crete, the Aegean Islands and much of the Byzantine Empire had been conquered too. By the first years of the thirteenth century economic and maritime control of most of the Mediterranean and its coasts had passed into Western European hands.

During the same period Norman-Northern French expansion had brought first England and then most of Wales, Scotland, and Ireland within the compass of this new Western European continental civilization. Nor was this all, for Scandinavia, the Baltic, and much of Eastern Europe up to Russia were also being firmly integrated in a religious, economic, and political sense into the continental Western European world. By the time of Innocent III, then, one can note that Europe's frontier in the broad sense of the word had been extended North, South, East, and West from its Carolingian heartland to include many areas which had previously either been somewhat remote from continental Europe or, as in parts of the Mediterranean, had actually earlier been part of the very different Byzantine and Moslem civilizations.

Now as Western Europe's frontiers expanded this resulted in much new land being thrown open to settlement or colonization. Behind the moving frontiers of the Reconquista in the Iberian Peninsula, during the eleventh, twelfth, and early thirteenth centuries, historians are beginning to appreciate the role of a peasantry who settled much of the newly conquered land in Aragon, Castile, and Portugal and made the reconquest permanent for the future. Similarly, as the German nobility moved east of the Elbe to conquer pagan Slavs and Balts the lands they seized were frequently settled by German peasants from the West. Norman-French conquest of England had as a sequel a similar movement of peasant cultivators into parts of Southern Wales, into Scotland below the Highland line, and into the Irish Pale, as Anglo-Norman nobles extended their influence into these remoter parts of the British Isles.

In some areas like Southern Italy, Sicily, and the Byzantine and Moslem East there was little mass colonization by Westerners, and the native peoples were not displaced. But even here thousands of

Western European nobles, soldiers of fortune, and merchants settled as a governing and commercial exploiting class who drew riches from their control of such areas. . . . The Italian and Provençal merchants who settled in Constantinople and the seaport cities of Syria, like the French, Provençal, German, and Italian nobles who set up their feudal principalities in the East and in Southern Italy and Sicily show the extent of Western European penetration of areas which had previously been closed to them.

These new frontier conquests, whether they were fully settled colonial areas or regions dominated by a Western European governing and commercial minority were not Europe's most important frontiers, important though they were. The important frontier was an internal one of forest, swamp, marsh, moor, and fen. It was this waste land which Europe's peasants settled and largely put into cultivation between the years 1000 and 1250. Due to their efforts the primeval forest which had covered a large part of Britain, Northern France, Belgium, Germany, Scandinavia, and Slavic Europe was hacked down and divided into assarts. Polders rescued maritime Flanders, Holland, and much of Northern Germany and Eastern England from the sea. A vast new area of virgin soil capable of sustaining a growing population was put to the plough or made available for pasturing increased flocks of sheep and cattle.

Nor was this all. Historical research in recent years has revealed an increased tempo of exploitation of mineral resources such as salt, silver, lead, zinc, copper, tin, and iron in Britain, France, Italy, Germany, and Scandinavia. New mining methods and other technological advances increased mineral production everywhere. The abundant timber and naval stores of Britain, Scandinavia, and the Baltic became more important commercially than ever before. The sea was exploited more systematically for its fisheries, especially the cod of Iceland and the Norwegian coasts and the herring of the Baltic caught in great numbers in this period off Swedish Skåne.

Can we wonder, in the light of this expanding internal and external frontier, that these years saw a steady growth of trade, of manufacturing, of urbanization. This was largely the result of new lands inside Europe's heartland and on the frontier being put into production, of greater exploitation of mineral and maritime resources, of the tribute which Islamic, Byzantine, and border peoples paid to enterprising Western merchants and conquerors. Western Europe lost its earlier isolation during these years and entered into the full stream of world commerce and trade.

Nor need we be surprised that these same centuries saw the development of a great Western European civilization, with its romanesque and Gothic art and architecture, its troubadour, chivalric, and fabliaux literature, its schools and universities which studied Roman law, medicine, and subtle scholastic philosophy. All were in part the by-products of an expanding prosperous Western European economy.

If one examines government, one notes similar progress. Feudalism in many areas during these years gave way to more advanced centralized government. The papacy established itself as a great international administrative system. Towns arising as new political entities developed urban institutions to fit the needs of their middle-class inhabitants. Even in the conservative countryside the manorial system, where it had existed, began to disappear, and Western Europe's peasant population by 1250 was everywhere rising from serfdom towards the greater freedom of tenant status. In the economic, the political, and the social and the cultural spheres these years were ones which saw steady advances for almost all the people of Western Europe.

In some ways, then, it is all the more surprising to note the changes which one finds in the following century, from 1250 to 1350, in most of Western Europe. These changes are beginning to engage the interest of a growing number of historians and have already given rise to a number of controversies. Let us briefly catalogue the nature of these new developments.

First and most noticeable, one finds during this century an end of the expansion and growth of Europe's urban communities. This is not true of Florence and perhaps Venice and some other parts of Italy, Barcelona in the Iberian Peninsula, and some towns in Southern and Northern Germany. But these are but exceptions to the general rule that these years saw a halt to the earlier trend towards increasing Western European urbanization.

Second, one can note within almost every town which has been carefully examined a growing separation of the burgesses into two distinct classes—one an urban patriciate of merchants and professional groups, the other an artisan proletariat. Venice in 1298 enshrined this difference in a Golden Book. Flanders reveals it in the struggle a little later centering around the personalities of the Van Artevelde family. Florence developed these differences into two recognized political parties, the *Popolo Grosso* and the *Popolo Minuto,* replacing to some degree the old Guelf-Ghibelline division. Study of thirteenth-century Montpellier or the cities of Germany reveals the same fundamental split in the urban population, which now leads to new discord and friction in the towns of Western Europe.

In the countryside a somewhat similar series of changes is apparent. The trend towards freedom stopped and in some places was reversed. Some peasants, taking advantage of their freedom and the new money economy, began to rent additional land from their land-lords and rise to the level of a yeoman class. Others, however, were less fortunate. They kept their freedom in most areas but without resources they sank to a cottar-bordar level as a rural proletariat of agricultural laborers. As one authority has said, the problem in the countryside in the fourteenth century was no longer peasant free-dom, but the price of agricultural labor. Soon we enter an era of peasant revolts, a symbol of a malaise and social discontent unknown to agrarian regions prior to 1250.

In political life one notes similar friction and basic instability. Ger-many and Italy afer 1254 relapsed into political anarchy and disunity. The rulers of the Iberian Peninsula, who had collaborated in win-ning victories over the Moors in the twelfth and early thirteenth centuries wasted their resources in family and dynastic internecine squabbles. In France, the enlightened monarchy of St. Louis gave way to the growing despotism of Philip the Fair and his ministers. Even in England, best governed of all during these years, the strong rule of Edward I gave place to the weaker rule of Edward II and the Despensers. Scandinavia, Slavic Europe, and Hungary were wracked by disorders in contrast to the relative stability in the late twelfth and earlier thirteenth centuries. The Avignon papacy with all its limita-tions succeeded to the strong Roman pontificate of the previous century. Politically as well as economically Europe moved from strength and stability to weakness and disorder.

One notices the same thing in the field of culture. The Gothic lost its originality and special strength, except in England, and a new naturalism modified the mediaeval sculptural styles of Northern Eu-rope. In Italy one leaves the mediaeval world of ideals exemplified by Dante to move into the more uncertain secularism and question-ing of Petrarch. North of the Alps chivalric literature lost its *raison d'être* as the practical, cynical Jean de Meun completed Guillaume de Lorris' idealistic *Roman de la Rose* on a new bourgeois note. Scholas-ticism lost its unifying intellectual role as the syntheses of Albertus Magnus, Aquinas, and Bonaventura were destroyed by the nomin-alistic logic of Ockham and Duns Scotus. New disturbing ideas of conciliarism were voiced by Marsilio of Padua and John of Jandum. The older mediaeval cultural pattern, like its economy and political life, was threatened with dissolution and decay.

It would be unwise not to recognize that the causes of these changes were infinitely varied and complex in nature. No single cause suffices to explain them. For instance, the nascent capitalism arising in important cities in Flanders, Southern France, and Italy was one factor which helped provoke class struggles between urban patriciates and proletariats everywhere and helped cause the dissolution of guild organizations. One cannot view the disintegration of Germany and Italy without recognizing how much this was due to the thirteenth-century struggles between popes and Hohenstaufens. Likewise one must note the importance of the national monarchies of France and England and their victory over Boniface as a cause of the ineffectiveness of the Avignon papacy. And there can be little doubt that the Black Death and Hundred Years' War lie behind many fourteenth- and fifteenth-century troubles which affected Europe.

Nevertheless, it seems probable that there was a more underlying reason than any of the foregoing—namely, the ending or closing of Europe's internal or external frontiers between the years 1250 and 1350, which influenced all segments of life in this period.

One can see this change best in examining Europe's external frontiers. By 1250 Western Europe had ceased to expand its influence in the Mediterranean. After losing control of most of Spain in the early thirteenth century, for instance, the Moors rallied to hold their mountain kingdom of Granada secure behind the mountain ramparts of the Sierra Nevada. On the other side of the Mediterranean the Moslem world recovered the Syrian coast from Crusading families who had clung to certain footholds there for many decades. In the Byzantine East Michael Paleologus by 1261 had regained Constantinople from the Latins and reconstituted the Byzantine Empire.

Many Western European footholds remained in the Orient. Cyprus, Crete, the Aegean Islands, and principalities in Southern Greece, protected by Italian sea power, remained Western. Activities like those carried on by the Catalan Companies show that opportunities still existed in this area for Western soldier adventurers to exploit. Also, there can be little doubt that Italian merchants were still the dominant economic power in both Mediterranean and Black Sea regions. One need only examine the careers of Marco Polo and other Italian traders who penetrated as far as China and the Indian Ocean during this century to be convinced of this fact. But it is equally true that after 1250 Western Europe increasingly found itself on the defensive in the Orient. It was not to it but to the rising power of the Ottoman Turks that the immediate future was to belong.

In Eastern Europe after 1250 one notices a similar contraction of Western Europe an influence. Continued Mongol control of Russia restricted Western influence to Novgorod, while disorder in Germany helped to stall the Teutonic *Drang Nach Osten* for many decades. Not until the second quarter of the fourteenth century was it resumed with the growing power of the Hanseatic League and Teutonic Knights in the Baltic and the beginning of Luxembourg hegemony in Bohemia. In Eastern Europe, as in the Mediterranean,

Western Europe found its influence waning, as Byzantines, Moslems, Slavs, and Balts resisted more successfully the pressures of Western European peoples. Even in the British Isles the story of the Bruces in Scotland and Ireland seems to show a resistance to Anglo-Norman influence, which had been all but irresistible earlier.

More serious, however, was the end of another frontier expansion—the internal one between the years 1250 and 1350. During this century in area after area of Western Europe unused land ceased to exist. In some places this was true by 1250. In others, like Southern France, it was a more gradual process not complete until well into the first years of the fourteenth century. As unused land was exhausted, however, Western Europe's peasantry (particularly in areas north of the Alps) lost the possibility of taking up vacant lands and raising their status. Forest, fen, marsh, and moor had at last been tamed and brought under cultivation and opportunities no longer existed for the hardy peasant to hack out an assart or drain low-lying swamp on terms more favorable than those available to him in his own village. No longer could the unearned increment of virgin land enrich monastic proprietor, noble landlord, and peasant cultivator alike. The boom in the countryside, which had lasted more than two centuries, came to an end. Few *villes neuves* or *bastides* remained to be founded. Instead, one finds emphasis upon forest laws, which were often conservation measures, necessary to protect what remained of the forests of France and England. Much research still remains to be done on agrarian population patterns, but some partial studies of Northern France suggest that by the fourteenth century there were probably as many people living in the countryside as were to be found there in the nineteenth century. A recent study of the villages of late mediaeval England also seems to show that in certain areas the population in this period was even greater than it is today. In Ireland and Scotland and Wales it seems clear that there was no increase in the area under cultivation after 1350 until the eighteenth century, when the arable area was increased at the expense of nearby pastoral clan societies.

Equally interesting is a fact which study of glaciers in Greenland, Iceland, and Norway has made clear. From about the year 1300 on for several centuries the climate of Northern Europe grew more severe. As it did, expansion of agricultural land toward the north ceased and the cultivated area even contracted in Norway, Sweden, and Finland.

We can sum up our conclusions as follows. After 1250 the external frontiers of Western Europe contracted and the internal frontier all but disappeared, except perhaps during the early fourteenth century along the borders of Eastern Germany and in Bohemia, where expansion continued to take place. With the end of the internal frontier ended the unearned increment of land which had enriched Western European society. With the contraction of the external frontier the riches which rulers, exploiters, and merchants (particularly those of Northern Europe) had drawn from Byzantine, Moslem and other peoples decreased as well. A Western European world which had been steadily expanding internally and externally down to 1250 saw its expansion halted and come to a stop as its frontiers closed.

It seem probable that the crisis produced by this fact lies at the root of the many changes that took place between 1250 and 1350. As free land gave out inside Western Europe, the peasants had no place to go now—few *villes neuves* or assarts beckoned the dissatisfied and the enterprising. Naturally the movement towards greater freedom came to an end. Instead, the peasantry had to face restrictions on their freedom, especially in parts of Germany, and their discontent began to be translated into a dissatisfaction with their lot which caused those peasant risings which were such a feature of fourteenth- and fifteenth-century Europe.

At the same time, the urban communities were equally affected by the end of this rural real estate boom which had fed their prosperity and expansion. Their growth ended and the crisis was made worse by the fact that smaller gains flowed into Europe from foreign areas, particularly Europe beyond the Alps. A Florence or a Venice or even a Barcelona might be prosperous, but other communities like Montpellier or Marseilles or Pisa were not. One can, as a matter of fact, see this urban depression by examining the building of cathedrals during this century. If one does, one notes an interesting fact. Between 1150 and 1250 in almost every community new cathedrals were built and older ones enlarged. Between 1250 and 1350, except in parts of Germany, this ceased to be so. Evidently Western European towns could no longer afford the building activity which seemed easy and natural a century earlier.

Now this end of urban growth and prosperity had a number of serious results which, in many cases, extended beyond the towns themselves. It ended a second safety-valve for Western Europe's rural population, already restricted by the ending of the internal frontier. Now dissatisfied peasants could not hope, except for a rare Dick Whittington, to find employment in a growing town labor force. Nor could peasant villages near towns count, as they had earlier, on a growing demand for their surplus agricultural produce to bring life-giving cash into their exchequers. There was now little escape available to the cottars and bordars who more and more became a depressed agricultural proletariat. Even a cursory examination of Piers Plowman reveals how bitter their lot often was.

These facts also help to explain why, in so many towns in Flanders, France, and Italy, there was friction and discord between the merchant patriciate and artisan proletariat during this period. It was no longer possible, as it had been earlier, for merchants to dispose of the goods which the town artisan guilds produced in increasing amounts except at a loss. There was no built-in expanding market for such production after 1250. Hence discord grew between producer and middleman which often took the form of civic disorder. At the same time in artisan guilds themselves it ceased to be always possible for journeymen to rise to the position of masters, as had generally been the case earlier. There was simply no market for goods produced by more than a few shops. Hence discontent within guilds, restrictive practices enforced more rigidly everywhere and that phenomenon of the late Middle Ages, the journeyman's guild. In the town as in the countryside opportunity for advancement had ended for many who had not been troubled by this problem earlier.

Even the nobility were adversely affected. Earlier new lands put into production had enriched noble landlords. Or younger sons had had the safety-valve of careers of adventures and the possibility of carving out estates for themselves in Spain, the New East, Slavic Europe, or the troubled border lands of Scotland and Ireland. Now this became less possible. No wonder such nobles in increasing numbers thronged the courts of rulers in the fourteenth and fifteenth century looking for preferment and position as their only hope of maintaining their place in society. Those idle nobles, whom we meet in Froissart or who formed the political machine manipulated by John of Gaunt, were created by the changed conditions of the period. Noble, burgher, and peasant alike were caught by the crisis of a society which had ceased expanding as the external frontier contracted and the internal frontier ended for most of Western Europe.

When one examines the papacy and royal governments of Europe during these years one sees the results of the closing of the mediaeval frontier with particular clarity. Up to the year 1250 or thereabouts the problems faced by the mediaeval papacy were essentially moral, religious, and political. Take, for instance, the Investiture Controversy, the Crusades, the struggle with German emperors over control of the Italian peninsula, or the problems of heresy in Southern France. After 1250 papal problems became increasingly financial, especially for the Avignon popes. At the same time we note a growing tide of criticism of the Church and papacy as corrupt, rapacious, and interested only in money. Such complaints had been made earlier, but not with the same force and unanimity. Now we find a rising tide of criticism, led by the Spiritual Franciscans, against papal annates, expectancies and the like, which were reiterated later in the century by monarchs like the kings of England and movements like those led by Wycliff and Hus.

Now careful examination of papal administration seems to show that the Avignon papacy with all its faults was much better organized than its Roman predecessor, so that, despite corruption, there was less waste in the collection of papal revenues. Why the outcry then? The answer seems obvious. A less prosperous Europe was less able to pay the costs of church government than had been the case earlier, and in the face of this fact the Avignon popes were forced to increase their pressure to collect the sums they felt necessary to run their papal Curia and their Church—a situation which was eventually to lead directly to the Reformation.

Nor were the popes alone in facing the dilemma of lowered revenues. The same problem faced the monarchs of Western Europe. This was no new problem, as all who have studied the financial difficulties that beset a Frederick Barbarossa or a John or Henry III of England well know. But after 1250 it became more acute. Rulers could no longer live on their own. They could not count on the appreciation in value of their royal estates or customs levies or court fines and the like to meet the expenses of their growing administrations. All of these had increased earlier as the result of an expanding Europe with expanding frontiers. This was now no longer so. Thus, a Philip the Fair of France tried to meet the crisis in part by reaching out for the rich Flanders towns or manipulating the coinage, that classic answer of a financially distressed government. Such expedients were, however, but temporary palliatives. The more general response to this problem was the development all over Europe of a new type of national taxation—whether it be in the Spanish monarchies, in Britain, in France, in Scandinavia or even in remote Bohemia. Rulers called on their nobles, middle class, and peasantry to help pay the cost of their growing administrations, until by 1350, this new type of taxation affected every segment of Western European society, although not always equally.

In the modern world Webb has pointed out a very similar phenomenon as the frontier has given out. When, as he has said, the sovereign has given out all the free land and none remains, it is necessary for him to begin to tax—taking back in another form the wealth he earlier showered out upon his people. This vertical movement of wealth, as he calls it, he regards as one of the results of the closing of the modern great frontier. Certainly exactly the same thing happened in mediaeval Europe, where new national taxation began at the very moment when the frontier ended there too. With this new taxation there arose all over Europe that late mediaeval phenomenon of representative institutions. This was caused in part by the need of the rulers to have the various classes of society vote them taxes and assist them in their collections until such time as the rulers felt powerful enough to dispense with such assistance. National taxation in late mediaeval Europe, then, and even representative governments, were in no small measure the result of the closing of the mediaeval frontier.

We might sum up the situation in Western Europe between 1250 and 1350 as follows. The crisis which Europe faced in this century was largely the result of the end of the mediaeval frontier. It was the crisis of a suddenly frontierless society. The results were serious indeed: the end of growing peasant freedom and tension in the countryside; a political, economic, and social crisis in cities which had ceased to expand; a church which had to concern itself so much with finances that it neglected its spiritual and moral leadership; and governments which had to meet this crisis by inaugurating large-scale taxation buttressed by representative institutions. That this was followed by that first of modern great wars, the Hundred Years' War, and that first of modern great plagues, the Black Death, simply compounded the difficulties Europe faced. We who, if we may believe Webb, face a somewhat similar frontierless existence may well reflect on how our European forebears met such a situation in the late thirteenth and fourteenth centuries and what the results were for the society and culture of Western Europe.

34. Cities and Social Classes

EDITH ENNEN

The population curve altered in the fourteenth century. The frequency of abandoned settlements in the countryside, the pause in the colonization movement eastwards of the peasantry, the abandonment of new town foundations and the arrested growth of many existing towns even to the extent of a considerable decline in urban populations are all indisputable signs of this negative trend. The plague was neither the original nor the sole cause of the crisis. In many individual cases the decline in population can be shown to have set in before the Black Death of 1348. With the high medieval mortality rate, only a small fall-back in births sufficed to bring a population reduction. Here we find a phenomenon which reflects human vitality and which requires biological investigation and proof. The plague accentuated the existing negative tendencies. There were famines on top of plague, notably that of 1315–1317 which affected the whole of northern Europe and may have contributed to the high death rate in the first great plague of 1348 by weakening the population.

Whether or not one is dealing with a general and century-long crisis in the later Middle Ages is a matter for dispute. The situation varied from one economic region to another. One must contrast signs of depression in Flanders and Provence with indications of progress in other regions, in south Germany, especially in Nürnberg, as well as in the Saar and Moselle regions and in Holland and

From Edith Ennen, *The Medieval Town* (Amsterdam: Elsevier Science Publishing, 1979), pp. 190–197. Reprinted by permission from Elsevier Science Publishing B. V., Amsterdam.

England. In France non-economic factors were at work, notably the Hundred Years' War. The chronology of the crises varied. In Barcelona its high-point was between 1431 and 1443 and was caused as much by the military ventures of King Alfonso as by the economic stagnation in Genoa. The meagre nature of the statistical work which has been done still makes a closer definition of "up and down" tendencies impossible. The question, in any case, cannot be solely answered by studying the towns. Thus, a conclusive answer to the question of whether there was a cyclical or a structural crisis, and whether the change in the agrarian economy was decisive, still cannot be given.

In north-western Europe, the late-medieval economic crisis expressed itself in the sharp rise and decline of different regions, in bitter competition for markets, and in the powerful reaction of the towns to advances in rural industries. Within the towns considerable social tensions accompanied the creation of an urban proletariat from displaced master-craftsmen and from apprentices who had lost all hope of ever becoming masters. There were sharp distinctions of wealth and ossification and stagnation in the economic sector.

• • •

Credit was essential for the smooth conduct of trade and production. Its use was a natural part of the chain of transactions from the purchase of raw materials to the sale of the finished article to the consumer. Industrial production for export was largely based on credit, either in the form of supplying craftsmen in their homes or of collective purchases by the guild. Credit linked one merchant with another. Creditworthiness was an essential prerequisite for a merchant's success. Interest was a natural accompaniment to it. Here we are faced with the teaching of the Church, and the Church had to come to terms with the prevailing situation. The doctrine that the existence of risk justified profit must be attributed to the scholastic theologians of the later Middle Ages. They began an extension of the theory of interest. The public sector also intervened in credit transactions: the favourite urban form of borrowing was the sale of rents.

A striking feature of the last part of the fourteenth century was the amount of social unrest. In Cologne in 1369–1370 the weavers brought about the overthrow of patrician control, and in 1396, after an embittered family feud between the Greifen and Freunden, they brought about a change in the constitution. The *Richerzeche* disappeared and the *Verbundbrief* formed the basis of the constitution until the imperial towns disappeared altogether as a concept. In the last years of the fifteenth century, unresolved differences brought about a renewed outbreak of trouble in the rising of 1482. In 1513 another insurrection led to the *Transfixbrief* which enlarged the clauses of the *Verbundbrief*. All the towns producing textiles for export suffered revolts by weavers in the fourteenth century: Constance and Augsburg in the south, Stendal in north Germany, and other towns from Flanders to Florence. There was unrest in the Hanseatic area, in the *Knochenhauer* (butchers) Revolt in Lübeck, in Danzig, Brunswick, in Nürnberg, Liège and Metz. The cliché "guild wars" does not sufficiently explain this phenomenon. Its antecedents are more complex. The movements led by the Parisian merchant, Étienne Marcel and the Jacquerie in France reflected the political crisis of a land at war as well as its serious social problems. Steinbach and Maschke have rightly warned against misunderstanding these movements. They were not the beginning of modern democracy. The political equality of corporations and not of individuals was in question. The work of Steinbach and Herborn for Cologne shows how quickly a closed society of the privileged reformed itself after 1396. Van Werveke has shown the same for Ghent. Here too, while the guilds were successful in controlling some or the majority of seats on the town council, they did not really rule the towns. In Ulm, Esslingen and other Swabian towns, the office of town mayor was still always held by a patrician although the constitution permitted a craftsman to be chosen. The cause lies in the operation of the principle of indispensability already recognized by Weber and more fully marked out by Maschke.

In many towns in which the guilds took control, in Strasbourg, Constance, Basel, and Augsburg, the patricians cut themselves off and formed an exclusive group. The result was that they declined in numbers. Urban society was organized according to occupation, and status symbols consisted in ways of dressing and in invitations to festivals and dances which were limited to chosen people. The dress permitted to each class was laid down by the town council. Patricians met in drinking societies. Their control of the town continued unweakened in trading towns without large export industries, for instance in Metz. Genoa too reognized only *nobili* and *populari* but no distinction between the *popolo grasso* and *popolo minuto* which was such a marked feature of Florentine society. Genoa also had the *albergo* which served as a social meeting place of the *nobili* and which corresponded to the German *Trinkstube* and from the fourteenth century there was also a popular equivalent to the *alberghi* of the nobility.

In central Europe egoism and conservation dominated guild life. The many apprentices with no hope of ever becoming masters also became an element likely to cause unrest and rebellion. They formed bands, and wandering apprentices became an ever-increasing phenomenon. The master craftsmen also combined, often on a regional basis in common cause against their apprentices. For example, in 1352 the bakers of Mainz, Worms, Speyer, Oppenheim, Frankfurt, Bingen, Bacharach and Boppard formed a super-guild to prevent an apprentice who had been dismissed by his master in one town from being able to find lodging and work elsewhere. The intertown guild also turned against married apprentices: if the wife of a baker's apprentice came to market and sold flour and cereal, no master in any of the eight towns might employ her husband. The practice of masters and their apprentices living together in the same house became less frequent. Solidarity among the apprentices themselves increased and had its outward manifestation in the uniform which they wore. The masters continued their opposition nevertheless. In 1442, for example, the furriers of Bavaria and Austria met to deny their apprentices every corporative right. In Strasbourg in 1404 forty-eight apprentice furriers from Bohemia and the Tyrol combined to form a separate brotherhood; in this very capital intensive business the chance of ever becoming a master was particularly remote. The master-craftsmen maintained that the urban authorities alone were empowered to settle conflicts between masters and apprentices. In 1465 this association of masters broadened when it acquired further links in Franconia, Swabia and the Rhineland. Unrest, strikes, and strife between master and apprentice filled the whole of the fourteenth and fifteenth centuries.

In Florence in 1378 disturbances turned into the revolt of the *ciompi* or woolcarders. This rising was of great interest to Renaissance historical writers and has been also to modern neo-Marxist researchers, although it has been correctly interpreted by neither group. This was no "proletarian revolution" with social revolutionary aims. In the July revolt, which resulted in a new political regime, people from all classes of Florentine society took part including patrician leaders from famous families like the Strozzi, Alberti and Medici; members of the industrial and mercantile middle classes and a great mass of wage earners. The revolt took its name from the woolcarders or *ciompi,* but every class of worker from the lower orders was represented—cloth dyers, fullers, finishers and small entrepreneurs who were not members of the Arte della Lana but their subordinate employees, namely *sottoposti.* Characteristically, three new guilds were formed to include them and these were added to the seven upper guilds and the fourteen lower ones. The aims and wishes of the *sottoposti* and *ciompi* were very mixed. Disappointment of the *ciompi* with the new conservative regime brought a further outbreak of trouble in August which produced no clear programme. As Brucker says:

It was a characteristic Florentine *imbroglio,* neither very bloody nor very destructive and as strongly influenced by personal hatreds and loyalties as by any spirit or sense of class. The historical significance of the Ciompi episode was its utilization by the Florentine patriciate to justify the increasingly narrow social base of politics and the progressive exclusion of the lower class from office.

In 1382 "order was restored."

At the same time the craftsmen of Ghent, supported by those of Bruges and Ypres, rose against the count, but he, with his allies the French knights, defeated them at West-Roosebeke in 1382. The overwhelmingly political character of the Ghent revolts in the fourteenth century is unmistakeable. In Liège the patricians were excluded from the town council. The corps of craftsmen who now wielded power had already begun to exclude apprentices and aliens. The entry fee for becoming a master was increased. This was a widespread development. The rule of the patricians was replaced by control by small artisan entrepreneurs. A proletariat grew up below them in the fifteenth century.

. . . The relatively greater prosperity of the major towns is revealed through statistics of poverty. The Brabantine accounts also provide evidence here. While the number of poor in Antwerp decreased between 1437 and 1480 from 13.5 percent to 10.5 percent, the proportion in Louvain increased from 7.6 percent to 18.3 percent, in Brussels between 1437 and 1496 from 10.5 percent to 17.1 percent. In smaller towns the number of poor rose as high as 36 percent. These poor came from declining industries or were made up of unskilled workers and immigrants from the countryside.

The time of most severe misery for the mass of workers coincided with the high-point of bourgeois luxury in the Low Countries. The most splendid buildings were erected by the prosperous upper class. In the meantime, the gulf between the moneyed aristocracy and the proletarian masses widened. The urban magistracy was no longer able to cope with the problems arising from poverty and the government had to intervene. In the fifteenth century, princes like Philip the Good intervened actively, if not systematically, against begging.

Poverty also had a place in the medieval social hierarchy: it gave the rich the possibility of doing acts of charity. The rich man was dependent on the intercession of the poor so that the poor man had prayers to offer in return for alms. The poor also formed their own associations. In 1454 a Brotherhood of Beggars was formed in Zülpich and was joined by cripples, the blind and other poor people. It raised fees from members and cared for the sick. The fierce struggle against the poor and beggars is an expression of early modern feeling and a product of the situation in early modern times. The beggar was still integrated into medieval society. Even if the lower classes in the Middle Ages were politically without rights and economically weak, frequent movement into the upper classes took place. Possibilities of saving and thereby advancement existed, especially for servants and apprentices. In Basel servants and craftsmen's assistants accounted for 17 percent of the population and 29 percent of all those who had to pay taxes. In general they formed what was the upper working class while among the wage earners, merchants' apprentices formed a lower middle class. Beneath the apprentices and servants were the day workers, unskilled workers, single women and, beneath them again, the beggars.

35. The Black Death and the Jews

PHILIP ZIEGLER

When ignorant men are overwhelmed by forces totally beyond their control and their understanding it is inevitable that they will search for some explanation within their grasp. When they are frightened and badly hurt then they will seek someone on whom they can be revenged. Few doubted that the Black Death was God's will but, by a curious quirk of reasoning, medieval man also concluded that His instruments were to be found on earth and that, if only they could be identified, it was legitimate to destroy them. What was needed, therefore, was a suitable target for the indignation of the people, preferably a minority group, easily identifiable, already unpopular, widely scattered and lacking any powerful protector.

The Jews were not the only candidates as victims. In large areas of Spain the Arabs were suspected of playing some part in the propagation of the plague. All over Europe pilgrims were viewed with the gravest doubts; in June, 1348, a party of Portuguese pilgrims were said to be poisoning wells in Aragon and had to be given a safe conduct to get them home. In Narbonne it was the English who were at one time accused. But it was the leper who most nearly rivalled the Jew as popular scapegoat. The malign intentions of the leper had long been suspected by his more fortunate fellows. In 1346, Edward III decreed that lepers were no longer to enter the City of London since:

... some of them, endeavouring to contaminate others with that abominable blemish (that so, to their own wretched solace, they may have the more fellows in suffering) as well in the way of mutual communication, and by the contagion of their polluted breath, as by carnal intercourse with women in stews and other secret places, detestably frequenting the same, do so taint persons who are sound, both male and female, to the great injury of the people dwelling in the city. . . .

But it is one thing to try to infect others with one's own disease for the sake of the extra companionship, another to spread the plague out of sheer devilry. When in Languedoc, in 1321, all the lepers were burnt on suspicion of poisoning wells, it was claimed that they had been bribed to do so by the Jews who, in their turn, were in the pay of the King of Granada. There were one or two cases, notably in Spain, where lepers suffered during the Black Death on suspicion of complicity but there do not seem to be any where the Jews were not accorded the leading role and the lepers cast as the mere instruments of their wickedness.

One reason for this was that nobody had cause for envying the lepers or economic reason for wishing them out of the way. It was very different with the Jews whose popular image was that of the Prioress's Tale:

> ... sustened by a lord of that contree
> For foule usure and lucre of vileynye,
> Hateful to Christ and to his compaignye.*

In Germany, and to some extent also in France and Spain, the Jews provided the money-lending class in virtually every city—not so much by their own volition as because they had been progressively barred from all civil and military functions, from owning land or working as artisans. Usury was the only field of economic activity left open to them; an open field, in theory at least, since it was forbidden to the Christian by Canon Law. In cities such as Strasbourg they flourished exceedingly and profited more than most during the economic expansion of the thirteenth century. But the recession of the fourteenth century reduced their prosperity and the increasing role played by the Christian financiers, in particular the Italian bankers, took away from them the cream of the market. In much of Europe the Jew dwindled to a small money-lender and pawnbroker. He acquired a large clientele of petty debtors so that every day more peo-

---

*..... supported by the Crown
For the foul lucre of their usury,
Hateful to Christ and all his company.

ple had cause to wish him out of the way. "It can be taken for granted," wrote Dr. Cohn, "that the Jewish money lenders often reacted to insecurity and persecution by deploying a ruthlessness of their own." It is fair to criticise the medieval Jews for exacting exorbitant rates of interest from their victims but it is also only fair to remember the extreme precariousness of their business, dependent on the uncertain protection of the local ruler and with virtually no sanctions at their disposal to enable them to recover their money from a reluctant debtor. To ensure their own safety the luckless Jews were forced to pay ever larger bribes to the authorities and, to raise the money for the bribes, they had to charge higher interest and press their clients still more harshly. Animosity built up and, by the middle of the fourteenth century, Shylock had been born. The Jew had become a figure so hated in European society that almost anything might have served to provoke catastrophe.

But though the economic causes for the persecution of the Jews were certainly important it would be wrong to present them as the only, or even as the principal reason for what now happened. The Jew's role as money-lender predisposed many people to believe any evil which they might hear of him but the belief itself was sincere and had far deeper roots. The image of the Jew as Antichrist was common currency in the Middle Ages. It seems to have gained force at the time of the First Crusade and the Catholic Church must accept much of the responsibility for its propagation. The vague enormity of such a concept was quickly translated into terms more comprehensible to the masses. In particular the more irresponsible priests spread rumours that the Jews kidnapped and tortured Christian children and desecrated the host. They were represented as demons attendant on Satan, portrayed in drama or in pictures as devils with the beards and horns of a goat, passing their time with pigs, frogs, worms, snakes, scorpions and the horned beasts of the field. Even the lay authorities seemed intent on fostering public belief in the malevolence of the Jews; in 1267, for instance, the Council of Vienna forbade purchases of meat from Jews on the ground that it was likely to be poisoned.

Today such fantasies seem ludicrous. It is hard to believe that sane men can have accepted them. And yet Dr. Norman Cohn has drawn a revealing parallel between anti-Semitism in the fourteenth century and under the Third Reich. On 1 May, 1934, *Der Stürmer* devoted a whole issue to alleged murders of Christian children by the Jews; illustrating its text with pictures of rabbis sucking blood from an Aryan child. Most Germans were no doubt revolted by such vicious propaganda but Buchenwald, Auschwitz and Belsen live vividly enough in the memory to save this generation from any offensive sense of superiority to its ancestors. Nor do the still more recent Chinese accusations that American airmen, in 1952, showered the countryside around Kan-Nan Hsien with voles infected with *Pasteurella Pestis*, the bacillus of bubonic plague, suggest that man's infinite capacity for thinking ill of man is in any way on the wane.

The Black Death concentrated this latent fear and hatred of the Jews into one burning grievance which not only demanded vengeance but offered the tempting extra dividend that, if the Jews could only be eliminated, then the plague for which they were responsible might vanish too. There was really only one charge levelled against the Jews; that, by poisoning the wells of Christian communities, they infected the inhabitants with the plague. The Polish historian, Dlugoss, claimed that they also poisoned the air but this view does not seem to have been at all widely shared. Some of the more fanciful reports alleged that the Jews were working under the orders of a conspiratorial network with its headquarters in Toledo; that the poison, in powdered form, was imported in bulk from the Orient, and that the same organisation also occupied itself in forging currencies and murdering Christian children. But these were decorative frills, the attack on the sources of drinking water was the central issue.

The emphasis on this accusation is surprising. With the exception of the Faculty of Medicine at Paris, which suggested that a minor contributory cause of the epidemic might be the pollution of the wells as a result of earthquakes, none of the contemporary experts seem to have tried to link infection with the drinking of tainted water. There were other ways of spreading the plague which must have seemed at least as plausible to medieval man. Alfonso of Cordova's vision of the infection of air by the release of a "certain confection" into a "strong, slow wind" has already been mentioned and in subsequent epidemics Jews were accused of passing around clothes taken from the dead or smearing walls and windows with an ointment made from the buboes of plague victims.

A partial explanation may be that many wells in built-up areas were polluted by seepage from nearby sewage pits. The Jews, with their greater understanding of elementary hygiene, preferred to draw their drinking water from open streams, even though these might often be farther from their homes. Such a habit, barely noticed in normal times, would seem intensely suspicious in the event of plague. Why should the Jews shun the wells unless they knew them to be poisoned and how could they have such knowledge unless they had done the poisoning themselves? This theory is supported by Tschudi who, in the *Helvetian Chronicle*, records not only that the Jews knew the wells to be contaminated by "bad, noxious moistures and vapours" but also that, in many places "they warned the people

against them.'' If they did, the warnings seem to have gone un-
heeded and certainly those who received them were little disposed
to feel gratitude to the Jews for their consideration.

There can be little doubt that the majority of those who turned
on the Jews believed in the literal truth of the accusations against
them. It might be thought that this certainty would have been shaken
by the fact that Jews died as fast as Christians; probably faster, indeed,
in their crowded and unhealthy ghettoes. But the Christians seem
simply to have closed their eyes to reality. Since the Jews caused the
Black Death it was ridiculous to suppose that they could also suffer
from it. Any appearance to the contrary was merely further evidence
of their consummate cunning. . . . But though such crude suspicions
might have been acceptable to the mob, they can hardly have been
taken seriously by the intelligent and better educated. Dr. Guerch-
berg has analysed the attitude of the leading plague tractators. The
most remarkable feature is how few references there are to the guilt
or innocence of the Jews. Konrade of Megenberg brusquely dismissed the accusations: ''Some say that this was brought about by
the Jewish people, but this point of view is untenable.'' In his *Buch
der Natur* he cites as evidence Jewish mortality in Vienna which was
so high that a new cemetery had to be constructed. Gui de Chauliac
was equally categoric. Alfonso of Cordova considered that, by all the
rules of planetary action, the Black Death should only have lasted a
year and that any subsequent extension must be the result of a
wicked plot. But he did not specifically accuse the Jews of being
responsible. The ''Five Strasbourg Physicians'' warned against poisoned food and water but it is doubtful whether they believed that
the poisoning was done deliberately by man. No other tractator paid
any attention to the possibility that some human agency was involved
in the spread of the plague, still less that such villains must be identified as the Jews.

On the whole, this reticence on the part of the tractators must be
taken to indicate that they did not believe the accusations. It is impossible that they did not know what had been suggested and, if they
had really thought that a principal cause of the plague was the poisoning of the wells by Jews, then they could hardly have failed to say
so in their examination of the subject. Their silence might imply
that they thought the idea too ridiculous to mention but it is more
likely that they shrank from expressing publicly an unpopular view
on an issue over which people were dangerously disturbed.

For it took considerable moral courage to stand up for the Jews
in 1348 and 1349 and not many people were prepared to take the
risk. The first cases of persecution seem to have taken place in the
South of France in the spring of 1348, and, in May, there was a

massacre in Provence. Narbonne and Carcassone exterminated their communities with especial thoroughness. But it is possible that the madness might never have spread across Europe if it had not been for the trial at Chillon in September 1348 of Jews said to have poisoned certain wells at Neustadt and the disastrous confessions of guilt which torture tore from the accused. Balavignus, a Jewish physician, was the first to be racked. "After much hesitation," he confessed that the Rabbi Jacob of Toledo had sent him, by hand of a Jewish boy, a leather pouch filled with red and black powder and concealed in the mummy of an egg. This powder he was ordered, on pain of excommunication, to throw into the larger wells of Thonon. He did so, having previously warned his friends and relations not to drink the water. "He also declared that none of his community could exculpate themselves from this accusation, as the plot was communicated to all and all were guilty of the above charges." Odd scraps of "evidence" were produced, such as a rag found in a well in which it was alleged that the powder, composed largely of ground-up portions of a basilisk, had been concealed. Ten similar confessions were racked from other unfortunates and the resulting dossier sent to neighbouring cities for their information and appropriate action.

So incriminating a confession settled the doubts or perhaps quietened the consciences of many who might otherwise have felt bound to protect the Jews. On 21 September, 1348, the municipality of Zurich voted never to admit Jews to the city again. In Basle all the Jews were penned up in wooden buildings and burned alive. "In the month of November began the persecution of the Jews," wrote a German chronicler. Henry of Diessenhoven has recorded the movement of the fever across his country. In November, 1348, the Jews were burnt at Solothurn, Zofingen and Stuttgart; in December at Landsberg, Burren, Memmingen, Lindau; in January, Freiburg, Ulm and Speyer. At Speyer the bodies of the murdered were piled in great wine-casks and sent floating down the Rhine. In February it was the turn of the Jews at Gotha, Eisenach and Dresden; in March, Worms, Baden and Erfurt.

In most cities the massacres took place when the Black Death was already raging but in some places the mere news that the plague was approaching was enough to inflame the populace. On 14 February, 1349, several weeks before the first cases of infection were reported, two thousand Jews were murdered in Strasbourg; the mob tore the clothes from the backs of the victims on their way to execution in the hope of finding gold concealed in the lining. In part at least because of the anti-Semitism of the Bishop, the Jews of Strasbourg seem to have suffered exceptionally harshly. A contemporary chron-

icle puts the grand total of the slaughtered at sixteen thousand—
half this would be more probable but the Jewish colony was one of
the largest of Europe and the higher figure is not totally inconceivable.

From March until July, there was a lull in the persecution. Then
the massacre was renewed at Frankfurt-am-Main and, in August,
spread to Mainz and Cologne. In Mainz, records one chronicler, the
Jews took the initiative, attacked the Christians and slew two hundred
of them. The Christian revenge was terrible—no less than twelve
thousand Jews, "or thereabouts," in their turn perished. In the
North of Germany, Jewish colonies were relatively small, but their
significance was no protection when the Black Death kindled the
hatred of the Christians. In the spring of 1350, those Jews of the
Hansa towns who had escaped burning were walled up alive in their
houses and left to die of suffocation or starvation. In some cases they
were offered the chance to save themselves by renouncing their faith
but few availed themselves of the invitation. On the contrary, there
were many instances of Jews setting fire to their houses and destroying themselves and their families so as to rob the Christians of their
prey.

Why the persecutions died down temporarily in March, 1349, is
uncertain. It could be that the heavy losses which the Black Death
inflicted on the Jews began to convince all those still capable of
objectivity that some other explanation must be found for the spread
of the infection. If so, their enlightenment did not last long. But the
blame for the renewal of violence must rest predominantly with the
Flagellants. It is difficult to be sure whether this was the work of a
few fanatics among the leaders or merely another illustration of the
fact that mass-hysteria, however generated, is always likely to breed
the ugliest forms of violence. In July, 1349, when the Flagellants
arrived in procession at Frankfurt, they rushed directly to the Jewish
quarter and led the local population in wholesale slaughter. At Brussels the mere news that the Flagellants were approaching was enough
to set off a massacre in which, in spite of the efforts of the Duke of
Brabant, some six hundred Jews were killed. The Pope condemned
the Flagellants for their conduct and the Jews, with good reason,
came to regard them as their most dangerous enemies.

On the whole the rulers of Europe did their best, though often
ineffectively, to protect their Jewish subjects. Pope Clement VI in
particular behaved with determination and responsibility. Both before and after the trials at Chillon he published Bulls condemning
the massacres and calling on Christians to behave with tolerance and
restraint. Those who joined in persecution of the Jews were threatened with excommunication. The town-councillors of Cologne were

also active in the cause of humanity, but they did no more than incur a snub when they wrote to their colleagues at Strasbourg urging moderation in their dealings with the Jews. The Emperor Charles IV and Duke Albert of Austria both did their somewhat inadequate best and Ruprecht von der Pfalz took the Jews under his personal protection, though only on receipt of a handsome bribe. His reward was to be called "Jew-master" by his people and to provoke something close to a revolution.

Not all the magnates were so enlightened. In May, 1349, Landgrave Frederic of Thuringia wrote to the Council of the City of Nordhausen telling them how he had burnt his Jews for the honour of God and advising them to do the same. He seems to have been unique in wholeheartedly supporting the murderers but other great rulers, while virtuously deploring the excesses of their subjects, could not resist the temptation to extract advantage from what was going on. Charles IV offered the Archbishop of Trier the goods of those Jews in Alsace "who have already been killed or may still be killed" and gave the Margrave of Brandenburg his choice of the best three Jewish houses in Nuremberg, "when there is next a massacre of the Jews." A more irresponsible incitement to violence it would be hard to find.

Nor were those rulers who sought to protect the Jews often in a position to do much about it. The patrician rulers of Strasbourg, when they tried to intervene, were overthrown by a combination of mob and rabble-rousing Bishop. The town-council of Erfurt did little better while the city fathers of Trier, when they offered the Jews the chance to return to the city, warned them quite frankly that they could not guarantee their lives or property in case of further rioting. Only Casimir of Poland, said to have been under the influence of his Jewish mistress Esther, seems to have been completely successful in preventing persecution.

An illustration of the good will of the rulers and the limitations on their effective power comes from Spain. Pedro IV of Aragon had a high opinion of his Jewish subjects. He was therefore outraged when the inhabitants of Barcelona, demoralised by the Black Death and deprived, through the high mortality and the flight from the city of the nobles and the rich, of almost any kind of civic authority, turned on the Jews and sacked the ghetto. On 22 May, 1348, he sent a new Governor to the city and gave orders that the guilty were to be punished and no further incidents allowed. A week later he circularised his authorities throughout the Kingdom ordering them to protect the Jews and prevent disturbances. By February, 1349, the new Governor of Barcelona had made no progress in his search for those responsible. King Pedro grew impatient and demanded immediate action. In a flurry of zeal a few arrests were made, including Bernal Ferrer, a public hangman. But the prosecution in its turn was extremely dilatory. Six months later no judgement had been passed and, in the end, it seems that Ferrer and the other prisoners were quietly released.

Meanwhile, in spite of the King's injunctions, anti-Jewish rioting went on in other cities of Aragon. There was a particularly ugly incident in Tarragona where more than three hundred Jews were killed. Here again Pedro demanded vengeance and sent a commission to investigate. The resulting welter of accusation and counter accusation became so embittered that virtual civil war ensued. In the end this prosecution too was tacitly abandoned. But the King did at least ensure that a new ghetto was built and intervened personally on behalf of several leading Jews who had been ruined by the loss of their houses and documents. When the next epidemic came in 1361 the Jews appealed to the King for protection and an armed guard was placed at the gates of the ghetto.

Flanders was bitten by the bug at about the same time as the Bavarian towns. "Anno domini 1349 sloeg men de Joden dood" is the chronicler's brutally laconic reference to massacres that seem to have been on a scale as hideous as those in Germany. In England there were said to be isolated prosecutions of Jews on suspicion of spreading the plague but no serious persecution took place. It would be pleasant to attribute this to superior humanity and good-sense. The substantial reason, however, was rather less honourable. In 1290, King Edward I had expelled the Jews from England. Such few as remained had little money and were too unobtrusive to present a tempting target. Some small credit is due for leaving them in peace but certainly it cannot be held up as a particularly shining example of racial tolerance.

36. Religion and Revolution

NORMAN COHN

Between the close of the eleventh century and the first half of the sixteenth it repeatedly happened in Europe that the desire of the poor to improve the material conditions of their lives became transfused with phantasies of a new Paradise on earth, a world purged of suffering and sin, a Kingdom of the Saints.

The history of those centuries was of course sprinkled with innumerable struggles between the privileged and the less privileged, risings of towns against their overlords, of artisans against merchant capitalists, of peasants against nobles. Usually those risings had strictly limited aims—the securing of specific rights, the removal of specific grievances—or else (like the famous *Jacquerie*) were mere outbreaks of destructive rage provoked by sheer misery. But risings could also occur which had quite a different scope. The Middle Ages had inherited from Antiquity—from the Jews and the early Christians—a tradition of prophecy which during those same centuries took on a fresh and exuberant vitality. In the language of theology—which seems here the most appropriate language—there existed an eschatology, or body of doctrine concerning the final state of the world, which was chiliastic in the most general sense of the term—meaning that it foretold a Millennium, not necessarily limited to a thousand years and indeed not necessarily limited at all, in which the world would be inhabited by a humanity at once perfectly good and perfectly happy. Offering so much solace of a kind which the official teaching of the medieval Church withheld, this eschatology

From Norman Cohn, *The Pursuit of the Millennium*, 2d ed. (New York: Oxford University Press, 1961), pp. xiii–xiv, 308–310, 314–319. Copyright © Norman Cohn, 1961, 1970. Reprinted by permission of Oxford University Press.

came to exercise a powerful and enduring fascination. Generation after generation was seized at least intermittently by a tense expectation of some sudden, miraculous event in which the world would be utterly transformed, some prodigious final struggle between the hosts of Christ and the hosts of Antichrist through which history would attain its fulfilment and justification. Although it would be a gross over-simplification to identify the world of chiliastic exaltation with the world of social unrest, there were many times when needy and discontented masses were captured by some millennial prophet. And when that happened movements were apt to arise which, though relatively small and short-lived, can be seen in retrospect to bear a startling resemblance to the great totalitarian movements of our own day.

• • •

. . . *Prophetae* would construct their apocalyptic lore out of the most varied materials—the Book of Daniel, the Book of Revelation, the Sibylline Oracles, the speculations of Joachim of Fiore, the doctrine of the Egalitarian State of Nature—all of them elaborated and reinterpreted and vulgarised. That lore would be purveyed to the masses—and the result would be something which was at once a revolutionary movement and an outburst of quasi-religious salvationism.

This salvationism, too, is of a peculiar kind, in that the salvation promised is terrestrial and collective. The Heavenly City is to appear on this earth; and its joys are to crown not the peregrinations of individual souls but the epic exploits of a "chosen people." And such a revolutionary movement is of a peculiar kind, in that its aims and promises are boundless. A social struggle is imagined as uniquely important, different in kind from all other struggles known to history, a cataclysm from which the world is to emerge totally transformed and redeemed. But this, again, is the very thing that in our time has most clearly characterised the two great totalitarian movements, Communist and Nazi, especially in their early, revolutionary stages. What has set these latter-day movements so utterly apart from the ordinary run of political parties in Europe—whether conservative or reformist—is precisely their way of endowing social conflicts and aspirations with a transcendental significance—in fact with all the mystery and majesty of the final, eschatological drama. In this sense the story unfolded in *The Pursuit of the Millennium* can be regarded as a prologue to the vast revolutionary upheavals of the present century.

Some suspicion of this has occurred to Communist and Nazi ideologists themselves. An enthusiastic if fanciful exposition of the heterodox German mysticism of the fourteenth century, with appropriate tributes to Beghards, Beguines and Brethren of the Free Spirit, fills a long chapter of Rosenberg's *Myth of the Twentieth Century*; while a Nazi historian devoted a whole volume to interpreting the message of the Revolutionary of the Upper Rhine. As for the Communists, they continue to elaborate, in volume after volume, that cult of Thomas Müntzer which was inaugurated already by Engels.* But whereas in these works the *prophetae* of a vanished world are shown as men born centuries before their time, it is perfectly possible to draw the opposite moral—that, for all their exploitation of the most modern technology, Communism and Nazism have been inspired by phantasies which are downright archaic. And such is in fact the case. It can be shown (though to do so in detail would require another volume) that the ideologies of Communism and Nazism, dissimilar though they are in many respects, are both heavily endebted to that very ancient body of beliefs which constituted the popular apocalyptic lore of Europe.

That peculiar faith which is of the very essence not indeed of chiliasm as such but of militant, revolutionary chiliasm—the tense expectation of a final, decisive struggle in which a world tyranny will be overthrown by a "chosen people" and through which the world will be renewed and history brought to its consummation—this did not disappear with the fall of the New Jerusalem at Münster. It continued a dim, subterranean existence down the centuries, flaring up briefly in the margins of the English Civil War and the French Revolution, until in the course of the nineteenth century it began to take on a new, explosive vigour, now in France, now in Germany, now in Russia. It is true that in the nineteenth century a naïve and explicit super-naturalism was gradually replaced by an orientation which was secular and which even claimed to be scientific, so that what had once been demanded by "the will of God" was now demanded by the "purposes of History." But the demand itself remained unchanged: to purify the world by destroying the agents of corruption. What is more, the agents of corruption were still identified with social groups which had been so regarded already in the Middle Ages: sometimes "the great ones" (now called "the bourgeoisie") and sometimes the Jews—with the clergy inevitably less prominent than they were, yet not wholly forgotten either. And as for the coming society itself—that too was still pictured much as it had been in the Middle Ages: as a state of total community, a society wholly unanimous in its beliefs and wholly free from inner conflicts.

*Thomas Müntzer was a religious visionary and a leader of the German Peasants' Rebellion (1325)—Ed.

Such was the tradition of apocalyptic fanaticism which—secularised and revivified—was inherited by Lenin and by Hitler.

• • •

In the Middle Ages the people for whom revolutionary chiliasm had most appeal were neither peasants firmly integrated in the life of village and manor nor artisans firmly integrated in their guilds. The lot of such people might at times be one of poverty and oppression, and at other times be one of relative prosperity and independence; they might revolt or they might accept their situation; but they were not, on the whole, prone to follow some inspired *propheta* in a hectic pursuit of the Millennium. These *prophetae* found their following, rather, where there existed a surplus population, rural or urban or both. This was as true of Flanders and northern France in the twelfth and thirteenth centuries as of Holland and Westphalia in the sixteenth; and recent researches have shown it to have been equally true of the Bohemia of the early fifteenth century. Revolutionary chiliasm drew its strength from the surplus population living on the margin of society—peasants without land or with too little land even for subsistence; journeymen and unskilled workers living under the continuous threat of unemployment; beggars and vagabonds—in fact from that amorphous mass of people who were not simply poor but who could find no assured and recognised place in society at all. These people lacked the material and emotional support afforded by traditional social groups; their kinship-groups had disintegrated and they were not effectively organised in village communities or in guilds; for them there existed no regular, institutionalised methods of voicing their grievances or pressing their claims. Instead they waited for a *propheta* to bind them together in a group of their own—which would then emerge as a movement of a peculiar kind, driven on by a wild enthusiasm born of desperation.

Because these people found themselves in such an exposed and defenceless position they were liable to react very sharply to any disruption of the normal, familiar, pattern of life. Again and again one finds that a particular outbreak of revolutionary chiliasm took place against a background of disaster: the plagues that preluded the First Crusade and the flagellant movements of 1260, 1348–1349, 1391 and 1400; the famines that preluded the First and Second Crusades and the popular crusading movements of 1309–1320, the flagellant movement of 1296, the movements around Eudes de l'Étoile and the pseudo-Baldwin; the spectacular rise in prices that preluded the revolution at Münster. The greatest wave of chiliastic excitement, one which swept through the whole of society, was precipitated by the most universal natural disaster of the Middle Ages, the Black Death; and here again it was in the lower social strata that the excitement lasted longest and that it expressed itself in violence and massacre.

But the rootless masses of the poor were not only shaken by those specific calamities or upheavals that directly affected their material lot—they were also peculiarly sensitive to the less dramatic but equally relentless processes which, generation after generation, gradually disrupted the framework of authority within which medieval life had for a time been contained. The one authority which was universal, embracing with its prescriptions and demands the lives of all individuals, was that of the Church. And by canalising the emotional energies of the laity, by directing their yearnings firmly towards an after-life in another world, the Church did indeed do much to impede the spread of revolutionary chiliasm. But the authority of the Church was not unquestioned. A civilisation which regarded asceticism as the surest sign of grace was bound to doubt the value and validity of a Church which was manifestly infected with *Luxuria* and *Avaritia.* Again and again during the second half of the Middle Ages worldliness amongst the clergy resulted in disaffection amongst the laity—and always that disaffection was most complete amongst the poor. It was inevitable that many of those whose own lives were condemned to hardship and insecurity should doubt whether ostentatious prelates and easy-going priests could really help them towards salvation. But if these people were alienated from the Church, they also suffered from their alienation. How much they needed the Church is shown by the enthusiasm with which they welcomed every sign of ascetic reform and the eagerness with which they would accept, even adore, any genuine ascetic. To be uncertain of the consolation and guidance and mediation of the Church aggravated their sense of helplessness and increased their desperation. It is because of these emotional needs of the poor that the militant social movements we have considered were at the same time surrogates for the Church—salvationist groups led by miracle-working ascetics.

Almost as much as to the Church, supernatural authority pertained to the national monarchy. Medieval kingship was still to a large extent a sacred kingship; the monarch was the representative of the powers that govern the cosmos, an incarnation of the moral law and the divine intention, a guarantor of the order and rightness of the world. And here again it was the poor who most needed such a figure. When we first meet the *pauperes,* in the First Crusade, they are already creating prodigious monarchs out of their own imagination: a resurrected Charlemagne, an Emico of Leiningen made emperor, a King Tafur. And to the poor any prolonged interruption or manifest failure of the royal power brought intense anguish from which they struggled to escape. It was "the poor, weavers and fullers" of Flanders who refused to accept the death in captivity of Count Baldwin IX and who became the most devoted followers of the pseudo-Baldwin, Emperor of Constantinople. The first horde of *Pastoureaux*, in 1251, were inspired by the prospect of rescuing Louis IX from Saracen captivity. And later, whereas in France revolutionary chiliasm waned as the prestige of the monarchy increased, in Germany the long decline of the imperial office fostered the cult of the saviour of the poor in the Last Days, the resurrected or future Frederick. The last emperor to possess all the aura of sacred kingship was Frederick II; and with his death and the fatal disruption known as the Great Interregnum there appeared amongst the common people in Germany an anxiety that was to persist for centuries. The career of the pseudo-Frederick of Neuss in the thirteenth century, the imperial lore that grew up around the flagellant leader Konrad Schmid in the fourteenth and fifteenth centuries, the prophecies and pretensions of the Revolutionary of the Upper Rhine in the sixteenth century—these things bear witness both to an enduring disarray and to the wild chiliasm that throve upon it.

When, finally, one comes to consider the anarcho-communistic millenarian groups which flourished around the close of the Middle Ages, one fact is immediately obvious: it was always in the midst of some great revolt or revolution that a group of this kind emerged into daylight. This is equally the case with John Ball and his followers in the English peasants' revolt of 1381; with the extremists during the early stages of the Hussite revolution in Bohemia in 1419–1421; and with Thomas Müntzer and his "league of the elect" in the German peasants' revolt of 1525. And it is true, also, of the radical Anabaptists at Münster—for the establishment of their New Jerusalem came at the end of a whole series of revolts, not only at Münster but throughout the ecclesiastical states of north-west Germany. In each of these instances the mass insurrection itself was directed towards limited and realistic aims—yet in each instance the climate of mass insurrection fostered a special kind of millenarian group. As social tensions mounted and the revolt became nation-wide, there would appear, somewhere on the radical fringe, a *propheta* with his following of paupers, intent on turning this one particular upheaval into the apocalyptic battle, the final purification of the world. . . .

A boundless, millennial promise made with boundless, prophet-like conviction to a number of rootless and desperate men in the midst of a society where traditional norms and relationships are disintegrating—here, it would seem, lay the source of that peculiar subterranean fanaticism which subsisted as a perpetual menace to the structure of medieval society. It may be suggested that here, too, lies the source of the giant fanaticisms which in our day have convulsed the world.

A Note On The Type

The text of this book has been set on the computer in a type-face called "Baskerville," based on the linotype face of the same name. The face is a facsimile reproduction of types cast from molds made for John Baskerville (1706–75) from his designs. John Baskerville's original face was one of the forerunners of the type-style known as "modern face" to printers — a "modern" of the period A.D. 1800.